Acts of Intervention

UNNATURAL ACTS: THEORIZING THE PERFORMATIVE

Sue-Ellen Case, Philip Brett,
Susan Leigh Foster, *general editors*

The partitioning of performance into obligatory appearances and strict
disallowances is a complex social code assumed to be "natural" until
recent notions of performativity unmasked its operations. Performance
partitions, strictly enforced within traditional conceptions of the arts,
foreground the gestures of the dancer, but ignore those of the orchestra
player, assign significance to the elocution of the actor, but not to the
utterances of the audience. The critical notion of performativity both
reveals these partitions as unnatural and opens the way for the
consideration of all cultural intercourse as performance. It also exposes
the compulsory nature of some orders of performance. The oppressive
requirements of systems that organize gender and sexual practices mark
who may wear the dress and who may perform the kiss. Further, the
fashion of the dress and the colorizing of the skin that dons it are
disciplined by systems of class and "race." These cultural performances
are critical sites for study.

The series "Unnatural Acts" encourages further interrogations of all varieties
of performance both in the traditional sense of the term and from the broader
perspective provided by performativity.

ACTS

OF

INTERVENTION

Performance, Gay Culture, and AIDS

David Román

Indiana University Press

Bloomington and Indianapolis

Some of these chapters have appeared elsewhere in a different form.
A version of chapter 3 was published in *Theatre Journal* 44:3 (1992): 305–327, and
appears here with permission of the Johns Hopkins University Press.
A version of chapter 5 was published in *Journal of Homosexuality* 26:2/3 (1993):
195–219, and appears here with permission of the Haworth Press.
A version of chapter 6 was published in *Entiendes? Queer Readings/Hispanic Writings,*
ed. Emilie Bergmann and Paul Julian Smith, 1995,
and appears here with permission of Duke University Press.

The photo of Ron Athey by Dona Ann McAdams appears courtesy of the Aperture
Foundation, reproduced from Dona Ann McAdams, *Caught in the Act: A Look at
Contemporary Multimedia Performance,* 1996.

The paper used in this publication meets the minimum requirements of American
National Standard for Information Sciences—Permanence of Paper for Printed
Library Materials, ANSI Z39.48-1984.

Manufactured in the United States of America

Library of Congress Cataloging-in-Publication Data

Román, David, date
Acts of intervention : performance, gay culture, and AIDS / David
Román.
p.   cm. — (Unnatural acts)
Includes bibliographical references and index.
ISBN 0-253-33370-9 (cl : alk. paper). — ISBN 0-253-21168-9 (pbk.
: alk. paper)
1. Theater—United States—History—20th century.   2. American
drama—20th century—History and criticism.   3. Gay actors—United
States—Biography.   4. AIDS (Disease) in literature.   I. Title.
II. Series.
PN2266.R66   1998
792'.086'640973—dc21   97-35808

1   2   3   4   5   03   02   01   00   99   98

For Richard Meyer

Keep watch, every night if you have to.

—"Sleeping under a Tree," Paul Monette

Contents

Acknowledgments

Immense have been the preparations for me,
Faithful and friendly the arms that have helped me.
—*Song of Myself*, Walt Whitman

THIS BOOK WAS written between 1991 and 1996. It is a product of the performance, AIDS, and academic communities of which I am a part and which compose my world. So many people have helped me during these past years, in fact, far too many to list in what already will seem a stretch of this genre's format. This book started off as an extension of my involvement with AIDS activism, which first began in 1986 in Madison, Wisconsin, while I was in graduate school. My friends at the Madison AIDS Support Network were instrumental in helping me begin to understand not only AIDS but, more importantly, how I could marry my emerging sense of responsibility with my actual capabilities. Michael Bemis, Will Handy, Mark Sweet, Jim Witalison, and Richard Kilmore showed me the ropes of community-based AIDS volunteerism and activism, and I remain grateful to them for doing so. I moved around a lot after I left Madison in 1987: Chicago, St. Paul, Los Angeles, Seattle, Philadelphia, New York City, and back to Los Angeles, where I now live. My affiliations with Chicago House, the Names Project–Chicago, ACT UP/Los Angeles, ACT UP/Seattle, the Seattle Bailey Boushay House, the Philadelphia AIDS Task Force, and the AIDS Prevention Action League in New York City have shaped my understanding of AIDS and have provided me a sense of community in the process. I especially want to pay tribute to the residents and staff of the Bailey Boushay House, one of the most remarkable places I have ever encountered, for allowing me to participate in their world during the two years I lived in Seattle.

Douglas Swenson, my partner from 1987 to 1994, pushed me to find a link between my professional interests and my political commitments and helped me discover a way to do so. His support during the difficult years of securing a Ph.D. and applying for academic appointments was unwavering. It was his suggestion that I shift my research focus from early modern theatre, the subject of my dissertation, to contemporary performance. This book began out of the conversations he and I would have about politics, AIDS, and performance. I hope that when Doug reads this book, he will recognize his many contributions.

Sue-Ellen Case and George Haggerty invited me to present my preliminary work on AIDS and theatre at the "Unauthorized Sexuality" conference they helped organize at UC–Riverside in 1991. Janelle Reinelt and Joseph Roach were the first to publish my work on AIDS and theatre in 1992. I am grateful for these initial opportunities and for these friendships, which provided me with the confidence to develop this project. Many other people invited me to present my work-in-progress at professional conferences, community forums, and university campuses. Parts of my research have been delivered to audiences at the MLA; ATHE; the Harvard, Rutgers, and University of Iowa lesbian and gay studies conferences; the NYU performance studies conference; the Swarthmore Sager Symposium; the Center for Literary and Cultural Studies at Harvard University; Northwestern University; Highways Performance Space; University of London; Rice University; CUNY Graduate School; University of California–Berkeley; University of California–Davis; University of California–San Diego; Outwrite; Pomona College; University of Washington; University of Pennsylvania; Duke University; Mount Holyoke College; Columbia University; University of Minnesota–Twin Cities; and University of Southern California. I am thankful for these opportunities and for the intellectual engagement from these audiences. I am especially pleased to acknowledge the Center for Lesbian and Gay Studies, which has been an important resource and community for me these past years.

I am also grateful to the editors who published earlier versions of some of these chapters: Bill Worthen and Janelle Reinelt, David Bergman, Emmanuel S. Nelson, Emilie Bergmann and Paul Julian Smith, and the various outside readers who commented on the work. Sue-Ellen Case, Susan Foster, and Philip Brett, the editors of the *Unnatural Acts: Theorizing the Performative* series, challenged me enormously to improve the manuscript. Their thoughtful comments and encouraging support throughout this process are deeply appreciated. A 1992 University of Washington Graduate School Research Grant enabled me to draft chapter 5, and a 1993–1994 University of Pennsylvania Mellon Fellowship in the Humanities enabled me to draft chapters 1, 2, and 7. The Philadelphia Gay and Lesbian Archives at Penguin Place and the AIDS Information Library in Philadelphia proved indispensible to this project. Thanks also to everyone at Indiana University Press, especially Joan Catapano and Grace Profatilov, and the outside readers for this project. Special thanks to Stephanie G'Schwind, who copyedited the manuscript and ushered it through production.

Many of the ideas in this book were initially shared with the students enrolled in courses I taught at the University of Washington and Yale University. Our class discussions greatly influenced my writing. The Yale students enrolled in the "AIDS and Literature" course, all of whom participated in the tenth-anniversary staged reading of Rebecca Ranson's *Warren* at Yale Cabaret in observance of World AIDS Day in 1994, deserve special acknowledgment. This project was nearly complete by the time I arrived at USC in 1995. My USC students, however, helped clarify many of my thoughts on *Rent* while providing the first forum to rehearse them. At each of these institutions—University of Washington, Yale University, University of Southern California—the students' own commitments to AIDS awareness and intellectual rigor have kept me focused.

Various friends and colleagues read and commented on this material throughout the writing process. I want to thank the following people for helping me write this book: Luis Alfaro, Stephen Best, Joe Boone, Gregg Bordowitz, Judith Butler, Susana Chávez-Silverman, Craig Chester, Carolyn Dinshaw, David Drake, Martin Duberman, John Fall, Brian Freeman, Ari Gold, David Halperin, Holly Hughes, Susan Jeffords, Dorinne Kondo, Michael Mayer, Tim Miller, José Muñoz, Cindy Patton, Janelle Reinelt, David Robinson, Doug Sadownick, Alberto Sandoval, Dustin Schell, Don Shewey, Karen Shimakawa, Matthew Silverstein, Paul Sutherland, Michael Warner, Evan Watkins, Bill Worthen, Robert Vorlicky, and Yvonne Yarbro-Bejarano. I am especially indebted to Jill Dolan, who read the entire manuscript and offered me invaluable suggestions for revision.

Many of the playwrights and performers I discuss in this book generously provided me with access to their work. I am especially indebted to the writers who opened up their archives to me. Two of them, Jeff Hagedorn and Jim Pickett, died before this book was completed. I hope my book will call attention to their work so that they may begin to receive the recognition they deserve. Thanks also to Tony Kushner, who invited me to the November 1, 1992, opening of *Angels in America* at the Mark Taper Forum, and to Rebecca Ranson for sharing with me her stories of *Warren*. I am also grateful to the various photographers who generously permitted me to reproduce their work: Dona Ann McAdams, Paula Court, Bettye Lane, Jennifer Girard, Rick Moffit, Chuck Stallard, Jill Posener, Barron Clairborne, Dylan Tran, Jay Thompson, Richard Armas, Michal Daniel, William Gibson, Martha Swope, Rink, Joan Marcus, and Lee Snider. Through their visual documentation of activism, theatre, and performance, these photographers have made crucial contributions both to my project and to the larger social history it records.

My parents, David and Myriam, and my two sisters, Connie and Brenda, have also provided support. Their inquiries about its progress—"So where's this book you're writing?"—inspired me to finish. This might not be the book they have been anticipating all these years, but I hope it gives them a better understanding of who I am.

Paul Monette, whom I considered a mentor, encouraged me to write and live well. His support was instrumental to me and I miss him. His own life and work remains my guide.

My friends have been behind this project from the very beginning. My friends in New York provide me a constancy in my life that I treasure. In part, it may be because they seldom move, but it is also because they have big hearts and lots of love. Dustin Schell, Craig Chester, and I share things that we try to keep between us, so I should probably leave it at that. Let me say only that I am happy to call them both my friends. Bob Vorlicky has enriched my life in many ways. I am deeply appreciative of my friendship with Alberto Sandoval; his intellectual curiosity, political commitments, and sheer resilience are unmatched among the people I know. Since I first met him in the late 1970s, Michael Mayer has been in my heart. Although I share shorter histories with Ari Gold, David Drake, Esther Newton, Carmelita Tropicana, and José Muñoz, I consider each of them a part of my necessary extended kinship circle. Holly Hughes is always there for me. Her own work is the best reminder to me of why performance matters.

My friends in Los Angeles provide me a sense of home. Joe Boone has offered me friendship longer than anyone else I know. His ongoing support has been crucial to my project and to my professional life. I am also lucky to have Dorinne Kondo in my life; her affection these past seven years keeps me coming back for more. Her contributions to my thinking are undoubtedly my greatest intellectual debt. Tim Miller is, there is no other way to phrase it, my best friend. His commitment to AIDS and performance has been one of the main inspirations for this book. The gifts of his friendship are many, and for all of them I am deeply grateful. All of these people offer me a sense of community which I need to acknowledge.

At the heart of my life is my partner, Richard Meyer. I should probably thank him for reading over this manuscript again and again and acknowledge the force of his intellectual rigor on my writing, but such thanks may obscure my greater debt to him. He has been my life's surprise. Richard's love and companionship sustain me. "With a thousand sweet kisses"—this book is dedicated to him.

Introduction

A N INTRODUCTION IS a preliminary performance which suggests that there is something more to come. AIDS, a crisis of such magnitude and boundless effect, would seem to need by now little if any introduction. The introduction to this book provides a map of the project, but the introduction is also meant to signal that the history it traces will exceed its design. AIDS, of course, is an epidemic which is still in process. Its limits are not knowable in the manner demanded of traditional objects of scholarly analysis.[1] At the same time, AIDS begs the question we ask of all dreadful performances—when will this ever end? Performances always and only end, and once enacted they vanish, leaving their trace in the official memory of performance we call theatre history.[2] AIDS performance foregrounds this vanishing act. So many of the performers, playwrights, spectators, critics, tech people, and others participating in the collective production of AIDS performance have already vanished along with their performances. This is a book that attempts to deal with this history we now must live with and live through: a history in which people disappear, performances vanish, but AIDS still remains. The specific challenge is to find a way to introduce these performances in a way that will mark their passing and recover what can survive.

Acts of Intervention is a book which examines the ways that gay men have used theatre and performance to intervene in the crisis of AIDS. Throughout the book, I argue that performance has participated in shaping our understanding and experience of AIDS. Foremost, this is a book about theatre and performance. The book focuses on the specific cultural field of the theatre and the particular possibilities made available through performance to address AIDS. I discuss dramatic texts and theatrical practices as instances of various cultural moments—in all their multiplicity and even contradiction—which have participated in the production of the ideology of AIDS in national, regional, or local contexts. But I am also interested in examining how AIDS has materially shaped the conditions and practices of theatre and performance. *Acts of Intervention* discusses not only the ways that theatre has provided a forum for gay male responses to the epidemic but also the degree to which these responses have in turn shaped the ideological formation of AIDS. *Acts of Intervention* does not aim to produce a canonical history of AIDS theatre and performance. For, as I argue, such a project does a great disservice to the cultural work of local and community-based performers, who may resist or abandon any hope for canon-icity. Because so many performances around or about AIDS have left little or no documentation, the critical task of constructing an AIDS theatre historiography comes up against immediate limitations. Rather than obscuring such limita-tions, *Acts of Intervention* will consider their effects.

Although *Acts of Intervention* does not set out to write the history of AIDS theatre, the book is organized in a loosely chronological fashion. It begins with an analysis of the performances and plays produced in the early 1980s and con-cludes with a discussion of the success of *Rent* in 1996. The book also examines some of the shifts in the representational and cultural understandings of AIDS throughout the past fifteen years. While I do not propose an exhaustive list-ing of performances, I do attempt to locate some forgotten and obscure perfor-mances around AIDS. The book is dedicated to writing the history of various local interventions of AIDS activism and performance which need to circulate more widely, performances which official history has in many ways and for many reasons either neglected or forgotten. Such a practice is in part my own way of coping with loss and disappearance. Memory—whether it be individual or collective—involves a dynamic dialectic between mourning what has passed and reviving what has been lost. The history of AIDS performance is located at just this juncture: between revival and disappearance. In our hope to retrieve a theatrical past, however, theatre historians may be able to replay only the very ephemerality that defines performance.

AIDS and Theatre Historiography

Key Words: Opening, Premiere; Performance, Production

Writing about AIDS performance raises questions concerning the practices of official documentation, of writing theatre history. Throughout this book, I ar-gue against some of the official histories of both AIDS and the theatre which obscure other histories which have remained undocumented. Furthermore, I ex-amine the relationship between that which has been represented and that which has been ignored. When thinking about AIDS it is tempting to look for a source or origin, a beginning, a key event or date that marks the official arrival of the epidemic. Finding the beginning of the story would provide an opening for the telling of its history. But the history of AIDS has no set point of origin. The epi-demic can be marked in any number of ways, from locating its first reportage in the *New York Times* or in scientific and medical journals, to remembering our first friend to die or the first protest or fundraiser we attended.

Likewise, the ephemerality of performance calls attention to the limits of its documentation. Theatre history attempts to confront this challenge by recovering the theatrical past and bringing it into consciousness. Writing about AIDS and performance can be only a partial recovery of a history with no point of origin and no predetermined place of destination. The theatre has its own set of conventions and practices that secure its arrival into an official theatre history; it too is invested in locating a set point of origin. The language used to describe the process of theatrical production, while familiar, if not seemingly fundamental, requires critical interrogation. Raymond Williams, the Marxist cultural critic, has taught us that ostensibly foundational terms are actually imbedded with specific ideological meanings. His *Keywords* has provided a critical model that has been imported by AIDS cultural theorists to demystify some of the foundational terms of dominant AIDS discourse.[3] Jan Zita Grover, for example, has written about the ways that the keywords of AIDS are "primarily the property of the powerful" and situates her project "to identify and contest some of the assumptions underlying our current knowledge [about AIDS]" in the spirit of Raymond Williams's cultural theories and in conjunction with AIDS activists, including people living with AIDS.[4] To map the limits of official theatre historiography as it pertains to AIDS performance, I follow Grover's example by turning to some of the keywords used to describe and/or mark the run of a theatrical production.[5] These four basic terms, when considered in relation to the question of a set point of origin, convey the investments the theatre upholds in establishing its official history. Furthermore, as I will argue, this discourse of the theatre produces certain effects that are similar to those produced by the official discourse of AIDS.

In theatre parlance, the opening night of a production signals an arrival; as such, it serves multiple needs and functions. An opening night, unlike a rehearsal or a preview, brings together various elements of the production process through the ritual of arrival. For the artists involved in the production an opening night is an opportunity to honor all the behind-the-scenes work of the production. Actors, directors, and designers, for example, exchange cards and gifts; friends, spouses, and supporters of the artistic team are invited to attend and usually bring flowers or other tokens of support. The presenting theatre or performance space invites patrons and donors to participate in the event as well. From these customs two things become apparent: First, an opening night is a type of exchange ritual that recognizes the support systems of the theatre; it calls attention to the idea of a community composed of artists and producers, theatre staff and management, sponsors and patrons, and select spectators who have some involvement with any of these people. Second, an opening night calls attention to the selective audience of the event; the audience is never arbitrary or random. The majority audience is composed of spectators already invested in the success of the production. Sometimes, in fact, depending upon the goals of the production, future producers and presenters also are invited to the opening night in the hope that the play will be produced elsewhere in the future. Given these two components, one can reasonably assert that opening nights are spectacles of communal investment and hope. Opening nights, inevitably given these conditions, call attention to the labor of production. If the performance at an opening is constructed as the culmination of the artistic process, the "opening" itself displays the theatrical apparatus of production, including the various and often competing social relations that link the artistic and economic activity of theatrical production. In other words, an opening night foregrounds the investments of those involved with the production of theatre.

Despite the profound symbolic significance of these factors, the primary construction of an opening night is to mark the entrance of a production into an official theatre history. The language of theatrical production explicitly addresses this process of entering into theatre history. And yet given the precision of this language, key dates in the process of production are often confused and conflated. Thus it may prove helpful to mark the distinctions between the terms *preview, press night, opening, performance,* and *production.* Opening night announces the arrival of the production into history; it is the night that theatre critics—who are barred from previews where the production may still be in development—are invited to review the performance. Productions, however, may also hold press nights. Press night performances generally precede opening night. These performances are also previews, performances where the artistic team fine-tunes the production in front of a paying audience. In the trajectory toward opening night, producers can "freeze" a production in previews in order for critics to begin attending performances for review. These "frozen" previews are called "press nights" and allow theatre critics and reviewers a certain flexibility in scheduling their theatre-going and in meeting their deadline schedules. Once the production is frozen, the artistic team must refrain from making substantive changes in the production. Generally speaking, the professional ethics of the print and media theatre review process demand that a play is not reviewed before it officially "opens." This is a courtesy extended by the press to the theatre, a courtesy which is reciprocated by the theatre to the press in the form of complimentary tickets to the opening night or press night. Critics and reviewers are invited to attend the opening night in order to maintain its construction as an official arrival and in order to confirm their own participation in the construction of a theatre history. Many, however, attend "press nights" and bypass the actual official opening. Reviewers in the daily print media, for example, often have their reviews written *before* the opening night, although these reviews are not published until the play officially opens. Thus, the theatre reviews that we read in the popular press are not necessarily reviews of the "opening night" performance. For theatre historians these reviews in the popular press are often the main documentation of the entire production's process and reception.[6]

A world premiere, much like an opening night, also announces an official arrival. A world premiere claims that the performance you are watching will be the first official performance of the play anywhere in the world. It declares authenticity and originality. Furthermore, a world premiere, unlike simply any "opening night"—except, of course, the opening night of a world premiere— presupposes historical significance. It assumes that somewhere at some time the play will be restaged. Once that happens, the production is forced to comply with more modest claims: the West Coast premiere, the Broadway premiere, the West End premiere, the Chicago premiere, etc. It also positions the play for revival, as in the fiftieth anniversary production or the restored or complete production. A world premiere can also signal the significance of the playwright, the director, or even the producing theatre. In all these cases, to call a performance a world premiere assumes a genealogy for the play that begins at the opening night of a world premiere. But, in truth, such genealogies obscure the materiality of the production's history—from its development to its opening performance. Moreover, these genealogical narratives conflate the unique and dynamic experience of any given performance with an absolute reading of a production; in this system, the opening night performance *becomes* the production and thereby erases the distinct features between them and the process by which this occurs.

A performance, in other words, is not the same as a production. A performance stands in and of itself as an event; it is part of the process of production. A performance is not an entity that exists atemporally for the spectator; rather, the spectator intersects in a trajectory of continuous production. A production is generally composed of a series of performances, including rehearsals, previews, and press nights. Even once the production opens, the performances of the run are never the same. The language of official theatre historiography—openings, premieres—conflates performance with production and sets up the fantasy that production and reception stop after the opening night performance.

I offer this diversion into keywords of the theatre in order to call attention to the challenges faced by theatre historians in constructing what Marxist theatre historian Bruce McConachie explains as "a more complete historical sociology of the theatre" which "would require extensive empirical and theoretical investigations into the sociohistorical conditions necessary for the emergence of various kinds of theatre, the relations between historical forms of theatrical expression and the dominant ideology of a historical period, and the functions of theatre in reproducing, modifying, or contradicting hegemonic relations of production."[7] For the theatre of AIDS, such a project provides the methodological means for viewing plays and performances as critical practices that shape our understanding of AIDS.

Official Histories

One of the reasons I highlight the differences between premieres and openings, and production and performance—keywords that, while relational, are not coterminous—is to put pressure upon the officializing history already in place around AIDS performance. With the mainstream and critical success of AIDS performance, it becomes necessary to question the ideological assumptions of the individuals and media that produce official critical reviews and pronouncements on the plays. I also want to call attention to the totalizing narratives naturalized as official histories both in the theatre and in our understanding of AIDS. "Narrativity," as theatre historian Thomas Postlewait explains, "is not merely a technique, borrowed from literature, but instead a condition of our temporal understanding of individual and social experience" (177). And not just for theatre history. In many ways, the discourses of theatre history resemble the medical discourses of AIDS.

The term *AIDS*, for acquired immune deficiency syndrome, as Jan Zita Grover explains, "was officially adopted by the Centers for Disease Control in 1982."[8] Grover offers a concise explication of the medical profession's process of identifying the various symptoms, diseases, and invading organisms, for example, that led to the official CDC adoption of AIDS as a term in 1982. But certainly, as Grover suggests, people were dying from the opportunistic infections we now associate with AIDS before the official arrival of the term *AIDS*. In this sense *AIDS* predates the official 1982 record of the CDC. Moreover, people who died before the official CDC definition died of complications due to AIDS despite there being no such thing as *AIDS* before 1982.[9] The point here is that AIDS existed before its official entrance into the historical register; while the specific cultural practices that produced the term *AIDS* may not have taken effect until 1982, viruses and infections were debilitating and killing many people before this date.[10]

A fragile genealogy of these events, in fact, can be constructed from lesbian and gay publications, medical journals, and the mainstream press. The first article in the gay press to refer to what we now know as AIDS was reported in the May 18, 1981, edition of the *New York Native*; the first writings in a medical journal appeared in the *Morbidity and Mortality Weekly Report* of June 5, 1981; and an article in the July 3, 1981, edition of the *New York Times* was that newspaper's first account of the epidemic. Each of these articles registers the epidemic's official entrance into historical consciousness and establishes the seemingly foundational basis for a print-media history. But these media occasions in and of themselves don't necessarily construct a history of AIDS. Like the theatre review process, which is based upon the logic of opening night performances, these reports can only mark their own participation and location in the process and production of HIV and AIDS. Indeed, the notion of a theatre opening as an official arrival relies on the same narrative construction as such key dates for HIV and AIDS as "day of diagnosis," "day of first opportunistic infection," or "day of HIV test results." The apparent stability of these constructions is belied, however, by the larger ambiguities of HIV infection and status. To test positive on one day does not necessarily mean that one was uninfected the day before; to test negative, moreover, does not automatically mean that one has not been exposed to HIV. HIV test results cannot trace the date of transmission or guarantee one's immunity in the future. Just as the idea of a theatre opening obscures the performance history of any given production by positing the fallacy of first arrival, so too do these dates of HIV or AIDS-related medical occasions pronounce and perform the signature of history on the body and thereby eradicate the process(es) of HIV and AIDS; theatre openings and premieres pitched as official arrivals signal the language of medical origins and vice versa. Each is based on a logic of sequential ordering that is both selective and self-serving and ideologically constructed as unmarked.

Insofar as AIDS is rendered an official historicizing vis-à-vis the dates of the body's responses to diagnostic procedures and tests, and insofar as a print genealogy of AIDS overdetermines the arrival of AIDS and obscures the process(es) of AIDS, AIDS will continue to be understood within the confines of these narratives of origin. Narratives of AIDS are always problematic, whether they arise from science or the media. Narratives of AIDS are always representations of AIDS, and as Cindy Patton makes clear, "representations of AIDS at every level—in the media, in the science, in the cultural assumptions manifest in the effects of institutional process—are multiple and discontinuous."[11] And while much could be said of the necessity of these official dates for organizing a personal response to HIV and AIDS—I am thinking not only of treatment options, clinical trials, and insurance coverages that depend upon this information to take effect, but also issues such as sexual options and decisions, support networks, and the various structures of feeling associated with information regarding personal health—it is important to recognize that the information gathered from the official occasions of HIV and AIDS may discipline us into certain responses. When physicians read the body they put into language an interpretation that is rendered definitive; these interpretations are naturalized as certainties under the muscle of science. No wonder, then, that so many people affected by HIV and AIDS now seek to challenge the discourse of science and offer differing interpretations of the body. Consider Michael Callen, who, after being officially diagnosed with AIDS in 1982, introduced a different way of thinking about AIDS, most notably, the then radical (and for many presumptuous) concept of the "long-term survivor" and the violently contested and revolutionary concept of safe sex. In *Surviving AIDS*, he writes: "Discovering a different way of thinking about AIDS at such a crucial turning point in my life provided a framework for me to justify believing that I might survive my disease. It was a life raft that kept me afloat in a sea of doom and gloom."[12] Like Callen, many gay men in the early 1980s began to offer tactics for survival. Unfortunately, these strategies were not always accepted or even acknowledged within the official narratives of AIDS.

Among the most significant of Cindy Patton's points in her tremendously valuable *Inventing AIDS* is her admonishment of the "amnesia surrounding the history of activism between 1981–1985" (19). Patton's concerns regarding revisionist AIDS histories serve as the basis for my comments here. While Patton's points are specific to AIDS service organizations, safe sex campaigns, and other early efforts within the lesbian and gay community to challenge government neglect, it is possible to extend her analysis to the history of artistic and cultural responses to AIDS. In this regard, the dominant historiographic narrative that positions *The Normal Heart* and *As Is*—both produced in 1985—as the earliest responses to AIDS in the theatre is not only inaccurate, it also does a grievous disservice to such artists, playwrights, and theatre collectives as Robert Chesley, Jeff Hagedorn, Rebecca Ranson, and San Francisco's *A.I.D.S. Show* collaborators, among others, whose AIDS performances were produced as early as 1983.

A theatre history around plays and performances which address AIDS therefore should avoid the impulse to offer an official AIDS theatre history. In fact, I would argue that an AIDS theatre historian should construct a model of analysis that cautions against the officializing rhetorical tendencies and totalizing narratives of theatre history in general. Such a project would be consistent with other projects on AIDS that describe the encounter with discourse about HIV and AIDS as overwhelming and perhaps unknowable in its totality:

> Inscribed since its appearance as profoundly unimaginable, as beyond the bounds of sense, the AIDS epidemic is almost literally unthinkable in its mathematical defeat of cognitive desire.
>
> But already we have here begun to make sense of AIDS, even if only in noting how it defeats our usual academic practices of careful, inclusive analysis. And we have also here assumed AIDS as an ongoing event, as something that moves within a history that is only partially *its* history.

The mathematical sublime thus quickly gives way in the case of AIDS to what we might call the historical sublime, for even more than the mathematical, the historical sublime marks reading—and our stake in it—as an activity framed equally by demand and defeat, as the ground on which we are condemned to negotiate the difference between that which can be comprehended by the capacities of the intellect and that which can only be apprehended as beyond, in excess, or pitted against such capacities.[13]

These are Thomas Yingling's words to describe the incommensurabilities between what we know and what lies beyond the reach of our cognition. Yingling's focus on the challenges that AIDS poses for our "usual academic practices" informs the problems faced when constructing an AIDS theatre historiography. Aware that our project is framed by demands and defeats, an AIDS theatre history should question the positivism imbedded in traditional theatre history.[14] This is not to say that we should abandon projects that attempt to recuperate an AIDS theatrical past; rather, our efforts to do so must acknowledge that a complete history of AIDS theatre is now improbable. We need to continue to document the theatre's responses to AIDS, collect and publish the various materials of people who have died of AIDS, and interview the living. But we also need to accept as axiomatic that the nature of a theatrical performance itself involves a sense of loss; performances are not repeatable. And it is this loss of the performance which fuels the practice of theatre history.

As in all aspects of AIDS and history, the task at hand for the theatre historian interested in AIDS plays and performances is to call attention to the overdetermined components that construct these official histories in the first place. I think we need to deconstruct these histories more carefully and locate our own critical practice as an act of intervention in the emerging institutionalization of an official AIDS theatre history. Once again, I quote Cindy Patton to make this point. Patton is discussing a disturbing trend among historical accounts of AIDS activism that privileges the political actions of ACT UP (AIDS Coalition to Unleash Power), the direct action group which emerged in 1987, at the expense of early AIDS organizing, and the revisionist history this type of historicizing engenders:

> These types of analysis of AIDS activism deny not only the immediate response of the gay male community to the AIDS epidemic in the early 1980s, but erase even more of the historical involvement in AIDS work of gay liberationists. . . . [The] implication that gay men sat around doing nothing but being "in rage" until 1987 ignores the radical roots of many of the current ASOs (AIDS service organizations), and the radicalism of people working inside what has become "the system." This is not to underestimate the differences and conflicts between ACT UP and the ASOs,

but outside observers and, increasingly, activists who have been told nothing of the early days of AIDS organizing, misunderstand the important
place of each in the fight against AIDS. One reason for this rapid revision
of AIDS organizing history is the reality that many of the early organizers
are now dead. (139)

For my purposes, the fact that many of the early playwrights and performers
whose work dealt in one form or another with AIDS are now dead, and that so
many of the artistic collaborators, producers, theatre staff, and spectators who
participated in these productions and performances are also dead and therefore
may leave no record of the events, already points to the futility of constructing
an accurate or total AIDS theatre history. Many early performances around
AIDS were simply that, performances without opening nights, world premieres,
or the critical review process that facilitates their official registration into theatre
history.[15] But this is still the case for many performances and productions
throughout the United States. As I will argue in chapter 7, even plays as celebrated and seemingly well documented as Tony Kushner's *Angels in America*
demonstrate the problems of these official practices. Likewise, many people
with AIDS are still unaccounted for by the CDC, AIDS service organizations,
and other institutions set up to administer to the needs of people with AIDS.
An AIDS theatre historiography must address and factor into account these limits of official documentation.

Acts of Intervention is primarily concerned with gay male performance and
the ways gay men have confronted AIDS through the theatre. The book does not
directly address the important works of other playwrights and performers who
have created work in response to the epidemic.[16] In this sense, the book already
falls short of being, or even aspiring to be, a complete AIDS theatre history.
Since the earliest days of the epidemic, gay men have been identified nearly ir-
reversibly with AIDS, a construct that has both perpetuated the decimation of
gay men throughout the 1980s and paradoxically facilitated the spread of AIDS
into non-gay communities in these years. The encapsulation of AIDS as "homosexual," despite the knowledge that HIV and AIDS surfaced simultaneously in
other populations not contained within the category of "homosexual"—IV drug
users, "Haitians," and hemophiliacs, for example—locked in the linkage between homosexuals and AIDS as a foundational logic in the cultural understanding of AIDS.[17] The force of this equation formulated in the early 1980s is
evident in the ways that AIDS has been represented in dominant culture. Cultural theorists such as Douglas Crimp, Jan Zita Grover, Cindy Patton, and Simon
Watney have gone to great lengths to describe and decode the ways that dominant culture has imagined gay men as the embodiment of AIDS. Simon Watney,

for example, explains how AIDS has been "embodied as an exemplary and admonitory drama, relayed between the image of the miraculous authority of clinical medicine and the faces and bodies of individuals who clearly disclose the stigmata of their guilt. The principal target of this sadistically punitive gaze is the body of the 'homosexual.' "[18] Douglas Crimp discusses the ramifications of this conflation of AIDS and gay men when he states that

> [w]hat is far more significant than the real *facts* of HIV transmission in various populations throughout the world, however, is the initial conceptualization of AIDS as a syndrome affecting gay men. No insistence on the facts will render that discursive construction obsolete, and not only because of the intractability of homophobia. The idea of AIDS as a gay disease occasioned two *interconnected* conditions in the U.S.: that AIDS would be an epidemic of stigmatization rooted in homophobia, and that the response to AIDS would depend in very large measure on the . . . gay movement. . . . "[19]

The effects of these representations, along with the other discourses by which we understand AIDS, led Paula Treichler to state in 1987 that we live not only in a medical epidemic but in an "epidemic of signification" as well.[20] These AIDS cultural theorists have taught us that AIDS cannot be separated from the discourses that construct it and, in fact, sustain it. The means to counter AIDS then needs to be explored in multiple sites of contestation and through various means of intervention. Early efforts to intervene in our understanding of AIDS set out to challenge the discourses which in fact rendered AIDS intelligible in dominant culture. One of the goals of these early efforts, which are by no means exhausted or unnecessary today, was to demystify and denaturalize the ideological underpinnings of the discourses that circulate as seemingly unmarked or neutral. *Acts of Intervention* aims to import these discussions into theatre and performance studies.

Theatre and performance studies is in a unique position to address questions about the relationship between AIDS and representation. Those of us who practice within this field have always needed to negotiate the often competing demands of examining the production process of performance on the one hand, and the task of critically interpreting performance on the other. In this sense, performance theorists have always had to interrogate embodied representations, particularly how embodied representations are *performed*. And yet when it comes to the topic of AIDS and performance, our discussions seem to remain primarily on the level of interpreting performance—that is, militating for or against certain representations—with little or no attention to the process or effect of performance within a larger social context. *Acts of Intervention* is interested in examining the effects of AIDS performance on the actual participants—performers and spectators—of this cultural practice. It asks how gay male performance participates in shaping gay men's relationship to AIDS.

AIDS cultural critics have taught us both the importance of critiquing the representations of AIDS that circulate in the culture at large and the need to expand the representational field of AIDS.[21] Theatre and performance studies can add to these discussions by continuing to examine the specific representations produced by the theatre and through performance. However, we can also contribute to these discussions by focusing on how these representations are produced and performed in the very space of performance, a space which we must generously imagine to include *both* the public sphere and the traditional stage.

Critical Generosity

If we now accept as axiomatic that AIDS has required us to rethink the traditional means by which we approach historical narratives, we should also consider how AIDS requires us to rethink the traditional means by which we criticize and interpret theatre and performance. Since the earliest years of the epidemic, gay men have used performance primarily for three specific yet interrelated purposes: first, as an educational means to challenge the misconceptions about AIDS; second, to build and sustain a communal response to the epidemic; and third, to pay tribute to those who have died. Most AIDS performances do not aspire to canonicity. Instead AIDS performances challenge our understanding of AIDS so that we better learn to cope with its effects. Nonetheless, many critics writing on AIDS performance, whether in academic or popular venues, base the very choices of what counts as AIDS performance on conventional concepts of theatre. Moreover, critics then go on to hold these performances up to an assumed and often uncontested standard of what constitutes "good" theatre. Good theatre, from this perspective, is understood to do primarily two things: stand the test of time and translate to as wide an audience as possible. In short, it should have "universal" appeal. Traditional theatre and performance criticism invests in a model of evaluation which is based on these canonical prejudices. The canonical biases which inflect most writing on AIDS performance begin with the reduction of AIDS theatre to a type of theatre; "AIDS theatre" becomes a generic category, a literary taxonomy which domesticates the radicalness of AIDS performance.

AIDS theatre and performance call for a new mode of criticism appropriate to the demands of the historical conditions of the crisis and the innovative artistic and political improvisations gay men have achieved in this time. The historical conditions which construct AIDS are continually shifting. As these conditions change, so must our evaluatory principles. A critical analysis which takes into account the changing cultural context of AIDS and performance might not conform to the traditional modes of theatre criticism. First of all, many people creating AIDS performances refuse to remain confined within the conventional bounds of theatre; or, less defiantly, may not even be aware of the traditional modes of theatre practice. People involved in the fight against AIDS perform various types of AIDS theatre, and they do this work in various, multiple, and unconventional settings. For these reasons, we need to allow our definition of AIDS performance to accommodate a more expanded and eclectic notion of what we generally consider to be theatre. *Acts of Intervention* examines mainstream and conventional theatre, including Broadway; performance art, solo performance, and interdisciplinary performance pieces; and community-based and/or community-specific projects, including AIDS educational theatre initiatives and/or site-specific performances. But it also examines various forms of performance which may not be immediately recognized as theatre, including various forms of AIDS activism. Chapter 1, for example, is devoted to documenting social responses to AIDS that tapped into, or even exploited, theatrical modes in the earliest years of the epidemic, the years *before* AIDS was represented on the conventional stage. Such an expanded definition of AIDS theatre underlines the distinct creative and political contributions gay men have achieved since the beginning of the epidemic. These AIDS theatres may choose to participate in the thematics of American drama, in the meditation of cross-cultural and transhistorical allegories of plague, or in the address of an incident so local that it may have little meaning outside its immediate context. These AIDS theatres may be interested primarily in raising money for AIDS causes and therefore take the form of a benefit or fundraiser, in contesting specific oppressive or discriminatory politics and therefore take the form of a protest or direct action, in educating peers about the risks of HIV transmission and therefore take the form of a play or community ritual, or in mourning loved ones and therefore take the form of a memorial service or candlelight vigil.

At best, critics writing on AIDS theatre and performance who attempt to index these works within preexisting artistic standards fail to account for the larger cultural work these performances set out to secure. At worst, they dismiss the efforts of gay men who prioritize in their AIDS performance political expediency or symbolic memorialization over artistic process. These approaches veil the fact that the idea of "artistic merit" is a culturally constructed concept primarily determined and sustained by a loose alliance of influential writers, academics, and artists. Debates about artistic merit begin to reveal the vulnerability of the concept of a fixed sense of artistic merit and the vested interests of those who set out to enforce and police it. To focus solely or even primarily on a performance's artistic merit is to obscure or trivialize the concern of how that performance may provide a necessary forum to address AIDS. The critical investment in aesthetics as the primary criteria sets up a false binary between art and politics that AIDS performance disputes. AIDS performance, like AIDS activism, emerged out of a community-based political movement that locates its history in the liberation struggles of lesbians and gay men. To lose sight of this fact is to seriously misunderstand the context of AIDS theatre and performance. This is by no means to suggest that the critic should abandon questioning the artistic qualities of an AIDS performance. Rather, the point here is that to focus on only the artistic process of an AIDS piece is a critical shortcoming. Our approach to AIDS theatre and performance should involve a consideration of both the artistic and political interventions these works may enact. Canonical prejudice, or the overinvestment in the cultural forms of the elite, should be supplanted by what I would call "critical generosity." Critical generosity is a practice that sets out to intervene in the limited perspectives we currently employ to understand and discuss AIDS theatre and performance by looking beyond conventional forms of analysis. Critical generosity therefore forces us not only to rethink the traditional criteria by which evaluations are made but also to acknowledge the ideological systems that promote canonical prejudice.

W hy generosity? What, in other words, is the necessity of generosity in the time of AIDS? Critical generosity is a response that resonates with the generosity of gay men who have used their own creative energy to intervene in the AIDS epidemic. This creative energy has materialized in the performance of AIDS activism in all its forms: from buddy programs and hotline counseling to ACT UP and PISD, from public speaking and corporate fundraising to tantric massage for PWAs and homecare for PWAs and their pets, from AIDS advocacy and lobbying efforts to AIDS healing circles and HIV-seroconcordant peer support groups, from red ribbons and AIDS quilts to die-ins and political funerals. Critical generosity participates and emerges out of the intrinsic generosity of this performance of AIDS activism. The works I have chosen to highlight in this book bring this mission of collective survival into the foreground. The critical task for me throughout this project has been to attend to the context and ambition of the performances under discussion. In this sense, my efforts to be critically generous can be understood as an attempt to honor the potential inherent in all AIDS performance to help us more effectively understand AIDS. Impelled by the epidemic, I am drawn to employing a mode of criticism that is neither adversarial nor polemical. Critical generosity understands that criticism can be much more than simply a procedure of critique or means for qualitative analysis. Criticism can also be a cooperative endeavor and collaborative engagement with a larger social mission.[22] This book aligns itself with lesbian and gay schol-ars who support lesbian and gay culture, and whose intellectual work helps sus-tain it. I have written this book not as a disinterested critic, but as a gay man living through the AIDS epidemic.

The idea that the intellectual writes from an objective vantage point is a fiction that needs to be continually contested and exposed. Our work is never objective; moreover, it affects the very artists under consideration—psychically, materially, spiritually. And yet despite this claim, critical generosity is never about conceding to the artist's intentions or authority. On the contrary, critical generosity puts pressure on the critic of AIDS performance to differentiate be-tween his or her activity—which is placing performance in its larger cultural, theoretical, and ideological contexts—and the creative activity of the performer. This sensitive critical dance—between honoring the intentions of progressive cultural work and pointing out its limitations or failures—foregrounds the stakes involved in writing about AIDS and theatre. Throughout *Acts of Interven-tion,* I have chosen to convey this tension rather than deny it. On this point, I agree with Jill Dolan, who writes, in the *Feminist Spectator as Critic,* that the chal-lenge for the progressive critic is not simply to nurture progressive work but also to address the limitations of even the most well-intended performance. For Dolan, this process may "institute a dialogue that resonates beyond the confines of an insular community," which, in turn, may enable radical cultural change.[23] Critical generosity attends to these effects and considers the ramifications of our intellectual work on the artists and communities involved.

My book on AIDS and performance, for example, is not only indebted to the theoretical interventions of AIDS cultural theorists but also to the wave of feminist performance scholarship which appeared in the 1980s.[24] Kate Davy's essays on lesbian performance, for example, demonstrate how performance can produce "spectatorial communities," an idea which resonates with my own proj-ect on AIDS. Davy writes about how

> performance pieces that construct lesbian spectatorial communities tend
> to drop from the performative address the heterosexuality that underpins
> hegemonic representations. . . . For spectators whose sole experience with
> dominant culture is one of either being erased entirely or foregrounded as
> tragically 'Other' against a (hetero)sexuality inscribed as fiercely norma-
> tive, the experience of being addressed as if inhabiting a discursive space,
> an elsewhere eked out in the gaps of hegemonic representations, is both
> profound and exhilarating.[25]

As we shall see in chapter 1, in the early 1980s, gay men and their supporters began through performance to build spectatorial communities around AIDS in-

tervention. Just as AIDS activism is indebted to the women's health care movement, which not only preceded the AIDS activism of the early 1980s but largely
enabled it, *Acts of Intervention* is indebted to the theoretical, political, and ideological interventions of feminist performance scholars.[26]

Finally, critical generosity should not be understood as a euphemism for
noncriticality, a naive celebratory propagandist rhetoric divorced from intellectual rigor. The intellectual rigor of critical generosity attends to the terms and
history of the AIDS crisis and not only (or primarily) the formal conventions
and genre analysis associated with high cultural production. This generous engagement with the different spaces where AIDS work is produced and with the
different communities this work may address brings forth a new means to understand the relationship between AIDS and performance. The practice of critical generosity therefore involves an intellectual engagement with the distinct
cultural contexts of performance. In this sense, critical generosity participates
in the necessary fiction of community. It is a criticism which locates its practice
in a participatory communal endeavor, what Cornel West has described as "a
new cultural politics of difference," where artists and intellectuals join forces
and talents to enact specific social change:

> The new cultural politics of difference are neither simply oppositional in
> contesting the mainstream (or malestream) for inclusion, nor transgres-
> sive in the avant-gardist sense of shocking conventional bourgeois audi-
> ences. Rather, they are distinct articulations of talented (and usually
> privileged) contributors to culture who desire to align themselves with de-
> moralized, demobilized, depoliticized, and disorganized people in order
> to empower and enable social action and, if possible, to enlist collective
> insurgency for the expansion of freedom, democracy and individuality.[27]

West claims that "prophetic criticism" is the approach appropriate for the new
cultural politics of difference "because while it begins with social structural
analyses it also makes explicit its moral and political aims" (31). Critical generosity responds to West's call for "prophetic criticism" since it also sets out to
confront the institutional regimes, including criticism, which disempower oppressed communities and individuals united to effect radical cultural change.
Like prophetic criticism, critical generosity pays attention to the conditions and
constraints of contemporary cultural production and to the potential of cultural
production to intervene in the political and public worlds under which people
now struggle to live. Hope is central to this struggle. *Acts of Intervention* invests
explicitly in the possibilities of hope. I realize that others may find this investment naive and even sentimental. In response, I would once again quote Cornel
West, who writes persuasively on the subject of hope in the context of what he

calls the "nihilistic threat—that is, the loss of hope and meaning" within black America:

> For as long as hope remains and meaning is preserved, the possibility of overcoming oppression stays alive. The self-fulfilling prophecy of the nihilistic threat is that without hope there can be no future, that without meaning there can be no struggle.[28]

While West's comments are specific to the systemic inequities oppressing African Americans, his ideas resonate in other cultural communities struggling to survive. *Acts of Intervention* provides the historical contexts by which hope was put into circulation by people united in the fight against AIDS. The consistent thread of AIDS activism and performance, as I argue, has been hope. Even those activists fueled by unmitigated rage invest in a degree of hope, if only the hope that their anger will prove effective personally and politically. With this in mind, I offer my practice of critical generosity in the hope that the various readers of *Acts of Intervention* may find in the book an affirmation of their own commitments to confronting AIDS or an invitation to begin doing so.

Acts of Intervention: A Critical Map

The first two chapters of the book provide an early cultural history of community-based responses to AIDS. Chapter 1, "Acts of Intervention," argues against the accepted wisdom that the theatre community failed to address AIDS in the early years (1981–83) of the epidemic. In various social performatives—fundraisers, benefits, memorials, vigils—theatre people employed performance as the primary means to raise money, educate those perceived to be at risk, and grieve for the dead. This chapter focuses on documenting these events and on developing a theoretical model for understanding the relationship between AIDS and performance. Chapter 2, "*One* and Counting: Early AIDS Plays" discusses early AIDS plays and performance pieces produced throughout the United States between 1983 and 1985. The chapter provides a more complete AIDS theatre history, one which includes an analysis of the critical reception and theoretical discussions which these plays and performances have engendered. And while the chapter is mainly historical in its approach, I address such issues as the politics of dramatic form and technique, representation and reception, and production and distribution, issues which are interrogated throughout the book. Together these two chapters seek to unsettle two problematic myths: that there was no viable AIDS activism before the arrival of ACT UP in 1987, and that there was no AIDS theatre before the 1985 productions of *As Is* and *The Normal Heart* in New York City.

The next five chapters of the book focus on specific instances of AIDS intervention in the theatre and through performance. They are case studies which can be read independently, although they are positioned in the book in a loosely chronological fashion. These case studies read dramatic texts and theatrical practices as examples of a cultural moment which convey not only the particular AIDS politics of their time but the specific interventions gay men performed. Chapter 3, "It's My Party and I'll Die If I Want To: AIDS Performance and the Circulation of Camp in the Late 1980s and Early 1990s," is concerned with the proliferation of camp both in the theatre and in the popular culture between 1987 and 1990 and the emergence of ACT UP in these same years. The chapter selects three key performances—Terrence McNally's *The Lisbon Traviata*, John Epperson's drag persona *Lypsinka*, and the Sodomy Players' production of *AIDS! The Musical!*—which thematize and explore the question of voice, and examines these productions in light of the theatrics of ACT UP. Chapter 4, "Solo Performance and the Body on Stage," addresses the phenomenon of gay male solo performance from the late 1980s to the present. The chapter explores how gay male bodies are rendered culturally intelligible and questions how AIDS solo performance might intervene in this process. The chapter begins by examining the ideological assumptions which have historically framed the terms of solo performance: performance art, performance, and theatre. The work of Michael Kearns, Ron Vawter, Tim Miller, and Ron Athey contest not only cultural myths of gay male bodies but the security assumed in the terms that are upheld to keep categories of performance discrete as well. These two chapters foreground performative tactics of identity and community in the age of AIDS.

The two next chapters, in building on these discussions, focus on performances by gay men of color. The intersections of "sexual minority" with "racial" or "ethnic" minority, particularly in relation to AIDS, raise a series of specific issues which I introduce here. Chapter 5, "Pomo Afro Homos' *Fierce Love*: Intervening in the Cultural Politics of Race, Sexuality, and AIDS," begins by looking at the ways that black gay men are represented in popular culture and how these representations inform discussions of AIDS and race. The chapter studies performances by the Pomo Afro Homos—three black, gay male artists— in this context. I argue that the work of the Pomos creates a space for a radical intervention in the cultural politics of AIDS. The Pomos, who toured their work across the United States regularly between the years 1990 and 1995, provide their audiences multiple simultaneous pedagogies depending on the specific subject position of the spectator. Chapter 6, "Teatro Viva! Latino Performance and the Politics of AIDS in Los Angeles," focuses on the specific AIDS cultural politics effecting Latinos in Los Angeles throughout the early 1990s. The chapter surveys the representations of homosexuality and AIDS in Latino theatre and culture and documents the various responses progressive Latino cultural workers in Los Angeles have achieved through activism and performance. These two chapters converse with other intellectual work which theorizes "minority" discourse; although these chapters seem to carry the book's burden of race, the issues raised in them are addressed throughout the project.

While the work of gay men of color is vulnerable to critical neglect, the work of Tony Kushner is vulnerable to a kind of critical excess generally reserved for only the most canonical writers. Chapter 7, "November 1, 1992: AIDS/*Angels in America*," discusses the first full staging of both parts of Tony Kushner's *Angels in America* (Part 1: *Millennium Approaches* and Part 2: *Perestroika*), which premiered in Los Angeles at the Mark Taper Forum on the eve of the 1992 presidential elections. But rather than offering a totalizing interpretation of Kushner's play, I isolate a single performance of *Angels in America* and speculate on the intervention made available to its audiences in that specific historical moment. The chapter looks at the occasion of *Angels* opening in light of a series of events converging on November 1, 1992. The chapter is inspired by the writings of Raymond Williams and the practices of performance studies. Throughout my discussion of this one performance of *Angels in America*, I consider the conditions of tragedy—in the modern world, on November 1, 1992— and the available means Williams and Kushner may provide us to move beyond it in light of AIDS. In this sense, the chapter is a meditation on hope.

The final chapter is concerned with the representations of HIV-negatives in AIDS theatre and popular culture. I survey the limited discourses surrounding negativity and point out some of the reasons why gay men might have left negativity unmarked. In theatre and performance, HIV-negatives rarely become the subject of the play. I not only consider the ramifications of this phenomenon, but I look to the conventions of AIDS theatre and performance for some answers to this problem. Therefore the chapter is interested in pursuing questions of genre: What are the effects of imagining AIDS as a tragedy? What do we make of the success and proliferation in the 1990s of comedies such as *Love! Valour! Compassion!* and *Jeffrey*? What is the relationship set up between genre and serostatus?

The final two chapters call attention to the success of AIDS theatre and performance and discuss plays that are widely produced and available in print. The continuing acceleration of HIV infections and AIDS fatalities among gay men along with the ubiquity of AIDS theatre and performance in the 1990s suggests that as the crisis of AIDS proliferates, gay men will persist in intervening in the epidemic. As I argue, these acts of intervention will prove most efficacious when they attend to both the dominant and subcultural understandings of AIDS in their specific cultural instance and location. Despite the historical trajectory as-

sumed in the organization of this book, I do not recommend reading AIDS theatre and performance as a narrative of progress. The commercialization of AIDS
theatre evidenced by the success of *Angels in America, Jeffrey,* and *Love! Valour!
Compassion!* in the 1990s is not—by any means—an indication that this work is
more important or valuable than its predecessors. Rather than viewing these plays
as the culmination of AIDS theatre and performance, we should be identifying and analyzing the specific network of factors that have enabled their mainstream arrival. The book's afterword on *Rent,* Jonathan Larson's 1996 musical
sensation, points to the kinds of questions we now need to consider given the
changing medical and cultural landscape of AIDS.

Throughout this book I have attempted to demonstrate how gay men have
intervened in the crisis of AIDS through theatre and performance. I have also
attempted to demonstrate how AIDS and our understanding of it have influenced our theatre. The ramifications of this dialectic materialize differently depending on the specific context of its reception by particular audiences. For this
reason, I will sometimes situate a particular performance through my own personal experience of the event as a means to mark not only the historical moment
of theatrical production but also a specific moment of its reception in my life.
Thus the book calls attention to the several histories of AIDS—including the
personal—which are unfolding simultaneously.

One final word on these unfolding histories and the issue of periodization.
While the book discusses performances between 1981 and 1996, I do not intend
Acts of Intervention to implicitly suggest, as others have begun to, that 1996 may
mark a turning point that has brought us very near to the end of AIDS. And yet
the current landscape of AIDS has radically shifted. As I discuss in the afterword, reports of successful new drug treatments along with drops in AIDS
fatalities in the United States have dramatically altered the way that AIDS is
understood and experienced by many people in this country—but not by all
people, and not even by all gay men. I end my book in 1996 for a number of
reasons, the most practical of them being that I simply needed to stop writing.
Throughout my writing process these past six years, I have struggled with the
need to continually update my research and historize specific modes of activism
and performance. I have also attempted to contextualize more clearly such emotions as hope and rage in relation to the AIDS crisis, feelings which are a little
more difficult to pin down since they emanate so unpredictably from within
our own individual selves and our dynamic and diverse communal worlds. The
challenge for me throughout this book has been to attend to the immediate historical impulses of the activism and performance under question and to allow
my own investments in those practices to remain visible. Speculations and pronouncements that we are approaching or have arrived at the end of AIDS have

been part of the historical response to AIDS since the early 1980s. Yet people continued—and still continue—to die.

At the end of his 1993 essay, "Sleeping under a Tree," an essay that addresses the need for sleep and his own insomnia given his particular mix of emotional anxieties, physical limitations, and treatment regimes, Paul Monette reimagines his insomnia as a form of resistance, his sleepless nights a time to monitor the world around him and those whom he loves: "Keep watch, every night if you have to."[29] I have taken these words to heart ever since reading them. They have moved me to go to the theatre, to activist meetings, and back to the computer more times than not. The book stops in 1996, as did most of the writing for it. While 1981–1996 may mark a period that will prove useful in some histories—it has for this one—it doesn't mark the end of AIDS. Paul Monette's words still resonate for me—I still keep watch—even as I complete this book.

Los Angeles
February 1997

Acts of Intervention

.

1

Acts of Intervention

July 3, 1981: "Sing Out on the 4th!"

"SING OUT ON the 4th!" demands the four-column Independence Savings Bank advertisement in the *New York Times* (fig.1). To further inspire readers' patriotism for the upcoming Fourth of July weekend, the ad provides the sheet music—musical notations and three rounds of stanza—for the U.S. national anthem, "The Star Spangled Banner." Such an ostentatious display of patriotism is ubiquitous in dominant media and only confirms the role of newspapers in what Benedict Anderson terms the idea of an "imagined community."[1] Newspapers provide the means to restore readers' confidence that the imagined world is "visibly rooted in everyday life." Newspapers organize the world, shape the idea of nationhood, and position the reader in relationship to the world as a national subject. The ritual of reading the newspaper, whether it is performed in the privacy and isolation of the home or in the openness of the public sphere, also highlights the act of reading as predominantly social. Although newspapers may be read in private, readers are assured that millions of others are simultaneously embarked in the same endeavor. In this sense, the "Sing out on the 4th!" ad in the *New York Times* foregrounds and assumes the mythos of community and nationalism. The ad is understood within this mythos, and, by extension, this understanding is naturalized in relation to the ad's form, venue, and assumed spectatorship.

The way the advertisement is laid out on the page resembles a coupon. You could ostensibly cut along the perforated lines and use the ad as a guide for the next day's national sing-a-long. Or perhaps you could pass it along to someone skilled at reading music or to someone who is unable to remember all the anthem's lyrics. In all cases, the ad begs for performance. Once clipped, the ad, like a coupon, is capable of reentering the cultural economy and outlasting (even if only shortly) its assumed obsolescence. The form is also essentially text-based. The image of the sheet music for the national anthem (the ad's "content") is framed by the ad's declaratives, "Sing out on the 4th!" and "Happy Independence Day," and signed by the Independence Savings Bank logo. The coincidence between Independence Day and Independence Bank secures a link be-

RARE CANCER SEEN IN 41 HOMOSEXUALS

Outbreak Occurs Among Men in New York and California — 8 Died Inside 2 Years

By LAWRENCE K. ALTMAN

Doctors in New York and California have diagnosed among homosexual men 41 cases of a rare and often rapidly fatal form of cancer. Eight of the victims died less than 24 months after the diagnosis was made.

The cause of the outbreak is unknown, and there is as yet no evidence of contagion. But the doctors who have made the diagnoses, mostly in New York City and the San Francisco Bay area, are alerting other physicians who treat large numbers of homosexual men to the problem in an effort to help identify more cases and to reduce the delay in offering chemotherapy treatment.

The sudden appearance of the cancer, called Kaposi's Sarcoma, has prompted a medical investigation that experts say could have as much scientific as public health importance because of what it may teach about determining the causes of more common types of cancer.

First Appears in Spots

Doctors have been taught in the past that the cancer usually appeared first in spots on the legs and that the disease took a slow course of up to 10 years. But these recent cases show that it appears in one or more violet-colored spots anywhere on the body. The spots generally do not itch or cause other symptoms, often can be mistaken for bruises, sometimes appear as lumps and can turn brown after a period of time. The cancer often causes swollen lymph glands, and then kills by spreading throughout the body.

Doctors investigating the outbreak believe that many cases have gone undetected because of the rarity of the condition and the difficulty even dermatologists may have in diagnosing it.

In a letter alerting other physicians to the problem, Dr. Alvin E. Friedman-Kien of New York University Medical Center, one of the investigators described the appearance of the outbreak as "rather devastating."

Dr. Friedman-Kien said in an interview yesterday that he knew of 41 cases collated in the last five weeks, with the cases themselves dating to the past 30 months. The Federal Centers for Disease Control in Atlanta is expected to publish the first description of the outbreak in its weekly report today, Dr. James Curran. The report notes 26 of the cases — 20 in New York and six in California.

There is no national registry of cancer victims, but the nationwide incidence of Kaposi's Sarcoma in the past had been estimated by the Centers for Disease Control to be less than six-one-hundredths of a case per 100,000 people annually, or about two cases in every three million people. However the disease accounts for up to 9 percent of all cancers in a belt across equatorial Africa, where it commonly affects children and young adults.

In the United States it has primarily affected men older than 50 years. But in the recent cases doctors at nine medical centers in New York and several hospitals in California have been diagnosing the condition among younger men, all of whom said in the course of stand and diagnostic interviews that they were homosexual. Although the ages of the patients have ranged from 26 to 51 years, many have been under 40 with the mean at 39.

Nine of the 41 cases known to Dr. Friedman-Kien were diagnosed in California and several of those victims reported that they had been in New York in the period preceding the diagnosis. Dr. Friedman-Kien said that his colleagues were checking on reports of two victims diagnosis, in Copenhagen one of whom had visited New York.

Viral Infections Indicated

No one medical investigator has yet interviewed all the victims, Dr. Curran said. According to Dr. Friedman-Kien, the reporting doctors said that most cases had involved homosexual men who have had multiple and frequent sexual encounters with different partners, as many as 10 sexual encounters each night up to four times a week.

Many of the patients have also been treated for viral infections such as herpes, cytomegalovirus and hepatitis B as well as parasitic infections such as amebiasis and giardiasis. Many patients also reported that they had used drugs such as amyl nitrite and LSD to heighten sexual pleasure.

Cancer is not believed to be contagious but conditions that might precipitate it, such as particular viruses or environmental factors might account for an outbreak among a single group.

The medical investigators say some indirect evidence actually points away from contagion as a cause. None of the patients knew each other although the theoretical possibility that some may have had sexual contact with a person with Kaposi's Sarcoma at some point in the past could not be excluded, Dr. Friedman-Kien said.

Dr. Curran said there was no apparent danger to nonhomosexuals from contagion. "The best evidence against contagion," he said, "is that no cases have been reported to date outside the homosexual community or in women."

Dr. Friedman-Kien said he had tested nine of the victims and found severe defects in their immunological systems. The patients had serious malfunctions of two types of cells called T and B cell lymphocytes, which have important roles in fighting infections and cancer.

But Dr. Friedman-Kien emphasized that the researchers did not know whether the immunological defects were the underlying problem or had developed secondarily to the infections or drug use.

The research team is testing various hypotheses, one of which is a possible link between past infection with cytomegalovirus and development of Kaposi's Sarcoma.

105TH YEAR: THE FRESH AIR FUND

Sing out on the 4th!

(Sing out)

Happy Independence Day

from

INDEPENDENCE SAVINGS BANK

1. *New York Times*, July 3, 1981, page A20.

tween patriotic ideology and capitalist investment that is, paradoxically, both the manifest and covert content of the ad. In this sense, investment is understood as a patriotic practice. The ad's venue—the *New York Times*—assures a wide readership and, moreover, one which Anderson would identify as an "imagined community" invested in the constructs of both nationhood and patriotism. Thus the ad's venue, in combination with the actual content of the ad, explicitly assumes a certain patriotic ideology which links national interest with security and ritual performance. The intended audience of the ad is, of course, no one less than everyone who reads the newspaper. However, the implied audience is the model citizen.

Alongside the "Sing out on the 4th" ad is a single-column news item which announces in its headline: "Rare Cancer Seen in 41 Homosexuals," the first reporting in the *New York Times* of what we now understand as AIDS. The juxtaposition of the ad and the news item on page A20 of the Friday, July 3, 1981, *New York Times* newspaper situates AIDS and patriotic performance, however arbitrarily, as independent, unrelated items *and* linked occasions within the U.S. cultural imaginary. Not surprisingly, the form, content, venue, and audience of the news item corresponds to the ad. The "imagined community" of the news item relies on the us/them binarism; the "us" is comforted by the presumed containment of the "contagion" in "them" by the following passage:

> Dr. Curran [spokesperson for the Centers for Disease Control] said there was no apparent danger to nonhomosexuals from contagion. "The best evidence against contagion," he said, "is that no cases have been reported to date outside the homosexual community or in women."[2]

The by now familiar popularized misconception of "risk groups" and "the general population" finds its first articulation in the nation's "newspaper of record" in Lawrence Altman's 18-paragraph news story. Within this story, Curran's comments universalize the experience of 41 gay men for the entire imagined "homosexual community" and sets into place the early perceptions of most medical experts and government officials that the rare cancer seen in those 41 homosexuals would remain, in Altman's phrasing, "among a single group."[3] The July 3, 1981, report on the "outbreak" of Kaposi's Sarcoma is constructed within what British AIDS cultural theorist and activist Simon Watney calls the contagion/seduction model of homosexuality. Watney explains how within this system, homosexuality is imagined as "a contagious condition, invisible and always threatening to reveal itself where least expected" and as the "spectacle of erotic seduction, in which 'innocent,' 'vulnerable' youth is fantasized as an unwilling partner to acts which, nonetheless, have the power to transform his (or her) entire being."[4] As in all contagion/seduction models, homosexuality must therefore be policed, disavowed, and/or contained to protect the assumed general population, which is constructed as based on heteronormative conceptions of the family, community, and nation. Mainstream media, including newspapers, enforce this view. Watney argues that the press constructs "an ideal audience of national family units, surrounded by the threatening spectacle of the mad, the foreign, the criminal and the perverted" (84).

And yet within the single group defined by the *New York Times* news story— gay men—an us/them binarism is also inadvertently constructed. Homosexuals are defined in terms of age ("the mean at 39") and location (New York City and the San Francisco Bay area) as well as sexual practices: "According to Dr. Friedman-Kien [one of the investigators], the reporting doctors said that most cases had involved homosexual men who have had multiple and frequent sexual encounters with different partners, as many as 10 sexual encounters each night up to four times a week." Friedman-Kien's profile of gay men with "rare cancer" allows for at least two possible means to implicate other gay men within his pool of 41 cases.[5] On the one hand, gay men who fit the profile are tacitly incriminated. On the other, the statistical limits of 41 gay men having "as many as 10 sexual encounters each night up to four times a week" exceeds the numbers in his pool. While Altman reports that "the cause of the outbreak is unknown, and there is as yet no evidence of contagion," contagion is implied by Friedman-Kien's profile. Altman writes that Friedman-Kien reported that of 41 cases known, nine were diagnosed in California and "several of those victims reported they had been in New York in the period preceding the diagnosis." Moreover, Friedman-Kien mentions that his colleagues "were checking on reports of two victims diagnosed in Copenhagen, one of whom had visited New York." The *New York Times* article reports that one of the primary doubts for a contagion theory for the medical investigators is that none of the men diagnosed with Kaposi's Sarcoma actually knew each other. But like the readers of the newspaper itself, who, unknown to each other, share the activity of their reading, an imagined community is constructed in terms of behavior and shared activity and located within New York City. The fiction of an imagined community is constantly evoked for the newspaper's readers in the text of the news story, in the Independence Savings Bank advertisement, and in the materiality of the newspaper itself. Readers must either accept or repudiate the identificatory possibilities within the "Rare Cancer" news story and in the relationship between that very news story and the adjacent four-column Independence Savings Bank advertisement. The newspaper seems to resolve this tension by directing its readers to the advertisement. The advertisement asks readers to perform a certain citizenship—"Sing out on the 4th"—and provides readers with the means to do so.

What we now understand as AIDS is first introduced in the *New York Times* alongside performance. Separated, at first, by the single-column's right-side line and, once more, by the moat-like white space between that very line and the perforations that enclose the sheet music for the national anthem, AIDS and performance are situated relationally within a national ideology of patriotism, citizenship, and community. Gay men are precariously implicated in the logic of page A20: either perform model citizenship or risk implosion with rare cancer. What's at stake is nothing less than the ideology of patriotic heterosexuality.

The celebratory command to "Sing out on the 4th!" seems to respond sequentially to the "Rare Cancer Seen in Homosexuals," whose subheading explains that an "Outbreak Occurs Among Men in New York and California—8 Died Inside 2 Years." The placement of the copy of the news headline with the ad headline within the same horizontal top column of the page uncannily places the two presumably "calendrical coincidences" in direct relation to each other.[6] If the news item makes explicit that the outbreak is contained within the "homosexual community," who then is directed to sing out on the Fourth and for what reasons? The cruel joke of the news item in juxtaposition with the bold "Happy Independence Day," on the Friday before the official national holiday weekend, shifts a potential time of leisure for hundreds of thousands of gay men into a potential time of terror. The members of an imagined community of gay men, in particular, are forced to locate their citizenship in either one of the positions of A20's binarism. AIDS and performance, as A20 insists, are relational terms in the continuous negotiation of national identity and model citizenship. The performance embedded in the "Sing out on the 4th" advertisement reads not only as a direct response to the "Rare Cancer Seen in 41 Homosexuals" but even more so as a foundational cultural instance that initiates a national AIDS ideology. Such a national AIDS ideology emerged from the cultural networks of power in the United States—the media, biomedical science, and government agencies—and is based upon their effects, disavowal, and repudiation on the one hand, and hyperbolic patriotism and moralizing on the other. It is not possible to ignore AIDS and performance, the two cohabitants of A20, as relational terms participating in the formation of a dominant AIDS ideology that will be assumed, contested, and continually negotiated within U.S. cultural politics throughout the history of the epidemic.

Gay male New Yorkers interested in performance had various options for the 1981 Fourth of July weekend. They could cut along the perforated borders of the national anthem and sing out on the Fourth—sheet music in hand—at the Pines, on the streets, or in their homes; or they could attend any number of theatrical productions in a vibrant New York theatre scene. On July 3, 1981, gay New Yorkers could choose between Charles Ludlam's *Love's Tangled Web* at the

Ridiculous Theater Company's home at One Sheridan Square; Elizabeth Taylor in the Broadway revival of Lillian Hellman's *The Little Foxes*; Ian McKellen in *Amadeus* (but only if you had advance tickets); Victor Bumbalo's new comedy, *Niagara Falls*; and two separate Joe Orton plays, *Entertaining Mr. Sloane* (directed by John Tillinger at the Cherry Lane in a production that would have Brad Davis replace Max Caulfield) or *What the Butler Saw*, which opened at the Upstairs Cabaret that night. The second installment of William Finn's "Marvin trilogy," *March of the Falsettos*, was at Playwrights Horizon; *Oscar Remembered*, a one-person play about Oscar Wilde's downfall, written and performed by Maxim Mazumdar, had recently opened at the Provincetown Playhouse; and the Glines's hit production of *My Blue Heaven*, by the lesbian playwright Jane Chambers, along with Caryl Churchill's *Cloud 9*, directed by Tommy Tune, were having successful runs. And, if this weren't enough, three plays written by gay men with gay characters and themes, Michael Bennett's musical *A Chorus Line*, Lanford Wilson's *Fifth of July*, and Albert Innaurato's *Gemini*, were playing on Broadway. Over sixty plays and performances were lit during the 1981 Fourth of July weekend in New York City.

The proliferation of lesbian and gay theatre in the United States evident in the early 1980s and, more particularly, available to New York audiences throughout the 1981 Fourth of July weekend resulted not only from the post-Stonewall liberation politics of the late 1960s and 1970s, but also from the emergence of community-based theatres throughout the country.[7] In New York City, this process began as early as 1958, with the founding of the Caffe Cino, and continued with the emergence in the 1960s and 1970s of other Off Off Broadway theatres such as La Mama, the Judson Poets Theater, the Glines Theater, and the Playhouse of the Ridiculous.[8] In these Off Off Broadway theatres, lesbians and gay men were able to begin offering alternatives to the standard fare of mainstream representation, what Don Shewey identifies as "frivolous fairies, psychotic bulldykes, and suicidal queens."[9] Early gay theatre proved an intervention in the perpetuation of these problematic representations. It offered a diversity of self-representations and it recuperated some of these clichés and placed them within a more queer-friendly context. Lesbians and gay men involved in early lesbian and gay theatre were able to initiate new structures for representation. These new structures challenged the concepts of traditional mainstream theatre not only in terms of content and representation, but also in terms of theatrical form, venue, acting, and spectatorship. New performance spaces sprang up in various locations throughout the city, providing artists the opportunity to work in conjunction with the communities most invested in the representations. At places like the Caffe Cino, the Ridiculous, and WOW Cafe, communities of actors, technical crews, and spectators were actually constructed around the idea and practice of performance. This, of course, is not unusual for the theatre, which in some ways demands the notions of collaboration in order to succeed. What is unusual, however, is that at these places lesbians and gays could work as *out* lesbians and gays. That many of the key figures and institutions of these early formative years of lesbian and gay theatre were thriving in the summer of 1981 is a testament not only to their talent and endurance but also to the success of their early interventions in expanding the representational field.

By July 3, 1981, lesbian and gay theatre was beginning to be both commercially viable and critically acclaimed. New playwrights and performers continued to appear on the scene and receive support from the institutional venues and networks set up in the early days of lesbian and gay theatre and in the wake of Stonewall. The options for gay men, in particular, during the 1981 summer holiday weekend were multiple. And if AIDS and performance were introduced in the *New York Times* that weekend as relational links that served the interests of a national heteronormative ideology that repudiated homosexuality at whatever cost, a foundational structure was already in place at the time to allow for a series of interventions. One intervention possible for gay men at the time was to clip out the sheet music for the national anthem and simply toss it away, throwing into crisis the representational iconography of patriotic performance and replacing the assumed performance with any of the other performances advertised in the *New York Times* and available throughout that weekend. Such a process of appropriating and recontextualizing the very forces of the regimes of power that construct AIDS, in particular those of the media, will be among the fundamental tactics of later direct action groups united in the fight against AIDS. But already in 1981, thanks to the efforts of an identity-based lesbian and gay political movement, gay men could respond to the ideology of patriotic heterosexuality and help shape an AIDS ideology that would grant multiple, various, and sometimes contradictory means of agency. Thus the advertisement to "Sing out on the 4th!" could be reconstructed so that rather than participating in the repudiation of homosexuality, gay men could actually declare it. Like the demo fliers and posters made ubiquitous by ACT UP and Queer Nation in the late 1980s and early 1990s, page A20 could be reconstructed to read as a call to action. "Gay Cancer Seen in 41 Homosexuals." "Sing out on the 4th!" "Meet at Washington Square Park at noon for a march and rally to demand more research and information!" But such direct acts of intervention, fueled by the fantasies available in hindsight, were not imagined at the time.

Acts of Intervention and the Space of Performance

Gay men, since the earliest days of the epidemic, have performed a continuous series of AIDS interventions. In the broadest sense, performance entails a wide-ranging spectrum of activity from mainstream commercial theatre to the rituals of everyday life. Performance, moreover, always entails production. Auditions and casting, rewrites and rehearsals, and staging and blocking, for example, all components of the production process and all loosely "performances" in their own right, are prime locations for intervening in our understanding of AIDS. The materiality of performance (actors, lights, sets, props) along with the venue or location—what I will be calling the space of performance—informs both the process of production and the performance of AIDS. Insofar as performance entails a deliberate enactment of social ritual, one could feasibly argue that all gay male social responses to AIDS are a type of performance, that many of these social performances are attempts to intervene in our understanding of AIDS as it takes its form and is sustained by the governing institutions of the dominating center of power, and that these performances— acts of intervention, really—contribute, immeasurably and in ways impossible to register effectively, to the continual cultural negotiations of AIDS, sexuality, and citizenship in the local, regional, and national spheres. Some of these performances have been staged in the theatre, others have been enacted in the streets; some of these performances have been recorded into the annals of U.S. cultural history, others have left no record of their production.

The earliest AIDS interventions—I am referring to performances and acts of 1981–84—were localized and temporal interventions that have left little or no trace of their production. Their intent to intervene in the dominant constructions of AIDS may have been in collaboration with fundraisers, early education efforts, protest marches, and memorial services; as such, they were performed in nontraditional performance settings including bars, community meeting centers, shared public spaces, and houses of worship. Their effects were meant to be direct and immediate. Their intent was not necessarily in calling attention to the merits of the performance itself, but rather performances were contained within the larger ritual structure of the fundraiser, the education campaign, the protest march, or the memorial service. The performance was in collaboration with a ritual that exceeded the performance, or, better stated, the performance participated in a larger ritualized performance—the fundraiser, the protest, the memorial—that itself was the primary act of intervention. Performance, in this sense, was part of the more encompassing ritual that helped organize people's response to AIDS both in space and in time. The intervention had less to do with the representation or content imbedded in the performance proper—the song, the dance, the act—and more to do with performance's potential to bring people together into the space of performance. And once people are gathered in the space of performance, the possibility of intervention proliferates.

But if the goal of early AIDS interventions was to gather people into the space of performance, wherever that may be, in order to raise funds, promote consciousness, initiate discussions, and to strategize and coordinate plans of support for those affected, the motivating and organizing force of the intervention was to stop the epidemic. In this sense, early AIDS performances can be defined as activist-identified. The fact that so little documentation remains for the early 1980s efforts suggests both the belief that AIDS would soon be resolved and that the motivation of artists, performers, and other early AIDS organizers was not contained within conventional aesthetic practices and archival systems. But the lack of documentation of these early intervention efforts also points to the widespread indifference to AIDS in the country at large, particularly among the media, whose failure to report on the epidemic kept these performance interventions from the public view.[10] The earliest AIDS performances were less invested in formal aesthetics, authorship, individual production, or the processes of critical reception—the standard fare of the arts—and more based upon the belief in the social role of the arts in promoting change. The artistic performance—the song, the dance, the act—served the mission of the intervention as either a commodity to draw people into the space of performance, as intermittent entertainment to fill the time between speeches, or, in the case of AIDS memorial services, as a tribute to the dead and those left behind.[11] The performance was not itself the *sine qua non* of the intervention. Rather, performance was part of the means of intervention. This anti-idealist notion of art also helps explain the lack of conventional performances about AIDS in the early 1980s. If, in the early 1980s, performance was located within the more encompassing process of social ritual, and if the artists, performers, and technical designers with an AIDS consciousness were participating primarily in the production of social ritual, it needs to be stated clearly and simply that the earliest responses *of* the theatre to AIDS were not then *in* the theatre.

It would be misleading, however, to suggest that the theatre community was so involved in fundraisers and benefits, consciousness-raising sessions and education campaigns, protests and rallies, and in planning AIDS memorial services and vigils that there was no available time or energy to represent AIDS on the stage. The level of denial in theatre communities across the country was omnipresent and real. In part, this denial was no different from that rampant throughout the United States in the early 1980s, even within lesbian and gay communities. Given this prevalence of AIDS denial, there was no reason to expect the theatre community to respond differently from any of the other communities hit hardest in the early years of the epidemic. The anxieties stemming from the fear of AIDS; the grief, if not the trauma, engendered by the number of losses of friends, lovers, and collaborators; and the assumption of many gay men in the theatre that they themselves would soon be dead, all contributed to the slow response in representing AIDS in traditional theatre venues.[12] But to make such a claim is not to say that theatre did not respond to AIDS early on. Theatrical representation is only one type of performance. Theatrical representation is only one means by which gay men through performance can intervene in the dominant ideologies that construct and sustain AIDS. The earliest AIDS performances were located not in the theatre but in the collaborative, community-based production of social rituals. These rituals set out to gather people into the space of performance in order to raise money for research and care; instigate AIDS awareness; establish community-based service organizations; facilitate discussion around such contested issues as sexual practices, behaviors, and identities; and honor the dead.[13]

1981–1983: Fundraisers, Benefits, Memorial Services, Candlelight Vigils

Fundraisers, the social ritual of gathering people into the space of performance to raise money, were, along with memorial services, the first acts of intervention in the fight against AIDS. Early AIDS fundraisers intended to raise money to support scientific research on Kaposi's sarcoma and provide treatment for gay men without money or medical insurance. AIDS activist and author Larry Kramer explains that the first AIDS fundraiser was actually the idea of someone from the medical profession, Dr. Friedman-Kien, who asked Kramer to begin organizing New York City's gay male community against the spread of Kaposi's sarcoma. Kramer reports that on August 11, 1981—five weeks after the *New York Times* article on "rare cancer"—he and three others (Donald Krintzman, Paul Rapoport, and Dr. Lawrence Mass) held the first fundraiser in his apartment:

> We called all the friends we could think of who had money for charitable contributions or were well known in the gay community and could help get the word around. Hundreds were invited, including every doctor with a gay practice. Eighty men came.

> Donald had prepared contribution circulars, and Dr. Friedman-Kien addressed the gathering and answered questions. He said he thought an epidemic was occurring (it was officially declared such in October by the government) [subsequently to be back-dated to June 5th by the Centers for Disease Control], that the causes were unknown, that there were a number of possible "culprits," none of which could be discounted.

> We raised $6, 635 as a result of the first night.

> Two committees were formed to carry forward the endeavors: one to organize a solicitation of Fire Island, chaired by Philip Gefter, and another

to plan a benefit dance, chaired by Edmund White. Each committee had over a dozen members. We all felt we were off to a good start.[14]

The August 11, 1981, fundraiser at Kramer's apartment and the efforts of a handful of volunteers on Labor Day weekend 1981 were intended to raise money, but they succeeded mainly in raising discussion about Kaposi's sarcoma. The Labor Day weekend fundraiser was a financial disappointment. Kramer reports that he, Paul Popham, and Rick Fialla stood at the door of the Ice Palace, a popular dance club, on Saturday night from midnight until 8:00 A.M. and collected a mere $126 from thousands of dancers. Cash boxes were also set up at the harbors, and brochures, detailing the epidemic, were distributed to "every door in the Pines and the Grove."[15] Randy Shilts reports that "the small band of organizers figured they'd be able to raise thousands from the 15,000 gay men who had congregated for the last blowout of the '81 season."[16] Unfortunately, the Fire Island fundraiser over Labor Day weekend raised only $769.55. And although checks were later mailed, by the end of the 1981 they had raised only $11,806.55. Edmund White's benefit dance committee ran into a series of obstacles: the leading gay disco, Kramer reports, was not supportive and "[a]ppeals to famous gay rock and disco stars, who would not be famous were it not for gay dancers, to appear at this benefit have been turned down."[17] Fundraisers are designed to raise money, but they are also designed to expand the field of support. Their intent is to identify new donors, subscribers, and supporters who extend beyond the confines of the familiar few. Kramer makes this explicit in his account of the Fire Island project when he writes that "we comforted ourselves that even if contributions were small at the Island, at least we were educating our community about KS, something few had known anything about before.[18] These early efforts to raise funds and consciousness led to the formation of the Gay Men's Health Crisis Committee, the earliest collaborative mobilization project to fight the epidemic. (The Gay Men's Health Crisis [GMHC] received its official corporate charter in the summer of 1982, and thus switched from a "committee" to a "corporation.")

Within seven months, GMHC was able to stage a more successful fundraiser to combat what was at the time termed Gay Related Immunodeficiency (GRID). The April 8, 1982, fundraiser, "Showers: A Benefit to Aid Gay Men with Kaposi's Sarcoma and Other Gay Related Immunodeficiencies," was attended by over 2,000 people who gathered to dance at the Paradise Garage and in the process raised over $52,000. (Still, only 500 names at the party were gathered for the mailing list.)[19] The multiple successes of the fundraiser dramatically shifted the AIDS consciousness of gay New Yorkers. "Showers" was the first in a series of large-scale benefits that would provide early activists the opportunity to address other gay men about the health crisis. In his address that night to the crowd, Paul Popham, the president of the Gay Men's Health Crisis Committee, assured attendees that the Crisis Committee would keep them abreast of the latest information on the "medical emergency."[20] Popham explained how over 150 had already died and "about that many more are very ill and may leave us, too." Money raised would go to fund specific research and to establish a free informational newsletter, "available to anyone anywhere, that explains in clear and simple language exactly what is known about all diseases thought to be related to our various activities." While the event was successful in raising money, it was also successful in disseminating important information, calming a growing hysteria while forcefully countering an equally growing apathy, announcing the long-term plans of the newly launched organization, and galvanizing more people around the health crisis than any other event up to that point.

The Showers benefit, which included live performances from such disco stars as Evelyn King and the Ritchie Family as well as a performance by the New York City Gay Men's Chorus, boosted the morale of a city under siege and put into motion a series of smaller, more localized fundraisers throughout Manhattan. On June 20, 1982, for example, Maneuvers—a newly opened gay bar in Chelsea—sponsored a special tea dance benefit with guest spots from, according to their advertisement, "all of New York's top D.J.'s."[21] The fundraiser was specifically for the St. Mark's Clinic's Lymphadenopathy Syndrome Project to detect immune deficiency in gay men. The special performance by members of the cast of Michael Bennett's *Dreamgirls* was, perhaps, the first theatrical performance at an AIDS fundraiser. Various New York theatre people also lent their support to the August 28, 1982, benefit cocktail party—attended by 330 people and which raised $18,000—at the Southampton home of artist Larry Rivers, including James Kirkwood, Edward Albee, Susan Sontag, Terrence McNally, Joe Pintauro, and Larry Kramer.[22] While it may be difficult to argue that such an event democratizes AIDS awareness and outreach, the $40-per-ticket benefit cocktail party significantly organized a group of visual and performing artists to respond to AIDS. Part of the effect of the benefit cocktail party, moreover, suggests one of the foundational axioms of issue-based fundraising, which exploits the celebrity endorsement model of political campaigning. The logic is that if famous people support an issue, then others less famous will support the cause, too. This trickle-down politics relies on the political compatibility of celebrities and their fans. The names listed on the invitation as the sponsoring host committee announces an eclectic "in-group" that one could ostensibly "buy" into. Despite the obvious problematics of such devices—including the conflation of the politics of the celebrity and of the fan, the question of who counts as a celebrity and who decides this, and the perpetuation of social hierarchies set up in the celebrity/fan system—it needs to be stressed that money *was* raised and people did take note of the seriousness of the health crisis and got involved.

Less elitist fundraisers involving performance and performing artists were held throughout the city in 1982 and more regularly beginning in 1983 at various cabarets such as Don't Tell Mama, which, after having already raised nearly $5,000 for AIDS research, hosted a three-evening performance in June 1983 in memory of the performer Billy Blackwell, and Jason's Park Royal, which sponsored "Cabaret Sings for AIDS," where over 25 cabaret acts performed and raised more than $1,000 in the process. Other New York City bars and establishments participated in the early fundraising efforts of 1982, including the Saint, a popular downtown disco, which contributed over $27,000, and Claire, the successful Chelsea restaurant, which raised nearly $17,000 by June 1983. Locales as diverse as the near legendary Pyramid Club in the East Village and the popular bar Uncle Charlie's on the West Side initiated their own fundraisers and expanded the field of support and the space of performance of AIDS intervention. Donations specifically to honor someone lost to AIDS were also organized by various groups in New York City. The Big Apple Softball League, for instance, raised $482 in memory of their colleague Timmy Kogut.[23] Individual performers, too, began to visibly identify as supporters of AIDS research and consciousness. Karen Akers, a dedicated cabaret singer who would become a veteran of the AIDS benefit circuit, explained in a plug for the April 12, 1983, "An Evening for AIDS" fundraiser at the Leo Castelli Gallery, that "we have to raise money, and we have to raise it now before more people are lost."[24] Singer Michael Callen, one of a handful of public people with AIDS, joined a cast of others, including Tammy Grimes and Rex Reed, to perform a joint benefit production of *Pal Joey* on May 22, 1983, at Town Hall for GMHC and Bandwagon of Vintage Musicals. Their collaboration may have been the first theatrical performance directly designed to benefit AIDS. Later that year, in August, Harvey Fierstein, the award-winning gay actor and playwright of the celebrated 1982 Broadway play *Torch Song Trilogy*, emceed a major theatre fundraiser at Studio 54 for the AIDS Medical Foundation. Broadway actors from such current shows as the *Pirates of Penzance*, Tommy Tune's *Nine*, *Mame*, *42nd Street*, and *On Your Toes*, including (again) Karen Akers, Maureen McGovern, Angela Lansbury, and Millicent Martin (who announced unconditionally her availability for AIDS benefits: "If anybody needs me for anything, I'll do it!") donated their time and talent for AIDS research.[25] These early fundraisers began to articulate a theatrical response to AIDS that, while stemming from a small but expanding circle of New Yorkers in the theatre and the performing arts, amplified the AIDS consciousness necessary to educate gay male New Yorkers and generate money for research.

But not only in New York City. In San Francisco, on June 13, 1982, one week before New York's benefit tea dance at Maneuvers, the Sisters of Perpetual Indulgence and Shirley MacLaine hosted the second annual outdoor Dog Show and Parade with performances by the Gay Freedom Day Marching Band, Twirling Corps, and Honor Guard and proceeds donated to the Kaposi's Sarcoma Clinic at UCSF Medical Center. The money raised was directed toward a national conference in San Francisco in late September.[26] And yet by July 1982, when the KS Foundation first opened it doors, the modest sum of only $2,745 had been raised at fundraisers throughout the city, a pattern that continued for much of the year and that prompted Charles Morris, the former owner of the *San Francisco Sentinel*, who was diagnosed with AIDS, to write the following:

> I think the gay community has to cut out all the bullshit fundraising and focus on AIDS. The gay rodeo in Reno raised funds for Jerry's Kids, we're collecting money for guide dogs for the blind, but we are ignoring our own. The government is allocating only 2.2 million dollars for AIDS research, but if we put our minds to it, the gay community could raise more than that in one month.[27]

While money was slow in coming, at least information about AIDS was getting out. In venues across the city, information concerning the growing health epidemic spread throughout the gay public world. In early September 1982, at the Nob Hill Cinema, porn sensation Leo Ford performed his erotic stage show with the Sisters of Perpetual Indulgence to benefit the reprinting of the Sisters' *War on VD* pamphlet (fig. 2). The benefit raised enough money to reprint 50,000 copies of the new safe-sex guidelines. If you missed the show or wanted a memento, the Leo Ford limited edition bronze sculpture—just under four inches, white onyx base—could be ordered for $125 with ten dollars from each sale donated to the KS Foundation.[28] The winner of the 1982 California Motor Club (CMC) annual carnival—decided by the amount of ten-cent votes accumulated during the event—was Chris Winkel, the chained slave stud who went soliciting for the KS Foundation.[29] Winkel, the first runner-up at the 1982 Mr. International Leather Contest, embodied the leather community's immediate response to AIDS. Karl Stewart's popular "My Knights in Leather" column, which appeared in *Bay Area Reporter*, regularly directed readers to various AIDS events in the Bay Area, including such early fundraisers as the November 21, 1982, "Out Damn Spot!" benefit at the Eagle and the Spring Equinox sex ritual party gathering at the Caldron. A November benefit for the KS Foundation at the Trocadero brought to the stage a potpourri of popular entertainers who donated their time for the first performance extravaganza on the West Coast. Performers ranged from the easy listening vocals of the Fifth Dimension and Carol

2. Leo Ford and the Sisters of Perpetual Indulgence at the Nob Hill Cinema, San Francisco, 1982.
© Rink Foto

Lawrence, the gospel music of Linda Hopkins, and the dance rhythms of Paul Parker to the disco beltings of such divas as Jeannie Tracy, Claudjia Barry, and Taka Boom, who told the *Bay Area Reporter* that "we'll do these over and over again 'til we get KS taken care of."[30] The evening included selections from the immensely popular local camp revue *Beach Blanket Babylon*, as well as performances by various other entertainers. Everything from airfares to hotel rooms were donated so that the entire proceeds of the door would go directly to the KS Foundation.

The largest early San Francisco fundraiser was "An Evening with Debbie Reynolds and Friends," which was organized and produced in less than a month. On June 23, 1983, Debbie Reynolds, Sylvester, Shirley MacLaine, George Kirby, Sharon McKnight, Morgana King, and an all-volunteer production staff joined forces to raise money for the AIDS/KS Research and Education Foundation, the first benefit for the new San Francisco–based national organization (fig. 3). The performance raised $43,000 and, according to the *Bay Area Reporter*, was

3. "An Evening with Debbie Reynolds and Friends," the first benefit for the AIDS/KS
Foundation, San Francisco, June 23, 1983.
© Rink Foto

"the most successful fundraiser in San Francisco gay history."[31] While the Foundation's fundraiser came out in the black, it did not sell out. Organizers had
to paper the house to give the illusion of a high-demand event, leading Randy
Shilts to claim that in 1983 "AIDS still lacked star quality."[32]

The Los Angeles version of the event, on August 28, 1983, at the Hollywood
Bowl, brought in only 2,000 people and left 15,000 seats unfilled. The benefit was
a disaster. Despite the impressive list of entertainers, controversy over the distribution of funds led to a virtual boycott by members of the lesbian and gay
community. Initially, half of the proceeds were to go to Saint Jude's Hospital, a
favorite Beverly Hills charity that had no patients with AIDS, no ongoing AIDS
research projects, and no interest in AIDS, except for a small interest in pediat-
rics. The objections from the lesbian and gay community led the promoter, Dick
Sheenhan, to drop Saint Jude's Hospital as a beneficiary, but not before serious
concerns about the event were raised. Lesbian and gay Angelenos felt that the
benefit was designed to promote the entertainment industry and alienate the

lesbian and gay community, who were virtually left out of all the planning.[33] In addition, the popular singer Sylvester, one of the participants in the San Francisco event, was barred from performing at the Los Angeles benefit because, according to his manager, the promoters claimed "it was not a gay show."[34] Even AIDS Project Los Angeles, one of the beneficiaries, could not endorse the event since the promoter "would not provide sufficient answers" about the distribution of profits.[35] From one perspective, the flop at the Hollywood Bowl demonstrated the limits of early interventions designed outside of the lesbian and gay community. The most successful AIDS benefits of the early 1980s resulted directly from the investments—financial, emotional, political—of the lesbian and gay community. Understandably, efforts seeming to exploit AIDS for personal gain and profit were immediately contested. In this sense, the actual intervention took the form of a boycott of the alleged AIDS benefit, an unfortunate and unnecessary irony in any year. But from another perspective, the Hollywood Bowl controversy demonstrated the anxiety of well-intending people around the issue of AIDS and, in particular, homosexuality. Steve Schulte, Director of the Los Angeles Gay Community Center, explained, for example, that the producers of Hollywood Bowl AIDS benefit "held the [first planning] meeting the same night as the board meeting of AIDS Project/LA."[36] The attempt to "degay" AIDS led producers to advertise in industry and trade papers, *Variety* and the *Hollywood Reporter*, and not in any of the several Southern California lesbian and gay publications. The word "gay" was apparently never mentioned in the entire evening. The KS Foundation benefits, furthermore, suggested the need for AIDS interventions to attend to the specific political dynamics of local systems at play in the immediate community under consideration. In other words, an intervention that worked in San Francisco might not work in Los Angeles.

And yet, despite these controversies, lesbian and gay people around the country gathered together in the early 1980s to fight AIDS in local communities and to raise funds for local and national AIDS research and service organizations.[37] In Chicago, performance benefits helped launch the Action AIDS program of the Howard Brown Memorial Clinic (HBMC). The September 25, 1982, cabaret fundraiser at the Riverside Club was the first in a series of six performances that culminated two months later with "Cornucopia," a one-evening, two-show, all-star cabaret extravaganza at Park West, featuring the national gay comedy team Herb and Potato; local Latin jazz musician Israel Torres and his thirteen-piece ensemble; female impersonators from Chicago's infamous Baton Show Lounge; and various other mimes, dancers, comedians, and singers. The performance series was a benefit fundraiser for the November opening of the HBMC's Action AIDS project and served as a galvanizing community action against AIDS for Chicago's lesbian and gay community. The "Cornucopia" benefit at Park West on November 20 raised over $11,000. At one point during the Park West double show, a letter from Tom Biscotto—the stage manager for the Goodman Theatre, who was in the hospital undergoing chemotherapy for Kaposi's sarcoma—was read by a friend. "In some ways, I'm a very lucky person," he wrote, thanking his friends in the lesbian, gay, and theatre communities for their love and understanding during his illness.[38] Biscotto was one of ten official AIDS cases in the state of Illinois at the time of the event. In the neighboring state of Michigan, with even fewer AIDS cases, the 1983 New Year's Eve benefit performances at the Douglas Dunes Resort, which included various singers and local performers, launched not only the New Year but set the stage for the community's commitment to raise AIDS consciousness in 1983.[39]

In Washington, D.C., early benefits in local gay bars were held for the Whitman Walker Clinic AIDS Education Fund. By the time of its first community AIDS forum on April 4, 1983, two months after the Fund's initial founding, $7,000 had been raised. In March 1983, the District of Columbia claimed a dozen AIDS cases of the nearly 1,100 nationwide. In April of 1983, a two-month series of benefit performances—a "battle of the beauties" drag competition—throughout the city was organized by Don Wainwright because, as he explained, "the time has come to educate Washington gays about the problem; this is a lot more serious than people think."[40] In Atlanta, one of the city's most successful early fundraisers was the June 20, 1983, lesbian-organized Sportspage benefit. Sportspage, the oldest lesbian bar in Atlanta, held a seven-hour entertainment marathon, with no "star power" to speak of, and raised over $3,000 for AID Atlanta. This lesbian-sponsored production, held in support of gay men, was the earliest lesbian-produced benefit for AIDS in the country.[41] Earlier that year, members from Atlanta's transvestite community raised over $2,000 for AID Atlanta at the Illusion Cabaret's benefit performance.[42] In cities throughout the United States, a community-based and community-driven AIDS information outreach and fundraising campaign emerged from the already organized lesbian and gay community social and political networks in place since Stonewall. Atlanta's strong response from the lesbian and transvestite communities demonstrated the advantage of cities already organized around lesbian and gay issues before the onslaught of the epidemic. Many of these cities had reported few AIDS cases at the time of these benefits. Consider two more examples from regions outside of the epidemic's epicenters. In Phoenix, the first major fundraiser in the Southwest was an all-night disco party at Profile in February 1983. The benefit raised money for the San Francisco KS Foundation and Phoenix's own Gay Community Center. In Minneapolis, a July 31, 1983, benefit concert by the Twin Cities

Men's Chorus raised $5,000 for the Minnesota AIDS Project, a state that, at the time, had only three reported AIDS deaths.

Throughout 1982 and 1983, critical years in the history of AIDS, in cities all across the United States, performance became the primary means for AIDS service organizations to raise money for research and direct services, distribute information and educate local constituents, and recruit volunteers to strengthen a grassroots community response to AIDS. Underfunded by federal and state government institutions, if funded at all, these grassroots organizations depended upon these benefits to bring people into the space of performance so that a community-based and community-directed position on AIDS could emerge to intervene in the disregard and denial of AIDS in the nation at large. Working within the multifarious vernaculars of specific local scenes—drag revues, disco parties, lesbian talent shows, concerts—early AIDS performances succeeded in establishing a counter-ideology to the mystifications of AIDS by the dominant regimes of power constructing AIDS.

Unquestionably the most galvanizing early AIDS fundraiser was the sold-out Ringling Brothers and Barnum and Bailey Circus at Madison Square Garden on April 30, 1983, which netted over $250,000 for GMHC and was attended by over 17, 600 people. According to Larry Kramer, the circus fundraiser was also up to that time "the biggest, most successful gay fund-raising event ever held."[43] Seymour Kleinberg, writing in *Christopher Street*, explained that "[p]lanning a benefit at the circus may smack of Society charity, but getting over 17,000 men (mostly) under one roof became a political landmark."[44] Kleinberg's point is significant here. The primary aim of early AIDS performance interventions was to gather people into the space of performance so that an AIDS intervention—educational, financial, political, psychological—could materialize. Randy Shilts reports the remarkable success of GMHC's earliest AIDS interventions:

> [I]n its twenty months of existence [GMHC] had distributed a quarter-million copies of its "health recommendations" brochure and put hundreds of volunteers to work as "Buddies," doing chores and providing a sympathetic ear to AIDS-stricken men. Over 100 volunteers had been trained to work on the group's crisis line. In San Francisco, the various services of education, counseling, and support were being handled by different groups with diverse emphases, but New York did not have such luxuries. GMHC was doing it all and had become the largest gay organization in the country."[45]

Clearly, GMHC deserved to throw a party for itself and raise money in the process.

Among the many acts at Madison Square Garden on April 30, 1983, perhaps none was more effective in shifting gay men's understanding of AIDS than Leonard Bernstein conducting the circus orchestra and opera diva Shirley Verrett in "The Star Spangled Banner" (fig. 4). Kramer confesses that "Leonard Bernstein walking across the length of the Madison Square Garden in his white dinner jacket to conduct the circus orchestra in the national anthem, while eighteen thousand gay men and their friends and families cheered, was one of the most moving moments I have ever experienced."[46] Less than two years before, when the *New York Times* first reported AIDS alongside the perforated sheet music to "The Star Spangled Banner," gay men had no counter-effective tactic to unsettle the ideology of heteronormative patriotism. On April 30, 1983, the lesbian and gay community, along with the ever-expanding AIDS community, joined forces to stage an unprecedented response to AIDS. Andrew Holleran captured the shift in consciousness for many at the circus when he wrote that:

> [Shirley Verrett] sang our anthem just as one hoped to hear it. It was a dream: a diva came and sang at your party. Thanks to the men of the Gay Men's Health Crisis, as we sang the words of Francis Scott Key amidst the spotlights, in the great cavernous space filled with hearts dedicated to the same goal, and not a few moist eyes—I felt two identities which are most often separated in time and place, merge: homosexual and American.[47]

An imagined community based upon a certain investment in a U.S. national identity, as Holleran's comments reveal, was reformulated and produced by GMHC and, in the process, internalized by thousands of others—including Kramer, Holleran, and, to some degree, even Kleinberg—as a relational tactic enacted to mobilize lesbian and gay citizens in the fight against AIDS. The result of this claim of national identity, itself an outgrowth of the identity politics of the gay rights movement, demonstrated both the possibility and necessity of a critical, mass, community-based AIDS intervention. To merge the typically dissonant identities—"homosexual and American"—into a more dynamic and proactive identity in the fight against AIDS shifted irrevocably the relationship of gay men to AIDS. Gay men meeting in the space of performance began to recognize that in the public sphere what mattered most was political power. And gathering over 17,000 supporters of AIDS consciousness and intervention in 1983, and at the circus no less, as Kleinberg concedes, was and could only be "a political landmark." The *New York Times* failed to report the occasion.

While fundraisers designed to raise money and consciousness are primarily exogamous in nature, that is, they are intended for as many people as possible without foreclosure, AIDS memorial services are generally endogamous rituals.[48] Memorial services for people who died of complications due to AIDS

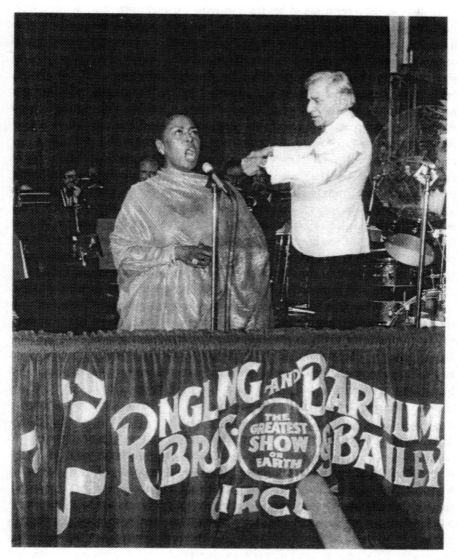

4. Shirley Verrett singing "The Star-Spangled Banner" with Leonard Bernstein conducting the circus orchestra at the April 30, 1983, GMHC Benefit at Madison Square Garden, NYC.
© Bettye Lane

were also, as they continue to be, fraught with various competing tensions, especially around kinship structures. Many memorial services for gay men who have died of complications due to AIDS deny both the person's sexuality and cause of death.[49] The strain between biological kinship structures and the kinship structures based upon "families we choose" sometimes, but not always, leads to two sets of memorials: one arranged by the biological family and one arranged by the family of choice.[50] Kath Weston, a lesbian anthropologist who writes on kinship, explains that for many lesbians and gay men "families we choose" refers to kinship relationships not determined by biology.[51] Often gay men who had died from AIDS complications were memorialized and buried in ceremonies obscuring their sexuality by their biological families in their hometowns while their friends and lovers, the families of choice, held simultaneous memorial rituals in other locations or locales. Remember, too, that many gay men with AIDS, especially in the earliest days of the epidemic, were abandoned by members of both sets of kinship networks. Weston explains how "when people told relatives and friends they had AIDS, kin ties were reevaluated, constituted, or alienated in the act, defined by who (if anyone) stepped forward to offer love, care, and financial assistance for the protracted and expensive battles with the opportunistic infections that accompany this disease."[52] Weston's account of this process begins to convey the complex psychosocial issues at stake for the person with AIDS. Feelings of isolation and dread, moreover, sometimes led to suicide. On December 16, 1982, for example, Richard Herbaugh—a twenty-nine-year-old gay man diagnosed with KS earlier that day—hanged himself in San Francisco's Golden Gate Parkway. Herbaugh's suicide note begins as a playscript, and he metaphorizes his suicide as a theatrical performance—"Greetings family and friends: Act 2 Scene IV: the curtain closes. Thank you, everyone. Thank you. . . . No lights, no sounds and no one to touch"[53]—only to rupture the performance metaphor in the very act of his death. With no imagined kinship structure to support him with his diagnosis, Richard Herbaugh decided to intervene. He had hoped to assist AIDS research through his suicide, his final wish—"offer my body to science for KS study only. Maybe they can conquer this evil soon"—was frustrated by the rigor mortis that had set in by the time his body was found the next afternoon. The corpse was useless for KS research. Despite his thwarted final wish, Herbaugh's death was not completely in vain. His suicide, one week before the 1982 Christmas holiday, alerted San Francisco's lesbian and gay people to the devastating and at times debilitating psychosocial issues of many people with AIDS, in particular, the weight of coming out as a person with AIDS.[54]

In early memorial services, performance provided a moving tribute to the deceased and served as the soundtrack to people's mourning. Memorial ser-

5. Public memorial service for Patrick Cowley at the Metropolitan Community
Church, San Francisco, December 9, 1982.
© Rink Foto

vices are designed to provide mourners with a cathartic experience, a sanctioned space where public and communal grieving releases emotions and
supplies ritualistic closure. In the process, memorial services enable the rebuild-
ing of community despite its loss. At the memorial service for the musician
Patrick Cowley, for instance, held at San Francisco's Metropolitan Community
Church on December 9, 1982, various friends and colleagues gathered to honor
Cowley's profound influence on dance music.[55] The *Bay Area Reporter* reported
that the "church was packed . . . to the rafters"[56] (fig. 5). Sylvester, one of
Cowley's collaborators and one of a number of singers at the funeral, broke into
tears and was unable to finish the spiritual he was singing. Another vocalist
stepped in and helped Sylvester complete the song, demonstrating both the
communal need to complete the grieving ritual and the power of collective support in the midst of AIDS. Cowley's memorial, which had gathered hundreds
of people into the space of performance, also served as a political forum, a reminder that while the event was a necessary communal ritual for grieving and
closure, it marked only one point in an ongoing political struggle. Rick Crane

of the KS Foundation took a moment during his eulogy to urge mourners to attend a rally and protest, later that same day, against Mayor Diane Feinstein's veto of the spousal rites bill earlier that morning.

In the course of the early 1980s, AIDS memorial services emerged as an increasingly common social ritual. Some of these services incorporated performance in new and original ways, often at the advance request or planning of the person with AIDS. People with AIDS began to produce their own memorials by selecting the speakers, music, readings, and venues and even shaping the service's structure.[57] This was the case already in 1982. James Howell, a dancer and choreographer affiliated with the Joffrey Ballet, left instructions in his will for his final ballet, *Ritual: The Journey of the Soul*, to be presented at his San Francisco memorial service.[58] Howell's insistence on his own AIDS memorial service as a form of celebration and public performance was lauded by one of San Francisco's gay newspapers: "Howell's gesture opens a new chapter on gays developing a style on how to die."[59] In 1981, a year before his death, Howell had suffered a near fatal bout of pneumocystis pneumonia. When he recuperated, he began work on *Ritual: The Journey of the Soul*, which had four performances in May of 1982 at his Sanchez Street dance studio. It was during this time that Howell became aware of the severity of his condition and chose to videotape the ballet. Howell died of AIDS complications on October 21. The video of his ballet was not shown until Howell's memorial service on November 7, 1982.

The forty-five-minute ballet follows the trajectory of a gay man's physical and spiritual life in six stages, beginning with "The Vision," the opening ensemble dance, and ending with "The Unfolding," the final dance for four male dancers. The ballet, a collage of various Zen beliefs and New Age ideas set to the music of Ligeti, Mike Oldfield, Satie, Albinoni, and Vangelis, traces the soul's journey through the body. The ballet choreographs the various energy blocks in the body the soul must pass through on its way to release. Two solo dances— the fourth and fifth parts of the ritual—suggest the soul's release from the body in death. In "The Awakening," the first of these dances, the body of the dancer is covered in fabric which he cannot, at first, discard. Toward the end of the dance, the body is triumphantly released from the struggle. The next dance, "The Ascending," involves a solo dancer who moves gracefully across the performance space. The dance ends with the soloist disappearing into an extremely bright and overpowering white light. From the perspective of the ballet's trajectory, the journey of the soul is now complete. *Ritual* was performed by Jim Howell's students. The video of *Ritual* was presented at Howell's memorial, an event that was, according to his friend, primary caregiver, and fellow dancer Robert Perkins, "a celebration of life."[60] Over fifty participants met at Howell's studio for the memorial service. They brought food and drink and

watched the ballet on a giant television screen. After the video, they shared stories and a meal. The memorial ended with everyone dancing—a direct defiance
of the somberness associated with conventional memorials and ultimately their
tribute to a friend. "It was a party!" Robert Perkins told me nearly twelve years
later, when I called him in San Francisco out of the blue to find out more about
Howell's story. "Make sure you mention that it was Jim's idea for it to be a celebration of life," he advised me during our conversation. White and blue bal-
loons filled Howell's studio just as they had when the dance was first performed
earlier that year.

Ritual: The Journey of the Soul may actually have been the first performance
about AIDS. Its intervention was local and temporary and experienced by a
small few. In the spring of 1982, Jim Howell composed and choreographed a
ballet that addressed his battle with AIDS. Its performances in May 1982 and
its presentation on video in November 1982, served two primary functions.
First, Howell set forth to contest the stigma of AIDS so pervasive in the early
months of the epidemic. Despite his illness, he taught dance in his studio until
one month before his death. Although AIDS was not explicitly mentioned during the ballet, Howell was public about his diagnosis. The context for the audience was linked with their knowledge of Howell's AIDS condition. The ballet's
focus on the limits of the body suggests Howell's own physical experience of
AIDS and his attempts to channel the energy of his soul to help his body deal
with AIDS. But, second, he also wanted to offer his community of dancers and
friends a means to respond to his approaching death. The presentation of the
video at his memorial was meant to counter the despair and grief associated
with death, in particular a death resulting from AIDS complications. Further,
the 1982 performances of *Ritual* in May and November, though presented in the
same space of performance and to many of the same people, served as a double
intervention. First, as a personal ritual for Howell himself, shared with a company of dancers and a small audience, the May 1982 performances were a way
for Howell to celebrate his own life and mark his own journey with AIDS. And
second, the November 1982 presentation of the ballet at Howell's memorial was
intended for his mourners—at Howell's insistence—as a means for them to reimagine AIDS, death, and the practices of memorialization itself. His November 7, 1982, memorial—"It was a party!"—was a celebration of his life and creative work.

From my own experience at AIDS memorial services, I have witnessed and/
or participated in a range of performances, including gay choirs and ensembles,
home movies of the deceased, highly produced video presentations, Chilean
folk performances, drag queen revues, communal dances, and even stand-up
comedy shows. All of these performances enact a certain and specific interven-

tion; generally one can argue that these performances set out to intervene in, if nothing else, the statistical abstraction of AIDS. In other words, the numbers have names, and these names had lives. These lives were rich in experience, personal interest, and whim; in dynamic concepts of self-identity, desire, and faith; in pleasures, quirks, and codes; and in loves, fantasies, and dreams. AIDS memorial services gather people into the space of performance—in houses of worship, in private homes, in leather vicinages, in favorite locales, in gay bars and discos, in secret sequestered provinces, in public parks, in candlelight vigils, in ritual fairy space, in dance studios, and, more recently with political funerals, on public streets—to pay tribute to the dead. Like all memorials, AIDS memorial services provide the living with the opportunity to grieve publicly over the loss of one of our own. And they provide us with the space necessary to attempt to reperform the bonds of kinship that enable the possibility of community. But in the specific case of AIDS, where notions of kinship and community are so often the very sites of contestation, the memorial services can serve to announce and honor the kinship structures established in support of the people with AIDS while they lived. Moreover, since people with AIDS—especially in the early years, but now as well—are stigmatized, abandoned, and feared, in life *and* in death, memorial services provide an important means to celebrate and valorize their lives.

By 1983, the ritual of the private AIDS memorial service led to public, communal outpourings of grief. Already many AIDS memorial services were becoming open to the public. Patrick Cowley's service in San Francisco already pointed to the need of others outside of his immediate kinship structure to participate in mourning rituals. The impulse to exploit the gathering of the assembled crowds led to the politicization of mourning. Large-scale public memorialization rituals resulted from these earlier exhibitions of support for individual deaths. Before the Names Project's unfolding of the AIDS Memorial Quilt at the 1987 March on Washington for Lesbian and Gay Rights, the most public AIDS memorializations were candlelight vigils. The first public AIDS vigil took the form of a national candlelight march on May 2, 1983. The march was organized and led by people with AIDS—according to the Centers for Disease Control, then numbering 1,366 cases with 528 already dead—in four cities across the country: New York City, Chicago, Houston, and San Francisco. In each city, people with AIDS were at the front of the march with a banner proclaiming "Fighting for Our Lives" (fig. 6). The marches in San Francisco and in New York City were estimated at over 6,000 people each.[61] People with AIDS addressed the crowds along with physicians, politicians, community activists, and local celebrities. In New York City, actor Susan Sarandon demanded that "the loneliness and isolation which has been connected with this disease must be

6. People with AIDS leading the first AIDS candlelight march and vigil in San Francisco, May 2, 1983.
© Rink Foto

stopped."[62] According to the *New York Native*'s reporting of the event, marchers walking from Sheridan Square to the Federal Plaza, led by a group of people with AIDS carrying a banner that read "Fighting for Our Lives," were followed by "members of the Big Apple Corps marching band with their instruments mute, except for the lonely beat of a drum. The band's own sign read "Support AIDS research funding before all the music is silenced."[63]

In San Francisco, mourners carried photos and placards with the names of loved ones who had died. Bobbi Campbell, a gay nurse and San Francisco's "KS poster boy," led the crowd in singing the traditional spiritual "Amazing Grace," a deliberate citational reference to Joan Baez's performance, five years before, at the public rally on the night of the murders of Harvey Milk and George Moscone. Campbell's political citation of Baez's performance, however, was misunderstood by many unfamiliar with the song's association with San Francisco's lesbian and gay political movement and overly familiar with its religious connotations. Various people, appalled by Campbell's choice of song, wondered in print about the representational politics of singing such a conversion-sounding spiritual. Campbell, in turn, chastised non–San Franciscans for expropriating the performance from its local context and, more generally, for questioning the motives of people with AIDS. In a letter to *Christopher Street*, Campbell conceded that "[s]inging will not deter AIDS" but argued that "[s]inging together can, however, encourage people who feel demoralized by their struggles."[64] In New York, marchers were unsure as to whether to sing and chant or remain silent and solemn throughout the duration of the march. Public memorials, like the more hermetic gatherings that constitute private AIDS memorial services, were unable to escape the contestatory politics of competing AIDS discourses in mourning the dead. First, the incident brought to the surface the emerging tension between various emotional responses to AIDS—in this case, between grief and anger, what Douglas Crimp would describe, some six years later, as a perceived opposition between mourning and militancy.[65] Second, the event called attention to the always contestable representational politics of performance and AIDS.

Across the country in New York City, San Francisco, Houston, and Chicago, people took to the streets to mourn their dead and to request funding for AIDS research. The Kaposi's Sarcoma Committee of Houston, for example, in its public notice announcing the vigil stated the following:

> The Kaposi's Sarcoma Committee of Houston invites you to a Candlelight Vigil for Public Health to memorialize victims of AIDS and to publicly request that funding for AIDS research, education, and coordination among all levels of government begin immediately. You may help to start this process by calling President Reagan at the White House Comment Line (202) 456-7639.
>
> > Monday, May 2, 1983
> > 8:30 PM
> > Reflecting Pool
> > Houston City Hall
>
> Bring a candle, container, and a friend and help us urge for support of national funding to help the AIDS Health Crisis.[66]

An estimated 3,000 people attended the Houston vigil. Members of the Diana Foundation, which underwrote the candlelight vigil, sold candles and raised $1,200 for the Montrose Clinic.[67] In Chicago, despite rain and cold temperatures, nearly 200 people turned out to march the one-mile route from Howard Brown Memorial Clinic to the Good Shepherd Parish Metropolitan Community Church. At the rally following the march, Tom Biscotto, the Goodman Theatre stage manager, who was too ill to attend the November 1982 Park West "Cornucopia" benefit for the Howard Brown Memorial Clinic, criticized a recent *Newsweek* portrayal of him as a victim. *Newsweek*, which had profiled Biscotto in its first AIDS cover story, wrote that before his diagnosis seven months ago,

"Biscotto seemed to have it all. . . . His life was full, his future bright. Today Biscotto, 35, doesn't know if he has a future at all."[68] In a direct rebuttal to the media's insistence on scripting the person with AIDS as victim, Biscotto proclaimed to the crowd that "my future, as far as I'm concerned, is still bright."[69]

Perhaps the most effective interventions of the candlelight vigils were the speeches by Biscotto and other people with AIDS. While the vigils were organized to memorialize people who had died and to request money for AIDS research, they also served as one of the first occasions for people with AIDS to address their issues in public. Organized by people with AIDS, the vigils provided them a space to formulate their own identities outside the constraints of the label of "AIDS victim" and to educate the community on what it meant to be living with AIDS. In New York City, Michael Callen told the crowds that "we need to be touched, we need you to talk to us."[70] Callen estimated that nearly thirty people with AIDS had started off with the march but by the end there were only five. "The others had left because of the stigma associated with the syndrome," he speculated.[71] Bob Cecchi, the other speaker with AIDS who addressed New Yorkers, read an open letter to President Ronald Reagan asking him to release federal funds for AIDS research and to provide national leadership during the health crisis. Cecchi closed his comments with an amazing rhetorical spin on the logic of heteronormative nationalism:

> Like our first president, you are the father of this country. Do you hear me when I say your children are dying? This problem transcends politics. In asking you to release monies, I am asking for an act of love. If you are my father, Mr. President, I am your son. Please help me save my life.[72]

In San Francisco, Mark Feldman, who along with Bobbi Campbell and Charles Morris spoke at the rally as people with AIDS, took a different approach when he admonished the president "for spending more money on the paint to put the American flag on his missiles than he's spending on AIDS."[73] On the following day, a national "Call-In" to the White House direct line to demand increased federal funds for AIDS research provided everyone the chance to address the president. According to the *Advocate*, a White House spokesperson admitted that "a lot of calls were received that day but no tally was kept. . . . This is not to discredit the [AIDS issue]."[74] But on May 3, 1983, the day following the AIDS vigil in New York City, San Francisco, Houston, and Chicago, a House appropriations subcommittee in a closed-door session passed supplemental funding for the federal health agencies but failed to include additional money for research on AIDS.

In May and June of 1983 cities continued to hold candlelight vigils and

7. June 13, 1983, candlelight vigil and citywide AIDS memorial service, Central Park band shell, New York City.
© Lee Snider

marches to keep AIDS issues active locally and nationally. On May 26, 1983, in Los Angeles, nearly 8,000 people met at the Federal Building to march down Wilshire Boulevard for increased federal action. It was the largest march in the country and was endorsed and supported by the National Association for the Advancement of Colored People and the National Hemophilia Foundation.[75] On June 21, 1983, 350 people marched to City Hall in downtown Seattle and packed the chambers as the City Council Committee met to consider a resolution to increase federal funding of AIDS research. Nine AIDS cases and four AIDS-related deaths had been reported in the state of Washington at the time. The committee voted unanimously to support the resolution. At the rally, the Seattle Men's Chorus sang "We Are a Family" from *Dreamgirls* and local gay musician Charlie Murphy performed his original music for the crowd. The Northwest AIDS Foundation, the largest AIDS service organization in the Pacific Northwest, was founded on that same day.[76] In New York City, about 1,500 people participated in an interdenominational AIDS memorial service at the band shell in Central Park on June 13, 1983 (fig. 7). The memorial included a eulogy for Kenny Ramsauer delivered by Geraldo Rivera, who had interviewed

8. June 13, 1983, Central Park AIDS memorial service, New York City. Participants are holding up placards with a number corresponding to a person who has died of AIDS in New York City.
© Lee Snider

Ramsauer on ABC's news show "20/20" shortly before Ramsauer's death in late May; a report by Ron Vachon, the former convener of the New York AIDS Network, on the events at the previous weekend's Fifth National Gay and Lesbian Health Conference in Denver; and a speech by Mayor Ed Koch, who in response to reports regarding the AIDS-phobic and discriminatory practices of funeral directors, promised to ensure that "no one discriminates against [people with AIDS or who have died of AIDS] in an unreasonable way."[77]

   In a highly effective theatrical reminder of the increasing number of AIDS deaths in the United States, people in the crowd defiantly held up poster cards, each displaying the number of a New York AIDS death (fig. 8). The highest number displayed represented the total number of people who had died up to that point, a direct and graphic allusion to "1,112 and Counting," Larry Kramer's manifesto for AIDS activism published three months earlier in the *New York Native.* The stigma around AIDS may have forced the numbers to stand in for the names, but for the people who carried the signs the correspondence between the number and the name was known. If the numbers conceded in part to the anonymity of AIDS in terms of government bureaucracies, for the community assembled the numbers were clearly identifiable with the people who had died.[78] In the early years of the epidemic it was not unusual for survivors to know the precise location of their dead in the tally of AIDS casualties. The tendency to conflate all deaths into a monolithic AIDS fatality, already in place in 1983, was staunchly resisted by the display of these numbers. And if in 1983 the names of the dead were not spoken aloud, at least the mourners intervened in the emerging statistical sublimity of those dead from AIDS by simply holding up the number and making *themselves* visible. Publicly and collectively, mourners announced their grief and rage by raising the numbers high above their heads. But they also performed an intervening surrogacy, standing up and standing in for the dead.

Such a mass public performance of the associative relationship between the living and the dead would not be staged again until its inversion in the Names Project, which was first unfolded at the 1987 March on Washington for Lesbian and Gay Rights, where those very numbers would be replaced by names, and the individual mourner eclipsed by the totality of the quilt's exhibit. Moreover, the structure of identification with AIDS for the person holding up the number was quite different in 1983 than it was in 1987. With no test available to detect HIV infection and to put into motion the subsequent construction of an identity—personal, social, political—informed by these test results, whatever one's status, the person standing up and standing in for the dead was implicated in the logic of associative AIDS contagion. Thus to hold up the number of an AIDS casualty was both an act of surrogacy and of community identification, and a direct resistance to the stigma of AIDS as it played out in the national public sphere. Mourners at the 1983 memorial service held up their numbered placards throughout the memorial service, replacing them only with hand-held candles for the vigil which directly followed (fig. 9).

Not everyone, of course, participated in these early sites of AIDS activism. In Washington, D.C., a local AIDS candlelight march and memorial service on June 19, 1983—Gay Pride Day—brought out less than one thousand people, a major disappointment for the organizers and participants. The low turnout for the candlelight march sparked a series of letters and editorials in the *Washington Blade* on AIDS apathy. Marchers were appalled that people at the bars refused to join the vigil. "No one was asking you to give up anything but an hour of your time to a very worthy cause," wrote one participant.[79] Washington AIDS organizers and activists, growing concerned about both the spread of AIDS and

9. June 13, 1983, Central Park candlelight vigil, New York City.
© Lee Snider

AIDS denial in their communities, attempted to generate more community involvement for the National AIDS Vigil scheduled for October 8, 1983. Editorials and outreach programs called on people "to stand up and be counted."[80] Organizers anticipated over 100,000 in the nation's capitol for the vigil and for the scheduled day of AIDS lobbying and the day for the National AIDS Forum, both of which preceded the vigil. The vigil co-chairs begged gays and lesbians "to recommit our energies and renew our resolve to conquering AIDS."[81] But controversies over the location of the vigil office, a space above Badlands, a popular Dupont Circle gay bar that discriminated against blacks, further fueled divisions in the local community. And the mismanagement of the event irritated gay activists from across the country. The week of the event, Boston's *Gay Community News* published a front-page article questioning both the organization behind the vigil and the general apathy around it. Rodger McFarlane, the executive director of New York City's GMHC, explained that "nobody out-and-out disagrees with the vigil, but there's no overwhelming support either."[82] The vigil had hoped to challenge the conflation of gay men and AIDS by explicitly addressing AIDS in nongay communities of color and among women. In the main promotion for the event the copy read:

> The one certainty about AIDS is that the disease has attacked black and white alike with no preference for a particular age group or sex. To date, 119 women have been counted among the 1,962 human beings affected. The media and the Falwells have designated this plague as a "gay disease"—a theory we wholly reject. That it has attacked gay males on a large scale is fact, but the heterosexual world is also feeling its deadly sting.[83]

Black and White Men Together and the Hughes-Roosevelt Democratic Club lobbied to have the offices moved to a more welcoming space for people of color, and Phil Pannell, the Human Rights Commissioner, threatened to have the Black Gay Community Conference, which was scheduled for that same weekend, boycott the event.[84] The controversies surrounding the vigil were similar to the debates concerning the 1982 Hollywood Bowl fundraiser fiasco. At the heart of the debates was the question of ownership and entitlement. Who gets to speak for AIDS? Who actually wants to? Who is invited to participate in the planning of AIDS events? The paradox of such contested claims of ownership over a syndrome so stigmatized that people refused to identify publicly in support of it only heightened the tensions within and among the various communities involved and highlighted the sometimes contradictory and even self-defeating practices of AIDS activism. In the end, only 1,500 people showed up in D.C. to participate in what was supposed to be the largest gathering of support for people with AIDS (fig. 10).[85]

But if the October 8th event was a disappointment ("an embarrassment," according to Rodger McFarlane, the director of GMHC[86]) as "a national demonstration to Congress and the President of the deep national concerns about this health crisis"—one of seven claims in the vigil's mission statement—it was a success insofar as it was able to gather together people with AIDS. Once again, people with AIDS demonstrated the significance of their presence and participation in public vigils for AIDS fatalities. The presence of a person with AIDS as a speaker and active participant challenged the equation of AIDS and death. In an interview before the vigil, Michael Callen explained that, although it is essential for the vigil to memorialize those who have died from AIDS, "there's too much emphasis on death."[87] Such a characterization of AIDS, Callen continues, "takes away from the will to struggle against it. And more than that, it's not consistent with our [PWA's] experience." Callen was not the only one to voice such sentiments. Seven people with AIDS spoke at the national AIDS vigil, the only people addressing the crowd. People with AIDS shared political,

10. First National AIDS Vigil, October 8, 1983, Washington, D.C.
© Bettye Lane

personal, and emotional aspects of living with AIDS; they voiced their dissatis-
faction with the government's slow response to AIDS, urging President Reagan
to appoint a federal task force on AIDS that would include people with AIDS;
they explained the necessity of the support systems they had established for
themselves, candidly speaking of their sexual histories and practices; and they
urged more people to become active in the fight against AIDS. In the process,
these seven PWA's provided a visual intervention into the dominant media image of people with AIDS as isolated bedridden victims awaiting death. This visual intervention was further dramatized when the group of PWA's unfurled a

11. People with AIDS displaying the "Fighting for Our Lives" banner at the first National AIDS Vigil on October 8, 1983, Washington, D.C.
© Bettye Lane

"Fighting for Our Lives" banner against the backdrop of the Washington Monument (fig. 11). Their willingness to circulate as counter-representations of people with AIDS was in direct relation to the people-with-AIDS self-empowerment movement that many of them had helped organize at the historic 1983 AIDS conference in Denver only months earlier.

The first national AIDS vigil designed to commemorate those who had died of AIDS served ultimately to support those living with AIDS. Arty Felson, a co-founder of the New York–based support group "People with AIDS," explained that the success of the vigil should not be reduced to the size of the crowd. For Felson, the vigil was about "a coming together [of people with AIDS] to share our support with each other, to share 'war stories,' and happiness at being alive."[88] In a sense, the vigil was not simply a chance for people with AIDS to educate the marchers, but an opportunity for people with AIDS to gather together and network with each other. Callen explained that "it will be very healing for all of us to get together and be with each other."[89] The establishment of a support structure where information about treatment, symptoms, and survival strategies could be shared emerged as one of the primary goals of the people-with-AIDS self-empowerment movement.

In 1983, candlelight vigils provided people with AIDS an opportunity to establish these networks locally, regionally, and nationally. The grassroots organizing of people with AIDS into networks of support in the first years of the epidemic was one of the foundational interventions of early AIDS activism— and the display of that network one of its most effective. At vigils throughout the country, people with AIDS took the stage, often as the only speakers. As such, the person with AIDS enacted a self-representation that countered the pervasive sensationalistic victimization image generated by the media. As a material presence, onstage and addressing the assembled crowd, the person with AIDS—a living, breathing body—intervened in the spectacle of AIDS and moreover, for the community assembled, inverted the performative and social dynamics of the traditional AIDS memorial service. Rather than being spoken about, the person with AIDS spoke both to and for. Ultimately, however, on these public occasions the person with AIDS spoke *as* a person with AIDS. The active agent of the performance, the person with AIDS spoke to the crowd, sometimes for the general concerns of all people with AIDS, sometimes as a surrogate voice for the dead, or sometimes for a specific act of intervention. In San Francisco at the October 1983 vigil, Dan Turner and Roger Lyon performed all these roles when at the AIDS vigil they unrolled a red scroll inscribed with the first names of all the 118 Bay Area residents who had died since June 1981, the retroactive date decided upon by the CDC as the official beginning of the epidemic (fig. 12). As Turner and Lyon recited the names of the dead, Michael Helquist recited the Mourner's Kaddish prayer offered at his lover Mark Feldman's memorial service earlier that year. The speakers expressed the message "People are dying, cut the red tape!" and urged the crowd to send the postcards distributed during the vigil to Washington to demand that the government "spend the money they have promised."[90] Moving outside the demoralizing representational field of death and dying, Turner exclaimed to the crowd: "I'm tired of being a nice guy. I'm tired of taking my medicine lying down. I'm still out ahead, and I've picked up a lover along the way!" In the process of expanding the space of performance to include the contested public sphere, the person with AIDS exploits the space of performance to challenge its horizon of expectation. No longer relegated to the confines of the coffin or the urn, the person with AIDS emerges into the space of performance as is, proliferating the crisis of representation around the idea of a person with AIDS. As a subject in social performatives, the person with AIDS speaking at candlelight vigils unsettled the traditional representational iconography of AIDS in the dominant media. The

12. Dan Turner (far left) and Roger Lyon (far right) unroll a red scroll with the names of 118 Bay Area residents who have died of AIDS as Rick Crane and Michael Helquist (center) read the names at the October 8, 1983, AIDS vigil in San Francisco. © Rink Foto

person with AIDS was, as Dan Turner explained to the assembled San Francisco crowd, "still out ahead" and "along the way" or, one could say, in production. In these early AIDS events, people with AIDS represented themselves less as victims than as dynamic subjects constructed through and against the pressures of social abjection and physical harm.

One final example of an early AIDS activist social performance: In July 1983, three gay men with AIDS—Michael Callen, Anthony Ferrera, and Roger Lyon—addressed a congressional subcommittee hearing on AIDS, the first time people with AIDS spoke before members of Congress. Each spoke directly about the need to clarify the misinformation circulating about AIDS and its transmission and the need for antihomophobic care. At one point, Larry Craig, a Republican representative from Idaho, spoke accusingly of the "homosexual lifestyle," asking if there was "an exodus" from the urban gay community because of AIDS. The three men each offered different rhetorical responses to Craig's concern of a mass exodus of gay men into the suburbs, middle America, or, perhaps, in Craig's imagination, Idaho. Ferrara shot back that "it's impossible to leave the Gay community," a statement which could have foreclosed the discussion. Lyon developed Ferrara's comment, explaining that "what we're finding in the Gay community is a very strong bonding, a coming together. I think AIDS has strengthened the Gay community." Callen, however, informed the assembled committee of the precarious position of gay people in the United States and redirected the question back to Craig: "Many of us moved to the cities to escape the prejudice we had experienced as gay and lesbian people. Where are we going to go?"[91] In cities across the country throughout the early 1980s, an impressive emergent AIDS activist community of lesbian and gay people broke out of this enforcement and took to the streets. Sometimes their numbers were astounding; other times they were very few. But intervention comes in many forms. In Davenport, Iowa, for example, no more than six people participated in an AIDS vigil and rally on the day of the 1983 National AIDS Vigil.[92] Callen's question—"Where are we going to go?"—was at once a direct and confrontational claim of social entitlement and an immediate refutation of an enforced exile from the political public sphere. But it was also a challenge to the early AIDS activist movement. Two years into the epidemic, Callen asks for an engaged and systematic plan for the continued fight against AIDS and AIDS-phobia.

Throughout the early 1980s, a dominant AIDS ideology in the United States emerged from the formulations of AIDS constructed by biomedical science, the media, and the government. This dominant ideology, while sustained by the regulatory regimes of power, was nonetheless multiple and contradictory as it took shape throughout the 1980s, accommodating competing tensions around cultural understandings of sexuality, citizenship, and disease as it systematically repudiated and disavowed the very terms of its construction. Performing artists, theatre people, and other cultural workers within the lesbian and gay community were continually implicated in the shifting national ideology of AIDS in multiple ways and, as such, both intervened in this ideology as it took shape and participated paradoxically in its perpetuation. Fundraisers targeted toward scientific research, for example, did not necessarily question the apparatuses and ideological markers of biomedical science nor, by extension, did they question the policies of the AIDS service organizations that they also helped finance. AIDS memorial services invariably gather people into the space of performance, primarily in order to honor the dead and the endogamy of their kin. AIDS memorial services are social rituals predicated on the materiality of death. Powerful, moving, and necessary social rituals, AIDS memorial services still rely on death for their ontology. (Without a death, they simply would not be.) Other social performatives without death and dying at their center, while emerging, were few and far between. While gay male performances attempt to counter the emerging official ideologies of AIDS in the United States, these performance interventions can never simply be oppositional to these ideologies or the myths engendered by them; rather these interventions coexist in dynamic and agitated reciprocity.

Methods of Intervention: AIDS Activism and Performance Theory

"We don't need to transcend the epidemic; we need to end it," Douglas Crimp states succinctly in his 1987 introduction to *AIDS: Cultural Analysis/Cultural Activism.*[93] Crimp is directing his concerns to the proliferation of artistic responses to AIDS that fail to exploit the arts' potential to actually save lives. While representations of loss and suffering in the visual arts, on the one hand, and arts fundraisers, on the other, serve important social and financial functions in the fight against AIDS, both fail to imagine the arts in proactive terms. Crimp is also skeptical of the critical methods established by the liberal left that champion works that only "express human suffering or loss," an unquestioned idealism that believes art will somehow transcend AIDS by producing a cultural renaissance redeeming those affected by AIDS. Crimp advocates for an activist art that "involves questions not only of the nature of cultural production, but also of the location, or the means of distribution, of that production" (12) and a cultural criticism more engaged with these issues of production, location, and distribution. Crimp's manifesto for an AIDS activist aesthetic and critical practice directly responds to the proliferation of representations of people with AIDS—in photography, literature, the media, and popular culture—that position the person with AIDS as a "victim" facing imminent death, or that in some way aestheticize the experience of AIDS within the constraints of generic tragedy. The idea that an engaged activist art is necessary to challenge the inertia of the art world's response to AIDS—let alone the AIDS myths which circulate in popular culture—assumes, as Crimp states, "that art *does* have the power to save lives" (7). The critique of representation, production, location, and distribution also relies on the belief that there are multiple sites of contestation in the fight against AIDS. By putting pressure upon the art world, activist artists and cultural thinkers can intervene in the ideologies embedded in dominant representations of AIDS. However, expanding the representational field is not enough. Activist art moves beyond (but does not relinquish) formal venues that traditionally house the arts—galleries, theatres, museums—and like community-based pedagogical interventions, activist art is local, sex positive, and skeptical of dominant systems constructing AIDS.[94]

In many ways, Crimp's call for an AIDS-activist aesthetic suggests the

methods and politics of materialist feminist criticism. Materialist feminist theorists have long challenged the institutional mechanics of production, location,
and distribution as they relate and contribute to sexist practices that remain
ideologically unmarked, naturalized as uncontestatory truths. Building upon
and expropriating from Marxist and Foucauldian critiques of institutional
structures and the construction of subjects, materialist feminism focuses its critique on social formations and historical forces—those that construct ideologies
oppressive to women—in order to demystify and challenge them. By calling attention to ideologies assumed and rendered natural or real, materialist feminist
theorists expose both the processes that give force to these ideologies and to
their naturalization in culture. Materialist feminist theory, like its precursor,
Marxist theory, insists on new social formations and believes in the possibilities
for social change. While Marxist theory focuses on the socioeconomic conditions of culture and ideology, materialist feminist theory foregrounds the role
of gender in the process of cultural production and the constitution of a subject.

In the case of theatre, materialist feminist criticism has focused on performance and textual interventions in the production of naturalized subject positions in the representational apparatus of the theatre. In *Feminism and Theatre*,
Sue-Ellen Case demonstrates the ways that traditional Marxist theory and feminist theory can combine to critique the specific historical contexts that produce
oppressive representations and/or conditions for women in the theatre. She
highlights the ways that feminist performance theorists and practitioners have
developed what she calls "a new poetics" that fundamentally alters the possibilities of production, representation, and interpretation.[95] Feminist performance critics, moreover, have challenged much more than the means of representing and interpreting women onstage. In U.S. theatre and performance
studies, feminist critics, as David Savran notes, "called for a radical reconfiguration of the discipline based upon their recognition that acting, play selection
and production, spectatorship, textual interpretation, the convictions of the
press, and hiring practices in theaters and universities have been deeply inscribed by patriarchal discourses and practices."[96] Materialist feminist performance theory calls attention to both the representational structures of the theatre and their ramifications. "Cultural production," Jill Dolan argues in her
groundbreaking study *The Feminist Spectator as Critic*, "is viewed as a framework
for the imposition of ideology, a framework which can be dissected and exposed
as complicit in the formation of systems of social relations."[97] Indebted to the
ideas of Brechtian theory, whose theatrical practices and theoretical methods
demand an interrogation of the material conditions of the theatre and a critique
of the Aristotelian-based conventions of realist theatre, material feminist performance theory and practice foregrounds and destabilizes the representational

apparatus of the theatre in order, as Dolan argues, "to demystify compulsory heterosexuality and the construction of gender as the founding principle of representation" (112).

Materialist feminist performance theory addresses Crimp's concerns regarding AIDS cultural production—form, venue, distribution—and adds explicitly the question of its reception. AIDS activist criticism, especially in theatre and performance studies, is indebted to the work of feminist theorists, many of them lesbians whose work addresses lesbian performance and lesbian representation. Just as AIDS activism is both inspired by and indebted to the work of lesbian and other feminists involved in the women's health-care movement and to the lesbian and gay liberation movement, AIDS activist cultural criticism is inspired by and indebted to feminist—in particular, lesbian—theory.

In theatre and performance studies, lesbian critics have achieved a level of engagement on issues of ideology and representation unmatched in gay male performance studies. Lesbian feminist performance critics have established a necessary investigation of the performative ramifications of lesbian representation in both mainstream and alternative theatres. Questioning the politics of representation and reception in a diverse field of performances, these critics persuasively argue that alternative venues which produce lesbian artists, rather than ghettoizing lesbian issues within an imaginary enclosed lesbian community, offer a critical practice that begins to articulate the diversity encoded by such problematic terms as *lesbian sexuality, lesbian desire*, and even the term *lesbian* itself.

Lesbian feminist performance theory provides a space for the collective negotiation and contestation of the lesbian subject. The rigorous debates between lesbians on the politics and means of lesbian representation and production enhance the possibilities for intervention. The engaged and sustained dialogue, and at times collaboration, between lesbian critics and performing artists demonstrates the relationships available to diverse cultural workers who gather into the space of performance to effect social change. The occasional rifts between lesbian theorists and performers point also to the stakes involved in sites of lesbian contestation.

For an AIDS-activist critical practice that is focused on theatre and performance, the pioneering work of feminist performance theory provides an invaluable model. Lesbian and feminist performance theory has long charted critiques of ideology and has intervened in this dominant ideology with new and original methods of analysis. "Feminists," as Elin Diamond explains, "in our different constituencies, with our different objects of analysis, seek to intervene in the symbolic systems—linguistic, theatrical, political, psychological—and intervention requires assuming a subject position, however provisional, and making truth claims, however flexible, concerning one's own representations."[98] Diamond's idea of intervention suggests that intervention is always performative—a tactical position assumed in relation to dominant ideology in order to question and abolish its effects. As such, her comment can be appropriated to begin to fulfill Crimp's requirements for a new AIDS-activist aesthetic and critical practice. AIDS activists, in our different constituencies, with our different objects of analysis, seek to intervene in the symbolic systems—linguistic, theatrical, political, psychological—and intervention, as Diamond and Crimp both make clear, requires us to *perform*, in multiple and often contradictory fields of power, our relations to dominant AIDS ideologies and our own experiences of AIDS. The early AIDS social performances—fundraisers, benefits, memorial services, candlelight vigils, and marches—already point to how interventions, directed against the emergent governing AIDS ideologies produced by the regulatory regimes of power in place in the United States during the early 1980s, were contested and reconfigured by people united in the fight against AIDS in a sustained effort to challenge and abort their effects. The acts of intervention of the early 1980s—locally, regionally, nationally—expanded and exploited the space of performance to address the contested public sphere. These acts of intervention assembled and recruited crowds of supporters willing to play their part in shifting the forces inventing and sustaining AIDS so as to survive and abolish AIDS. The theatre, indebted to the social performatives of the early 1980s, began to accommodate many of the impulses of these early AIDS interventions, producing its own series of interventions in and against the conventions of its practice. The earliest AIDS plays and performances built upon and expropriated many of the tactics of these early AIDS interventions in order to wield their own power to shape our understanding of AIDS. And while many of these plays and performances too closely resembled or promoted the representation of suffering and loss evident throughout the culture of the 1980s, many also began to exploit the specific mechanics involved in theatrical production and provided their own contribution to fighting AIDS.

2

One and Counting

Early AIDS Plays

Let me tell you right now—my objective is to illuminate and not depress.
I am here to tell you that there is a spirit which banishes all fear.[1]
—*The A.I.D.S. Show*

Early AIDS Plays: 1983–84

IF THE EARLIEST AIDS interventions were performative occasions that gathered
people into spaces outside of the theatre in order to raise funds, educate
people, and honor the dead, it should not be too surprising that the earliest
AIDS plays were also produced as fundraisers, education campaigns, and memorials. On August 14, 1983, *One*, a thirty-minute monologue depicting a gay
man with AIDS, premiered at Company, a Chicago gay bar, and reopened on
September 6 for a one-week engagement at Chicago's Organic Theatre Cabaret.
One was produced by Lionheart, Chicago's lesbian and gay theatre. One year
later, in September 1984, *Warren*, a one-act play about a gay man who dies of
AIDS, opened at Seven Stages Theatre in Atlanta. In San Francisco, a group of
theatre artists formed Artists Involved with Death and Survival (A.I.D.S.) and
presented the first workshop of *The A.I.D.S. Show* at Theatre Rhinoceros on September 6, 1984. And in New York, productions of Robert Chesley's controversial
play *Night Sweat* and Stephen Holt's *Fever of Unknown Origin: A Kind of Love Story*
premiered in 1984 with mixed results. Each of these early AIDS plays contributed to the interest of the theatre industry in producing AIDS plays on mainstream stages, an interest that materialized in 1985 with the original productions of *As Is* and *The Normal Heart* in New York City. These early AIDS plays
set out to inform audiences of the physical, emotional, and social effects of
AIDS. Their efforts to reach audiences demonstrated the theatre's capacity to
participate in the shifting ideologies concerning disease, sexuality, and citizenship in the United States during the formative years of the AIDS crisis.

The earliest of these plays set out to intervene on local fronts as specific community-engendered responses to the epidemic. Their success as local interventions led to their adaptation in theatres throughout the country. *One* was written by Jeff Hagedorn, a white gay man, to "dispel some of the irrational fear surrounding AIDS"[2] and to raise money for Chicago's recently established Howard Brown Memorial Clinic's Action AIDS Project. *One*, which was performed as a benefit at Company, raised $500 for Action AIDS.[3] *Warren* was written by Rebecca Ranson, a white lesbian, to memorialize a friend and collaborator who died in April 1984.[4] *The A.I.D.S Show*, a two-hour compilation of skits and songs written by thirteen lesbian and gay male writers, sketched out over twenty vignettes dealing with AIDS issues and, according to the late Chuck Solomon of Theatre Rhinoceros, "trie[d] to cover the health crisis from as many different perspectives as possible."[5] By the end of 1984, *One* had been produced in San Antonio, Los Angeles, Schenectady, Milwaukee, New Orleans, and Kansas City. In each of these cities, *One* was produced as an AIDS benefit raising a total of over $20,000 by the end of 1984.[6] By the end of 1985, *Warren*, which involves a cast of eight, had been staged in Honolulu, Rochester, Philadelphia, New Orleans, and Los Angeles, in each case as a benefit for a local AIDS service organization. Initially scheduled for only four performances in September 1984, *The A.I.D.S. Show* ran nearly continuously in San Francisco for over a year, moving from the studio theatre in the basement, where it was, as Miranda Joseph explains, "showcased for community groups which might select sections of it for use at their own events," to the main stage, where "it went into an extended run at the theatre and became the first of a four-play cycle."[7]

The irony that the first play to be marketed as an AIDS play would be titled *One* is immediate. The play announces a count-off not unlike Larry Kramer's speeches or publications in the *New York Native* that begin with, and are titled after, the number of AIDS cases at the time of his writing—"1112 and Counting," "2339 and Counting."[8] The title also suggests the display of numbers at early AIDS vigils. *One* claims its entrance into representation and theatre history as a first, suggesting that nothing precedes it and that instead everything will follow. It intimates that there will be other plays, many other AIDS plays, to come. *One*, yes, but not the only one. Nonetheless, at the same time the play nearly self-consciously announces its singularity, its isolation in the representational field.[9] *One* performs its outness, its entrance into public discourse defiantly. Like the early people-with-AIDS self-empowerment movement, which pressed for and mobilized public recognition of the idea of "a person with AIDS," *One* imagines and puts into motion the idea of "AIDS theatre." Its insistence on being codified as an AIDS representation is not negotiable. *One* emphatically locates itself at the juncture of vulnerability and impudence.

13. Carl Forsberg in the original Lionheart Theatre production
of *One*, by Jeff Hagedorn, Chicago, August 1983.
© Jennifer Girard Photography

One portrays an unnamed gay man recently diagnosed with AIDS who presents his experience directly to the audience (fig. 13). The tone is conversational,
a stream-of-consciousness monologue which shifts tones depending upon the
issue at hand. He wonders who might have infected him and worries about
whom he might have infected; complains about his doctor ("he's an idiot sometimes") and the nurses at the hospital; and shares an amusing story about his
mother, who, when hearing of his illness, smokes a joint with him. He speculates on the slim chances of his survival and considers suicide. Although the

character shares anecdotes from his past, from his childhood to his sexual exploits, the focus remains on the present and on the effects of AIDS on his personal relationships:

> It never occurred to me that a disease could change everyone in your life. It's not just your own life that changes. It's the lives around you. Relationships . . . contort themselves. They seem like entirely new things. I have trouble recognizing them as continuations.[10]

Despite named references to ex-lovers, parents, and friends, much of the monologue is composed of moments such as these, generalizations that defy specificity.

One is neither autobiographical nor is it the story of any particular person. Hagedorn obscures the playwright from the representation, making no claims for autobiography and offering no revelations about his own health. The effect of having the hero deliberately unnamed, and of having the character performed by an actor and not the playwright, allows the audience to potentially identify with the representation. Hagedorn is explicit about his intentions. In an interview he explains that

> everything I was reading seemed to ignore the fact that these patients were people, seemed to imply that the moment they acquired this disease they became less than human. Even gays were referring to the victims as "those backroom boys." If the community does it, the rest of the world can only be worse, so I wanted to write something as universal as possible—so everyone who looks at it can say, "That's me!" or, "That can be me." Theater, an emotional medium, is the best for dealing with these irrational reactions, for demystifying these prejudices.[11]

By presenting spectators with a supposedly blank slate, Hagedorn hopes they will become more aware of their own emotions about AIDS, discover their capabilities and limits, and act accordingly. Hagedorn leaves the question of support up to the spectator.

With the need to cast an actor, the production cannot help but call attention to the distance between the actor and the role. *One* sets out to represent AIDS so that spectators can begin to deal with AIDS more directly. The unmarked representation of the protagonist—is this a true story? is it based on the playwright? someone the playwright knows? someone I might know?—allows spectators to mark the character from their own experiences. The play holds no aspirations other than to have audiences imagine AIDS from the perspective of a person with AIDS. The person with AIDS is depicted as someone who is, as Hagedorn describes, "an average, normal human being who happens to have this disease."[12] Audiences are asked to empathize with the person with AIDS. Hagedorn explains that "the point of the play" is to present the person with AIDS so as to "make you like him."[13]

By presenting AIDS as it is experienced by the protagonist, Hagedorn asks audiences to rally around the representation of AIDS. The monologue sets out to solicit the spectator's compassion by presenting the protagonist's emotions, mainly anger and fear, but also his resilience; the play begins with the statement "I have acquired a disease that means I am going to die" and ends with the affirmation "I'm alive today and I'll be alive tomorrow and the next day." Audiences are invited to imagine themselves as the protagonist's support network and, in the dynamics of such projections, encouraged to make themselves available to support actual people with AIDS. The fact that *One* was performed in association with an AIDS service organization provided audiences with an immediate location to offer their support either through volunteerism or donations.

But the choices set up in *One* for audiences also put into motion the totalizing impulse to universalize the character's experience as *the* experience of AIDS. The mechanics of production already point to some of the embedded biases of the spectator. In Chicago, as in most cities, the character was played by a white actor. Whiteness, as an unmarked racial category, presumes a series of universals that disavow the ways that race and ethnicity factor into our understanding and responses to AIDS. The idea that race and ethnicity might shape a person's experience of AIDS was not explored in early AIDS discourse. The elision of the two categories—race and sexuality, or, more precisely, white and gay—sustains the white normativity that defined urban gay culture at the time. Race, as a category of analysis in AIDS performance, would not be forcefully addressed until the early 1990s.

Despite the play's contradictory tensions—universalizing AIDS in order to allow for direct spectatorial engagement, on the one hand, and distancing audiences from the representation by having the character unnamed, on the other— and the political problems they each may engender, *One* should be recognized primarily as an intervention in the representational politics of AIDS. Still there are problems embedded in the representational and production choices of Hagedorn's play, problems that cut both ways. Thinking through the ramifications of whiteness as an unmarked racial category raises a series of concerns specific to the ethnic and racial identifications of the audience, questions that may unsettle Hagedorn's intent to "demystify prejudice" and limit the possibilities of Hagedorn's intended educational outreach.[14] Hagedorn's attempt to universalize AIDS, moreover, collapses the distinct experiences of people with AIDS. Unfortunately this is the burden of both visibility politics and interventions that arise from productions intended to expand the representational field.

Once a production gains entrance into representation, that representation is burdened as definitive.

Hagedorn's short play helped launch the representation of AIDS in the theatre and introduced audiences throughout the country to the theatre's capacity to initiate discussions and debates around AIDS while raising money for AIDS services in the process. A few months before his death in 1995, Hagedorn wrote to me describing these early productions:

> I think the early productions were pretty incredible since they were not generally done by theaters (I demanded it always be done as a fundraiser), so most of the people who arranged for productions took all those pains because they wanted to get word out or spur action. The play was rarely performed in theaters. It was taken to schools groups, youth groups, we did it as a sermon in the middle of a church service, it was done in bookstores and living rooms, it was used to train counselors just as we were gearing up for this fight. For instance, the Kansas City production (1984) was used to create an AIDS group there. Phil Palma, who made all the arrangements, was a real estate man who read a notice about the play, contacted me for a copy of the script just out of personal interest and 3 months later put on a rather elaborate benefit. They raised $7,000 (which was a lot of money then) and there was not an AIDS group to give it to, so they created it. I thought this was theater fulfilling its function better than I had ever seen.[15]

If evaluated solely on the standards of artistic merit, *One* falls short. It introduces no new formal or aesthetic devices; relies quite heavily on the conventional tropes of melodrama and realist drama; and, other than introducing the person with AIDS as a character for representation, plays predictably. And yet as a community-based artistic project, Hagedorn's play successfully challenged the theatre to begin addressing AIDS directly on the stage. *One* suggests that before AIDS performances can begin to question the institutions that sustain AIDS, performances need to begin to unsettle the theatre's own complicity in the denial of AIDS. Therefore, Hagedorn's immediate act of intervention was to actually stage AIDS in the first place. Furthermore, that *One* was able to circulate so quickly in lesbian and gay community-based sites and alternative-performance venues demonstrated audiences' willingness to support such projects.

While *One* focuses on the story of only one person with AIDS and foregrounds exclusively his experience of AIDS, Rebecca Ranson's 1984 play *Warren* focuses on the responses of the friends and family of the character with AIDS to his diagnosis and subsequent death. In the year that separates these two representations, we move from the singular and lonely representation of *One* to a cast of characters whose response to Warren's illness and death become for the spectator possible points of identification. Rather than focusing exclusively on the experience of AIDS for the person with AIDS, Ranson asks audiences to situate themselves in relation to the person with AIDS. The conventions of realist theatre, in particular tragedy, depend on spectatorial identification for the cathartic release of pent-up emotions made possible in the denouement. Ranson frames her play within this theatrical tradition. *Warren* displays various responses to AIDS that range from a father who, initially troubled by his son's sexuality, grows to accept his son by the play's end, to his stepmother, who, despite her ignorance of homosexuality and AIDS, wants to learn and understand more about both, to Warren's leather-friend Sam, who rages against the injustices for gay men in the age of AIDS. Characters are placed within a continuum of support, and audiences, by extension, are asked to locate their own positions accordingly. Ranson provides two equally developed, although initially discrete, kinship structures: Warren's family of origin, represented by his mother, father, and stepmother, who all live in Tennessee, and Warren's San Francisco family, composed primarily of other gay men. Rebecca, Warren's long-time lesbian friend, who lives in the South, is the bridge between these two worlds. By the end of the play, both sets of people join to form a support system for Warren and for each other—"EVERYONE: We wanted to keep Warren with us."[16]

Based on a true story, Rebecca Ranson's play is essentially about her friendship with Warren. The play, she explains, "could be part of his legacy."[17] In this sense, Ranson's choice to present a representation that would be "true to life" also explains her choice for realist models of conventional tragedy. Realism allows for the emotional identification with the characters. In the initial 1984 Atlanta production, some of the stage props were Warren's actual possessions. Unlike *One*, where the representation of AIDS circulates as seemingly unmarked, Ranson deliberately names the source of the play and of the various characters in the representation. The play, subtitled "a true story," is unequivocally a memorial to Ranson's friend, Warren. By emphasizing the personal dimensions of her play, Ranson provides spectators a theatrical occasion where emotions are central. Ranson admits that *Warren* is not "great art; I think it's good ritual."[18] This choice to forego "great art" for "good ritual" is a noteworthy practice that seems to characterize many of the earliest AIDS plays. Although they seem to concede an unnecessary binarism between art and ritual, these playwrights anticipate Douglas Crimp's call for an activist art divested from conventional aesthetics and commodification systems. Ranson's fresh insights into her play's function as first a personal ritual—"I've called it my way of doing a funeral for a friend"[19]—and also as social ritual for others affected by AIDS—"A lot of people felt it was a religious experience"[20]—positions audi-

ences as participants rather than merely spectators. In this subtle shift of audience role, Ranson is able to maneuver the various interventions intended by her
play. Audience members, as participants, are led into the space of performance
to observe and enact—as in a memorial service—the bonds of kinship on display, but, unlike the endogamy performed in private services, Ranson invites
audiences to claim Warren for themselves. "There's a strange collective connection for me when I've been in the audience," Ranson explains. "It has to do with
sharing Warren with an audience; it's *their* Warren—their person or friend or
lover who has AIDS."[21]

Warren also works as a pedagogical intervention in expanding audiences'
understanding of AIDS. In 1984—despite increasing numbers of AIDS cases
in cities and states across the country—AIDS was very much perceived as a
disease specific to large urban gay communities. *Warren* makes explicit that
AIDS happens everywhere and not only in New York, San Francisco, and Los
Angeles. Audiences in Atlanta, Honolulu, Rochester, Philadelphia, and New
Orleans, the cities that along with Los Angeles first produced the play, had to
come to terms with the realities of AIDS in their communities. *Warren* helped
them do so. After the first staging at Seven Stages in Atlanta, audience members,
including AIDS researchers from the Centers for Disease Control, shared their
feelings and experiences with each other and the cast, playwright, and director.
One actor explained that although "the script may not be that strong, the emotions that it touches, the feelings that it reaches are so great . . . that's what
makes it work."[22] The Philadelphia performances, only nine months later, a
weekend benefit run on June 7–9, 1985, for the Philadelphia AIDS Task Force,
were praised in the local gay press for their educational potential in humanizing AIDS.[23] Dr. Marshall Kreuter, the former director of the Division of Health
Education at the CDC, claimed in 1984 that *Warren* was especially beneficial in
raising AIDS awareness. In an interview with the *Advocate*, Kreuter argues that
the play "should be helpful in getting people aware of, and sensitive to, a variety of psychosocial issues related to the AIDS dilemma."[24] Ranson was invited
by the CDC to present her play at the first International AIDS Conference in
Atlanta in 1985.[25]

Finally, *Warren* demonstrates the alliances formed between gay men and
lesbians in the midst of the epidemic. Ranson stages this alliance as the key relationship in her play. Rebecca and Warren, the two central characters, are old
friends who met in the Southern town where Warren was raised and Rebecca
still lives. After he came out, Warren moved to San Francisco. The play shifts
from these two locations as the friends take turns visiting each other. Although
Rebecca and Warren do not always share the same interests or values, they are
committed to their friendship:

REBECCA: Are you still going to bars?
WARREN: Sometimes.
REBECCA: I don't understand you men.
WARREN: You will if you come to California.[26]

Warren pays tribute to the efforts of lesbians in support of gay men in the early years of AIDS. Throughout the play, Rebecca is the point person for Warren's two support systems, his biological family in the South and his gay male friends and lovers in San Francisco. By the end of the play, Rebecca has returned to San Francisco, and, after Warren's death, has resolved to write a book about AIDS:

REBECCA: I spent a month in San Francisco, time with Kelly and Sam.
Joe died while I was there at home with Sam the way he wanted.
I interviewed patients on the AIDS ward. I'm writing a book about them.

Warren, like *One*, circulated across the country in communities not necessarily associated with AIDS. Both plays relied on constructing universals that found expression in the realist conventions of the theatre. Sentimental, melodramatic, nearly maudlin, these two plays nonetheless were able to continue the work set out in 1981 by AIDS activists in New York City and San Francisco. Performed not *at* fundraisers, memorials, or education campaigns but *as* fundraisers, memorials, and education campaigns, *One* and *Warren* intervened as local pedagogies that aimed to unsettle emerging AIDS mythologies in communities not associated in the popular imagination with AIDS. The conventions of realist theatre and the impulse to universalize AIDS, while problematic ideologically, at the time served the political interests of the playwrights to introduce AIDS as a subject for the theatre. Hagedorn and Ranson also introduced for many spectators a person with AIDS, if only in representation. Many audiences, while familiar with AIDS, had little or no experience with AIDS. *One* and *Warren* enticed audiences to invest in the characters with AIDS, to follow the trajectories of their lives and illness, and, in the case of *Warren*, to respond emotionally to their deaths. At the end of these plays, audiences may still not have met a person with AIDS but they now know and have loved the person with AIDS represented on stage.

For the spectator with AIDS a different identification dynamic occurs. While on the one hand, the idea that the experience of AIDS merits representation and emotional investment can be viewed in some ways as empowering, on the other hand, the representation of death participates in the demoralization associated with the AIDS-equals-death equation ubiquitous in the cultural logic, regardless of its reality. Neither *One* nor *Warren* forcefully critiqued the

"AIDS victim" ideology, nor did they set out to. Their focus on educating audiences about AIDS inadvertently ignored the issues specific to people with AIDS. Seemingly unfamiliar with the emerging and contemporaneous people-with-AIDS self-empowerment movement, these plays do not address the possibility of a person living with AIDS. Although *One* does not end in death but rather with the character's affirmation of life, the assumption that AIDS equals death is introduced in the play's first line and is sustained throughout the performance. And while an AIDS diagnosis in 1983 or 1984 was largely perceived as a near immediate death notice, the people-with-AIDS self-empowerment movement had already been launched in New York and San Francisco and vigorously set out to revise the cultural psyche which preferred "AIDS victim" to "person with AIDS." The prevalence of people with AIDS organizing and addressing rallies and candlelight vigils, education campaigns, and media occasions as early as 1982 already began to contest this labeling, although it wasn't until 1985 that people with AIDS actually collectively addressed these issues in the theatre.

While *One* and *Warren* were produced by community theatres in a diverse group of cities throughout 1984, San Francisco's *The A.I.D.S. Show*, a community-based theatrical collaboration, premiered at San Francisco's Theatre Rhinoceros. *The A.I.D.S. Show* was initially imagined in early 1984 by Theatre Rhino's founding artistic director, Allan Estes, C. D. Arnold, and Robert Pitman as a street theatre piece about AIDS for the 1984 Democratic National Convention. *The A.I.D.S. Show* was funded by the city arts council but postponed due to Estes's AIDS-related death in May. The project was revived months later under the direction of Leland Moss.[27]

The performance is loosely framed around a series of skits portraying the responses and shifting understandings of AIDS within a small group of friends celebrating New Year's Eve from 1980 to 1984.[28] In between these skits, other scenarios are performed by the ensemble cast, many as monologues. Thus, one character, Murray—inspired by Arnold's offstage phone friend in Harvey Fierstein's *Torch Song Trilogy*—in one-sided phone calls to Arnold documents the adjustments of sexually active gay men in the age of AIDS. From his defense of the Baths in 1981 ("it is NOT disgusting, it's liberated!") to his defense of phone-sex in 1984 ("it is not disgusting, it's liberated!") Murray is able to proclaim quite proudly in his final conversation with Arnold that "gay men are the most adjustable species on the face of the earth."[29] Other skits stage safe-sex negotiations and complaints, the effects of AIDS denial, nostalgia for body fluids, various issues of people living with AIDS—including women and people of color—and a host of other topical issues concerning AIDS. Throughout *The A.I.D.S. Show*, audiences witness gay characters, many of them people with AIDS, and their relations addressing AIDS in a series of competing and often contradictory discourses, but the effect, in the end, is a performance highly determined to promote AIDS consciousness in the vernaculars of San Francisco's gay communities. Songs with titles such as "Rimming at the Baths" and skits referring to fisting, orgies, and other radical sexual practices offer no apology or accommodation for their sexual explicitness. *The A.I.D.S. Show* project demonstrated the possibility of the theatre to raise AIDS consciousness in a gay-affirming and sex-positive manner. The collaborators relied upon the local vernaculars of San Francisco's urban gay culture to get their messages about AIDS across to audiences. The skits ranged from full-fledged camp to gutsy, sexually explicit material that presented a community's response to AIDS in all its contradiction. Like *Warren* and *One*, *The A.I.D.S. Show* also included scenes of emotional despair and suffering. The mixture of genres and modes—comedy, tragedy, melodrama, agitprop—and the short, self-contained vignettes enabled *The A.I.D.S. Show* to adapt to the latest AIDS information and cultural response.

The A.I.D.S. Show, while intervening in the sex-negative and "AIDS victim" ideologies of the early 1980s, also provided a major break in tone. The invocation of humor and camp mixed with the emotions of suffering and loss authorized gay men to face the epidemic by whatever means possible. Peter Adair, who adapted *The A.I.D.S. Show* with Robert Epstein for PBS in 1986, explains the effects of this shift in tone and focus for gay men: "It expressed a lot of things we hadn't been able to articulate. . . . The whole play is a celebration of gay culture."[30] In this sense, *The A.I.D.S. Show* can be understood as a type of ritual healing. For a community under siege, *The A.I.D.S. Show* offered its San Francisco audiences a space to gather and regroup. *The A.I.D.S. Show*, according to Chuck Solomon of Theatre Rhinoceros, "was intended to reach out to the community and deal with fears as well as present information on AIDS, look at the politics of the disease and how it affects lovers and families. It's not unusual that people in the audience who are strangers will put arms around one another when a particularly emotional part comes up."[31] Performed in the vernaculars of its intended audience and specific to the local and topical issues of San Francisco's diverse lesbian and gay community, the collaborators succeeded in gathering people into the space of performance to enact community. A tribute to their endurance in the age of AIDS and to the lives of lost friends and lovers, *The A.I.D.S. Show* entertained and comforted its audiences without compromising its politics of AIDS awareness and indictment.

"Let me tell you right now—my objective is to illuminate and not depress," Michael, a character with AIDS, announces to the audience in the first words of *The A.I.D.S. Show*. "I am here to tell you that there is a spirit which banishes all fear." Beginning in the fall of 1984 and running nearly continuously for over a year at Theatre Rhinoceros, the members of Artists Involved with Death and Survival illuminated the lives of gay San Franciscans by hosting a community ritual that was part mourning and part celebration, part camp and part tragic. *The A.I.D.S. Show* was both critically and commercially a success. The support from audiences was demonstrated by the continual extensions of the production run, its sequels, and its spin-off plays. Much of the play's commercial success had to do with the marketing strategies and audience development already in place at the Theatre Rhinoceros. But it was the collaborative efforts and skills of its artists and production crew to engage AIDS issues that facilitated *The A.I.D.S. Show*'s enormous achievement in galvanizing San Francisco's lesbian and gay community.

The earliest theatrical representations of AIDS in New York City were less enthusiastically received. Robert Chesley's *Night Sweat: A Romantic Comedy in Two Acts* was first presented by the Meridian Gay Theatre on May 24, 1984. Chesley dedicated his play to the memory of Rhino founder Allan Estes but, as Chesley confesses in his introduction to the published script, "my best buddy told me he wished I had never written it."[32] *Night Sweat* was trashed by *New York Native*'s theatre reviewer Jeffrey Matson, who wrote that "the scattershot dramaturgy . . . combined with the play's ugly vision and insulting depictions, especially of the AIDS victims (I realize that this is not the preferred term, but it does reflect the self-image of the characters), adds to a needlessly downbeat evening and seems a shameful offering from New York City's only regularly producing gay theater organization."[33]

Night Sweat deals with the decision of a person with AIDS, Richard, to check into the Coup de Grace Club, a place where gay men with AIDS go to be voluntarily killed. For $10,000 gay men receive the "experience"—a wholly theatricalized fantasy-death sequence that involves graphic sexual practices chosen by the patron and enacted by the suicide service. Chesley's highly bizarre and chilling drama avoids the formal constraints of realist theatre or even the more overtly political devices associated with Brechtian theatre.[34] Instead, the play is staged in metaphorical and surrealist excess. Consider, for example, the dream sequence which opens act 2:

> The mad scene from *Lucia di Lammermoor*—the introduction to the cabaletta, cutting directly to the ornamented reprise. A man in stunning Lucia-mad-scene drag lip-synchs to Sutherland with great and tender emotion. Among the onlookers are a Leatherman and a Man In Evening Dress, who begin to waltz gracefully together. At the end of the scene, Lucia stabs herself for real; there is a copious flow of blood from his breast as he staggers, falls and dies. The Leatherman and Man In Evening Dress kiss each other and part as the lights fade. (45)

Tish Dace, in one of the only positive reviews of the play, wrote: "I don't know which is the more exciting: seeing what new variation on his theme Chesley will invent in each new scene or worrying about whether our hero will survive another two minutes."[35] The combined effect of the play's nonrealist form with the play's graphic display of sadomasochism, suicide, and despair alienated audiences eager for the more positive and/or heartwrenching AIDS representations of *The A.I.D.S. Show*, *Warren*, or *One*. In a city besieged by AIDS, a play about a suicide service for gay men with AIDS was bound to be dismissed in 1983.

Chesley, too, was implicated already in the polemical debates around AIDS and sexual practices in New York City's gay community. In a series of letters beginning in 1982, written in response to Larry Kramer's published essays on Kaposi's Sarcoma in *New York Native*, Chesley emerged as one of the defenders of gay male sexual practices, relentlessly questioning Kramer's alleged "gay homophobia and anti-eroticism."[36] *Night Sweat* in many ways continues these debates; eschewing the mainstreaming strategies of GMHC and the alarmist erotophobia of Larry Kramer, Chesley opts to stage, as he explains in the play's introduction, the psychosocial "night sweats" of urban gay men instead:

> So what is *Night Sweat* about? It's about a community which based a significant part of its identity—and economy—on a celebration of sex now facing a lethal sexually-transmitted disease. It's about the so-called "self-destructive lifestyle" of the '70s and early '80s, and the relation of this to the psychological connection between sex and the death wish. It's about paralyzing fear. It's about loss of hope. It's about underlying gay self-hatred and masochism. It's about the necessity of accepting oneself and one's needs. (10)

The persistence of the equation of sex and death, specifically as it is constructed to exist in coterminous relation with AIDS, is internalized and eroticized by Chesley's characters. Although Chesley's depiction of deeply disturbing and yet sensually ecstatic "suicides" for gay men with AIDS may have provoked some audience members to question their own fears and fantasies—Tish Dace goes on to claim that "the idea of avoiding AIDS' terminal agonies and having some fun to boot is highly seductive"[37]—the representational politics of *Night Sweat* for audiences in the early 1980s ultimately were out of sync with the emotional and political needs of most gay men at the time. *Night Sweat* was perceived as nihilistic and irresponsible. Matson's review, for example, challenges Chesley's lack of hope; he writes: "That [representation of] hopelessness is a lie and an insult to a community that has responded strongly to this crisis. Both persons with AIDS and their support organizations have reacted with compassion and courage."[38] *Night Sweat* carried the burden of representation for being the first AIDS play staged in New York. In his attempt to represent the fears and anxieties of many urban gay men in the uncensored vernaculars of gay male sexual culture, Chesley was misunderstood as indicting gay men.[39] His interest in tapping into the gay psyche, in all its confusion given the nightmare of AIDS, was underappreciated at the time.[40]

Stephen Holt, veteran comic playwright, actor, and Ridiculous alumnus, faced different obstacles with his AIDS play, *Fever of an Unknown Origin: A Kind of Love Story.*[41] Holt began writing *Fever* in the spring of 1984 in response to a friend's AIDS diagnosis in February of that year. Holt rejected his earlier ventures with comedy to write a play that would address both AIDS denial and the experience of being a person with AIDS. The play traces the journey of "a gay aerobics teacher who is unhappy though sought after—until he contracts AIDS."[42] By the end of the play, the person with AIDS has died but not before finding love with the play's main character, the celibate Henry. Henry, a formerly rejected suitor—"overweight, balding"—"finds that the disease, despite its horror, forces them to overcome their different forms of isolation."[43] In spite of the peculiar erotophobic pairing of the person with AIDS with the "overweight, balding" celibate character and, as a result, the underlying assumption that both are in some ways undesirable, Holt sets out to represent a positive depiction of love in the age of AIDS. Holt actually attempts to address the looksism endemic in gay culture and exacerbated by AIDS by centering his tragedy on Henry, "a person who has no value according to the gay value system" and is victimized by "this problem of image over substance."[44] Holt situates Henry metonymically with the character with AIDS in order to demonstrate the effects of looksism and AIDS-phobia, their relation, and the possible means to overcome them. The two men find love despite (and partially because of) the health crisis. Their relationship is, as the play's subtitle reminds, "a kind of love story."

Holt finished writing the play in May and, with enthusiastic support from Theater for the New City, the play was rushed into production for a September 1984 opening. Stuart Timmons, writing in the *Advocate*, documents the play's reception:

> Partly due to its "tiny" budget and mostly, Holt feels, due to the fact that the subject was then taboo, *Fever* got scant coverage. The one mainstream critic who came to see it, Marilyn Stasio, from the *New York Post*, wrote a review that never saw print, and Holt's play closed after a brief run.[45]

Unlike the other early AIDS plays—*One* in Chicago, *Warren* in Atlanta, *The A.I.D.S. Show* in San Francisco, and even *Night Sweat* in New York City—*Fever of an Unknown Origin* did not emerge from either a lesbian and gay community-based theatre or an AIDS service organization affiliation. These other early AIDS plays, regardless of the political implications of their representations, came directly out of the communities most affected by AIDS. As such, they attempted to intervene on a number of fronts, with differing success, in both a troubling national AIDS ideology invested in maintaining—at whatever cost—heteronormative patriotism and in locally specific ideologies resulting from the internalized effects of these national AIDS myths.

Even though *Fever* failed to hold a successful run and was virtually insignificant in the debates and shapings of an AIDS consciousness for gay male New Yorkers in 1984, *Fever* attested to the possible support from New York theatre companies in staging AIDS plays. Theater for the New City is not a gay theatre.[46] Its interest in Holt's play demonstrated a shift in the efforts of the theatre industry in New York City to support not only fundraisers for AIDS but also plays that address AIDS explicitly. The occasional success of gay male theatre in non-gay theatres and venues in New York City, most notably Harvey Fierstein's critically acclaimed and commercially viable back-to-back Broadway hits, *Torch Song Trilogy* and *La Cage Aux Folles*, occasioned an interest in gay themes unprecedented in U.S. theatre.[47] In 1984, AIDS began to emerge as a viable subject for the theatre in New York City. These early plays set the stage for the phenomenal critical success of the two most widely recognized AIDS plays of the 1980s, both produced in 1985: William Hoffman's *As Is* and Larry Kramer's *The Normal Heart*.

As Is and *The Normal Heart*:
Commercial Viability and Arrival in 1985

Although neither *As Is* nor *The Normal Heart* was staged until 1985, their respective playwrights had been working on them for several years. William Hoffman started writing *As Is* "sometime in 1982,"[48] and Larry Kramer wrote the first draft of *The Normal Heart* in the summer of 1983.[49] Their productions, at such noteworthy theatres as Circle Repertory Company and The Public Theatre, generated an avalanche of press in both gay and mainstream publications, including major reviews in the *New York Times*. For the most part mainstream critics lauded the plays for introducing AIDS to the stage, virtually unaware of the various plays and performances already in circulation throughout the early 1980s. Since both plays were produced at major established venues and employed well-known actors, directors, and technical designers, a lack of critical coverage would have actually been more unusual. Indeed, the critical attention directed toward both these plays, but especially *The Normal Heart*, was unprecedented for any cultural text about AIDS at the time. In the years since their premieres, the plays have continued to generate a deluge of critical interest.[50] For my purposes, I see the primary intervention of these plays in terms of their effect on the theatre industry and, subsequently, because of this effect, their ability to mainstream AIDS to a wide range of audiences. *As Is*, which premiered at Circle Repertory on March 10 before opening on Broadway on May 1, won the 1985 Drama Desk Award for outstanding new play, a 1985 Obie Award for distinguished playwriting, and was nominated for three Tony Awards. *The Normal Heart*, a New York Shakespeare Festival production, opened at the Public Theater on April 21, 1985, and has since been staged across the United States and in various countries throughout the world.

As Is contains many of the themes introduced in the earliest AIDS plays, in particular the renegotiation of kinship structures amid AIDS. Rich, the play's principal character with AIDS, interacts with various friends and family members in an attempt to construct an appropriate support system. The play rehearses familiar themes of AIDS rituals and performances—the demystification of dominant AIDS myths, especially regarding people with AIDS; the contradictory responses of secondary characters, both gay and straight, including denial and fear; and the panoramic display of gay male urban culture—but it also introduces some new components to the theatre of AIDS. *As Is* foregrounds paraperformative representations of gay male responses to AIDS. Scenes depicting AIDS support groups and AIDS hotline interactions called attention to the rituals and resources of the New York City AIDS community. Furthermore, the play foregrounded the possibility of living with AIDS. Although death is ubiquitous in the play, from the death of a supporting character to the constant references to others who have died offstage or outside the plot-lines, the central character with AIDS is alive by the play's end. Indeed, in the final moments of the play, Saul, Rich's former lover, talks Rich out of suicide and, in an unprecedented scene in AIDS representation, participates in a mutual seduction scene. The reaffirmation of desire in the age of AIDS is staged in the new politics of safe play and in the unlikely setting of a hospital room:

SAUL: Would you like to?
RICH: If we're careful. Do you want to?
SAUL: I'd love to. What do you think?
RICH: I think it'd be okay.
SAUL: What'll we do?
RICH: I don't know. Something safe.
SAUL: We'll think of something.
RICH: Close the curtain.[51]

Despite the limits of their negotiation and the unexploited opportunity to educate audiences explicitly on safe sex practices, Hoffman's presentation of the person with AIDS as a sexually viable partner and a desiring subject worthy of

pleasure without shame was a major intervention in the prevailing ideology of
the person with AIDS as diseased pariah. Throughout the play, various characters yearn for the days before AIDS when the possibilities of sexual pleasure
were unmitigated by a fear of death, so much so that most critics, as we shall
see, read the play as nostalgic. And although many characters are nostalgic for
the years before AIDS—who wouldn't be, after all?—to reduce the play to a nostalgic elegy for sexual promiscuity refutes the possibility of the play's intervention in conservative sex-negative ideologies both inside and outside of gay male
cultures. Instead of lamenting the end of sex, *As Is* stages, as John Clum observes, "the triumph of desire, now qualified and modified, in the new world."[52]
Love and sex in *As Is* commingle in a dynamic relation that intervenes in the
sex/death logic characteristically associated with gay men and AIDS. In its ostensibly apolitical approach—the play does not address institutional AIDS neglect or challenge overtly any dominant regimes—and in its humorous tone, *As
Is* humanizes AIDS without gesturing toward universals.

Such seemingly contradictory impulses to humanize AIDS and to insist on
sex-positive approaches to gay male erotics proved to be amenable to mainstream audiences. According to John Glines, the play's producer, and a veteran
of gay theatre, *As Is* grossed more than $90,000 by September 1985, surpassing
Glines's previous hit, *Torch Song Trilogy*, at the same point in its run.[53] A survey
conducted by the League of New York Theater Producers and Theater Owners
discovered that, overwhelmingly, audiences attended *As Is* to learn more about
AIDS.[54] While *As Is* prevails in humanizing AIDS, it is anything but polemical.
The play addresses various AIDS issues and challenges various AIDS myths;
however, the play does not critique any of the institutional structures that sustain AIDS. Hoffman admits that for him the play was a type of therapy, a way to
cope with his own fears and anxieties.[55] By foreclosing overtly political issues,
As Is was able to generate an overwhelmingly positive response from mainstream critics whose opinions can make or break a show. Thus critics as influential as Frank Rich of the *New York Times* and Clive Barnes of the *New York Post*,
in their newspapers' first reviews of an AIDS play, could celebrate the play's
representational politics and artistic merit. Even John Simon, the consistently
sour voice of theatre reviewing, could write in *New York Magazine* that *As Is* was
"the best new play of the season."[56]

Such critical attention ensures box-office potential, but it does not guarantee
commercial success. So what else facilitated the play's popularity with diverse
audiences? Jan Zita Grover explains that "remarkable shifts in both the quantity
and nature of depictions of AIDS took place in 1985."[57] From *Life* magazine's
notorious July cover story, "Now No One Is Safe from AIDS," to Rock Hudson's
public announcement and subsequent AIDS death, from the marketing of the
HIV-antibody test to the saga of Ryan White, and from the premiere of the first

made-for-television AIDS movie, *An Early Frost*, to the first international AIDS conference in Atlanta, AIDS reentered popular discourse in 1985. Given the hysteria and anxiety emerging from the resurgence of media attention, more people were concerned about AIDS and were willing to seek out, as the Theater Producers and Owners Survey indicates, information about AIDS.

Developed by the prestigious Circle Repertory Company, which was founded by many of the Caffe Cino alumni, directed by Marshall Mason, and produced on Broadway by Lucille Lortell and the Shubert Organization, *As Is* reformulated the conventional theatre industry's response to AIDS. Leading producers were now willing to go further than fundraisers and benefits and invest in an AIDS drama that, while stemming from the gay community, mainstreamed AIDS awareness to a general audience. If nothing else, *As Is* legitimated AIDS theatre as commercially and critically viable: "The Blue-haired ladies just love it. When we first sold out the Wednesday matinees, that told us we've got a cross-over audience," Glines reported enthusiastically to the *Advocate*.[58] Finally, the cross-over success of *As Is* was facilitated by the legitimacy of the venues in which it was produced, which in turn made the play eligible for the important theatre nominations and awards announced each spring. Circle Repertory's reputation for artistic merit and Broadway's capacity to generate media combined to market the play to a mainstream audience generally unfamiliar with community-based lesbian and gay theatre. The success of *As Is* prompted adaptation for public television in 1986.

The success of *As Is* was not an isolated incident. Larry Kramer's play *The Normal Heart*, the most notorious AIDS drama of the 1980s, opened at the Public only a month later. Kramer's play, a pièce à clef about his involvement with GMHC, galvanized audiences into polemical debates about AIDS. In the tradition of agitprop theatre, *The Normal Heart*—unlike any other AIDS play up to that point, and arguably since—relentlessly castigated the various structures of power contributing to the AIDS crisis. Kramer implicated political leaders both in the lesbian and gay community and in the local and national political spheres. Essentially a history play, *The Normal Heart* selectively tells the story of AIDS in New York City from 1981 to 1984. The play follows the narrative of Ned Weeks, a character loosely based on the author, as he attempts to educate other gay men about the burgeoning AIDS crisis. Through the character of Ned, Kramer rails against "every perceived enemy in sight."[59] Among the targets he pursues are the *New York Times*, for failed coverage of the epidemic; New York City mayor Ed Koch, for ignoring AIDS issues; the National Institute of Health (NIH) and the Centers for Disease Control, for complete mismanagement of AIDS research; and the board of GMHC, the organization he helped found in 1981, for alleged cowardice in dealing with each of these sources of power.

Despite the play's vilifying polemical rhetoric and the near Shakespearean engagement with the political systems that sustain AIDS, *The Normal Heart* best exemplifies early AIDS plays that attempt to normalize gay behavior within the context of a larger humanity. Ned Weeks, the play's protagonist and the Kramer surrogate, speaks the ethos of this sentiment when he claims, "I don't want to be considered different."[60] In fact, Kramer has his characters go to great lengths to demonstrate just how conventional they are in terms of how they live their lives. They just "happen" to be gay, "happen" to be dying of AIDS.

And yet, paradoxically, the Ned Weeks character rages against the sins of promiscuity and argues for the domestication of gay sexuality within the traditional model of heterosexual marriage and monogamy—"why didn't you guys fight for the right to get married instead of the right to legitimize promiscuity?" (85)—implying that gay men are getting what they deserve for rebelling against heteronormative structures. David Bergman's insightful discussion of Larry Kramer's "rhetoric of AIDS" stresses this problem in Kramer's writing. Bergman argues that

> Kramer's one alternative to "fuck[ing] yourself to death" is a marriage-like relationship between men, suggesting that gay survival relies on approximating heterosexual behavior. Kramer blames the victims of lovelessness for their own predicament, and their deaths on a life of mindless, unrestrained sexuality. In *The Normal Heart*, Ben, the heterosexual brother of Ned Weeks, says "you guys [homosexuals] don't understand why there are rules and regulations, guidelines, responsibilities," and Ned lamely agrees (68). For Kramer, gay sexual behavior is "the equivalent of eating junk food" (79), irresponsible because it disobeys the rules, regulations, and guidelines that govern heterosexual relations. He fears . . . its very uncontrollability.[61]

The Normal Heart can be seen as a play that participates in a double mission. On the one hand, Kramer is urgent in his demand to disseminate to a large, mainstream audience necessary information about AIDS. The production notes to the published version of the play explain how the information about AIDS was conveyed: "walls of the set, made of construction-site plywood, were whitewashed. Everywhere possible, on this set and upon the theater walls too, facts and figures and names were painted, in black, simple lettering" (19). The theatre became the public arena where social issues about AIDS were offered for discussion and debate. Mark Gevisser, for example, explained how "gay New Yorkers used the theatrical space opened by Kramer and producer/director Joseph Papp as a vital source of information, as a forum for anger."[62] On the other hand, Kramer seems equally committed to dramatizing what his protagonist claims is a "culture that isn't just sexual" (114). Indeed Kramer goes so far as to have Ned Weeks and his lover marry, offering the traditional closure of conventional narratives of heterosexual love.[63] Kramer's choice to use theatre as the medium for his ideas successfully engaged its mainstream audiences to feel for the play's protagonists by universalizing such issues as love, sexuality, and death. Furthermore, Kramer's choice of realist techniques of engagement and empathy secured such a response.

Douglas Crimp, one of the few gay critics to challenge the play, finds most disturbing Kramer's employment of these elements of nineteenth-century realist theatre: "The genre employed by Kramer will dictate a reactionary content of a different kind: because the play is written within the most traditional conventions of bourgeois theatre, its politics are the politics of bourgeois individualism."[64] I would add to Crimp's critique that in this type of theatre, as Raymond Williams argues, we see "the transformation of the tragic hero into the tragic victim."[65] Williams argues that in liberal tragedy, the question of agency shifts indelibly from the context of history and community toward the singular achievement or failure of an isolated individual whom Williams identifies as "the individual liberator" (95), and the primary emotion evoked in this type of tragedy is pity. With this in mind, the problem which emerges in Kramer's play becomes ultimately the reinscription of gay men, especially those with AIDS, as victims. And like the victims of bourgeois tragedy, who anticipate the liberatory effects of "the individual liberator"—in Kramer's play, the Ned Weeks character—people with AIDS and gay men simply die pitiful deaths. Crimp's critique of *The Normal Heart* is significant not so much as a complaint against Kramer—complaints against Kramer are as ubiquitous as Kramer's own vilifications—but, rather, for calling attention to the ramifications of the playwright's choice, in 1985, to assimilate within the confines of mainstream theatre production.[66] Just as feminist theatre in its early phases attempted to stage positive representations of women, Kramer, like many of his contemporaries, invests in the attributes of realist theatre to postulate positive images of gay men without considering the effects of the realist form.[67] Furthermore, to complicate the issue, Kramer's play offers yet a second traditional closure typical of realist theatre: death. Realist drama is so embedded in the prevailing ideology of naturalized heterosexuality in dominant culture that it offers no representational position for gay men or lesbians which is not marginal or a site of defeat. The inadvertent irony of Felix's death immediately following his marriage to Ned Weeks is inescapable.

Still my point here is neither to contest Kramer's choice of genre nor disclaim the play's activist base. At its historical moment it was politically necessary to stage AIDS in order to educate mainstream audiences as well as to document and initiate discussion about AIDS from a gay male outlook. Realism, whatever its political limits, was a familiar strategy for representation and would render the play accessible to a far-reaching range of spectators. From this perspective *The Normal Heart* succeeded in its mission, having been staged almost continuously at the Public from 1985 to 1986 and thus reaching a wide audience. Nonetheless, one of the implications of this style of play—the "way we live now" syndrome—is that the representation of gay men with AIDS only solidifies dominant cultural images of gay men. As Stuart Marshall writes on the images of gay men within television and print media, "Death and homosexuality are now inseparably linked in public consciousness."[68] The new convention of the "AIDS victim" housed within the limits of realist drama where he meets inevitable death contributes to what Marshall describes as a form of demoralization: "This representation [of the "AIDS victim"] is too close—it taps our most profound fears in this terrible crisis and its calculated effect is demoralization" (21).

The 1985 critical and commercial success of *As Is* and *The Normal Heart* in New York led to productions of the plays in theatres across the country and fueled an interest among other lesbian and gay community-based theatres in other early New York AIDS plays whose initial runs proved unsatisfactory. Both *Night Sweat* and *Fever of an Unknown Origin*, for example, went on to have successful production runs in California in gay community-based venues. In local, regional, and national theatres unfamiliar with the work of lesbian and gay playwrights and AIDS activists, *As Is* and *The Normal Heart* eclipsed the earlier AIDS performances both inside and out of the theatre. *As Is* and *The Normal Heart* came to be understood as the first AIDS plays and continue to be imagined as such. AIDS activists across the country encouraged theatres and universities to mount productions of these plays, especially of *The Normal Heart*. In Madison, Wisconsin, the 1986 University of Wisconsin's Department of Theatre and Drama's production of the play was held as a benefit fundraiser for the recently launched Madison AIDS Support Network and proved to be one of the most successful means for the agency to recruit volunteers. The relationship between the University theatre community and the emerging AIDS community—while not yet overlapping—initiated a vibrant exchange of support, dialogue, and resources that lasted well beyond the run of the play. The Madison production proved successful on a number of fronts: as a fundraiser, as an educational forum, and as a galvanizing community-building event.[69]

Not all communities producing *The Normal Heart* had such luck. The 1989 production at Southwest Missouri State University in Springfield, Missouri, led to a community protest against the play and the arson of the home of Brad Evans, the president of SMSU's student group formed to support the embattled production. State representative Jean Dixon claimed that the play's purpose was "to promote the homosexual life-style as a viable, legitimate life-style,"[70]—a charge that quickly garnered support from the Springfield residents, who formed Citizens Demanding Standards to block the university production. Evans's activist response to these criticisms led him to form People Acting with Compassion and Tolerance (PACT) in support of the play. Evans, along with others from PACT, planned a candlelight vigil in conjunction with the play's opening "to honor those who have died of AIDS and those who have it now."[71] In the process, Evans and the other activists demonstrated that acts of intervention often expand and exploit the space of performance, that they gather people into the space of performance so that direct challenges to AIDS-phobia can materialize and effect social change. It was during the AIDS candlelight vigil that Evans's home was set on fire and burned to the ground. The eight-performance run of *The Normal Heart* at SMSU sold out in less than four hours; Springfield audiences were forced to contemplate the relationship between Kramer's play and its own community response as well as their own positions and actions in relation to both AIDS and AIDS-phobia. Evans's capacity to draw on early AIDS activist social performatives to garner support for a theatrical performance about AIDS was a first. Still it is a peculiar and unusual irony that a vigil ostensibly for people with AIDS was really for a theatrical production about AIDS. The relationship between the social rituals enacted in public space and the performances produced for the conventional stage is one of reciprocity and mutual influence. Social rituals and theatrical productions, while not coterminous, are relational; sometimes, as in the case of *The Normal Heart* at SMSU, they are actual extensions of each other, and their meanings can be understood only in the light of their symbiotic relation.

Critical Assessments of Early AIDS Plays: Audience, Locale, Production

The specific responses to *The Normal Heart* in New York City, Madison, and Springfield make explicit the point that the productions of AIDS drama should not be reduced to a monolithic preconception of these plays. Rather, specific plays need to be evaluated within the context of the locale of their production and reception and with regard to the historical moment of their production. Rebecca Ranson points to this need when she describes the first production of *The Normal Heart* in Atlanta and her own response to her play *Warren* four years after its initial run:

At the local Alliance Theater, the audience had sobbed and sobbed over Larry Kramer's *The Normal Heart* the night [I] attended. Then "[the audi-

ence] got up and left," feeling like "they did what they needed to do for
AIDS." . . . *Warren* provided "a tremendous catharsis for grieving on some
level, but it did not provide anything that I thought got people going. . . .
We keep letting people off the hook . . . we keep moving them, exciting
them, and then they had their experience, and it is not going to go anywhere."[72]

Ranson's comments call attention to the idea that intervention demands continual renegotiation and that its effects in one moment in history may not serve
the interests of future needs. But, as both the SMSU controversy and the University of Wisconsin success also demonstrate, the same play that falls politically short in Atlanta may turn out to be a primary and foundational intervention in Springfield, Missouri, or Madison, Wisconsin.

Critical discussions of these early AIDS plays fail to account for the specificity of their productions and focus discussion instead on textual interpretation. Partly this results from the tendency of literary critics to rely on published
playscripts which are more easily rendered stable or simply available. But the
conflation of published script with the play's production history leads to a critical overinvestment in text. Thus literary critics and theorists end up accommodating AIDS performances into the generic or thematic taxonomies of traditional literary categories, failing to exploit the possibility of performance to
unsettle the very comforts of these systems. The primacy of *As Is* and *The Normal Heart* in these accounts suggests as much. While there is no doubt that both
these plays revolutionized the concept of AIDS drama and, to some degree, inaugurated the national discussions of AIDS and theatre, if for no other reason
than the fact that they were produced and reviewed by the established machinery of the U.S. theatre industry, AIDS performances, as I have argued, predate
the official 1985 arrival of these plays. Moreover, these critical discussions of
early AIDS plays burden *As Is* and *The Normal Heart* as foundational discourses
for discussions of AIDS in the theatre. The plays are interpreted without any
consideration of the historical context of both AIDS and performance. More
often than not, the two plays are imagined and discussed in symbiotic relationship, as a binarism that locates *As Is* on one end of a continuum and *The Normal
Heart* on the other.

The limits of this binary become clear when critics argue for or against the
two plays' supposed effects. D. S. Lawson, for example, sees the binarism established by rage and remembrance, which he sets up as two discrete emotions,
the "twin avenues of dramatic reaction to the [AIDS] situation."[73] For Lawson,
The Normal Heart is a rage play and *As Is* a remembrance play: "Kramer's invec-
tive typifies the rage many feel at this microscopic killer and at the society that

for so long ignored (and continues to ignore) the health and destiny of its gay brothers and sons and fathers and friends. Hoffman's nostalgic play defines a mode of remembrance, of sadness over freedom and innocence and pleasure lost; it is a wistful elegy for a world we can now only remember and hope to recapture."[74] Lawson proceeds to discuss the thematics and tone of a number of plays produced in New York City since 1985, situating plays according to these two emotions. And while Lawson advocates for the necessity of both rage and remembrance tendencies, and concedes that they may occasionally cohabit in the same play, he concludes his discussion with a pitch for plays that "reject the theatrical techniques of dramatic realism and strike out into territory unknown on the popular stage" (154).

Joel Shatzky, in an essay published in the same anthology, offers a similar model for understanding AIDS plays when he claims that *As Is* and *The Normal Heart* "established the basic approaches to the dramatization of the AIDS epidemic: personal reaction and public outrage."[75] Unlike Lawson, who concentrates on textual interpretation, Shatzky provides a useful discussion of the 1985 critical reception of the two New York City productions. The mainstream critical response, he demonstrates, instigated the binarism by comparing the two plays to each other. Unfortunately, Shatzky then proceeds to reinscribe the binarism in his critical discussion of the plays. Despite his brief acknowledgment of earlier AIDS plays, Shatzky reaches the same conclusion as Lawson.

By concentrating on thematic and formal concerns, these critics fail to account for the elements of material production, historical context, and political intervention. And while their discussions provide interesting and enlightening readings of the plays, the focus on aesthetics and traditional modes of literary criticism sets up a false binarism between the two plays and imposes a misdirected critical engagement that strips both plays from their immediate interventionist possibilities. Neither critic discusses the politics of rage or remembrance in proactive terms. Instead, the classification system suggests a type of generic prototype for AIDS writing. John Preston, the influential gay writer and editor, has warned against this type of criticism directed toward AIDS writing. At the 1990 Outwrite Conference in San Francisco, Preston declared that

the purpose of AIDS writing has to be found outside of any conventions that contemporary criticism and publishing might try to impose on us. The canons are proven to be ineffective, inappropriate. What is "literature" becomes a meaningless academic question when what is defined can't accommodate what is happening in our lives. . . . Those of us who are writing about AIDS can't worry about these definitions anymore. We can't be concerned with careerism, with academic acceptance, or having the fashions of the day dictate how we write. We can now only deal with being witnesses.[76]

The influential editor of gay literature, Michael Denneny, supports Preston's position when he declares that "AIDS writing is urgent; it is engaged and activist writing; it is writing in response to a present threat; it is in it, of it, and aims to affect it."[77] Both Preston and Denneny align themselves with Douglas Crimp's earlier 1987 manifesto for an activist art and critical practice. These critics refute traditional interpretive models, seeking out a more politically engaged context for AIDS writing.

Some theatre criticism on these earlier AIDS plays offers a method of analysis that seems more compatible with an activist critical practice. James W. Jones, for example, discusses *As Is* and *The Normal Heart* in the context of other representations of AIDS in film and television. Jones, unlike Lawson and Shatzsky, foregoes literary classifications for an engaged critique of the representation of the person with AIDS, concluding his discussion with the "danger of assigning the gay person with AIDS, and, by extension, all gays, to the category of Other."[78] Don Shewey, the editor of the 1988 anthology *Out Front: Lesbian and Gay Plays*, demonstrates the historical and social context for the early AIDS plays. He writes that the "script for these works seemed a mere pretext for the gathering of individuals collectively seeking information about the mysterious disease, seeking an outlet for anger, anxiety, and grief. These plays had a powerful impact on an audience that needed to bolster a still shaky sense of gay self-acceptance in order to face the medical horrors and political backlash sure to come."[79] For Shewey, AIDS plays in the mid-eighties gathered people into the space of performance to counter the mystification of AIDS in the popular imagination. His subsequent discussion of three plays from the mid-eighties—*The Normal Heart*, Robert Chesley's *Jerker*, and *As Is*—calls attention to the multiplicity of perspectives evident and necessary in the theatre's engagement with the reality of AIDS. The theatre in "asserting its ancient function as a public forum in which a community gathers to talk about itself,"[80] can take the lead in communicating essential information for the survival of its people.

Joseph Cady, in his review of the 1990 anthology of AIDS plays *The Way We Live Now*, offers a historical overview of AIDS plays and argues against the tendency of various critics and editors who "attempt to detoxify the stigmatized subject [of AIDS] via association with famous writers."[81] He wonders why "no popular group or documentary theater about AIDS is represented" in the anthology and why "plays developed within a gay community-theatre context" are excluded.[82] Cady reminds us of the need to foreground the community-based origins of AIDS plays. Shewey and Cady, in their prospective pieces, insist upon foregrounding what some of the other critics writing on AIDS theatre elide, the fact that early AIDS plays emerged out of the already politicized lesbian and gay movement. Moreover, by grounding their observations in the sociopolitical contexts of the lesbian and gay movement and the AIDS crisis, Shewey and Cady suggest that AIDS plays will continue to proliferate as necessary interventions, countering theatre scholar John Clum's unfortunate speculation in 1992 that "AIDS drama, so important in the mid-eighties, may have served its purpose."[83]

In making such a comment, Clum replaces one mode of classification based on thematics and formal methods with another equally problematic mode of classification based on venue and audience. Clum positions contemporary theatre in direct antagonism to the political activism of the late eighties. He imagines the two sites—the theatre, the streets—as discrete and oppositional:

> ACT UP demonstrations dramatize the AIDS crisis through vivid theatrical metaphors played out where decisions are made—on Wall Street, in the headquarters of drug companies, and at medical conventions. In doing so, they prove the power of theater but also come up against its limitations, as drama tends to play to the already-converted and seems to have little effect on those who need conversion. For over twenty years, theater people have lamented the inability of political theater to do more than validate those in the audience who share the playwright's opinions. ACT UP has redefined political theater for the age of mass media. It has shown that theaters are not places to effect social change: theater is a more effective tool for shocking people into awareness of key issues when it is taken out of its conventional home. (81)

The history of AIDS plays and performances directly refutes Clum's assertions. Plays such as *One*, *Warren*, and *The A.I.D.S. Show* galvanized communities across the United States; performed as fundraisers and benefits for emerging AIDS service organizations, as educational forums for people concerned and affected by AIDS, and as public grieving rituals to memorialize people who had died of AIDS, these plays established the foundation for an engaged AIDS political theatre. Rather than conceding to the alleged ineffectiveness of any given site of power, AIDS activists have—since the beginning of the epidemic—demonstrated the need for continual and simultaneous interventions. AIDS activists understand that the fight against AIDS must be fought in multiple sites of contestation that, while prioritized according to political need, are never relinquished or abandoned, and finally, that these interventions are often addressed with competing and even contradictory tactics. AIDS activists in the theatre, more specifically, have effected multiple and simultaneous interventions each targeted to the specific, and always different, local political needs of the intended audience and locale. AIDS plays performed in the theatre intervene differently depending upon this need and upon the specific ideologies already in place in the communities that produce them; the productions of *The Normal Heart* in New York City, Madison, and Springfield reveal as much. Moreover, the history of AIDS performance, as I have argued, emerged out of a more expansive understanding of the space of performance on the one hand, and a more encompassing appreciation for the political possibilities of community-based theatre projects on the other. The simultaneity of interventions in conventional theatre and in the more readily identifiable public sphere cannot be isolated or set up in direct opposition. Instead, they are related sites of contestation, spaces of performance that unleash the possibilities of intervention and its material effect.

Sometimes performance may actually locate itself at this juncture between confined conventional theatre space and open contested public space. Let me cite and recuperate one other early AIDS performance to make this point. On the afternoon of September 28, 1983, a community ritual conceived, produced, and directed by local conceptual artist Jay Critchley was performed at Provincetown Harbor Beach. In the midst of the summer's hysterical AIDS media reporting that named Provincetown as Ghost Town, Critchley, in collaboration with choreographer Paul Fonesca, conceived of an environmental theatre piece which included "dance, movement, sand sculpture, costume, readings and percussion, all closely enmeshed with references to the local seashore environment and the history of this little village."[84] *Immunity Mandala* was designed, as Critchley explains, to "look at the AIDS epidemic on many levels."[85] A structured thirty-five-minute theatre piece, which began with an elaborate and detailed ceremonial landing of a fishing boat carrying seven of the performers, who were greeted with percussion and dance by the performers on shore, and ended with the ritualistic exorcism of AIDS hysteria, *Immunity Mandala* both expanded and exploited the space of performance to intervene in "the fear, shame and spiritual ills that had invaded many of the participants and audience over the past months."[86] Over one hundred people participated in the event as either performers, spectators, or inadvertent and unsuspecting cohabitants of the performance space/beach. The centerpiece of the performance was the construction of the mandala circle with colored sand, a sacred space for regeneration and balance that became the centralized location for the rites of community healing. Dancers, singers, dogs, seagulls, and eventually the tide moved in and out of the circle in a ritual designed to engender hope and to honor the life cycle. Critchley, in the "role" of shaman, dedicated the ritual to the people of Provincetown, reminding the assembled crowd of the centuries of strong village women "who sat in vigil waiting for fishermen who often did not return from the sea," and connecting the history of the village with the vigils of gay men and their friends "awaiting solutions and answers we may never get."[87] *Immunity Mandala* offered a very specific and local community an opportunity for communal healing and energizing in the midst of AIDS. In the open air and on the beach, the performance itself cohabited with the other rituals of life less specifically marked as performance on that sunny afternoon. *Immunity Mandala* participated in the daily occasions of living: free, open, communal. In effect, the performance offered its participants a temporal respite from the sensationalist media conflation of Provincetown with AIDS and, in the process, may have rejuvenated a community with the simple reminder of the life systems available to, and all around, them.

This rupture of the binary constructed as "theatre space vs. public space," or its analogue, "non-effect vs. effect," is already put into motion by many other early AIDS performances—the theatrical, political, public, and social occasions that gathered people into the space of performance to direct specific acts of intervention. Some of these performances were even performed in public spaces rendered as unconventional spaces of performance, spaces located and understood more readily within the geographies of progressive movements for social change or communal grieving rituals. Alisa Solomon, in her 1989 tribute to ACT UP, identifies this expansion of the space of performance as "activists tap[ping] into theatre's special union between representation and community."[88] Solomon's insightful discussion of ACT UP's social performatives and theatrics, intelligently grounded in both theatrical precedents (Brecht, Artaud, Guerilla theatre) and earlier and ongoing political movements (feminism, antiwar efforts, civil rights), points out that political theatre never really has, as Clum imagines, any set "conventional home." But even Solomon's account of ACT UP disregards the political and performative importance of activists engaged in the fight against AIDS before 1987. It is not arguable that ACT UP evokes the "ancient theatrical impulse of empowering a community through ritual."[89] But ACT UP, for all its accomplishments in the late eighties, is as indebted to the social performatives of the early 1980s—the fundraisers, benefits, memorial services, safe-sex campaigns, candlelight vigils, and rallies—as it is to the early AIDS theatre pieces produced throughout the United States, including immediately ephemeral and highly localized environmental theatre pieces such as *Immunity Mandala*.

Each of these ritual occasions of the early 1980s made explicit the need to exploit performance's political and communal potential, and each helped set the groundwork for the later interventions we have come to understand as the direct actions of AIDS activism. And if the goal of much of this direct action was to exploit the mass media communications systems that construct and circulate many of the mythologies that inevitably shape our understanding of AIDS, in order to reconstitute or reconfigure those understandings (or ideologies) as they take shape, other performances in the 1980s opted to focus on performance's incommensurability with documentation and media recirculation. The simultaneity of these two seemingly oppositional activist approaches—theatricalizing the social performatives of AIDS activism for media documentation and circulation on the one hand, and exploiting performance's very incompatibility with documentation on the other—rather than setting into place an imagined value-laden hierarchy, instead actually demonstrates performance's adaptability for concurrent but distinct modes of intervention. More directly, this simultaneity calls attention to the *process of production* in any social performance designed to expand the possible means of imagining AIDS and the various locations of agency for performers—activists, artists, people with AIDS—united to revise the cultural psyche that sustains AIDS. The theatre remains a viable site for these deliberations and interventions. In particular, the theatre's process of production, generally obscured in dominant venues and ensembles and even, by extension, in the production of AIDS activism so heavily concerned with entering and disrupting the field and technologies of mass media representation, emerged in the years between 1985 and 1988 as a means of agency for people with AIDS. By shifting the focus from performance and its reception to the actual process of production, AIDS ensembles expanded the intervention possibilities of the theatre in the midst of AIDS.

AIDS Theatre Collectives:
Artists Confronting AIDS in Los Angeles

Despite the proliferation of AIDS plays emerging from lesbian and gay community-based theatres, regional theatres, and established New York City theatres in the early and mid-1980s, it was not until much later that theatre collectives designed primarily by and for people with AIDS appeared on the scene. That the cultural instance that gave rise to community-based HIV theatre companies also gave rise to the emergence of a new community-based direct-action AIDS activism is not coincidental. The need to expand and exploit the possibilities and locations of AIDS activism coincided with a need to expand and exploit the representational field of AIDS. The same momentum of grassroots lesbian and gay organizing that resulted in the establishment of AIDS service organizations led to the reconfiguration of an AIDS activism that focused less on providing social services for people with AIDS or establishing educational outreach programs and more on direct confrontation with the regimes of power that sustain AIDS, including occasionally even the ASOs themselves. In the theatre, a similar trajectory took shape. AIDS theatre and performance emerged in the early 1980s from the lesbian and gay community-based theatres—themselves a direct result of the long-standing lesbian and gay community-based grassroots political movement—to service and collaborate with newly established ASOs. With the 1985 success of *The Normal Heart* and *As Is*, AIDS plays began to formulate as both a genre with a familiar thematic and formal structure and a mainstream and regional commodity. And while community-based theatre organizations continued to develop and stage these and other plays, it was not until the Artists Confronting AIDS production of *AIDS/US* in 1986 that people with AIDS assembled in the theatre to enact a new and unprecedented intervention in the production and understanding of AIDS discourse.

Artists Confronting AIDS (ACA), a Los Angeles community-based arts organization, was founded officially in 1985 by playwright James Carroll Pickett and playwright, director, and actor Michael Kearns in order "to explore how the arts can affect the AIDS crisis and how the AIDS crisis affects the arts."[90] Artists Confronting AIDS held its first meeting in February 1986 and launched its first official production, *AIDS/US*, in April 1986 (fig. 14). *AIDS/US* depicted the lives of thirteen different people impacted by the AIDS crisis, seven of whom were diagnosed with AIDS. All thirteen of these people shared the experience of production and performance, telling their stories to each other and negotiating community through the process of production—casting, reading, rehearsal, performance, and reception. Pickett and Kearns, two white gay men, had been producing gay theatre in Southern California since early 1983. Their 1983 productions of Kearns's play *The Truth Is Bad Enough* and Pickett's play *Bathhouse Benediction*, while not specifically AIDS plays, addressed various gay male cultural issues and established their reputation in Los Angeles for sophisticated and politically engaged gay theatre.[91] Their 1985 productions of *Warren, Night Sweat,* and Pickett's *Dream Man*, a monologue concerning a phone-sex-industry worker, introduced AIDS issues on the stage for the first time in Los Angeles. Their collaborations on these productions led to the formal establishment of Artists Confronting AIDS, an unprecedented collective in the history of theatre and one that continues to thrive in the 1990s. According to Pickett and Kearns, the initial idea of ACA was to raise money for AIDS research. Pickett and Kearns, already established names in the Los Angeles theatre scene, invited a number of local artists to meet and see what could be done about AIDS in Los Angeles. Jim Pickett explained that "at the time, we were scared. We were *very* scared. I think part of the motivation for forming the company was 'I don't want to go through this alone.' 'Are other people feeling this way?' "[92] Neither Pickett nor Kearns was aware of his serostatus at the time the

14. Michael Kearns and James Carroll Pickett of Artists Confronting AIDS, Los
Angeles, 1986.
Photo by Thomas Cunningham courtesy of Michael Kearns

group was formed, but both were suspicious. Pickett, who died of AIDS complications on July 3, 1994, tested HIV-positive in 1988; Kearns, who remains
asymptomatic, tested positive in 1990.

The early productions under the banner of Kearns and Pickett were conventional theatre pieces typical of the work emerging from lesbian and gay theatres across the country, community-based theatrical productions with professional actors, technical crew, and directors. With the production of *AIDS/US* in
1986, Pickett and Kearns abandoned the standard trajectory of professional
theatre, whose goal remains the exhibition of a completed and perfected artistic
product for critical and commercial consumption, in order to accent and exploit
the process of production for the participants involved. In other words, *AIDS/
US* focused first and foremost on the experience of production and performance
for the *AIDS/US* company. Kearns explains that the crucial experience of *AIDS/
US*, true of any work in the theatre, is for the actors and collaborators: "Yes,
we're doing it for the audience, and yes, we hope to educate, and heal, and all
those other wonderful words, but we're educating ourselves, healing ourselves,

15. Performers in *AIDS/US,* an Artist Confronting AIDS collaborative presentation, Los Angeles, 1986.
Rick Moffit

getting in touch with who we are among ourselves. . . . That focus is our experience *before* we open. The play can be deemed a success *before* a critic or audience ever comes to see it."[93] *AIDS/US* did not cast actors. The actual thirteen people whose stories were depicted on the stage performed themselves (fig. 15). In order to invite as diverse a group of people as possible for *AIDS/US,* Pickett and Kearns contacted different AIDS service agencies, friends, and networks. The intent was to identify as many people as possible who wanted to express themselves in an artistic manner about the disease. The result was a company that included Pat and Vicki Reynolds, a white mother and her nineteen-year-old daughter, who had lost their husband and father to AIDS; Luis Maura, Steve Tracy, Tom Trimm, Don Staiton, Jerry Minor, and Andrew Hiatt, six ethnically, professionally, and generationally diverse gay men with AIDS; Helenclare Cox, Andrew's mother;[94] Susan Habif, a white social worker; Lyn Hilton, a white woman with AIDS, who had lost her husband to AIDS; Anthony Bruno, a white gay man identified with the leather community and an AIDS widower; and Melrose Sprague, an HIV-negative African American woman and AIDS fundraiser.

AIDS/US was scripted from interviews by James Carroll Pickett and Michael Katz, and directed by Michael Kearns.

Throughout rehearsal and performances, cast members needed to have cots backstage to relieve fatigue; there were even times when cast members were too ill to rehearse or perform. One of the members of the ensemble, Lyn Hilton, died near the end of the production run. While *AIDS/US* is clearly about survival and self-empowerment, Hilton's death during the performance run played into the cultural logic equating AIDS with death. The sad irony that a play about AIDS survival would inadvertently include an AIDS death was inescapable. Rather than elide their efforts to unsettle the hegemony of the AIDS death representations in future performances, Hilton's part was kept in the show for the remaining performances by Dale Raoul, who announced that she was an actress reading Hilton's words. Hilton's story was still very much her story and part of the company's story now as well. No one spoke more than a few lines at a time, and only occasionally did people respond to each other. Instead, the script was formulated around certain key themes: support systems, symptoms and hospital experiences, survival techniques, love and sex, and denial. *AIDS/ US* very simply gave people with AIDS and their supporters an opportunity to tell their stories on the stage. All cast members remained on stage for the performance, offering support to one another as they stepped into the spotlight to tell their stories. Some cast members read from scripts. The fact that the company was composed of nonactors was neither erased nor exploited by the production.

The performance of *AIDS/US* begins with the introduction of the company, who announce immediately their relationship to AIDS:

> ANDREW: I was living in San Francisco when I was first diagnosed in January '83. I'm Andrew.
> TOM: I'm Tom. I was first diagnosed with ARC two years ago. In December I got the AIDS diagnosis. I'm 25 years old.
> PAT: Don died a year ago. I'm Pat. We were married 24 years.[95]

Like the AIDS candlelight vigils, rallies, and other public occasions where people with AIDS addressed an assembled crowd, the process of production and performance of *AIDS/US* made explicit the needs and concerns of a select group of people with AIDS and others affected by AIDS. The company invested in presenting primarily two goals: first, to empower all people affected by AIDS to tell their stories; and second, to establish and perform kinship and support structures and pay tribute to those available or already in place for people with AIDS or people who had lost someone to AIDS. Unlike earlier AIDS plays that rely on actors and that moreover obscure the relationship between the actor and the representation of AIDS, the company of *AIDS/US*—as "real" people living with AIDS—enact these very networks of support in the actual process of production. This crucial difference—"real" people vs. supposedly unmarked actors (playing either "real" people or constructed representations of people with AIDS and their families)—shifts the goals of production from the audience to the company. The production process of *AIDS/US* explicitly enacts kinship and support systems for people with AIDS, but it does not rely on its audiences to validate its efforts. In the tradition of grassroots community-based arts, *AIDS/US* assumes its audience as a support system, an extension of the company. *AIDS/US* relies on the presumption that, while the experience of AIDS is unique and specific, AIDS is everyone's issue.

The focus on the company's experience of production—individually and collectively, through rehearsal and during performance—casts *AIDS/US* as a form of performative therapy, a collective empowerment ritual that authorizes people to fashion and share identities based on, but not limited to, their experiences with HIV and AIDS. Such a project touches upon the principal mission of the community-based arts-practice movement, a movement which is, as Arlene Goldbard explains, "based on the belief that cultural meaning, expression and creativity reside within a community, that the community artist's task is to assist people in freeing their imaginations and giving form to their creativity."[96] Community-arts-based practices such as *AIDS/US* refute the idea of the artist as genius. This romantic construction of the individual artist as an intuitive and transcendent genius, so embedded in the Western cultural imaginary, is replaced in community-arts practices with the practice of collective artistic expressions. Through performance, communities—however defined or determined—produce social rituals, which according to John McGrath "enrich cultural identity, amplify marginal voices, attack cultural homogeneity, increase community self-determination and challenge the dominant power structure."[97]

In many ways, it could be argued that community-arts practices such as *AIDS/US* overinvest in the idea of "community" without ever questioning its rhetorical, political, and performative employment, let alone the term's inability to accommodate all the various identities imagined under its usage. As Cindy Patton explains, the idea of community has specific limitations when it comes to AIDS:

The term *community* has been nearly evacuated: the illusory unity of a "gay community" has been highlighted by the failure of mainstream AIDS groups to work effectively outside the white, middle-class gay-male

core group. In addition, co-optation of the term by mainstream media—
"heterosexual community" or "white community"—has robbed the term
of its references to shared histories of oppression.[98]

The replacement of the notion of artist as genius with the concept of community
as agent for social change can also be a romantic one and, even more so, a concept that plays into a particularly traditional American mythos. Michael
Warner, for example, writes that the notion of a lesbian and gay community
is "generated in the tactics of Anglo-American identity politics and its liberal-
national environment, where the buried model is racial and ethnic politics. . . .
Community also falsely suggests an ideological and nostalgic contrast with the
atomization of modern capitalist society. And in the liberal-pluralist frame it
predisposes that political demands will be treated as demands for the toleration
and representation of a minority constituency."[99]

The concerns voiced by Patton and Warner point to some of the limits of
the representational consequences of *AIDS/US* and other community-based performatives. Concepts of community are heavily reliant on concretizations of the
authentic. The idea that there is an intelligible understanding of the authentic
or "real" HIV community or the authentic or "real" person with AIDS, and that
this understanding escapes the representational systems of the dominant media, burdens the production of community-based arts practices with the cum-
bersome problem of self-justification and explanation on the one hand, and the
taxing fear of expropriation on the other. Needing to name oneself as a person
with AIDS, for example, already presumes an identity-based organizational
politics and, moreover, runs the risk of having that very fragile identity abused
and violated through acts of misreading or appropriation.

Thus the formation and practice of an HIV community-arts project based
on the so-called authentic HIV and AIDS experiences of actual people and the
subsequent onstage presentation of this experience by the people who have
lived it suggests that the representation on stage is not a representation at all—
that, instead, what is staged remains in some way outside the representational
systems through which we have come to understand AIDS. As such, the
AIDS/US project reifies an ownership of AIDS that may leave its audiences off
the hook. If audiences of *AIDS/US* are privy to the "real thing" in the performance of *AIDS/US*, the possibility of audiences' *disidentification* becomes an option
as well. To assume an authentic experience of AIDS outside representation sets
up authenticity in a new authoritative and problematic way that may actually
disrupt the possibilities of an efficacious performative intervention in our understanding of AIDS. The critical reception of *AIDS/US* by the Los Angeles
press demonstrates this tendency to differentiate from the representation. Vari-

ous critics invest in reviewing the production not as a theatrical representation but as an authentic, unmediated experience. The reviewer for the *Los Angeles Times* reports that "[e]ven for an audience that knows of AIDS only secondhand, the show is a powerhouse . . . this is the genuine article."[100] The *Daily News* critic proclaims that *AIDS/US* "is not a performance,"[101] and the writer for the *LA Weekly* states that " 'critical distance' is meaningless" and goes so far as to undermine his own critique of the play's "human potential jargon" by confessing that he "doesn't have the disease, at least not yet."[102]

The idea that *AIDS/US* speaks a certain set of truth claims about AIDS that escape understanding unless one "has the disease" goes against the mission of the company. Artists Confronting AIDS assumes, naively perhaps, that AIDS is everyone's issue, that there is no hierarchic ownership of AIDS. Nonetheless, the choice to work with nonactors sets this trap of authenticity where critics position *AIDS/US* as "the genuine article" and not as an innovative AIDS interventionist tactic. That *AIDS/US*—itself a reconceptualized discursive means of understanding AIDS—is implicated in the means of its articulation, whether through the systems of the theatre or through the systems of an identity-based politics, is unavoidable. Rather than surrendering critical engagement, audiences of *AIDS/US* could consider the following questions: In what ways does the performance of *AIDS/US* exploit the identificatory impulse inherent in identity-based politics in order to maintain its strategic effort to galvanize a communal response to AIDS? In what ways is the ownership of AIDS, so immediately anchored in the "authentic" experience of the *AIDS/US* company, democratized and made available to the audience through the performance? In what ways does *AIDS/US* allow for critical engagement *and* emotional identification? Or, if these questions are unanswerable, in what ways does *AIDS/US* set out to avoid expropriation or the tolerant tendencies of the liberal pluralist frame?

Many of the answers to these questions are addressed in the process of production itself. While *AIDS/US* makes no effort to offer radically innovative theatrical devices, its very primal ritualistic impulse to gather an assembled crowd to relay and share experience already ruptures some of the more traditional conventions of mainstream theatrical representation. In part, this begins with the announcing of an unequivocal subject position defined by AIDS. The self-identification of the company in the first moments of the performance invites audiences to produce their own subject positions in relation to AIDS. In the event that spectators are not able to assume an "AIDS identity," the production—by casting people from the community without AIDS—problematizes that position for them. In other words, one does not need to have an AIDS diagnosis to have a relationship to AIDS. This point is again brought to the surface at the end of the performance, when cast members turn to each other in a chain-like response of acknowledgment and support:

> DON: We are thirteen people united.
> ANDREW: United by what AIDS is . . .
> ALL: Us!
> HELENCLARE: I love you, Andy.
> ANDREW: I love you, Anthony.
> ANTHONY: I love you, Susan.
> SUSAN: I love you, Lyn.[103]

And so on, until every cast member is acknowledged. Throughout this process, company members hold hands. The performance concludes with the company's collaborative proclamation to the audience: "And we love you!" Hands extended across and over the stage, the imaginary line between audience and company is finally obliterated. At the end, everyone assembled in the space of performance is enraptured by the handheld link into the communal embrace that completes the ritual. Such performative gestures enable community to surface as an intervention in the fight against AIDS, if only temporarily in the limited space and time of the performance that is *AIDS/US*.

The representational intervention of the production, which culminates in this finale, enacts a community-based response to AIDS that includes the audience. However, this entrance into representation obscures the production process, which is designed to serve the interests of the company members and not necessarily the spectator. The immediate and direct intervention of *AIDS/US*—to bring together a select group of people with and affected by AIDS in order to refashion life-affirming and empowering identities based on these experiences—is not evident in the actual performance of *AIDS/US*. It is for this reason that Kearns and Pickett are vehemently opposed to any type of documentation of the performance of *AIDS/US*. The documentation of performance inevitably involves a certain translation of performance and its effects into another medium—film, video, text—which, in turn, has its own effects and history. In this sense, it is not possible to document the process of producing the main interventions—the empowering rituals of negotiating and creating kinship and support through the exchange of AIDS stories—without conflating the production with performance and without translating performance into something other than performance. In short, documentation *produces* something else. While the primary intended intervention can be communicated and explained—in interviews, critical essays, or published reviews, for example—it cannot be reproduced. The intimate experience of fashioning identities and negotiating support remains in the production process of *AIDS/US*. What is staged in the performances of *AIDS/US* is only one component of that process.

While the idea that performance is only one component of the process of production is true of all theatre, it becomes increasingly poignant in productions by HIV ensembles and companies. Various cast members, for example, focused on the process of production to stay alive. Many of their reasons for joining the *AIDS/US* company—to concretize the will to live, to articulate a personal response to AIDS, to establish or expand networks of kinship and support—began in production. Michael Kearns explains that, throughout the rehearsal period and during the production's performance run, "[many of the people with AIDS in the company would say:] 'I'm staying alive to do next week's show.' Well on video you don't have to stay alive to do next week's show."[104] The process of production enables this desire to live to endure; onstage performance mainly represents this desire and its achievement. For cast members and others in the company involved in the performance's production, the collective experience of this process is only partially representable in performance. The tension between the process of performance's production, which focuses exclusively on the company, and the reception of the representation emerging from the performance of the production, which is directed primarily to the spectator, is partially resolved in the experience of live theatre, where actors and spectators negotiate need. Such negotiations between performer and spectator are arguably the ethos of theatre and, according to Artists Confronting AIDS, can be experienced only in the theatre. Documentation of the experience of company members, and their exchange with the audience, is not possible.

The efforts of Artists Confronting AIDS to resist representation positions *AIDS/US* as a seemingly authentic experience of AIDS located outside of representation, as "the genuine article" unmediated by representational systems, an impossible position for any performance regardless of AIDS. But by keeping their focus on production and not on the representation embedded within performance, Artists Confronting AIDS is capable of challenging the hegemony of representational systems constructing AIDS. They offered a new model for AIDS theatre that foregrounds the process of performance's production rather than the reception of performance's representation. The focus shifts from the experience of the spectator (reception) to the experience of the company (production). What Artists Confronting AIDS offers the theatre of AIDS is the possibility to enact multiple, albeit specifically localized, interventions. Although the primary goal of the company is to expand the space of performance for people with AIDS and HIV, Artists Confronting AIDS challenges audiences in a variety of ways.

Other interventions directed toward the audience and inevitable in the materiality of production emerge with *AIDS/US*. The pedagogical intervention begins for audiences with the decision to attend a performance cast with people
with AIDS. People often called the theatre concerned about contagion, asking
whether it was safe to attend the theatre and if AIDS could be "caught" by being
in the same room with someone with AIDS. With prospective spectators developing interest in *AIDS/US*, the box office became an AIDS hotline dispensing
information to quell these fears. Once these ticket holders were in their seats,
the theatre became an emotional laboratory, especially for those about to mix
for the first time with someone self-identifying as a person with AIDS. Even on
the basic level of placing a reservation for tickets or asking a friend to attend a
performance, prospective spectators were coerced into speaking aloud the title
AIDS/US, an implication that locates spectatorship already within a community
based on an identity-politics model. The *US* in *AIDS/US* carries equal weight in
the title. *US* presupposes a shared link, a common experience and identification.
And yet rather than rehearsing the familiar binarism generally at play between
those with AIDS and those without, the *US* remains unmarked. Who is the *US*
in *AIDS/US*? *US* does not directly refer to anyone specific. But when spoken
aloud, the person who speaks the title is immediately included in the possessive
terms of the pronoun. The slash bar between the two terms of the title connects
the very terms that it appears to separate. The bar becomes the index of the cultural work put into motion throughout the production; it is the symbol of the
relationship between AIDS and us. If the bar between *AIDS* and *US* appears in
print as a type of prophylactic between the two terms of the title, which is to
say as the title appears in print it seems to keep these terms discrete, it loses
such force when spoken aloud. Crudely put, it is not possible to ask for tickets
to *AIDS/THEM*. To speak the title *AIDS/US* is to be already implicated in one
of the pedagogical interventions of the production. The title *AIDS/US*, moreover, suggests the relationship founded on page A20 of the July 3, 1981, *New York
Times*. It, too, converges AIDS, performance, and nationalism. The *US*, of course,
speaks national identity. This time, however, the discursive structures are reori-
ented to allow for agency amid AIDS rather than its disavowal or foreclosure.

The process of production then is also available to the audience, albeit differently. Thus documentation is not able to capture the process of *AIDS/US* for
the audience either. Audiences are invited to share in the *AIDS/US* company's
final process of production: performance. Performance involves fragility, urgency, temporality—qualities articulated by the company and defining their
lives in the midst of AIDS. Performance is about shared intimacy and its collective negotiation and exchange; it sets into motion the circulation of mostly invisible energies between and among the performers and the audience. The pro-

cess of the production of this energy materializes through the body: sweat, laughter, tears, applause. But these effects, once visible and audible, make explicit only their performance and not their process of production, which remains outside of the representational field. By divesting from both representation and documentation, *AIDS/US* makes explicit the political efficacy of the performance's process of production.

While many of the earlier AIDS performances and social performatives between 1981 and 1984 escaped critical documentation in major medias because of the calculated negligence of the various institutional regimes of power throughout the 1980s, later social performatives set out to exploit mainstream media through regular, sustained, and always innovative manipulation. ACT UP's brilliant and savvy media-friendly soundbites, graphics, and theatrics relied, to a large degree, on the operatives of visibility politics. The documentation of visibility politics and its tactics—in both mainstream and alternative media—served multiple and specific purposes that varied according to who held the camera and for what end. For AIDS activists, mass-scale representation through mainstream documentation facilitated the circulation of intervening information about AIDS from an engaged activist perspective. Activist video collectives of the late 1980s, such as Testing the Limits (TTL) and Damned Interfering Video Activist Television (DIVA TV), also helped document an activist response to the epidemic for others interested in imagining interventions in other locales and, equally important, reversed the gaze of surveillance back onto the police, the CDC, the FDA, or whatever power structure was at hand. Activists videotaping a demonstration would focus on both the action itself and the police response to it. DIVA Catherine Saalfield explains how when "ACT UP organizes a demonstration, DIVAs organize to be there, document, provide protection and countersurveillance, and participate."[105] Videotaping becomes a means for AIDS activists to bring evidence of police abuse into a court of law, a means for AIDS activists to study and critique their actions, and a means for AIDS activists to celebrate their accomplishments with others unable to participate for whatever reasons in the action. Documentation served the interests of the activist intervention, and in some cases, became the primary intervention itself.[106]

ACT UP/New York, given its location and access to national television newsrooms and networks, set into motion the AIDS activist investment in dominant media's documentation of its actions. ACT UP/NY's manipulation of news industries kept AIDS issues circulating in national news networks. Local ACT UP chapters throughout the country followed suit, sometimes even basing the entire political efficacy of the action on whether or not it made the local television newscasts. Like the earlier social performatives that employed performance to serve the intervention—fundraisers, benefits, memorials, rallies, candlelight vigils—ACT UP manipulated performance to service its own intervention. Through its "theatricalization of rage,"[107] ACT UP appropriated performance to call attention to the specific issue at hand—needle-exchange programs, AIDS housing, NIH policies on treatment expediencies—enabling that information, which is *performed* by activists, to receive documentation for mass circulation in major media markets. ACT UP depended upon the organizing tactics of visibility politics and invested in expanding strategies of representation. To ACT UP was therefore essentially to act out, insofar as acting out is understood to mean performing oneself into the visible field of representation, however unwelcome it may be for those it confronts.

Performance, by its very nature and against its own investments in representation, resists documentation, despite performance's own paradoxical attempts to document itself through its own reiteration night after night during a sustained production run. Performance, in fact, is incommensurate with documentation, even though documentation itself may be, as ACT UP's video collectives demonstrate, a performative practice. And while performance can be documented—in text, video, or interpretation—once so, it becomes another form of representation, no longer performance but its translation. For Artists Confronting AIDS, documentation is unable to capture the interventionist strategies of the process of production. Documentation overly determines the final stage in the process of production, which is performance, and the effect of performance, which is representation. The process of performance's production is both temporal and spatial. The focus on performance and representation burdens the process of production to rely on a sequential logic that may not be, as the *AIDS/US* series points out, adequately visualized. In this sense, the process of performance's production escapes representation.

One of the ways that Artists Confronting AIDS has been able to unsettle the hegemony of representation in discussions of performance on the one hand, and to counter the fact that performance cannot be reproduced through documentation on the other, is by proliferating the production process. Since *AIDS/US* in 1986, James Carroll Pickett and Michael Kearns have produced *AIDS/US II* (1990) and *AIDS/US/Women* (1993). *AIDS/US/Youth* is in the planning stages. In their efforts to exploit the possibilities of performance's production process, Artists Confronting AIDS has been able to form, much like ACT UP, coalitions. Instead of documenting the representations of any given performance in a production run for mass circulation, ACA mounts more productions for circulation. New people are invited into the process of production, forming coalitions with previous cast members, technical artists, theatre managers and volunteers, and former audience members familiar or involved with the previous *AIDS/US*.

AIDS/US II closely follows the production process of its antecedent, as does *AIDS/US/Women*. The focus remains on the process of production for the company members involved. With all new people involved in the productions—except for Pickett, Kearns, and Helenclare Cox, who appears in all three—Artists Confronting AIDS brings forth the expanding demographics of AIDS through the production and performance process. ACA also addresses their losses to AIDS, six of the seven people with AIDS from the initial *AIDS/US* (1986) had died by 1990. The different *AIDS/US* productions trace many of the shifting AIDS ideologies between these years as well. In 1990, for example, more treatment options and support networks for people with AIDS were available. Furthermore, an AIDS consciousness was more deeply entrenched throughout the city of Los Angeles, although there was still a lack of attention to the relationship and reality of women and AIDS. Many of the people with AIDS in the later companies did not share the unmitigated optimism of the initial production; their stories are less about beating AIDS and more on how they plan to continue living with AIDS. Moreover, in the four years between the first two productions—1986 to 1990—Pickett and Kearns learned that they were HIV-positive. Their previous collaborator, Michael Katz, had also died an AIDS-related death.

The follow-up productions, always performed in the Los Angeles area and usually either for free or as an AIDS benefit, have included intravenous drug users and their partners, a homeless person with AIDS, a lesbian transvestite AIDS activist with HIV, a homosexual priest with AIDS, a lesbian ex-convict, and a mother and child with AIDS, along with various others from the demographic pool of *AIDS/US* (1986). Rather than working from the additive model of liberal pluralism, which accommodates difference by marginal inclusion, the *AIDS/US* series reconfigures the structure in which the stories are related. The structure of the production and performance is determined by and dependent on the needs of the specific company. Later productions, while similar in format to *AIDS/US* in that they involve company members sharing their AIDS experiences, allow for different forms of telling stories. In *AIDS/US II* a mother and father who lost a child to AIDS sang a song the mother wrote about the loss. In *AIDS/US/Women*, two of the lesbian AIDS activists with HIV, who were both involved with ACT UP/LA, insisted upon introducing more direct confrontational tactics in both the production and performance process. In performance, for example, the chant "Say it out loud: Women get AIDS!" became one of the organizing tropes of the performance format.[108] This rupture of the initial *AIDS/US* model, which did not directly challenge social and political institutions, announced both a shift in AIDS activism and an accommodation of the preferred tale-telling tactics of the two lesbians involved in the production.

The support structures established in earlier productions sustained themselves with the continual presence of Helenclare Cox, who first appeared in *AIDS/US* (1986) with her son Andrew and who appeared in *AIDS/US II* to tell the story of her new relationship with yet another Andrew from the *AIDS/US II* company, who, at the time of the production run, was living in her home. By the time she appeared in *AIDS/US/Women*, she had buried both Andrews. Steve Tracy, an actor who died of AIDS and who was part of the company of *AIDS/US* (1986), circulated in the stories of his close friend and *Little House on the Prairie* costar Alison Arngrim, a company member of *AIDS/US II*. But the main consistency throughout these productions has been Jim Pickett and Michael Kearns. As the founding directors of Artists Confronting AIDS, Pickett and Kearns have demonstrated the ways that the production of performance can act as an intervention in the way that AIDS is imagined by people with AIDS, their supporters and survivors, and the local communities they live in. By concentrating their efforts on the local, Artists Confronting AIDS directly challenged the residents of Los Angeles to participate in the shaping of a local AIDS ideology that would serve the interests of people with AIDS. Through the production of performance, Pickett and Kearns would provide for themselves and other people living with HIV and AIDS a means to gather into the space of performance to establish support systems, produce healing rituals of love, and resist the documentation of their lives as mere statistics lost in the sublimity of AIDS. "*AIDS/US* has given me life," explained Reverend Steve Pieters, a long-term survivor diagnosed with AIDS in 1982 and one of the company members of *AIDS/US II*; "and love and compassion," added his fellow cast member Tony Apodaca.[109]

Beginning in 1986, Artists Confronting AIDS provided people with AIDS and others affected by AIDS a process that enabled its participants to experience "life, love, and compassion." The production of performance made explicit the theatre's capacity to effect social change if only in the local and temporal space of *AIDS/US*. *AIDS/US* productions remind their participants and audiences that while representation engenders its own ideological effects, so too does the process of production. For people with AIDS and other members of the company, "life, love, and compassion" result from the immediate effects of the process of production. Representation, whether understood as a representation or mistaken for the authentic, materializes through bodies performing on the public stage. But by shifting the focus, for those involved, from performance and representation to the actual process of production, Artists Confronting AIDS intervened in the ways by which AIDS theatre and performance imagines intervention. In this sense, the *AIDS/US* series does its main work outside the representational field, exploiting and expanding the site of intervention to include the space of production, that unofficial process that allows for the rehearsal of AIDS on the terms set by its participants. And it was through these rehearsals of identities and communities in the midst of AIDS that yet another space for survival appeared.

By 1987, AIDS theatre ensembles, in the spirit of the Los Angeles–based Artists Confronting AIDS, had surfaced in New York City and San Francisco. Although these collectives, largely composed of people with HIV and AIDS, performed in major urban centers with already established theatre industries, their work was exclusively confined to noncommercial venues and small audiences. By 1987 as well, a handful of new plays and performances about AIDS had begun to circulate throughout the country. But these plays were atypical. Lesbian and gay companies, university theatres, and regional theatres produced plays such as *Warren* or *The Normal Heart*, but few commissioned new theatre work on AIDS. In the next chapter, I will look at how both gay theater and AIDS activism of the late 1980s moved away from the realist, testimonial, and/or memorializing modes that characterized early AIDS plays and early AIDS activism. More specifically, I will look at how camp, a defiant form of gay humor, resurfaced in gay culture within the context of the epidemic.

3

"It's My Party and I'll Die If I Want To!"

AIDS Performance and the Circulation of Camp in the Late 1980s and Early 1990s

OVER THE TELEPHONE, Bob, a playwright, tries cheering up Robin, his ex-lover who has AIDS. Robin, however, is interested in neither nostalgia nor comfort. "If you have to do something," he explains, "write me a funny AIDS play."[1] So ends *Pouf Positive* (1987), Robert Patrick's short and powerful one-act that concludes his epic oeuvre *Untold Decades*. Patrick, of course, grants his character's request by offering *Pouf Positive* as that same "funny AIDS play." Robin's acerbic and witty monologue, from which the entire play is composed, self-consciously articulates a set piece of theatre criticism, calling for a theatre that extends beyond the classical realist tragedies that characterize the majority of plays about AIDS produced by gay men. Through Robin's request, Patrick also reminds audiences that the seemingly incongruous, indeed audacious, pairing of AIDS and humor need not run counter to a politics of representation set forth by AIDS activists. In fact, 1987, the year Patrick wrote *Pouf Positive* was also the year that Larry Kramer—author of the celebrated AIDS play *The Normal Heart*—shifted gears and inaugurated the spectacularly effective, and often seriously funny, AIDS theatrics, the direct action AIDS activist organization ACT UP (AIDS Coalition to Unleash Power).[2]

If 1987 marks a turning point in AIDS activism, it also marks a participatory and simultaneous transition in the history of AIDS theatre. *Pouf Positive* stands as the first AIDS play based entirely on what we familiarly and awkwardly term *camp*, incorporating the survivalist strategies of an earlier, pre-Stonewall gay model of responding to oppression, violence, and discrimination with post-Stonewall outrage, irony, and wit.[3] Whereas earlier staged productions representing AIDS and people with AIDS worked from the universalist impulse invested in soliciting both sympathy and understanding,[4] Patrick's aim, not unlike ACT UP's own, was to focus on the anger against the limited discursive fields by which we live with and struggle against AIDS.

While ACT UP had expanded to include more than fifty chapters in the

United States between 1987 and 1991, American theatre had been far less successful during this period in interrogating AIDS as it was represented by such
dominant cultural institutions as the media, biomedical science, and the state.[5]
My purpose in this chapter is both to examine how gay playwrights and performers positioned themselves against such dominant representations and to
provide a critical practice of reading camp in light of the AIDS crisis. How
did theatrical (re)circulations of camp function as strategic interventions in
the battles surrounding the representations of gay male identity and AIDS in
the late 1980s and early 1990s? To address this question, I will focus on three
different productions of the period: Terrence McNally's *The Lisbon Traviata*,
Lypsinka's *I Could Go on Lip-Synching*, and the Sodomy Players' collaborative
performance of *AIDS! The Musical!* Although only one of the plays actually concerns itself with AIDS, all three position a gay response to the epidemic, trigger
various impulses in gay and mainstream spectators, and, when read collectively, suggest the role that camp has begun to play on American stages as well
as in a popular culture fissured by the issue of AIDS. As I will discuss, AIDS
emerges in *The Lisbon Traviata* and *I Could Go on Lip-Synching* as a structuring
absence. Although these works never specify AIDS as a theme, they may nonetheless be understood as (indirectly) addressing the epidemic. These theatrical
works resonate forcefully as responses to AIDS once they are placed within
their larger cultural contexts. The chapter concludes with a discussion of an
AIDS play that arrives on the scene, like the AIDS theatre collectives before it,
informed and deliberately motivated by the AIDS activist movement of the historical period in question.

Domestic Quarrels (or the Opera of Everyday Life): *The Lisbon Traviata*

"You can say all you want about Maria,
no one's ever accused her of causing AIDS."[6]

—*The Lisbon Traviata*

In the initial New York production (1985) of Terrence McNally's *The Lisbon Traviata*, the play concludes with the troubled diva-identified protagonist
Stephen stabbing his lover, Mike, who is breaking up with him. In the critical
moment of Stephen's performance, he provides his own soundtrack; first Maria
Callas's "Sempre Libre," from Verdi's *La Traviata*, and then her "Humming Chorus," from Puccini's *Madame Butterfly*. It is in one of these operatic moments—
reenacting the role of women in opera, in which, Catherine Clément argues,
"women sing their perpetual undoing,"[7]—that Stephen stages his own dénouement. McNally revised the ending for the second production (1989), in part he

admits because critics were disturbed by the bloodiness of the finale and in part because he simply "hadn't gotten it right."[8] In the second version, Stephen neither stabs Mike nor spins the Puccini aria. Instead, the lovers have "a terrible, tremendous moment between them. The only sound is Maria Callas singing *La Traviata*."[9] Yet, one year later, in what McNally views as the definitive version of the play, he restored the violent conclusion of the first production, albeit in a slightly modified form, focusing less on the Jacobean qualities of the finale and more on the nuances of Stephen and Mike's relationship and Stephen's friendship with his opera cohort, Mendy.

The instability of McNally's text, evident in its various editions, suggests the difficulties of staging gay relationships and friendships, but even more points to McNally's struggle with the available discursive means of staging gay relations, gay subjectivity, and death in the late 1980s. That is, *The Lisbon Traviata* enacts the same problematics of representation spurred by Patrick's *Pouf Positive* and ACT UP; the play attempts to reconstitute the means by which gay men, in particular, articulate both singular and collective identities at the same moment that dominant cultural institutions repudiate them.

Although *The Lisbon Traviata* hardly mentions AIDS, McNally does not avoid the subject entirely. Rather, AIDS informs the reality of its protagonists as a shadow that threatens to intercede at any moment; it is the woeful component underlying the play's tragic capabilities. Like Violetta's consumption in Verdi's *La Traviata*, AIDS in *The Lisbon Traviata* provides the means by which opera's grand dénouements can be realized. Both *Traviatas* are, after all, about love.

The tragedy embedded in *The Lisbon Traviata*, however, emerges from the comic first half of the play, which highlights the friendship between Stephen and Mendy, the uproarious camp who, while unloved, has found some sense of solace and companionship in the recordings of Maria Callas. In the argot of high camp, Stephen and Mendy spend the earlier part of the evening dishing various divas, recordings, concerts, and, occasionally, mutual acquaintances, passing the time listening to opera before Stephen's tenuous date with a younger waiter sometime later that evening:

> STEPHEN: Are you still looking for that *Medea*?
> MENDY: Here's Dallas, the first La Scalas with Lenny, Covent Garden, the night she met Onassis, *O notte tremenda, notte d'orrore*, but where's the last La Scalas?
> STEPHEN: Mendy, I don't want to hear *Medea*. Any of them. I hate *Medea*. I loathe *Medea*. I despise *Medea*.
> MENDY: Even with Maria?
> STEPHEN: Even with Ethel Merman. It's boring music.

MENDY: Maria was never boring.
STEPHEN: She was in *Medea*.
MENDY: You're going to hell for that.
STEPHEN: I already have. I'm just here on a pass. (18)

It is during these moments that the play's major themes unfold. While the two skirt around the issues that are really at stake in their lives, Stephen casually mentions how he has just acquired a rare and pirated recording of Callas's 1958 Lisbon performance of *La Traviata*, which the obsessive Mendy insists he must hear—immediately. And here is where the personal drama begins to disclose its presence—the coveted recording is at Stephen's apartment, where Stephen's soon-to-be ex-lover is entertaining a date, someone who cares very little for opera, although ironically he may have actually heard Callas's performance as a boy growing up in Lisbon.

The first act centers on this dual tension underlying the play's major theme of loneliness and the need for intimacy: Will Mendy ever hear the Callas recording? How will Stephen cope with his lover's new date? Mendy, who admits that he is "too much for some people," wants to be loved, but lacking that, finds comfort in the grand passions of opera and his unwavering fidelity to La Divina. Stephen is less resigned than Mendy; he sees his relationship with his lover, which began with an intensity worthy of opera, as a kind of real-life equivalent to the grandly expressed couplings in the operatic canon.

While the play's title would indicate that McNally's master plot is the Verdi opera, it becomes clear as the work develops that McNally positions his play in relation to all opera. And although it would seem that the elevated place that opera holds in the arts (for many, opera is the apex of refined cultural tastes) is what defines these urban gay men, it is essentially opera that undoes them. Opera, and the diva-identification of its enthusiasts, pushes the comic matrix of the first act toward the tragic conclusion of the final act. For this is precisely the ideology of all opera, as Clément eloquently argues in her important feminist critique of the art form:

> Beyond the romantic ideology, lines are being woven, tying up the characters and leading them to death for transgression—for transgressions of familial rules, political rules, the things at stake in sexual and authoritarian power. That is what it is all about.[10]

For Clément, the only lament available for women is death: "that is opera's innermost finality" (22). Clément's insights into the sex and gender systems encoded in opera point to what many feminist theorists, including Gayle Rubin, Luce Irigaray, and Eve Kosofsky Sedgwick, have called the "traffic in women" among men.[11] Patriarchal masterplots involve women as the symbol that is passed between men in the homosocial negotiations that provide the constraints by which patriarchies exert their hold over women. Yet women are not the only ones undone by opera; a quick perusal of opera plots and themes demonstrates how any difference from the reigning ideologies of patriarchy are aestheticized, contained, or indeed destroyed. Feminist analysis may clarify the equally problematic phenomenon, evident in *The Lisbon Traviata*, whereby gay men assume a tragic identification with and thereby appropriate the place of women in the patriarchal economy shared by opera and Western culture at large.

Gay men, as McNally's play reminds us, are situated in a peculiar relationship to dominant culture. As Eve Kosofsky Sedgwick points out, twentieth-century culture has structured homosexual identities through "two conceptual impasses or incoherencies, one concerning gender definition and the other concerning sexual definition."[12] This recurring conflation of gender and sexuality promotes such a confusion that gay men must continually negotiate their subjectivity in and against this process. *The Lisbon Traviata* dramatizes this challenge and demonstrates one of its results. Facing the no-win situation of identification within a binary sex/gender system of difference, McNally's characters find recourse in the abstracted although highly gendered subjectivity of the tragic heroine.[13] While Mendy and Stephen attempt to negotiate an identity that is based on, but not limited to sexuality—that is, a sexuality that is not itself essentialized—they aspire to an identity that finds cultural recognition in the highly aestheticized stylizations of difference in the world of opera. On one level, this process seems to connect with the dynamics of all bourgeois drama and to precipitate the result that Bertolt Brecht finds most loathsome of classic realist theatre—namely, cathartic release. Or, to put it in another way, in the world of opera Mendy and Stephen find a means to counter the forces of heteronormativity. Yet Stephen and Mendy seem unaware that these same operatic ideals are defined by the ideology of compulsory heterosexuality. Musicologist Mitchell Morris calls attention to this problem in his discussion of the politics of the opera queen:

> The greatest fault of the traditional opera queen's perspective is its tendency to deny even the possibility of social and political action, thus in effect acquiescing in the status quo. As long as the opera house provides a space—a closet, we might say—in which the spirit may soar free, everyday injustices seem to matter much less. This separation between opera house and "real world" effectively neutralizes most of the potential social impact of the oblique interpretations that "queer" the opera; the best remedy for this split is the reminder that all aesthetic choices inevitably imply ideological choices.[14]

Notice how Mendy comments on Stephen's process of identification as Stephen describes his first meeting with his lover:

> STEPHEN: The moment I saw him, even before he'd seen me, before we were introduced, I knew he was going to be the one. He was my destiny and I was his. I saw my future flash before me and it was all him. It was like the first act of *Carmen*. Don José sees her, she throws him the acacia flower, and his fate is sealed.
>
> MENDY: Carmen isn't gay.
>
> STEPHEN: She is when a certain mezzo's singing her.
>
> MENDY: What did Mike throw you?
>
> STEPHEN: Wouldn't you like to know?
>
> MENDY: I love your choice of role models. Carmen and Don José. They were a fun couple.
>
> STEPHEN: We're turning into . . . who? I can't think of anyone who ends happily in opera.
>
> MENDY: Hansel and Gretel. (20)

Mendy's continual undercutting of the master plot that Stephen uses to situate his own relationship indicates that he, at least, recognizes the pitfalls of compulsory heterosexual identification. However, Mendy himself finds no effective means to resist the pervasive ideological discourse of perversity that accompanies nonheterosexual identification. Given the context of AIDS that permeates this play, such perversity, moreover, is associated with death. Both Mendy and Stephen are unable to fashion selves that allow them a means to express, let alone pursue, their desires. If Stephen finds voice in the heroines of opera, Mendy's *modus operandi* is drawn from the divas who sing them. Mendy, as Wayne Koestenbaum points out in *The Queen's Throat*, is "drowned in diva idolatry."[15]

In sum, Stephen and Mendy find refuge in opera, either in the heroines of the plot or in the tragic lives of the women who sing them (fig. 16). But this place of refuge is itself oddly diseased, contaminated by the associative miasma of identification. Opera undoes the female characters caught in the negotiations between men, it undoes the women who sing them, and it undoes the gay men who identify with either. Identification can lead only to alienation, marginalization. There is no entrance into this system where the lament is not death.[16]

The language by which Mendy and Stephen give voice to their desire, moreover, is formulated around the camp argot of a historically specific subset of the urban gay male experience—a survivalist strategy deployed against a society that, as social historian Allan Bérubé explains, "questioned [gay men's] status as men, stereotyped them as effeminate, and harassed them for their sexual-

16. Nathan Lane as Mendy and Richard Thomas as Stephen in
the Mark Taper Forum production of Terrence McNally's *The
Lisbon Traviata*, Los Angeles, 1990.
Photo by Jay Thompson courtesy of the Mark Taper Forum

ity."[17] Mendy and Stephen spend hours volleying back and forth in their own
campy stichomythia, one punctuated with the learned details of opera, establishing a zone where they seemingly control the social and discursive spaces
that determine their relationship. The discourse of camp offers Mendy and
Stephen a means to displace their anxieties about intimacy, relationships, and
AIDS onto an exquisitely ornate discourse of opera expertise. The potential for
emotional support in their friendship gets rerouted into a competitive structure
of diva worship.

By the end of the drama, Stephen has murdered his lover and Mendy is
locked in his apartment. Mendy at least now owns the coveted *Lisbon Traviata*
recording. But what is Mendy's future? "All great beauties are finally alone.
Look at Maria. That apartment in Paris became her tomb" (21), Stephen explains

to Mendy early on, telling us more about Mendy's own future than of Maria's. His isolation seems symptomatic of his addictive relation to opera. Thus, as Koestenbaum explains, "[i]n his most extreme incarnation, as Mendy in *The Lisbon Traviata*, the opera queen is unfit for love, and the taste for opera is seen not only as compensation for lost love objects, but as the very catalyst of loss" (30). In *The Lisbon Traviata*, McNally presents characters who are caught in the gridlock of master plots and their resulting archetypal pathologies. McNally fails to let his two main characters, gay men in the midst of an epidemic, recognize that (their) everyday lives are at once more negotiable—and less tragic—than opera. The fact that in this finale, Stephen's lover—a doctor and the only character in the play who voices AIDS awareness—lies dying suggests that gay male identities are further threatened within the world of the play. In *The Lisbon Traviata*, McNally posits contemporary gay identity as a tragic spectacle of love and loss.

Read My Lips: Lypsinka and the Politics of Nostalgia
"What I call nostalgia, a lot of people call 'post-modernism'."[18]
—John Epperson

John Epperson's claim (in the epigraph above) to the terrain of current theoretical interrogations of popular culture immediately positions his camp-infested, one-person tour de force *I Could Go On Lip-Synching* as a resounding site of origination (fig. 17). Epperson's drag persona, Lypsinka, is strategically situated at the matrix of camp and nostalgia on the one hand, and the postmodern politics of discursive narrative productions of the self on the other. His show is a self-described "parody of a cheesy Las Vegas lounge act."[19] Epperson continues:

> When people find out that I'm a "female impersonator"—a term I don't particularly like—they ask who do I do, and I tell them I don't do anyone. I made up my own character. I made an elaborate soundtrack of all these different voices and Lypsinka is all those people rolled into one. She's also a living cartoon, very animated, very high energy. It's a very stylized form of theatre and because it's so artificial and ritualistic, it approaches performance art. But I just see it as plain entertainment with a unique twist. Everything is lip-synched, even the dialogue. I don't utter a word.[20]

Epperson, whose career as Lypsinka began in the downtown clubs of Manhattan, has since met with wide critical acclaim. *I Could Go on Lip-Synching* was reviewed favorably in the mainstream press and Epperson's performances as Lypsinka continue to prove financially successful. Madonna has served as a financial backer.

17. Theatre program for Lypsinka's *I Could Go on Lip-Synching*,
Los Angeles, 1991.
Courtesy of the Callboard Theater

The curious phenomenon surrounding Lypsinka's achievement, however, has less to do with Epperson's obvious talent and more with the commodification of camp that his work implies, its recirculation in both gay and mainstream venues, and Epperson's insistence on its apolitical appeal. Just as in *The Lisbon Traviata*, in *I Could Go on Lip-Synching* camp is staged in all its excess. Furthermore, Lypsinka's *I Could Go on Lip-Synching* reminds its spectators, and in particular, its gay audiences, of camp's availability in fashioning an identity in relation to, and perhaps even in spite of, societal mechanisms that normalize compulsory heterosexuality.

Despite this deconstructive edge, the ruling impulse behind *I Could Go on Lip-Synching* is anchored in a politics of nostalgia. On the one hand, Epperson demands from his audience a type of cultural literacy that is similar to that which McNally presumes in *The Lisbon Traviata*. Both Epperson and McNally present diva identification as a familiar, if not the defining, trope for gay men of a certain class and education. Thus, recognizing opera heroines, sopranos, lounge acts, and Hollywood icons is the litmus test for the ideal spectator. Many gay men do share the vocabulary of Mendy, Stephen, and Lypsinka;[21] but many others do not, and that suggests the class and racial barriers these productions generate. On the other hand, the very nature of Epperson's production—Lypsinka never speaks—necessitates that the spectator identify with these voices from the past. If the combination of camp discourse and opera trivia enabled the audience of *The Lisbon Traviata* to speculate on the efficacy of camp's discourse in relation to AIDS, the glamour-based iconography of *I Could Go on Lip-Synching* is staged as the only operable mode available for gay men to begin imagining a voice with which to sing. In other words, since Lypsinka never speaks, the audience is given no other position than identifying with and then contextualizing the prerecorded voices that give shape to the performance. Revival, Lypsinka seems to be saying, equals survival. It is precisely this enforced nostalgia that permeates the entire production.

Specifically, the show itself serves as a brief but concentrated lesson in the endless litany of tragic torch singers, spunky Hollywood actresses, glitzy showbiz girls, and syndicated TV heroines of the Eisenhower era who have served, for many years, as fetishized icons for some gay men. Epperson indulgently marches in an outrageous diva-ridden parade consisting of nearly thirty female voices from the archives of American popular culture. These range from major singers to minor talents, from the immediately recognizable to the now obscure: Judy Garland to Dolores Gray, Pearl Bailey to Cyd Charisse. The inclusion of women who never quite achieved mass recognition is preserved through Lypsinka's citational performance. In this sense, Epperson may be seen as a kind of camp archivist. Yet the voice of the minor performer reverberates with the pathos of her failure to become a major star. By not specifying these women by name, Epperson's archival project retrieves not the performer herself but the historical mode and period of her performance. Even Epperson's most explicit citation remains oblique. *I Could Go on Lip-Synching* references the 1962 film, *I Could Go on Singing*, Judy Garland's last completed movie and an over-the-top production of song and pathos in its own right.[22]

In *I Could Go on Lip-Synching*, Epperson offers a blitzkrieg of hyped femininity so that the spectator can participate in the icon-shaping that the show encourages; that is, as Lypsinka, Epperson writes himself into the very same diva fascination in which he/she holds his audience unconsciously complicit. The structure of the narrative invites the audience to witness the star-making machinery at work, tracing the trials and tribulations of Lypsinka as she embarks on her road to stardom. Epperson's artistry is a craft of self-consciousness; this mimicry of divas is interrupted only by the implicit desire that Lypsinka be recognized as a famous, legendary "voice" despite the audience's obvious awareness of Epperson's lip-synching. Indeed, as Lypsinka, Epperson exaggerates his lips with wicked, bewildered expressions mocking the formal constraints of lip-synching and further calling attention to the conventional rules of the genre.[23] Still, by the end of the performance, after having simulated various icons from the past, Lypsinka joins the ever growing conga line of pop celebrity. The show concludes with Lypsinka's own arrival at the mythic landscape of stardom, or as the evening's program claims: "the well-worn comeback trail takes her from the burlesque to Vegas to Paris to, at last, a glorious career in Hollywood as the Lypsinka we know and love today."[24] With this ending, it becomes clear that Lypsinka needs the lost voices of these minor celebrities to remain unrecognizable so that she, Lypsinka, can emerge as diva. If the voices were exclusively those of recognizable stars, Epperson would be merely citing their specific performance styles. For Epperson it is not enough to serve as a persuasive stand-in, a believable Judy, a powerful Merman. He needs to become his own persona through the seemingly endless citation of both major and minor voices. Epperson is at once the nostalgic archivist of female celebrity and, as Lypsinka, a version of the diva herself.

Although much could be said about the obvious gender blurring typical of female impersonation and its own complicated relation to camp, I would like to focus on the relationship between camp and nostalgia, especially since Epperson himself sees them as central components of his show. *I Could Go on Lip-Synching* embarks on a retreat into history, one that may be best described as a hermetically sealed moment that precedes AIDS, and one that is additionally reinforced by the formal design of Lypsinka's performance. Nostalgia is first solicited from the coded icons Lypsinka mimics and further triggered by the awareness of the historical marking of camp and drag in gay and lesbian history. For many gays, especially those who are older, Epperson brings up a familiar and important style, which may have lost its initial potency and immediate urgency. While the gay bar along with drag entertainment have long been essential for gays (and lesbians) as a refuge from the culture of the closet, obviously since Stonewall gay men have had many more options for meeting and communicating. Furthermore, the social spaces where drag and camp were first assigned have expanded so that camp culture has now permeated the mainstream. Thus, Lypsinka (re)occupies that place in gay culture and (re)provides that once flourishing space for gay men. This is not to say, of course, that camp and drag have lost their initial appeal. Instead I am suggesting that Lypsinka's camp and drag is more readily familiar as the camp and drag of a lost era. The more recent radical drag of both gays and lesbians is a deliberate departure from earlier "apolitical" entertainments of piano bars and burlesque reviews. This newer drag, a topic outside of my scope, is much more about the visibility politics of current gay movements, although it needs to be noted that a radical drag and camp agenda has been operative since long before the birth of any Queer Nation.[25]

I Could Go on Lip-Synching serves as a fantasy for a certain gay spectatorship yearning for the "simplicity" of life before AIDS. Lypsinka's choice of emulated icons supports this longing—although, in the process, Lypsinka alienates generations, classes, and ethnicities of gay men and lesbians who may not recognize Tallulah Bankhead, let alone Dolores Gray. In many ways, Lypsinka's coded and specialized iconography and vocabulary validates the subject position of mainly older, white gay male spectators. Lypsinka's own discursive narrative production of the self, based on camp and drag, furthermore recalls an earlier generation's strategy of self-defense:

> [Camp] could simultaneously distance [gay men] from the humiliation they endured as social outcasts while creating an alternative moral order and culture in which gay men were in control. . . . These styles reflected the self-consciousness of some gay men as sexual or gender outsiders and helped them define themselves as "insiders" of their own secret world.[26]

Whereas the nostalgic recollection of these strategies of self-defense and survival may function nostalgically for some spectators, even for a younger or unfamiliar gay spectator astute enough to recognize the historical significance of camp and drag, these memories also point to the problematics of camp's commodification in contemporary culture for gays and lesbians. The social significance of camp and drag, available to gay men and lesbians, may not be apparent to a mainstream audience.[27] Mainstream spectators, some with no sense of gay and lesbian history, may leave with impressions that see gay men *as* entertainments. The success of drag on Broadway in the 1980s, in such commercial hits as *Torch Song Trilogy, La Cage aux Folles*, and even *M. Butterfly*, demonstrated the demand by mainstream audiences for this type of gay performance to such an extent, as Mark Gevisser argues, that "gay culture is presented to mainstream heterosexual America as a drag show."[28] The survivalist quality that so marks camp and drag for the gay spectator is reconfigured and depoliticized in the commodification process.

Epperson seems well aware of this market, exploiting the popularity of camp and drag for all his spectators. Lypsinka's performance marks a self-conscious retreat, for performer and gay spectator alike, into a pre-AIDS moment, recalling an era when camp and drag were, arguably, sources of empowerment, survival, as well as entertainment. On the one hand, it's admirable how Lypsinka proposes that these same modes of self-representation—camp and drag—which have always been available to gay men, may in fact now be useful for gay people surrounded by AIDS. The politics of nostalgia, therefore, may enable a familiar, and ostensibly successful, battle for gay men fighting AIDS. Yet, on the other hand, there's something emphatically apolitical about Lypsinka. Epperson himself claims that "some people opt to be [political]. I don't. I set out to entertain."[29] From this perspective, the politics of nostalgia only lengthens the distance between past and present, locating nostalgia in the liminal plane of the neither here nor there. The spectator is brought to that location and asked to participate vicariously in Lypsinka's narrative production of the self, one based entirely on camp and nostalgia. Yet vicarious participation suggests a type of implication. Lypsinka suggests that we, too, seek that same self-conscious retreat into a glorified past, one fueled more by fantasy than by any claim of truth. Ask any of these same older gay spectators about these romanticized days of gay life before AIDS, for instance, and they'll tell you that these were not all days at the beach or, even, nights at the movies.

I Could Go on Lip-Synching is located in this hermetically sealed zone of a glorious, apolitical nostalgia. Epperson acknowledges as much when he asserts, "The closest I get to a political comment in my show is with Shirley Bassey singing 'This Is My Life' and then cutting to Norma Zinger singing 'This Is My Country' and then abruptly cutting into Tallulah Bankhead asking, 'What have you been doing? What *have* you been doing?' "[30] This final number is punctuated throughout by Lypsinka's silly gestures—she clutches, like a purse, a box of *Life* cereal and guarantees that laughs, not necessarily ideas, are left with the spectators. Still, the assertion of Lypsinka's life in these final moments secures our response to the begging question, what have *we* been doing? In fact, Lypsinka answers the question for us. We, of course, have been watching her. And by the finale—Lypsinka's arrival and success in Hollywood—the answer becomes clear, especially as we watch her *in* Hollywood, that lip-synching is the promoted voice, indeed the only available voice (if we can even call it one), for gay men's success at the moment. The stunning and eerie epiphany of this ending resonates as the curtain drops and the house lights brighten; the audience once more returns to the streets of reality where silence, as we are all too often aware, does equal death.

To his gay audience, Epperson presents lip-synching as the only available discourse and divas as our only models. To survive in the grueling presence of AIDS, gay men have few choices here: nostalgic retreats into a formulated and artificial collective memory; croonings with the coded beltings of a tortured but fabulous past; or most uncannily, lip-synching Lypsinka's own lip-synching. By the end of the performance, Epperson has brilliantly staged his own celebrity and gay men have one new diva to emulate, mimic, and adore— Lypsinka herself. Such a proposition, to lip-synch Lypsinka, while clever seems odd—although perhaps that is just the point. In *I Could Go on Lip-Synching* camp circulates as a perpetually available site of origination; a location to which gay men can retreat temporarily and reclaim that mythic truth of identity and agency that may never have really been there in the first place.

While Epperson positions camp as the mechanism which instigates a certain apolitical nostalgia, AIDS activists at this point intervene with a radical cultural critique of nostalgia and its assumed frivolity with their "Read My Lips" graphic, which fuses camp and nostalgia in order to serve their own purpose. Along with various other agents in the late 1980s, ACT UP participates in the lip-synching phenomenon characteristic of the period. From Lypsinka to presidential campaigns, network-television game shows to same-sex kiss-ins, at the close of the 1980s, U.S. popular culture was immersed in an unprecedented fetish for lips. In part, this preoccupation with lips derived from the insidious AIDS hysteria of contagion and the popular misconception of HIV transmission through kissing. Though AIDS was just one player in a crisis of authority affecting the nation, its role, nonetheless, cannot be overestimated. In the spring of 1988, for example, ACT UP New York staged the spectacular Nine Days of Protest throughout various locations in New York City, Newark, and Albany as part of the national action called forth by the recently established national AIDS network, ACT NOW (the AIDS Coalition to Network, Organize, and Win). The action was part of a nation-wide demonstration calling attention to the various local and national issues that contribute to AIDS and AIDS-phobia. Same-sex kiss-ins emerged as one of the most successful tactics highlighting homophobic responses to AIDS.

On April 29, 1988, ACT UP New York staged a kiss-in with a fact sheet, "Why We Kiss," to educate the public on homophobia and AIDS. Among its five reasons was the declaration that "we kiss as an affirmation of our feelings, our desires, ourselves." Gran Fury, "a band of individuals united in anger and dedicated to exploiting the power of art to end the AIDS crisis,"[31] produced posters of same-sex couples kissing declaring Read My Lips, which then be-

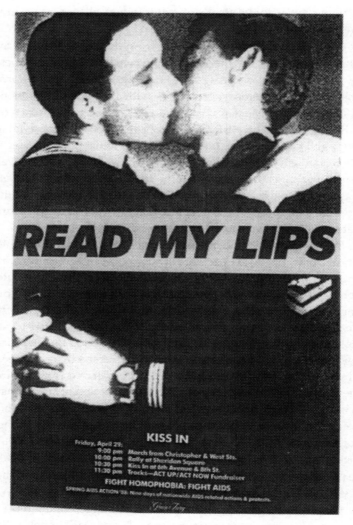

18. "Read My Lips" (boys), designed by Gran Fury, 1988. ACT
UP poster for the April 29, 1988, Kiss In.
Gran Fury

came available nationally as T-shirts sold to help finance ACT UP.[32] The graphic
used for the men's poster and T-shirt was a World War II photograph of two
kissing sailors in full uniform (fig. 18). The text Read My Lips was strategically
centered to capture attention and anchor the visual message. As Richard Meyer
writes of this graphic, "the recovery of homoerotic imagery from the first half

of the twentieth century ties the contemporary act of same-sex kissing to a larger legacy of queer culture and self-representation."[33] Later in 1988, in a presidential election, George Bush would boast his campaign slogan, "Read My Lips: No New Taxes," joining Lypsinka, Gran Fury, and the countless ACT UP members and supporters in the unending crisis of authority, discourse, and representation that the whole phenomenon of lip-synching indicates. To emphasize this specific cultural anomaly and its location in the public imagination, one need only recall that around this same time a popular network-television game show, *Putting on the Hits!*, actually awarded prizes to contestants who best lip-synched familiar chartbusters on the airwaves.

The Read My Lips men's graphic powerfully and cleverly recontexualizes the image of the two kissing sailors for an AIDS activist agenda. Just as Epperson reaches back into the archives of popular culture and pulls out Lypsinka, Gran Fury resurfaces with, as Andrew Ross has put it in his discussion of camp, "the rediscovery of history's waste."[34] And just as Lypsinka speaks through the voices from the past, the image of the two kissing World War II sailors gives voice to the activism of their 1980s cohorts. Yet differences abide. In Lypsinka, a peculiar variation on the activist slogan Silence = Death seems to have taken effect. I have argued that in *I Could Go on Lip-Synching* Epperson employs the politics of nostalgia and finds himself perpetuating a discursive paralysis that finds no exit, except as fantasy or diversion, for performer or spectator, in the inescapable context of AIDS. That camp and nostalgia can combine with an AIDS activist politics, however, is evident in the Read My Lips graphic.

T-Shirts and posters, of course, like Lypsinka, don't really speak. But as images that circulate like money in and out of diverse fields, they carry messages that can be relayed and easily consumed. The message of the Read My Lips graphic is so simple that it literally instructs us how to respond. If, for gay men, reading Lypsinka's lips results in an inevitable "who's that girl?" bewilderment and positions the chapped lips of near forgotten divas as our only voice, the Gran Fury graphic solidly and audaciously reminds us that those (re)circulating sailor lips are ours to claim as well. Just as gay men leave Lypsinka's show encouraged to proliferate Lypsinka's own production, a sort of "We Could All Go on Lip-Synching," gay men sporting the Read My Lips graphic proliferate the same-sex kiss, giving voice to our collective desires.

Many would argue that Lypsinka's show is more firmly in the tradition of gay performance as entertainment. And, indeed, there is much to be said for the utility of entertaining the troops in the age of AIDS.[35] Gay men, as Bérubé has documented, have a long tradition of staging camp as a means to entertain those on the front lines of war. Furthermore, to be constantly reminded of AIDS and its horrors could have an equally demoralizing effect for those who are in the midst of mourning. In fact, there are some gay playwrights who feel obliged to avoid the subject of AIDS entirely, seeing their responsibility during the epidemic as one of offering seemingly apolitical productions that provide a refuge from the reality of AIDS. "Who needs to see someone die of AIDS on stage? Who needs to have their heart broken again?" wonders playwright and producer John Glines.[36] The 1991 Off-Broadway revival of Robert Patrick's 1964 play *The Haunted Host*—one of the earliest openly gay plays—suggests the proliferation of the trend of both camp and nostalgia. And yet for many others convinced that representations and their larger ideological effects are the central agenda for gay and lesbian politics, the retreat into, or perhaps from, history has serious problematic ramifications. In the late 1980s and early 1990s, activist groups ranging from ACT UP and Queer Nation to GLAAD (Gay and Lesbian Alliance against Defamation) went to great lengths to raise these issues of representation, holding both gays and straights accountable for the perpetuation, deliberate or inadvertent, of negative stereotypes and limited representations of lesbian and gay experiences. Productions as diverse as *The Lisbon Traviata* and *I Could Go on Lip-Synching* only fueled the battle over representation precisely because of their availability to gay and straight audiences alike. Whether or not either play engages in AIDS issues directly, because they circulated within mainstream venues across the country, the characters they represented inevitably participated in the ideological constructions of gay men and AIDS. Regardless of any prefatory disclaimer or insistence on the performances' apolitical tactics, these productions derive from a larger, more complex cultural position that cannot be separated from the politics shaping our responses to AIDS.

(In)House Music: Act(ing) Up in *AIDS! The Musical!*

"You've had the disease, you've been to the demonstration,
now see the musical!"[37]

—promotional slogan for *AIDS! The Musical!*

The peculiar logic of the announcement for the Sodomy Players' 1991 production of *AIDS! The Musical!* rested on the presumption that attending their pushy pairing of AIDS and entertainment *was* the next step for AIDS activists. Such a strategy proved successful for the world premiere of the production at Highways Performance Space in Santa Monica, California, on August 2, 1991 (fig. 19). That the opening night performance was a benefit fundraiser for ACT UP/Los Angeles helped validate the producer's claim that seeing the musical was complicit with AIDS activist politics, thus guaranteeing its eventual sold-out status.[38] But *AIDS! The Musical!* went much further than simply subtle, crafty marketing strategies, for it located, in the vexed and troubled arena of

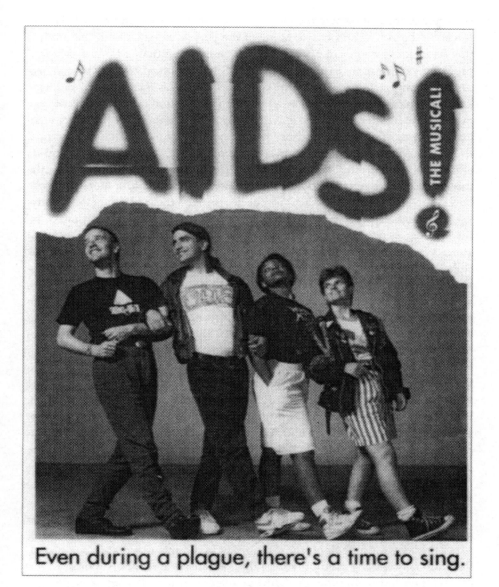

19. *AIDS! The Musical!* promotional postcard for the August 1991 production at Highways Performance Space, Santa Monica.
Photo by Suzanne Tallon courtesy of Highways Performance Space

representation, a site where the issues facing lesbians, gays, and/or AIDS activists could be voiced and heard. Many of the people affiliated with the production were active members of ACT UP/LA, suggesting that *AIDS! The Musical!*
provided yet one more instance of the AIDS activist credo "By any means necessary." Camp, too, prevailed. Unlike *I Could Go on Lip-Synching* or *The Lisbon
Traviata*, where camp emerged as a possible intervention into the crisis of (gay
male) representation in the age of AIDS only to be subsumed by the larger ideological effects of either compulsory heterosexuality or the politics of nostalgia,
AIDS! The Musical! managed to maintain both camp's outrageousness and its
efficacy as a survivalist discourse. *AIDS! The Musical!* demonstrated how the
theatre could accommodate both entertainment and activism, or more precisely,
how camp could serve AIDS activist politics through the medium of the theatre.

The musical, written by Wendell Jones and David Stanley, with music by
Robert Berg, is described in its press release as "an all singing, all dancing, all
queer voyage into a world of AIDS activism, new age gatherings, sleazy sex
clubs, radical fairies, lesbian love, and fags bashing back!"[39] It charts the emotional, spiritual, and political development of Thomas, a person with AIDS who,
at the musical's opening, loses his lover, Bob, to AIDS. But before he dies, Bob
opens the production exclaiming in his last words: "I always wanted death to
be like a big musical with angels and songs."[40] Moments later, to defuse the emotional charge of Bob's death, the actor playing him shouts to the audience in
Brechtian fashion, "Ladies and gentlemen, sisters and brothers, girlfriends all,
the Sodomy Players are proud to present *AIDS! The Musical!*" reminding us that
what we are about to witness is only a production, a representation, of AIDS.
With the by-now-standard AIDS death out of the way in the very first number,
a complete reversal of the operatic movement toward death evident in *The Lisbon Traviata*, the focus shifts to highlight the person living with AIDS and his
picaresque wanderings through contemporary gay culture. The focus on living
with AIDS is deliberate; according to the playwrights, "We didn't want to contribute another tired, tired, tired boring tragic AIDS play."[41] Jones and Stanley
insist on reimagining AIDS performance within the context of the AIDS activism of their historical time. At various points, performers break out in song
either to give voice to their personal desires or to comment on the actions staged,
therefore successfully manipulating any predictable audience response to the
production's music. In order to challenge the prevailing ideology of AIDS perpetuated by dominant culture, *AIDS! The Musical!* employs activist tactics in
both the thematic and narrative aspects of the play, in its Brecht-based theatrics
and, most effectively, through its employment of camp.

The major plot motivation centers on Thomas's madcap, Alice-in-Wonder-
land-like romp through the diverse currents that together may constitute "gay

culture." While he endures the six-month lag for regular health care through the county medical system, Thomas discovers and explores political activism, spirituality, violence, and healing in a gay and lesbian community torn apart by a decade of deaths and governmental indifference. On his journey, Thomas finds himself singing, dancing, and pulled in different directions by apolitical AIDS buddies, dogmatic political activists, skirted spiritual gay men, closeted talk-show hosts, burnt-out ERA leaders, and an east Texas transsexual named Lurleen Devoreaux. The music covers a full span of popular styles ranging from country western and Morrissey-like ballads to new age chants and rap. Supporting actors perform various characters who exemplify distinct facets of gay identity and together give life to the concept of a queer community. In order to implant the concept that identity is both dynamic and performative, characters themselves, like the actors who play them, highlight different aspects of their identities at different moments, making it difficult to locate a fixed and assigned role. Thus, for example, the hunk whom Thomas meets at the Flesh Pit underground sex club directs him to the radical fairy gathering at the beach on the following day. Thomas travels to and from these divergent fields of gay culture to emerge by the end of the musical with an identity that builds from the best of all these queer locations. While the principal voyage is undoubtedly Thomas's, the writers show other characters in the same process of political and spiritual awakening. Lisa, a white lesbian and former ERA spokesperson, embarks on a journey of her own after meeting Vanessa, an African American lesbian AIDS activist who rekindles Lisa's political activism. As the production unfolds, activists end up becoming more spiritual while spiritualists, in turn, become more political. Various identity markers are announced, appropriated, and fashioned in an ongoing give-and-take by the characters. This is unlike the circles of lip-synching endlessly entrapped in Lypsinka's performance. The fluidity of identity construction in *AIDS! The Musical!* enacts a postmodern recreative politics, rather than an imitative politics of nostalgia.

To their credit, Jones and Stanley insist on the complexity and paradoxes of gay life in the early 1990s, avoiding any overly romanticized notions of contemporary gay culture. Instead, the episodes are staged as fully dramatic contradictions. For example, at the first ACT UP/LA meeting Thomas attends (rendered entirely in rap), members argue vehemently and with malice, to the extent that one actor comments, "AIDS, the spectacle, it's not so wonderful." Yet after such heated exchanges as "You don't trust me / You disgust me," or the defensive posturing of "ACT UP members aren't hostile to newcomers, just to each other," the feuding activists pull through to demonstrate against inadequate health-care funding. The cacophonous members of the ACT UP/LA meeting that closes the first act—including the voices of women and people of color—

find a collective voice in the "Paint the City" scene that begins act 2. In one of the musical's most powerful scenes sung by the company, Thomas participates in his first ACT UP action—a covert operation to commit vandalism by painting bloody hand prints on city property—and sings of the importance of their action with fellow activists:

> Paint the city, gonna paint the city, paint the city
> till it's dripping red.
> Paint for all the walking wounded, paint for my friends
> who're dead.
> Paint, paint, paint, paint the city
> Paint, paint, paint, paint the city red.
>
> Paint for Larry, gonna paint for George,
> Paint for Henry, gonna paint for you.
> Cover this city in pain and anger
> Paint the truth to get our message through!
> Paint, paint, paint, paint the city
> Paint, paint, paint, paint the city red.

While the characters sing, they also hang signs that carry such slogans as "Full Funding for AIDS Programs," "Stop Right Wing Fascists," and "Women's Right to Choose." Placards with the sketched faces of Jesse Helms, Lou Sheldon, William Dannemeyer, and George Bush, inscribed with such accusations as "killer," "shame," and "bloody," are painted and posted throughout the performance space during this scene. The effectiveness of this metatheatrical scene lies primarily in the reenactment of the ACT UP theatrics combined with the Brechtian explanatory, simple song.

Throughout *AIDS! The Musical!* voices sing from specific subject positions as well as from communal choruses that, rather than obliterating differences, call attention to the common goals among diverse members. The songs also vary in tone. In the evening's most impressive solo moment, Carlos, a PWA, responds in song to his buddy's obsessive care-taking habits of providing him everything but what he actually wants:

> Momma, I need a gun for my birthday
> Momma, I'm sure a gun could blow this tension away.
> This world is filled with sorrow and pain,
> I find it harder each day to maintain.
> The strength I need to help me stay sane . . .
> I'll pick the folks who have to scream "OWW!"
> When I shoot them with my gun POW!
> Momma I need a gun for my birthday.

The deadpan humor of the PWA singing "Momma I Need a Gun" is as poignant as it is outrageous and angry. The actor who sings the song also happens to be the company's most gifted singer, yet the director deflates the serious emotional intensity of the song's formal composition by having the actor employ campy gestures of trigger-happy fantasies of usurpation and annihilation. Anyone who hates queers or is made nervous by people with AIDS is shot. The conventional solo, standard in musicals as a means to convey the emotional depth of character and as the device to bring the spectator into the character's psyche, is so manipulated in the production of *AIDS! The Musical!* that spectators have no firm grounding from which to safely enter the emotional identification process typical of classic realist theatre. Instead, spectators are left with the contradictions of the performance, constantly challenged to speculate on the *issues* raised rather than the *emotions* generated from the plot.

The Brechtian legacy invoked by the production's manipulation of conventional theatre practices and devices places *AIDS! The Musical!* in the tradition of a political interventionist theatre that demands that its spectators question the normalizing effects of dominant ideological institutions. Brecht's famous "alienation effect" serves to distance the spectator from the mystification process by which dominant ideology maintains its grip on oppressive social conditions. While Brecht's concept of "epic theatre" directly challenges the class conditions perpetuated and secured by dominant culture, his ideas have long served various oppressed groups throughout the world. Cultural materialist feminists have demonstrated the efficacy of Brecht's strategies for a theatre committed to the representational restructurings of gender relations and gendered identities. Jill Dolan explains the potential of Brecht's ideas for such a project:

> Estranging the spectator from the conditions of life outlined by the representation denaturalizes the dominant ideology that benefits from such "natural" social relations. Ideology circulates through a text as a meaning effect which can be deciphered by a spectator freed from the dreamlike state of passive receptivity. If the representational apparatus is ideologically marked, its material aspects must be brought into full view and denaturalized for the spectator's inspection. The mystification of social arrangements is exposed and the spectator is presented with the possibility of change.[42]

Although Dolan here is appropriating Brecht's ideas for her own feminist-based interrogation of the cultural conditions and representations of women in dominant culture, her use of Brecht provides AIDS activists with a materialist model to consider for their own work. Thus, building on this legacy of political theatre, a materialist AIDS activist criticism would consider the material conditions and social relations that construct the discourses by which dominant culture speaks about AIDS. The goal of a materialist AIDS activist criticism is to destabilize the assumptions that underlie the dominant mythologies of AIDS and intervene in the social and institutional arrangements that contribute to the AIDS crisis.

Within this critical framework, the political critique of *AIDS! The Musical!* becomes more apparent and the potential political intervention more immediate. *AIDS! The Musical!* recuperates the politics of Brecht's epic theatre and appropriates his concepts for an AIDS activist agenda. The intentional manipulation of the formal, compositional motifs of musical comedy, the shifting yet dynamic interplay of actor and role, and the informative educational basis of the production are mixed with the deliberate invocation of campy, outrageous humor. All combine to articulate an activist position in the representational crisis around AIDS. For the spectator, *AIDS! The Musical!* offers a location from which the various issues surrounding AIDS can be discussed, debated, and argued. Before the start of the second act, for example, a woman takes the stage to announce the continuation of the play, but before doing so she anticipates some of the questions spectators may have of the specific constituency the musical seems to ignore:

> You know, a lot of people have been asking us, "Why don't you have any straight people in your show?" The answer is really very simple, "Because we don't have to." The media in this country has ignored homosexuals for years. This show is about that community. . . . Thank you, and now, Act II of *AIDS! The Musical!*

Such casual disregard for women, people of color, and other marginalized groups affected by AIDS can certainly be seen as an unnecessary insult. My sense here, however, is that the playwrights are focusing instead on how one community—the diverse queer community of Los Angeles—copes with the epidemic. And unlike the majority of AIDS representations in the popular media circulating in the early 1990s—from Kimberly Bergalis to the melodramatic mothers in the television special "Our Sons"—which focus on "innocent" heterosexual "victims" or the responses of heterosexual siblings, *AIDS! The Musical!* refuses to accommodate the comforts of a nongay spectatorship by softening its queer elements. Such a direct confrontation succeeds in raising the issues that inform our understanding of AIDS. Straights and gays leave the theatre forced to consider both the dominant representations of AIDS in the media as well as the implications of excluding other communities affected by AIDS in any representation that invokes AIDS.

The most effective tactic to disturb our understanding of AIDS is directly

addressed to the gay community whom the creators of the musical want to depict and address. Indeed, the musical deliberately plays on this potential exclusion of in-house "others." First, while the major plot concerns Thomas, a white
gay man with AIDS finding his own voice and sense of identity in the midst of
the epidemic, the writers are astute enough to include other gay men who also
have AIDS, including men of color. Yet the real *coup de théâtre* (and the major
political trump card) in *AIDS! The Musical!* arrives at its conclusion when we
learn that Lisa, the white lesbian activist and friend to Thomas, also has AIDS.
Moreover, her illness has been overlooked by all of her friends, associates, and
suggestively, her audience. The revelation that Lisa has AIDS offers its gay audience the sting of complicity in its own perceptions of AIDS. Throughout the
1980s and early 1990s, women with HIV were consistently neglected in the
dominant discourses of both AIDS and AIDS activism. As Cindy Patton argues,
"the erasure of women's needs is systemic, grounded in a complex array of media representations of the HIV pandemic, cultural beliefs, and research and policy paradigms which are deeply gender biased and not easily changed."[43] Recall
that in 1991, at the time of *AIDS! The Musical!* the opportunistic infections
specific to women with HIV were not officially recognized by the CDC.[44] Jones
and Stanley effectively introduce Lisa's diagnosis in order to challenge the effects of their own production. Lisa's AIDS diagnosis unsettles the musical's narrative trajectory, which has centered on Thomas. In a brilliant moment of dis-
turbance, the conclusion implicates the performance and its audience for
focusing on Thomas at Lisa's expense.

Despite the effectiveness of *AIDS! The Musical!* for its specific lesbian, gay,
and/or AIDS activist constituency, and even in its capacity as an educational,
albeit voyeuristic, device for a mainstream audience, the production raises some
of the same problems of representation as *The Lisbon Traviata* and *I Could Go on
Lip-Synching*. Mainly, the concern falls on the efficacy of camp and its translat-
ability for mainstream spectators. In the case of *AIDS! The Musical!* camp
functions for its specific, self-proclaimed audience of gays and lesbians as an
invigorating, informative, and in-house representation. Camp, in this sense, is
utilized as yet one more Brechtian alienation-effect by which the performance
maintains its politicized edge. Yet, for mainstream viewers unfamiliar with the
coded survivalist strategies of a lesbian and gay community, or even unaccus-
tomed to a radical theatre, camp upsets the emotional leverage most associated
with AIDS representations in the popular culture. From this perspective, camp
solicits a very different distancing effect that may result in a form of dismissal.[45]

Furthermore, in the commodification process of theatre in a mainstream
economy of late capitalism, the radical, upfront politics of camp which resonate
in *AIDS! The Musical!* risk becoming neutralized. For example, in the review

published in the *Los Angeles Times*, critic Robert Koehler begins by awarding the production the "Bad Taste Title of 1991."[46] While it could be argued that Koehler is engaging in his own campy repartee, this seems unlikely given the cryptic review which follows. On the one hand, he applauds the *esprit de corps* of the company—"You also have to chuckle over an evening that exudes the spirit of a Mickey Rooney–Judy Garland musical where the rallying cry is 'Hey kids! Let's put on a show!' " He also imagines the audience might undergo "terrific therapy" especially for those of us with the disease, or those of us who know someone with the disease. Yet, on the other hand, he faults the show for not living up to the aesthetic standard which he classifies under the rubric of "a real musical." In this regard, the major complaints are set against the casting, the score, and the overall "intent" of the production, as the following excerpts variously indicate:

> While the game plan is to attack the disease, public apathy, and the po-
> litical enemies of gays and lesbians with wit and song, it's undercut
> by truly peculiar casting: The good voices are demoted to small, support-
> ing roles, and the weak, often inaudible (due to the over-cranked vol-
> ume of the taped score) sometimes tone-deaf voices are awarded with the
> leads. . . .
>
> It's a work-in-progress, and then some. Jones, Stanley and Berg are tossing
> around lots of ingredients right now, but they haven't decided what it is
> they are actually cooking. . . .
>
> But now that they, Jones, Stanley and Berg, have pushed down the barrier
> that says you can't treat AIDS comically, they have to get down to the hard
> business of crafting a real musical. (F9)

However valid this critique of the cast's talent as singers may be, the critic misses the deliberate and camp aspect of such casting. He also misses the po-tency of the writers' obvious agenda—clear to the majority of its gay audi-ences—that a different type of theatre as well as a new spectatorial relationship to the material elements of production are necessary to engage the audience critically on the issue of AIDS. Rather than letting the spectator revel and be drawn in by the virtuosity of voice (think of Mendy and Stephen listening to Maria Callas), the casting of nonsingers, or amateur voices, in prominent roles ensures an anti-escapist engagement with the issues addressed throughout the performance. Furthermore, much of the camp element is stressed in these (tone deaf) moments. Humor, too, emerges from such deliberate shrills. Camp in *AIDS! The Musical!* informs both the narrative elements of the plot and its pro-duction.

Rather than seeing the Brechtian-based and interventionist performative strategies employed as a means to interrupt the mystification processes of AIDS by the mainstream media, this review, itself published in the mainstream media, only reifies the very power structure that systematically obscures any radical AIDS agenda. The radical politics of AIDS activists are reduced to the infantalized attention-getting antics of the neighborhood clique. Unlike *The Lisbon Traviata* or *I Could Go on Lip-Synching*, where the material elements of the productions—costumes, sets, lighting, etc.—deliver the effects of finished and marketable products, *AIDS! The Musical!* relies on its work-in-progress-like quality to deliver its message. Its grittiness—in "peculiar casting," minimal setting, rehearsal-like tone, for example—contributes to its major intention: to politicize representations of AIDS from a queer activist point of view. The sheer energy generated from the community-based collective that brings *AIDS! The Musical!* to the stage informs its audiences of the necessary fusion between art and life, camp and politics, performance and activism. At the end of the musical, cast members returning for their curtain call begin singing "Silence equals death! Action equals life! We are alive!" inviting members from the audience to join them in song and dance and opening up the performance space in a reminder that the activist performative gestures of the cast are available to anyone interested in fashioning oppositional images and representations for a group of people in the midst of crisis. *AIDS! The Musical!* teaches its audiences that activist performance doesn't need to be about virtuoso talent or diva behavior. Activist performance invites the nonprofessional into the space of performance, which always exists within the contested public sphere. The (in)house music engendered by the performance proliferates the possibility of further interventions in the representational struggles around AIDS that we all face in the 1990s.

In each of the plays discussed—*The Lisbon Traviata*, *I Could Go on Lip-Synching*, and *AIDS! The Musical!*—I have argued that the imaginative impulses of the gay men who have created these texts inform audiences, particularly gay audiences, of the possible discourses available to us when faced with the omnipresence of AIDS. Each of these moments in contemporary theatre, however situated around the issues of AIDS, participates in the constitutive role of ideology through the production and dissemination of our responses to the epidemic and, by extension, in the degrees by which our own responses give shape to the ideological formations around AIDS. This participatory exchange or, rather, play between the formation of an AIDS ideology and the ideological forces that give shape to our responses to AIDS finds direct address in the theatre where performative constructions of identity and articulations of a subject position are offered to the spectator in a complex fusion of identification, entertainment, self-determining agency, and/or a call to action. The various possible

positions for gay men that these three productions invoke—whether they be
the problematic, and tragic, identification with the gendered master plots of
compulsory heterosexuality; the ambivalence of the politics of nostalgia; or
the invitation to sing and act (up)—announce camp's availability in articulat-
ing and disseminating a gay male response to AIDS, however divergent its employment.

Near the conclusion of Robert Patrick's *Pouf Positive*, Robin, the protagonist,
announces to his playwright friend: "It's my party and I'll die if I want to!"[47]
reclaiming an agency for gay men and all people with AIDS during the epidemic and recirculating camp as a means to intervene in the dominant discourses governing AIDS representations. The theatre, as Robin believes and
Patrick insists, holds the capacity to service a community—in this case, mainly
gay men who are fashioning selves and communities to best cope with AIDS.
Mendy and Stephen, Lypsinka, and the characters of *AIDS! The Musical!* are,
after all, only markers in the contemporary institutional and discursive practices that we engage as we confront the epidemic. McNally, Epperson, and the
Sodomy Players Collective, however, participate in the larger ideological constructions of gay male representation and thus can inform that ideology as it
takes shape.

As spectators, we too are involved in the production and distribution of the
discourses that comprise the social phenomenon we call AIDS. In the theatre
especially, our engagement involves a certain complicity that we must either entertain or resist. Our task is to locate our participation so that we can question
it and then formulate, in our own voices, the available avenues of opposition to
the positions we eschew or the available courses of support for those we embrace. Camp, as one alternative, already points to the complexity of the situation of constructing selves, as well as to some of the possible pleasures. Such a
project—to intervene in the dominant representations governing AIDS—must
involve a serious interrogation of the discourses, imagined or available, by
which we fashion our identities to counter AIDS. The shared project to fight
back and intervene in AIDS is available to all of us who participate in the collective and localized enterprise we call theatre. No doubt, for many of us, it's
the role of a lifetime.

Throughout this chapter, I have been interested in examining the ways that
gay men have strived to construct identities through performance to counter the
effects of AIDS. In this regard, solo performance, perhaps more than any other
dramatic form, would seem to be an ideal means to address the question of identity within the context of the epidemic. In the next chapter, I discuss gay solo
performers who address AIDS in their work. The chapter highlights the poten-

tial interventions made available through a specific genre, but it also points to some of the genre's limitations. As we shall see, solo performance provides new means for gay men to confront AIDS through performance but also raises a distinct set of concerns, not least of which is the status of the material body on stage.

4

Solo Performance and the Body on Stage

Flesh and Blood (Part 1)

THE PERFORMER Ron Vawter, costumed in eclectic robes and scarves draped loosely across his body, is dancing ecstatically across the stage. It's October 1993 and Vawter is performing his solo tour de force *Roy Cohn/Jack Smith* at New York City's Kitchen, a piece he has toured for nearly the past two years and now plans to retire after the completion of this brief run. Vawter is performing the final moments of the Jack Smith segment when suddenly he trips and scrapes his leg. I am sitting in the front row watching a slight trickle of blood flow down his leg, unsure if this is part of the performance or if, in fact, Vawter has hurt himself inadvertently. My doubt reminds me of the constant tension between the representational and material bodies on stage. I observe Vawter intensely, attentive to whatever cues his expressions may reveal to help me interpret this confusing moment. Within seconds, it becomes clear to me that Vawter's fall is not scripted into the performance although its presence is now surely part of *this* performance. His momentary hesitation, suggested by his own stolen glance at his bleeding leg, is quickly resolved and most likely unnoticed by others sitting further back in the performance space. His performance proceeds without any further disruption. And yet, for me, Vawter's own fleeting acknowledgment of his bleeding leg unsettled the theatre's representational impulse designed to mask the material body—the flesh and blood—of the performer. Although Vawter seems able temporarily to dismiss his slightly bleeding leg, I cannot. For the rest of the performance, I no longer imagine Jack Smith. I only see Ron Vawter performing Jack Smith. The spectacle of Jack Smith's flamboyance, brilliantly performed by Ron Vawter, is usurped by the spectacle of the performer's bleeding leg. The performance now carries the added layer of being about not only Roy Cohn and Jack Smith, but also about Ron Vawter.

Roy Cohn/Jack Smith is Vawter's solo exploration into the lives of three white gay men with AIDS: Roy Cohn, the notoriously closeted McCarthy era lawyer; Jack Smith, the notoriously outrageous performance artist and filmmaker; and Vawter himself. Vawter's presence is marked primarily by the frame of the piece; he begins the performance by introducing himself as a person with AIDS and welcoming us into the performance space, and then he explains that this evening's performance is being filmed. At the end of the performance, he returns to thank us for attending and urges us to consider the realities of other people living with AIDS, in particular women. At no point in the piece does he tell us anything else about himself. And yet the performance itself marks Vawter's presence since his is the only body actually staged. In other words, it wasn't Jack Smith's leg that was bleeding, or that was represented as bleeding, it was Ron Vawter's. Like most, if not all, of Vawter's public, I am aware that he has been living with AIDS and that consequently (and crudely) the HIV virus is in his blood.[1] His bleeding leg makes me wonder if this is then yet another instance of "HIV upstaging"—HIV's belligerent tendency to ham it up and take over the stage. I left the Kitchen feeling as if I had witnessed—along with Vawter's own amazing performance—the uncanny performance of HIV itself.

Before returning to my discussion of Ron Vawter, I want to raise some questions concerning gay male solo performances about AIDS that I will then address in this chapter. My experience of Vawter's performance, informed by the reality of his bleeding body, brought to the forefront issues of living and acting, materiality and representation, authenticity and surrogacy, and the ways in which efforts to either obscure or call attention to these acts, by performers and/ or spectators, help shape our understanding and response to AIDS. Since gay men's bodies are already burdened as the markers of AIDS, what then happens when gay men—living with AIDS, HIV-negative, HIV-positive—employ their material bodies in performance to conjure AIDS? In what ways can gay male solo performance intervene in the dominant constructions and ideologies that sustain AIDS? Related to this line of inquiry are questions of artistic form. How does gay male solo performance differ from more traditional theatrical forms and practices? What relationship does it have with conventional theatre? How useful is it to separate performance art, performance, and theatre as three discrete forms?

These questions, concerned with some of the material and formal problems of performance, ultimately suggest questions regarding the body in performance; in solo performance the body of the performer emerges as the primary site of representation, interpretation, and, consequentially, possible intervention. The cultural anxieties concerning the body in general—and the bodies of gay men with or without AIDS, in particular—circulate continually around AIDS performance. In this chapter, I will discuss three solo performers whose work addresses the vexed issue of gay male subjectivity during the AIDS crisis. Ron Vawter, Michael Kearns, and Tim Miller each employ distinct artistic means to confront AIDS through solo performance. The fact that each of these

three performers is also a white gay man will also be addressed. I also consider
the ways that race, sexuality, and gender are culturally read through the body
of each performer and how, in turn, that reading participates in shaping our
understanding of AIDS. Finally, I conclude the chapter with a discussion of Ron
Athey's *Four Scenes from a Harsh Life*, a performance that exemplifies the problems that arise when the white gay male body marked by (and with) HIV performs on and alongside the body of a gay man of color. As we have already seen,
stylistic modes such as camp and dramatic forms such as realist theatre convey
specific histories and distinct ideological effects that need to be read within the
contexts of their cultural moment and location. In order to more fully appreciate
the interventions made possible by the artists under discussion, I begin with a
brief survey of issues specific to solo performance.

Performance Art, Performance, and Theatre

The tendency of cultural critics to bracket solo performance into set generic
categories such as performance art, performance, and theatre, terms laden with
specific and generally masked ideological biases as well as with their own traditions and aesthetics, exacerbates the difficulty of using these terms to describe
the work of various gay male solo performers whose work deals with AIDS.
Rather than exonerating myself from the debates about these terms, I attempt
to consider the factors that have led to this categorical crisis.[2] Interrogating the
ideological underpinnings of these categories and the discursive structures that
insist upon these notions as discrete may illuminate some of the interventions
solo performers attempt to achieve through live performance and may also
point to some of the ways that cultural institutions and structures—funding
sources, print and media reviewing industries, programmers and curators—
both facilitate and obstruct these works.

Performance art is a term that may reveal more about the politics of cultural
criticism than it will about the art itself (even when performers attempt to locate
their performance in the midst of these discursive politics). Performance art has
eluded critical fixity in part because of its historically enigmatic, slippery status
within the arts. As C. Carr, a leading historian and critic of performance art,
explains in *On Edge*, a compilation of her writings published in 1993, "The category [of performance art] is still relatively uncodified."[3] While this lack of codification exists in terms of the formal, aesthetic, and material anachronisms of
performance art, when compared to more conventional art practices, Carr's notion is misleading if one considers the cultural politics associated with the term.
If such artists and supportive critics find performance art's ontology in its alleged ambiguity, that it should be understood as an empty and malleable vessel

that defies the very process of codification, then less supportive and hostile critics go to great lengths to stigmatize the category by embedding political meanings in it that then valorize the category accordingly. These ideologically charged meanings render performance art *as* describable and categorizable. Performance art's tendency to position itself as a type of performance tabula rasa makes it vulnerable to cultural inscriptions that describe it as an abject practice.

Since performance art has so escaped critical definitions, it may be useful to provide a brief overview of the way in which performance art has been described historically. Performance art is often understood as live art by artists, and according to Roselee Goldberg

> the history of performance art in the twentieth century is the history of a permissive, open-ended medium with endless variables, executed by artists impatient with the limitations of more established art forms, and determined to take art directly to the public.[4]

Partially because of its structural flexibility, performance art has often been a successful medium for artists to directly engage in a critical commentary on established social practices as well as widely accepted artistic conventions.[5] While some of the earlier advocates and producers of performance art viewed the medium as radically outside of theatrical conventions and related more to the visual arts, more recent critics have seen the possible intersections between the visual arts and the theatre as blurring any separationist categories.[6]

One of the results of this convergence is the (re)emergence of the term *performance* in differentiating the type of work popular in the U.S. avant-garde throughout the 1970s and early 1980s and understood as "performance art" from the equally historically rich kind of grassroots community-based projects now ubiquitous among disenfranchised groups who prefer to call their work "performance." Part of this shift in terms results from artists' interest in setting their work apart from certain historical (and academic) debates about theatre and the visual arts. But part of this shift results from other more immediate cofactors, such as money and location. In the earlier years of performance art, now described as "classic performance art," visual artists influenced by Happenings and/or emerging from the Conceptual and Body Art movements began to forcefully explore the open-ended possibilities of "live art."[7] Jackie Apple characterizes this work as

> image rich, movement-based, multi media, sometimes site specific, both solo and collaborative group endeavors . . . investigatory, exploratory, experimental, improvisational, metaphoric form engaged in all sorts of ritual, alchemy and transformation. Like collage and assemblage, it takes what is at hand and makes something else out of it, turning the pedes-

trian into the phenomenal. Be it minimalist, flamboyant, irreverent, medi-
tational, political, conceptual, etc., performance art is foremost a percep-
tual intervention.[8]

While performance art, as Apple suggests, historically foregrounded questions
of aesthetics, primarily form, performance, the current and more favored term
among practitioners, drops the "art" and its subsequent privileging of aesthetics from "performance art" to foreground questions of identity and community.
This is particularly true for performers who emerge from oppressed groups
who see their work as overtly political in nature.[9] Throughout the 1980s, in response to the neoconservative shift engendered by the Reagan years, various
marginalized communities—the urban poor, people of color, out lesbians and
gays—found in performance a means to explore issues of identity, community,
and coalition building.[10] Many of these people, while unfamiliar with classic
performance art, were committed to exploring the politics of identity through
performance.[11]

The performance artists of the 1970s and early 1980s, of course, also invested in these terms, but the idea of identity and community was shaped
around the shared and fundamental identity as "artist." Artists in the 1970s,
such as Chris Burden, Vito Acconci, and Dennis Oppenheim, following the tradition of the European avant-garde, made work primarily for the art world, or
more specifically, other artists. But already in the 1970s, other artists, especially
women artists involved and conversant with issues from the feminist movement, began to explore more autobiographical and explicit political works. This
work was nurtured in such locations as the Women's Building in Los Angeles,
where performances by Cherie Gaulke, Suzanne Lacy, and Faith Wilding,
among others, differed substantially from the often hermetic performances of
artists interested in questions of aesthetics. *Performance art* functioned as a term
that could accommodate these various modes of performance and, moreover, include the works of women artists such as Rachel Rosenthal and Linda Montano,
who often defied either of these categorizations.[12]

Nonetheless, already by the 1970s, performance as a practice akin to the
folk arts—storytelling, singing, mythmaking—reasserted its claim within the
local cultural field. Generally unconcerned with questions of aesthetics for
the sake of aesthetics alone, performance as folk art and community ritual proceeded simultaneously—sometimes overlapping, sometimes in contradiction—
with gallery or museum-driven performance art, and was similarly undocumented and ignored outside of its specific community. Left alone on the margins
of mainstream culture, grassroots performance and performance art flourished.
As an organizing term, *performance art* seemed to envelop both "classic perfor-

mance art" and local grassroots performances, both of which began to be documented without differentiation in the groundbreaking periodical *High Performance*, founded by Linda Frye Burnham in 1978. *High Performance* was founded to enable performers to learn of each other's work and for those interested in the field to learn of work that may have had a limited or obscure run. The periodical was not interested in establishing a genre of performance; it was founded to circulate information about the various kinds of performances enacted throughout the United States and elsewhere.[13] The seemingly belligerent aversion to defining performance art in the 1970s was nearly universal. Ellen Zweig suggests that *performance art* was used as a term in the 1970s "precisely [in] that almost anything could fit. It was an empty frame within which both the object (the art) and the context (a socially constructed world) might be transformed."[14]

For the most part, the questions around performance art in the decades that followed remained within a specific and arguably hermetic community.[15] C. Carr, however, discusses the commodification of this community-based practice—how "money changes everything"—and provides an indispensable account of the ways that performance art began to be defined by outside forces at first interested in exploiting the practice as a market trend, and later, as we shall see, by those who catapulted the generally ignored practice into the cultural wars of the late 1980s.[16] In this sense, it is important to note that *performance*—whether the term is used to refer to performance art or community-based performance—is not itself outside of the problems of the theatre. The current commodification of performance and performance art ensures that any subversive component inherent in the forms loses much of its capacity to engage in radical critique once it enters more mainstream venues and mass-cultural spectatorships.[17] Jeanie Forte, a feminist performance theorist, asks:

> Just how much does the work retain any potentially subversive impact once it has achieved commercial viability? . . . Yet if performance artists are doomed to relative obscurity, playing only to audiences of "the converted," how will societal consciousness be raised (or abrased) on a larger scale? Should this even be a conscious goal?[18]

Although Forte questions exclusively the politics of women's performance, her concerns about commodification are central for any oppositional strategy "entrapped" within the dynamics of mass culture. Gay men need only be reminded how earlier stagings of the subversive capacity of camp and drag were appropriated into mass culture as mere entertainments by mainstream national theatres.[19] Furthermore, commodification doesn't necessarily refute subversion but rather repositions performance within a context that at once recognizes the medium's own implication within mass cultural systems of representation and reception. It's not as if performance art or performance can be placed outside the inspection by which they hold traditional art accountable, nor can the two be placed outside of the operative tensions of popular culture. Instead, it becomes necessary to consider the degrees of opposition either performance art or performance offer within cultural practices at large, and, as Philip Auslander comments, recognize how performance *"problematizes,* but does not *reject,* the representational means it shares with other cultural practices."[20] These are vital considerations for gay male performers who address AIDS in their work. The short history of gay drama in the age of AIDS has already demonstrated how one type of drama intended as political intervention—the humanist depiction of suffering and loss—can have problematic ramifications when mainstreamed.

Central, too, to the debates about performance and theatre, although this topic is less discussed, are the economics of the theatre. Much of what is labeled performance or performance art would be labeled theatre if it were produced in a more traditional venue. The venue of the performance directly affects the critical reception, audience expectation, and funding sources of the performing artist's work, let alone the category under which the performance is understood. In short, a solo performance at a Broadway theatre—Anna Deavere Smith, Jackie Mason, Lynn Redgrave—is never mistaken for performance art, but a solo performance in the East Village—Danny Hoch, Holly Hughes, Robbie McCauley—is rarely received as theatre unless it moves to an off-Broadway theatre. These categories—performance art, performance, theatre—reveal more about the economics of the performing arts than they do about the formal categories they supposedly define. The economic history of performance enables the categories to emerge in the first place. It is no coincidence that the current preference for the term *performance* over *performance art* caught on with the machinery of the critical review process, which seemed more than relieved that the "art" half of the term *performance art* could be dropped out. Without the accompaniment of its valorizing coterm *art,* critics and spectators could more easily dismiss performance as having no "artistic" value. If earlier artists who defined their work as "performance art" were derided as pretentious or academic, artists who identify their work as "performance" now run the risk of being accused of unprofessionalism. The question "Where's the art?" emerges as the central preoccupation of skeptics of performance. Often these performances fail even to get critically reviewed. The totalizing project of theatre history, which relies on these reviews, therefore may perpetuate this process of dismissal. Since these performances may not participate in the official practices of theatre business—opening nights, world premieres, press junkets—they lack access to the legitimating mechanisms which ensure their critical reception and official documentation.

Often the issues posed by questions relating to categorization—performance art, performance, theatre—are temporarily resolved by not only the politics surrounding performance venues but also the very geographical location of the venue. In New York City, for example, performance happens downtown; theatre happens uptown. Each geographical location is understood as containing a specific constituency based on class presumptions that extend and play into the maintenance of this binary. The economics of performance involves such concerns as funding, sponsorship, marketing, and critical review, all separate endeavors that converge in an interdependent network that both enables and legitimates the production of performance. In New York City, for example, the uptown/downtown divide sets up a false trajectory on artistic merit based on venue. A performance is a work-in-progress or a nontheatrical event until it re-appears on an established theatrical stage. Or, as in the case with annual programs such as the Brooklyn Academy of Music's Next Wave series or the Serious Fun Festival at Lincoln Center, performances that are imported into mainstream venues allow spectators both to slum through the downtown scene and to confirm their own traditional standards of performance in the process. The actual venue of the performance, along with its geographical location in the city, inscribes the performance into already marked (albeit veiled) ideologies based on the artistically conservative conventions and tastes of a cultivated, mainstream, elite audience. Critics and curators, too, opted for the term *performance* over *performance art*, in part to escape the gridlock of the "Is performance art theatre?" debate but also to recognize the deluge of solo performers who began to populate local, regional, and national public stages. For many people, performance art evokes, as one curator explains, "images from the '70s of someone hitting himself with raw meat."[21] For some critics, the shift in terms from *performance art* to *performance* is a deliberate attempt to differentiate between works that are in dialogue with classic performance art and works that are not. Jackie Apple, the critic most adamant in sustaining these distinctions, goes so far as to claim that in the 1990s, "real performance art has become an endangered species."[22] Other critics, on the other hand, conflate the terms for specific arguments against the theatre. These critics argue that performance, although not theatre proper, holds the capacity to provide a radical critique of precisely the issues of representation, subject-position, and performer-audience dynamics that are staged in the theatre.[23] Occasionally, critics suggest that *performance* and *performance art* are interchangeable terms, and fail to locate these terms in their specific political and cultural histories. In this sense, the terms are linked by affinity. For these critics, performance art and performance share a commonality simply because supposedly neither is theatre. The result of this strategic conflation of terms is that part of the specific political and cultural histories of these categories now includes this very slippage. In other words, in order to understand the categories one now needs to understand the history and politics of their convergence. Despite efforts to distinguish these two occasionally overlapping categories in terms of their politics, histories, traditions, and constituents, performance art and performance now are located on one side of a binary opposite theatre.

The politics surrounding the economics of performance directly affect artists as well. One of the ramifications of the theatre/performance binary is that solo performers must position themselves and their work within this preexisting system. Some solo performers such as Eric Bogosian and Diamanda Galas refuse the category of performance artist, while others, including many others who are less established, embrace it. In either case, the fact that solo performers must now respond to the binary indicates the institutional muscle of theatre industries, which disciplines artists into or against the very categories that the apparatus upholds. Moreover, these categories and their power to shape artistic identities are maintained through conventional funding sources. The National Endowment for the Arts (NEA), for example, no longer has a grant category for solo performers. Up until the mid-1990s, solo performers could apply as "solo theatre artists" in the "theatre program" funding source of the NEA. Solo performers who address AIDS in their work, like those who ostensibly do not, must maneuver themselves around these categories and their effects in order to exploit the possibilities engendered by the system that sustains them. In the case of gay male performers who address AIDS, already thrust into the vexed cultural politics that surround the categories of "gay men" and "AIDS," the added burden of situating their work within or against the theatre/performance divide imbues the artists with the political ideologies inherent in each of these terms. How these solo artists negotiate these issues will be the focus of the rest of the chapter.

Solo Performance and AIDS

The spectacle of AIDS is, as Watney explains, "constituted in a regime of massively overdetermined images, which are sensitive only to the values of the dominant familial 'truth' of AIDS and the projective 'knowledge' of its ideally interpellated spectator, who already 'knows all he needs to know' about homosexuality and AIDS."[24] The conflation of AIDS and homosexuality, or more precisely, the "male homosexual body," distanced an alleged "general public" from identifying AIDS as a threat to anything other than the stability of the bourgeois family, the emblematic sign of the nation. This logic, as Watney makes clear, was based on a system of identification. "But the substantive process of identifying," Watney argues, "operates in two modes: the transitive one of identifying the self in relation to the difference of the other, and the reflexive one of identifying the self in a relation of resemblance to the other. The homosexual body is an object that can only enter 'public' visibility in the transitive mode, upon the strictly enforced condition that any possibility of identification with it is scrupulously refused."[25] The purpose of the enforced abjection of the homosexual body is nothing less than a means to secure more forcefully the "fragile stability of the heterosexual subject of vision."[26] In other words, the spectacle of AIDS serves to secure a larger erasure of the gay male subject. It "promises a stainless world in which we [gay men] will only be recalled, in textbooks and in carefully edited documentary 'evidence' as signs of plagues and contagion averted—intolerable interruptions of the familial, subjects 'cured' and disinfected of desire, and 'therapeutically' denied the right to life itself."[27] I quote Watney at length because his ideas, while responding to the specific AIDS ideologies of the mid-1980s, help contextualize the cultural work of gay male solo performers during this period and since. Gay male solo performers use their homosexual bodies in order to enter into the spectacle of AIDS so as to upstage it. In performance, as Peggy Phelan puts it, "the referent is always the agonizingly relevant body of the performer."[28] Gay solo performers set out to expand the representational possibilities of the male homosexual body on stage.

The referent of the body of the performer in AIDS performance has a history that can be located in the initial efforts of people with AIDS who in the early 1980s began to unsettle the cultural myths surrounding gay men with AIDS. I argued in chapter 1 that these efforts were most effective when gay men with AIDS entered into the public discourse about AIDS. In the community-based rituals in which people with AIDS and their supporters first assembled—memorial services, social protests, fundraising efforts, and candlelight vigils—people with AIDS challenged the representations and discourses that had marked the dominant understanding of AIDS. At the same time, gay men in the performing arts, whose relationship to AIDS was often unmarked, took to the stage to raise funds for research and care, educate people about AIDS, and pay tribute to the dead. But already by 1983, gay men in the performing arts took to representing AIDS.[29]

These earliest solo performances, along with the presence of people with AIDS at community-based social rituals, were the first public embodiments of AIDS outside of the systems that represented people with AIDS as hospitalized victims, emaciated bodies, and disease-ridden threats to the so-called "general population." By representing themselves within a specific AIDS activist consciousness, gay men with AIDS were able to intervene in the ways that AIDS was rendered visible—and thus intelligible—in culture. The AIDS activism of the early 1980s also bore witness to the acts of solidarity, affinity, and often surrogacy that gay men whose health status was either unknown or unmarked, enacted to share (and thus lessen) the burden of stigma and shame that people with AIDS in both the private and public sphere were forced to endure. Gay male performers and actors, who entered into the representational system of AIDS in community-based solo pieces, marked their bodies in such a way as to conjure AIDS and to unsettle the primacy of the limited and demoralizing images of AIDS circulating in the national sphere at the time. In Watney's phrasing, these were the first interventions into the "spectacle of AIDS." Given their narrow circulation, these earliest solo performances could contest the spectacle of AIDS only for their own localized and limited audiences. Since these representations emerged from what was beginning to be labeled gay theatre, the specific categories of performance art, performance, and theatre were in many ways amorphous. The category of gay theatre itself conflated these categories under its own political agenda; gay theatre, like gay men in general at this time, had little cultural power and was imagined as innately artistically perverse. And yet within this abjection of gay theatre, gay men found a space to enact an intervention that began to call into question gay men's own perceptions of AIDS. In fact, this was the central point of contestation for these solo performers and actors; if nothing else, these self-representations and performances initiated a major shift in AIDS representation, especially in regard to gay men's identification and internalization of the "spectacle of AIDS."

The combined efforts of people with AIDS and gay male performers representing or conjuring AIDS allowed other gay men vulnerable to AIDS to locate themselves on a new AIDS identificatory continuum that challenged the identification process established by dominant culture at the beginning of the AIDS crisis. Dominant culture, as Watney argues, assumes the heterosexual family unit as nationalist icon on one end of an identificatory continuum and gay men as a threat to this ideology on the other. But for gay men, as I have demonstrated in chapter 1, this identificatory continuum implicated all gay men as abject and set into place yet another transitive identificatory system within it, which forced gay men to locate themselves against this abjection. The logic of the *New York Times'* page A22 coerced gay men in the early 1980s to set up their own continuum, one that located those with "rare cancer" as abject extreme and those who saw themselves as outside of the local, age-specific, and morally incriminating number-of-sexual-partners profile of the article at the other end of the continuum. Early gay male solo performances in theatres, bars, community spaces, and alternative performance spaces enabled gay audiences to enter into a more nuanced identification with AIDS that did not rely on the specific us/them binarism of dominant culture. If gay men were already understood as the abject other within dominant culture, in the representational logic of the us/them binarism within gay culture, that is, within the "gay men with AIDS/gay men without AIDS" system, solo performers sometimes positioned their bodies on the cusp of the binarism to challenge its extreme either/or options. Suddenly, uninfected gay men could begin to negotiate reflexive identification with the gay man with AIDS when represented by a mediated third person—the gay actor or solo performer.

In solo performance, the reflexive model of identification has historically been the primary choice for performers and playwrights. I have already discussed in chapter 2 how Jeff Hagedorn's *One* manipulated the spectator to identify with the representation of the person with AIDS. *One* inaugurated a series of one-person plays that continue to this day to stage the experiences of people with AIDS. Moreover, the casting agencies and directors for AIDS plays tend to hire actors whose sexuality (let alone HIV status) is generally unmarked to act the role of the person with AIDS. These choices tend to exploit the spectator's reflexive identification with the representation of the person with AIDS. Several solo performers and playwrights, however, have introduced other means of identification, exploiting the unique capability of solo performance and one-person plays to manipulate identification with the representation constructed by the gay male performer alone on the stage. These out gay performers, already marked by their homosexual bodies, challenge the dominant AIDS ideologies of their specific historical, cultural moment and the ways that AIDS is understood by their intended audiences. Many of the solo performers who are living with HIV or AIDS are also public about their HIV status or their AIDS diagnosis and use this information to unsettle the comforts of both transitive and reflexive models of identification and to expand the field in which AIDS is constructed and understood in the national public sphere. I now turn to the work of some of these artists who exemplify this process.

In *Intimacies* and *More Intimacies*, Michael Kearns, one of the cofounders of Artists Confronting AIDS, performs a series of fictionalized monologues of people with HIV or AIDS. Kearns, a white gay man who is HIV-positive, has been producing AIDS theatre since 1985. His AIDS-theatre career as an actor, previous to *Intimacies*, which premiered in Los Angeles in 1990, had been playing primarily the role of the gay man with AIDS or the gay friend of the person with AIDS, a necessary intervention throughout the 1980s but for Kearns, no longer politically or artistically challenging. AIDS theatre throughout the 1980s focused nearly exclusively on the white gay male experience of AIDS; other than the community-based HIV-theatre companies that included gay men of color, nongays, and women, such as *AIDS/US*, which Kearns produced and directed, most AIDS plays and performances contributed little to expanding the representation of the person of AIDS from the white, middle-class, generally thirty-something, urban gay man. Kearns, one of the most prolific and persistent AIDS theatre artists of the 1980s, felt it was now necessary in the 1990s to tell other AIDS stories and to use the network of power he had helped establish to do so. *Intimacies* was inspired by Kearns's own empathy for those whom he describes as the "the disenfranchised faces of AIDS, not the usual media darlings."[30] His identification with the other faces of AIDS—"a junkie, a whore, the homeless, the unloved"—led him to create characters who could begin to expand the representational field of people with AIDS and who, in turn, would challenge the gay community's own understanding of AIDS. Kearns performs characters of different racial and ethnic backgrounds; "the questionable political correctness of a white character playing an African American or a hearing actor playing a deaf character, or a man playing a woman is not only deliberately controversial," Kearns explains, "it has become my modus operandi."[31] *Intimacies* and *More Intimacies*, which premiered in 1992 and follows a similar format but with new characters, include fictional characters who are nongay-identified men who have sex with men, hemophiliacs, a teenage street hustler on drugs, a lesbian IV drug user, a hearing-impaired gay man and various others. Throughout these monologues, Kearns explains the social factors that have conditioned AIDS for these characters and that have rendered them either invisible or abject within the popular imagination. His efforts to call attention to the ways that racism, sexism, and classism contribute to the AIDS epidemic are unique to AIDS theatre.

By bringing forth into representation other people with AIDS who do not fit the profile of the white gay man with AIDS, Kearns attempts to demonstrate to his audiences their own misconceptions of other people with AIDS and AIDS in general. Kearns's effort to offer a more expansive portrait of people with AIDS can be seen in tandem with his earlier efforts to accomplish this mission in *AIDS/US* (1986) and *AIDS/US II* (1990). If the earlier *AIDS/US* series staged actual people living with HIV or AIDS and others affected by HIV and AIDS, why then create and perform fictionalized characters now in the 1990s? Why not simply continue to produce the self-representations of these other people with AIDS? I raise these questions to call attention to the politics of speaking for others and then offering these voices as fictional representations of the disenfranchised faces of AIDS. While on the one hand, Kearns's interest in *Intimacies* is to identify and perform the stories of others affected by AIDS who have been denied self-representation through a type of performance surrogacy, he is also, on the other hand, invested in exposing the embedded racism and sexism associated with AIDS in dominant discourse and within the gay community. *Intimacies* succeeds at directing the spectator into reflexive identification with the representation through Kearns's own positioning of his white gay male and HIV-positive body. An actor such as Kearns is already familiar to Los Angeles audiences of community-based AIDS theatre projects and Los Angeles AIDS activism. While Kearns has also worked in film and television, he is best known as the first out HIV-positive actor in the Hollywood industry. In other words, his body is already self-marked as gay, as HIV-positive, as actor, and as AIDS activist within the gay male community. Furthermore, in Los Angeles, Kearns has consistently acted the role of the white gay man with AIDS in the various community-based AIDS theatre projects. In this sense, Michael Kearns *was* the representational face of AIDS for many people in Los Angeles throughout the 1980s.

The various characters of *Intimacies* and *More Intimacies* are performed by Kearns without the help of wigs, costumes, or makeup. Instead, Kearns uses a simple red scarf to signify the character (fig. 20). Kearns never attempts to obscure his own presence on stage; audiences watch Kearns perform these characters as the actor Michael Kearns. The only referent for the spectator that suggests Kearns is not the character in the monologue—other than the text itself—is the red scarf. Kearns uses the scarf differently in each monologue to convey a sense of the character and to distinguish the characters from each other. Wrapped around his head, the scarf is a symbol of hair and signifies an African American female prostitute; draped across his shoulders, the scarf transforms into a sacramental cloth and signifies a closeted Catholic priest; and so on. At the end of the performance, during his curtain call, Kearns reworks all of the gestures of the scarf associated with the characters in order to pay tribute to them. Once this closing tributary ritual is complete, Kearns departs from the stage, leaving the scarf behind on a chair that he has used throughout the performance. It is as if Kearns means to leave the characters behind, a reminder to the audience and to himself that he is not one of the characters that he performs. The final image of the lit red scarf, the referent of the identification between the performer and the character, is held in relief, leaving the audience to speculate on their own identification with the scarf now that Kearns no longer is associated with it.

The spectator is drawn to identify with the characters in three ways. First, by the monologue; second, by the actor; and finally, by the associative logic of the scarf. The monologues are all gritty, often humorous, self-portraits that end in a type of epiphany for the character. Each of the characters shares an emotionally charged story of his or her experience with AIDS that ends with a cer-

20. Michael Kearns performing Paul in *More Intimacies*, Los Angeles, 1992.
Courtesy of Michael Kearns

tain form of acceptance. Paul's monologue, which closes *More Intimacies*, ends
in an affirmation of his deafness and of his HIV status:

> I went to this meeting. There was a room, filled with gay, deaf men, using
> sign language, communicating passionately. They were all infected with
> HIV. We sat in a circle and everyone told his story—in sign. Even though
> I didn't fully understand I got enough . . . (*Live in deaf accent, accompanied
> by signing*) I finally learned to sign. . . . This guy in the group says, "Deaf-
> ness is a gift." He also believes being gay is a gift. And having HIV is a
> gift. His name is Billy. He's the opposite of me. But I love him. . . . [32]

Kearns begins his monologue with a voice-over spoken in "natural voice," and
by the end, after the monologue explains that Paul has learned to sign, Kearns
concludes Paul's monologue "live in deaf accent, accompanied by signing." The
final words of the monologue and of the performance of *More Intimacies* are in
sign only: "Feels great!" Kearns's attempt to perform Paul's story positions the
spectator so as to identify with Paul's struggle to find his voice, a voice which
is located in the language of American Sign. That Kearns has been able to imag-

ine Paul, perform him, and learn his language conveys more than Kearns's artistic talent. Kearns teaches his audiences that people with AIDS must be met on their own terms, through their own voices, and situated in the context of how they experience their own relationship with AIDS. By the end of the performance, the identificatory impulse of the spectator shifts from the transitive to the reflexive through the monologue's narrative power and the performer's artistic deliverance. Kearns uses his body as a temporary surrogate for others with AIDS who for specific reasons are rendered abject within the gay cultural imaginary. Kearns exploits the privilege of his race and gender to serve as an entrance for white gay men to begin to identify with others unlike them. I asked Kearns about this process in a personal interview:

> The key to the performance is the white boy, Michael Kearns. Without that consciousness the metaphor would be lost. I invite—as the privileged, attractive, white man who has almost as many privileges as anyone else other than a white heterosexual man—audiences to take the journey and play these roles with me. No makeup, no costume, nothing. So, in other words, I show you that if I can become these characters, you have no excuse for not being able to either.[33]

With *Intimacies* and *More Intimacies*, Kearns complicates the notion of community. Without pitting communities against each other, Kearns suggests that white gay men with HIV may find solidarity and community not only with other gay men but also with other people living with HIV and AIDS. Gay male spectators with HIV or AIDS are invited to seek affinity with these other people with AIDS outside of the gay community, and conversely, non-white gay men living with HIV or AIDS are invited to seek affinity with white gay men who are HIV-positive or living with AIDS. The red scarf becomes the emblem of identification. Alone on stage, it invites others to stage and perform their identifications, an endless set of performances that reveal both the relentless devastation of AIDS acceleration in the world and the available possibilities of resistance to this fact with the practice of an identificatory politics of affinity and community. The red scarf is left alone on stage, an invitation for others—anyone, everyone—to take the scarf and perform their own AIDS stories, or the AIDS stories of others with whom they may identify.

Kearns's next solo project, *Rock* (1992), is based upon his own identification with Rock Hudson, who died of AIDS complications in 1985. Unlike *Intimacies* and *More Intimacies*, which present fictionalized people with AIDS from marginalized communities who remain outside of mainstream representation, *Rock* addresses the ways that AIDS is constructed through the dominant media. In *Rock*, Kearns contextualizes his own position as an out, HIV-positive, gay actor in Hollywood. Throughout the piece, Kearns performs various characters—some fictional, some biographical—who have shaped their identities around key moments in Rock Hudson's life. He includes stories of a young gay man who came out the very day Rock Hudson died, Marilyn Monroe, and a gay Hollywood voice coach. The characters are each defined through their relationship with Hudson, whose life in some capacity has affected them. Rather than performing Hudson, Kearns begins to forge a composite portrait of Hudson through the associative relationships Hudson's life and career provoked. Throughout this process, Kearns is able to provide a historical framework that comments explicitly on Hollywood homophobia and the limited forms of agency gay actors have historically had to counter it. His own intervention in this system is marked by his use of video footage of his appearances on television. *Rock* combines footage of Kearns's roles on television from classic "Cheers" episodes in the 1980s to his interview with Tom Snyder on the "Tomorrow" show in 1975 as the "Happy Hustler" and even a scene from one of his gay male porn roles. Most effective, however, is the video footage, which frames his performance, of his appearances on "Entertainment Tonight," where he speaks as an openly HIV-positive gay actor in Hollywood.

Rock begins with a videotape of Kearns's appearance on "Entertainment Tonight," which aired nationally on December 17, 1991. In the clip, Kearns explains how the death of Brad Davis and the fact that Davis kept his AIDS diagnosis hidden from the public for fear of discrimination inspired him to come out nationally about his HIV status. The short clip shows Kearns talking candidly about his life and career. He continues this discussion once the stage lights come up and reveal Kearns on stage as Michael Kearns, the actor we have just seen on tape. Kearns immediately contextualizes the performance by critiquing the various medias—television and print, specifically—that construct the dominant representations of people with AIDS. His own vulnerability to expropriation is staged as he discusses the ways that his own story is now a "story" in the media. But rather than stop here, Kearns goes on to first discuss and then demonstrate the available means of intervention that actors with HIV are able to perform in order not to be appropriated by the dominant media system. In doing so, he offers the first AIDS solo-performance piece that comments directly and specifically on the politics of the representational systems in mainstream and alternative medias that construct the AIDS celebrity posthumously.

In *Rock*, the primary site of contestation for AIDS performance is mainstream representation itself and the means of intervention is solo performance. Kearns's concerns with representation are in and of themselves not new. His innovation lies in his ability to use the ways that he himself has been complicit with representation—as an actor, as an activist—as a means to critique the very systems that construct him *as* a representation. In this sense, Kearns fore- grounds the fact that he is an actor—like Brad Davis, like Rock Hudson—and that actors, by the very nature of their need to perform a role, must negotiate continually their relationship between self and character. The fact that he is an HIV-positive actor foregrounds his associative identifications with Brad Davis and Rock Hudson. He places himself in a history of AIDS representation and discourse around the topic of Hollywood and AIDS. This history is primarily general; that is, he self-consciously intervenes in the media reporting of AIDS and Hollywood as a "story" that is told in the midst of hysteria and shock by explaining on television and on stage how he is not yet, or soon to be, dead. But it is also personal. He tells of interviewing Brad Davis on his ideas about acting in the early 1980s and of meeting Rock Hudson at a bathhouse in 1983. This identification with Davis and Hudson as actors with HIV recontextualizes the dominant representations of Davis and Hudson and offers a context from which to understand Kearns's own identity. Rock Hudson, for example, serves as a re- minder to Kearns of what he could have become—a closeted gay actor whose struggle with AIDS is revealed only through his illness and imminent death. Kearns, rather than incriminating Hudson for being closeted, is more interested in exploring the conditions that secured Hudson's closet.[34] Therefore, the iden- tification works both ways. Not only could Kearns have been like Rock Hudson, but in a different context, Hudson may have been able to be more like Kearns. Ultimately, *Rock* asks the question whether Rock Hudson's death enabled Kearns to constitutively formulate an AIDS identity in the first place. Had Hud- son not died in the way that he did, would Kearns as an HIV-positive gay actor have formulated his activist/artistic identity in the way that he has? Is there any- thing redeemable in Hudson's death? These questions, specific to the industry of Hollywood, seem at first hermetic. But Kearns makes sure to emphasize that Hollywood is an industry that produces mainstream representation, and main- stream representation produces and circulates the dominant images of AIDS. Kearns's project intervenes in this system and counters the images of dominant media as they take shape. In an interview, Kearns explains his reasons for com- ing out nationally as an HIV-positive actor:

> Several things made me make the decision, but one of the things was that I felt that it was vital that if I was ever going to announce this HIV positive status, that I had to do it when I was working at 100 percent capacity, at my optimum, as opposed to announcing it when I was in any way debili- tated, because I wanted to have the energy to present in a healthy, positive, non-stereotypical way. I didn't want to say: "I'm dying now and I'm gonna talk about being HIV positive." I want to say: "I'm alive now; I'm doing

X amount of shows a week; I'm at my pinnacle creatively as an actor and so on (and by the way, I'm HIV positive)."[35]

The identification with Rock Hudson and the critique of the media industry are perhaps the two most apparent political pedagogies of Kearns's performance. *Rock*, however, also addressed the question of HIV/AIDS discrimination in the workplace. Kearns's focus in *Rock* is the civil rights of HIV-positive actors, but his overall message extends to all people living with HIV or AIDS. "Anyone with HIV who chooses to work a job for which they are qualified should be able to do it, including actors," he insists.[36] After his curtain call, Kearns thanks the audience and concludes his performance with video footage from yet another one of his appearances on "Entertainment Tonight." This time Kearns is interviewed for his recurring role as an HIV-positive character on the prime time show "Life Goes On." Kearns's work on this show, which has since been canceled, marked the first time in network history that an out HIV-positive actor was employed to act on television. "HIV does not equal death," Kearns tells the camera of the national entertainment-news program. "HIV merely changes your life."[37] *Rock* is framed by the archival footage of these national television interviews, a reminder that the body of the gay man with HIV always enters public consciousness as a representation with political and ideological meanings. Through solo performance, Kearns proves that these representations that circulate in the national understanding of AIDS are contestable, never neutral or natural, and always in need of continual contextualization. Since they circulate in the national sphere as one of the primary means by which we position ourselves around AIDS, they affect our individual and collective unconscious. Michael Kearns performs *Intimacies, More Intimacies,* and *Rock* across the United States in alternative performance spaces, college campuses, and community centers.[38] His solo performance work is an act of intervention in the dominant cultural systems that construct AIDS. Although performed locally, Kearns's solo work achieves its national effect through the process of touring. And when placed in the context of the simultaneous local, regional, and national performances of other solo performers who tour, his work, like the work of his peers, intervenes in the hegemonic spectacle of AIDS.

Solo performance is, in a peculiar way, a misnomer for the work of individual performers. As Kearns's work begins to suggest, solo performance can never be understood in isolation. Even Jeff Hagedorn's *One*, perhaps the first AIDS representation in the history of AIDS theatre, was understood only in relation to other performances of people with AIDS in the public sphere. Moreover, solo performance, as *One* demonstrates, already involves a dialectical relationship between the performer and the representation staged. Even if the performer is

performing autobiographical material, the relationship between the representation of the body in performance with the body represented in the narrative of
the performance creates a tension that reveals that solo performance already involves two competing and often even contradictory representational referents:
the already marked body of the gay performer, which is a representation in and
of itself, and the representation performed by and through the performer's
body. Solo performers cannot escape this condition of an already dual-repre-
sentational referent. Ron Vawter's solo performance *Roy Cohn/Jack Smith* works
with this paradox and introduces a new narrative choice in gay male solo performance in the process.

In *Roy Cohn/Jack Smith*, Ron Vawter performs two historical figures who
died of AIDS (figs. 21 and 22). Unlike Michael Kearns, Vawter's project has the
actor actually perform the historical figure. The work of Michael Kearns demonstrates two of the primary means by which performers with HIV and AIDS
narrate AIDS in performance. In *Intimacies* and *More Intimacies*, Kearns creates
fictional characters with AIDS. In *Rock*, he creates fictionalized histories for historical figures with AIDS, which are conveyed by other characters associated
with the person. Although Kearns is public about his HIV status, it is only in
Rock that he situates his HIV-positive status within the context of his performance. In *Roy Cohn/Jack Smith*, Vawter discloses immediately before each performance that he is a person living with AIDS. His performance is framed by
this announcement. "I want the audience to know there is another personality
at work in the room, apart from those created ones," he explains in an interview.[39] This other personality, Ron Vawter, plays a crucial role in situating Roy
Cohn and Jack Smith—two men he positions at opposite ends of a homosexual
continuum but who share the effects of the "forces of repression" on their personalities—as people with AIDS. The two separate sections, separated by an intermission, portray Roy Cohn and Jack Smith before their AIDS diagnoses.
AIDS is never mentioned in the performance. In the first section, Vawter performs Roy Cohn. Cohn is delivering a speech attacking homosexuality at a dinner sponsored by the American Society for the Protection of the Family in 1978.
The event is based on historical fact. The script, however, is fictional, written by
Gary Indiana, yet based on research of Cohn's life and writings.[40] The second
section is a recreation of a 1981 Jack Smith performance, *What's Underground
about Marshmallows?* Smith, who is perhaps best known for the 1964 cult classic
film *Flaming Creatures*, was a pioneer of the East Village 1960s arts scene.[41] In
the forty-minute performance as Jack Smith, Vawter re-creates Smith's unique
and flamboyant style of performance.

Vawter explains that *Roy Cohn/Jack Smith* is an essay on oppression. He is
interested in presenting these figures as two extreme but linked examples, or

21. Ron Vawter performing Roy Cohn in *Roy Cohn/Jack Smith,*
New York City.
© Paula Court

results, of the forces of homosexuality's repression in American culture. Their excessive overcompensations—Cohn's disavowal of his own sexuality and his repudiation of homosexuality in general, Smith's flamboyance as a type of defense mechanism—suggest personalities that are, in Vawter's view, "warped by this repressive society that told them their natural sexual impulse was wrong."[42] One extreme of this phenomenon, Cohn, abused power at the expense of other gays; the other extreme, Smith, exaggerated his marginalization through his flamboyance. According to Vawter, "rather than hide his homosexuality, [Smith] pushed it forward to such a ferocious and exhibitionist degree that it became

22. Ron Vawter performing Jack Smith in *Roy Cohn/Jack Smith,*
New York City.
© Paula Court

another form of hiding."[43] For Vawter these two men are powerful reminders of
the forces of oppression gay men had to battle before AIDS. Still it is AIDS that
ultimately unites them. Cohn died in 1986 and Smith in 1989. Vawter accentuates their association as two very different gay men who were first destroyed
by the forces of repression and finally by AIDS. "AIDS and repression are two
separate malignancies, but because the virus has loomed so large over the last
ten years, I wanted to remind people that there have long been other forces at
work leading to another kind of death—a spiritual death," Vawter explains.[44]

While Vawter may set out to remind audiences of the social conditions that oppress gays, he cannot escape the question of how AIDS factors into his performance. Despite focusing on events that happened before either Cohn or Smith knew of their AIDS conditions, events which for Vawter demonstrate the effects of sexual repression, AIDS remains the central organizing trope of the performance. The AIDS politics of *Roy Cohn/Jack Smith* are complicated primarily in two ways. In foregrounding the force of repression in Cohn and Smith, for audiences already aware of the fact that Cohn and Smith died of AIDS and reminded of this fact through Vawter's pre-performance comments, a causal relationship between societal repression and AIDS is suggested if not assumed. In this way, the logic presumes that repression itself causes AIDS. Since the text of *Roy Cohn/Jack Smith* does not explicate the social and political factors that have conditioned AIDS, the "two separate malignancies" are linked as two locations on the trajectory of homosexuality. The cultural repression of homosexuality, according to Vawter, results in "warped personalities" that, in turn, make Cohn and Smith vulnerable to AIDS. While Vawter provides a fascinating historicization of a specific event in the histories of these two individuals, he leaves out any direct commentary on what these two men may signify culturally or how they should be contextualized within an AIDS history.[45] Whether or not Cohn and Smith stand in for the "homosexual" or for the "gay man with AIDS" remains a central question of Vawter's performance.

This question of the signification of representation haunts all solo performance. Solo performers who address AIDS in their performances must continually negotiate between two distinct performative stances: the universalizing of AIDS and the individuating of AIDS. Solo performers are especially vulnerable to charges that their AIDS performances are either individuated to such a degree that they remain hermetic, that is, the performance is only about the performer's own experience, or that the performer's work universalizes AIDS to such a degree that the specific and always various conditions of AIDS are disavowed. The tension between these two competing and often contradictory modes of performance and interpretation highlights the second complication around the AIDS politics of *Roy Cohn/Jack Smith*. Vawter challenges the interpretive logic of his performance, which links repression and AIDS, within a causal relation by the use of his own body and experience with AIDS. He manipulates interpretation through this experiential performative. Speaking to audiences before each performance as Ron Vawter, a person with AIDS, he seemingly situates himself outside of the performance of *Roy Cohn/Jack Smith*. And yet it is precisely because Vawter addresses the audience as Vawter, that he himself becomes part of the performance of *Roy Cohn/Jack Smith*. Stephen J. Bottoms develops this idea:

[Vawter] stresses, in his introductory spiel to *Roy Cohn/Jack Smith*, that these performances are not impersonations of the men in question, but very personal, subjective responses to them. Vawter thus explicitly inserts *himself* into the performance, as the common factor in the two monologues, and it is possible to view the transition from one to the other as being obliquely representative of his own personal journey of liberation, from self-repression to self-expression.[46]

The performative representations of Roy Cohn and Jack Smith are always mediated by Vawter's own body, a body with AIDS, which therefore makes *Roy Cohn/Jack Smith*, as Vawter insists, a piece about "three white gay men with AIDS." Vawter introduces and marks his body as that of a "white gay man with AIDS." He permits his own body to inhabit the representational referent of "white gay man with AIDS," inviting his audiences to read his body through the familiar apparatus known as the spectacle of AIDS. Rather than obscuring his own material presence, Vawter marks it discursively. Unlike Kearns, who in *Intimacies* and *More Intimacies*, sees his gender and race as enabling him to actually expand the representational possibilities of people with HIV and AIDS by performing identities outside of his own, Vawter seems to suggest the opposite. In performance, Vawter racializes and genders his body—and names it as a body with AIDS—immediately. Nonetheless, Vawter's discursive tactic of marking his body as a body with AIDS permits the possibility that Vawter's performance will be subsumed by the power of the spectacle of AIDS, that despite Vawter's intention to intervene in this system, his performance may instead reify it. This is the burden of representation all performers with AIDS must face.

The problem of appropriation into the spectacle of AIDS must be dealt with by all AIDS performances regardless of their intended intervention into the dominant AIDS ideologies of their times. The question performers must address is not so much how to avoid appropriation, but rather how to manipulate the process of appropriation. There will always be, in any political performance, degrees of subversion and degrees of appropriation. Performers negotiate this condition and intervene accordingly. AIDS performance runs the risk of heightening the spectacle of AIDS even, paradoxically, as these performances attempt to challenge and critique the ways AIDS is understood culturally. Vawter's means of intervention into the spectacle of AIDS is at once individuating and universalizing. Vawter provides for himself intraperformative moments of distantiation from representation and extraperformative materials of identification and interpretation. Each of these performative modes works differently in performance for the performer and for the spectator. In his portrayal of Roy Cohn, for example, Vawter seemingly inhabits the psyche of Cohn. But as James Leverett points out, Vawter's performance of Cohn is interspersed with long pauses that suggest Vawter's distance from the character he is performing. Leverett explains how this process is manifest in the Roy Cohn section:

> The pauses gave the undulating monologue a missing formality; it became a kind of sonata. Here was no abstract conceptual coup, however. The new form emerged from the immediacy of creation, from what was there—and who. The words belonged to a fiction of Roy Cohn, but the pauses were solely the domain of Ron Vawter.
>
> He stopped, stepped back from the lectern, took a drink, then stayed there for a long time, completely still and silent, looking out. Where was he then? I don't know. It wasn't in the fiction, certainly, but it wasn't in our—the audience's—reality either. Wherever he was, our hearts rushed there unconditionally, leaving us barely breathing and wide open.[47]

For Leverett, this silence "is a great mystery" and results from Vawter's artistic genius: "All of Ron's art came from there." Vawter's pauses into silence unsettle the governing impulse behind *Roy Cohn/Jack Smith*, which directs audiences to accept the representation as an effect of historical truth. The silence, as Leverett explains, reminds the spectator of the material presence of the actor, Ron Vawter. And yet, just as Roy Cohn is interrupted in these momentary pauses, so too is Vawter.

Vawter's attempts to negotiate his identification with and against Roy Cohn and Jack Smith become apparent in these silences. Audiences, however, are never privy to Vawter's actual process in this system. Instead, the spectator becomes aware that such a dynamic tension informs Vawter's performance throughout. In the Jack Smith section, Vawter performs with the ashes of Jack Smith's body, which are mixed in with his makeup, literally on his face. Vawter also has a tape of Smith's actual performance playing on the earphones that he wears throughout the Smith section to help him with his timing. Smith's voice and his ashes infiltrate Vawter's conscious to such a degree that Vawter sees the section as a type of trance: "it feels as though there is a second will at work. Although I am very aware of what I do on the stage."[48] The audience, however, is not aware of either the ash ritual or the voice recording. Such an intraperformative ritual suggests Vawter's investment in identifying with Smith. If earlier he uses his body to reference AIDS and conjure Roy Cohn, he now, in the Jack Smith section, literally puts Smith on his face. In his recreation of Smith's performance, Vawter performs an act of surrogacy:

> So when I was starting to work with Penny [Arcade] on researching Jack, she let me have some of his ashes, and because Jack's sense of how to paint

himself for a performance was so extreme and in a way was a kind of warpaint itself, I thought well, I'm going to use the ash, I'm going to return him to his own makeup. So I use the ash for every performance. I mix it with the glitter I put on my eyes and it charges me. It empowers me in a way that—I mean, when I'm sitting there and I know that Jack is on my face literally and I hear him coming through the earphones and I'm amidst this whole world of his I've carefully engineered to have around me—the slides, the reconstruction of space—something spooky comes through.[49]

Vawter's self-induced channeling of Jack Smith through the ashes and the earphones are never explicated to his audience during the performance. All of this information about intent and material practice is revealed through interviews and press coverage of Vawter's performance. In performance, the act of surrogacy is individuated and unmarked. Vawter knows that Smith's ashes are on his face and that his voice is playing on the earphones; the audience does not. Vawter's personal identification and relationship with Smith is neither explained nor even acknowledged during the performance. The deliberate privatizing of Vawter's personal process keeps the performance from being overly individuated. Nonetheless, as Vawter makes clear in his interviews, the individuation of AIDS motivates the performance. From this identification, Vawter then is able to offer his most explicit AIDS intervention. Once again, he uses his body to make his point. People with HIV and AIDS should not give up, he argues, nor should they be discriminated against because of their status or diagnosis. As a self-identifying performer with AIDS, Vawter joins the longstanding history of people with AIDS entering the public sphere to challenge misconceptions about AIDS.

The solo performances of Michael Kearns and Ron Vawter, only two of the many gay male performers with HIV who have produced AIDS performances, directly challenge the systems that construct AIDS. Their work, which differs considerably in terms of content, form, and production, establishes a model for performance engaged in unsettling the dominant spectacle of AIDS. By challenging the systems that render their status intelligible, they begin to intervene in the limited ways that seropositive people and people with AIDS are imagined. Of course, not all gay solo performers who produce AIDS work are HIV-positive or living with AIDS. Moreover, those who are HIV-positive or living with AIDS are not always public about this information. Remember, too, that in the early 1980s gay men had no idea of their serostatus or that they even had a "status": HIV testing was not introduced until 1985. Despite the availability of HIV testing since the mid-1980s, many gay male solo performers may choose, for any number of reasons, to keep their sero-status unmarked in performance.[50]

Although there are now many gay performers who are public about their HIV status or AIDS diagnosis, most performers do not announce their sero-status at all. Historically, many gay male performers who were either untested or HIV-negative and who chose to leave their sero-status private, did so in solidarity with people living with HIV and AIDS.[51] This is especially true of performers in the late 1980s and early 1990s, the most effective years of ACT UP. Many of these performers felt it was politically necessary to produce AIDS performance regardless of their own status. Tim Miller, who cofounded PS 122 in New York City and, later, Highways Performance Space in Santa Monica, California, comes out of this political context. Since the early 1980s, Miller has offered diverse audiences around the world innovative solo pieces that have reinvigorated the field of performance and have influenced an entire generation of performers in this country and abroad. Although he has consistently addressed various important social issues in his work, it is his performance pieces of the early 1990s—*Sex/Love/Stories* (1990) and *My Queer Body* (1992)—which focus on sexuality and AIDS, that I will be discussing. Miller has written and performed solo pieces that both document the response of gay men in the time of AIDS and, even more effectively, inform the methods by which queer bodies fashion sexual identities and political roles during this epidemic.

Miller's solo performance *Sex/Love/Stories* dismantles any sense of direct mimetic transference of his life into performance by offering the following prefatory disclaimer: "I remember so many things, some of them even happened."[52] In *Sex/Love/Stories*, he describes in poignant and powerful detail what it was like for him to come of age—artistically, sexually, politically, and spiritually—in the 1980s during the advent of AIDS. He incorporates various performance modes—movement, voice, and visuals—in order to invite the spectator to witness and participate in the shaping of a communal response to AIDS. The work is primarily autobiographical, but the effect is directed against an over-identification with the performer and focused instead on prompting spectators to tell their own stories and participating in direct actions to fight AIDS. Two moments in the performance exemplify this process. The first segment concerns a literally "stripped down" interrogation of gay male sexuality in the midst of AIDS, while the second offers a utopian possibility emerging from such a necessary, radical self-critique of the body.

In the section that follows the powerful *ubi sunt* component, where Miller questions his own survival amid a litany of the dead, he returns from the wanderings of urban sexual explorations to the most local of all geographies, that of the naked body. In a dialogue with his flaccid penis, Miller details the price that gay men have paid in light of AIDS and its cultural representations. Initially, what is striking in this scene is how the demoralization of gay men faced with the contemporary realities of AIDS sets up a seemingly irreconcilable distance between sexual desire and sexual possibility. Miller's penis refuses to "get hard" despite the encouragement offered by Miller's reasoning. Yet, for a mainly gay audience offered the voyeuristic moment of surveying Miller's naked body, what occurs here is an immediate "stimulation" which results from the gay gaze toward the conventionally desirable naked male body.[53] Miller manipulates this response by beckoning the spectator to at once notice his penis— "will he get hard, and if so what then?"—and not notice his penis—the "embarrassment" of impotence. While the spectator is implicated in the physicality of this moment, the narrative that accompanies Miller's nakedness disturbs this objectification of the gay male body. In Miller's piece, the gay male body is repositioned away from what Stuart Marshall describes as the "demoralization" typical of traditional AIDS representation.[54] *Sex/Love/Stories* effects a gradual shift from the personal landscape of Miller's body to the larger social arena of the gay body politic. Miller recuperates the sexual without apology and returns to his audience the repoliticization of the body that has been appropriated and reinscribed by dominant discourse as diseased:

> Get hard, because it still feels good to be touched . . .
> get hard because there is so much that is gone . . .
> get hard, because you can remember you are alive . . .
> get hard because every time I come I think of the men I've loved
> who are dead . . .
> get hard because I am a queer and it is good and I am good and I
> don't just mean in bed . . .

If Larry Kramer's protagonist in *The Normal Heart* posits the gay body politic as demanding "a recognition of a culture that isn't just sexual" and points to history for his evidence, Miller reinscribes the sexual and demands a recognition of a culture that isn't just transhistorical. He uses his body to at once arouse gay men's desire and politicize that desire in the process. By the end of the section, performer and spectator shift from the physical demoralization of gay male desire in the age of AIDS to its important role in reinscribing a sex-positive and gay-affirmative sexuality.

While the "Get Hard" segment of *Sex/Love/Stories* reclaims for gay male sexuality an enabling capacity for self-determination, the "Civil Disobedience Weekend" section, which ends the performance proper, offers a utopian rendering of what happens when gay men who celebrate their sexuality meet. At its root, "Civil Disobedience Weekend" suggests the powerful and transformative ramifications of men loving men, or at least men having sex with other men. The piece begins with the retelling of the incarceration of a group of gay activists and artists jailed for demonstrating in front of the Los Angeles Federal Building on issues ranging from AIDS negligence to government censorship of the arts.[55] Men are separated from women and sent to their separate cells. Despite the authorities' attempts to stifle the erotic and the political, the gay men left in the holding cell engage in a wild orgy of safer-sexual expression that ends not only with the collective orgasm of the all-male group but also the spilling of the seed for a new world order where AIDS activists and artists gain political stature and rule. AIDS activists, gay artists, even gay professors, "bring each other off," giving new meaning to the chant of "Action equals life." With an impromptu gathering of the Los Angles Philharmonic providing the sound-track for a complete global restructuring (Beethoven's Ninth Symphony), Miller euphorically describes the results of their demonstration. Thousands of people, speaking dozens of languages are dancing in the streets; the federal police have resigned and joined ACT UP; Gorbachev and Yeltsin have sent a memo to the activists with the hope of establishing an international democracy led by artists and activists; George Bush, on the other hand, has fled the White House; and what's left of the U.S. government has decided to place AIDS and other domestic issues as the top budget priorities. Even national monuments across the country have been transformed, now honoring those who fought for social justice and an end to the AIDS epidemic.

Undoubtedly, much of this piece plays humorously—indeed, can be viewed as satire at its most provocative—and this seems to be the point. Miller effectively distances the viewer through campiness, self-effacement, and direct narrative undercutting. Thus, while the gay spectator may find direct identification in the fantasies (both the sexual and utopian), Miller troubles this moment by positioning the fantasy *as* fantasy. This is, after all, an imaginative retelling of an event that can possibly be rendered as "real" only from the perspective of the future. And yet, what remains important to note is how Miller refuses assimilation as an option and posits direct usurpation as *the* fantasy or the not *yet* real.[56] This is a remarkable departure from the assimilationist positions represented in gay theatre between 1989 and 1991, the main years during which Miller toured the piece.

My Queer Body, his next full-evening performance piece, continues his exploration of desire and identity in the age of AIDS. In *My Queer Body*, he presents a cartography of desire that, while serving as the basis for his storytelling, emerges by the end of the performance as the foundation for an awakened American ethic of democracy (fig. 23). His work engages the most urgent needs of our society in a style and ambition that recalls both Walt Whitman and Allen Ginsberg. Like these poets, Miller's work is both deeply subjective and thoroughly visionary. And yet it is also anchored in the traditions of the theatre.

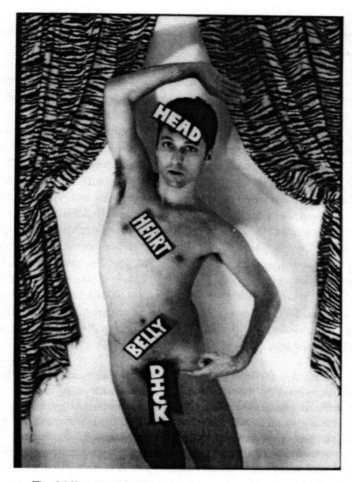

23. Tim Miller, *My Queer Body*, 1992.
Chuck Stallard

While *My Queer Body* invites comparisons to the literary heritage of American culture, especially American poetry, Miller's presence and movement on stage marks and announces *My Queer Body*'s theatricality. In this way, his performances challenge traditional generic classifications and constraints. *My Queer Body* imagines a theatre where the body's poetry—its movements and desires, its scars and wounds—can be reconciled with the poetry of its soul. The results from such performances are moments of deep, collective epiphany. Both *Sex/ Love/Stories* and *My Queer Body* bear witness to our vexed historical moment;

they are elegies for the dead that remind the living to, in his words, "Live the days. Value every kiss. Love well. And savour your body's blink between being born and dying."[57]

The performance begins with Miller entering into the performance space touching, describing, and (metaphorically) collecting various body parts from the audience. This short prelude includes the naming of body parts and the conjuring of a collective consciousness around the three terms of the title—*my, queer,* and *body*—and ends with the lines: "We have summoned the body! The Body is here." The performance contains various stories Miller recuperates from his body—"My skin is a map, a map of my world, my secret world"—from a humorous account of his conception, his first date with a boy in high school, an account of a civil disobedience event in Los Angeles, to a retelling of the "Get Hard" section from *Sex/Love/Stories,* and concludes with a fantasy sequence with Miller invited to perform at the inaugural cultural event of the first black lesbian president of the United States. Throughout the performance, Miller explores the possibility of queer agency in the midst of AIDS. The performance is also a moving meditation on grief; *My Queer Body* invokes many of Miller's former lovers and friends who have died of AIDS and details Miller's own complex emotions around AIDS. At one point in the performance, Miller is telling a harrowing story of a violent AIDS protest in Los Angeles. Protesters are bashed and beaten. Miller goes into the audience to tell the story:

> When we started tonight we called up some places on our bodies. Some things happened to those places too. Somebody said fingers. (*Touches people with each body place*) Your fingers were smashed by a horse's hoof. When hundreds of L.A.P.D. on horseback trampled through us, hurting lots of people. Your beautiful arm struck with a cop's nightstick. Your wrists swelled real bad from the tightness of the handcuffs after you were arrested and were kept in the basement of the parking structure at the Century City Hotel. Your beautiful ass got dragged along the pavement. All our spirits battered by the fuckheads in charge. My face up against the wall of art.[58]

He escapes the violence, led by the California bear—who jumps out of the burning state flag and proposes amid the chaos: "Tim, let's get outta here"—to the desert. Once there he enters a volcano, only to find the horror of AIDS inescapable. Naked and back on stage drenched in a red light, Miller proceeds to perform an excruciatingly grief-ridden account of his losses and his fears. He stops the performance and returns to the audience and sits naked on someone's lap:

> This is the most nervous part of the performance. Here, feel my heart. I
> see my face reflected in your eyes. I am here with you. My body is right
> here. You are right there. Here, feel my heart. I still feel alone. A little afraid
> of all of you.[59]

At the height of this moment, Miller shares his vulnerability and asks for support. The moment is perhaps the most profound pedagogical intervention of his
performance—"Here, feel my heart." From this simple directive, the possibility
of deep connection arises. And from this deep connection, so does the possibility of community. *My Queer Body* refers, of course, to Miller's own body, and
the stories, however real or fictional, are the stories inscribed upon it. But the
performance goes beyond individuation in its collective call to action and community. In the end, *My Queer Body* is a parable of loss and reclamation. It asks
audiences to tell the stories of their own queer bodies. Miller's performance invites all queers to find the maps on their skin and share the journey of their
bodies with one another.[60]

Michael Kearns, Ron Vawter, and Tim Miller—like most solo performers—
have toured extensively. Unlike staged plays, which are revived or adapted after their initial run, solo performers perform their own work in diverse venues
and for equally diverse audiences continually. They rely on hosting institutions
to sponsor their performances. The categorical crisis of performance—performance, performance art, theatre—becomes evident in the way that each of these
performers is categorized within the national culture. Kearns, for example, despite his credentials in film and television and his theatre reputation in Los
Angeles, performs in community-based venues and colleges when he tours. For
these reasons, within the national theatre imaginary, his work is usually understood as community-based "performance." Vawter, who also worked in film and
television, has toured in more established venues. Art houses, museums, and
theatres have sponsored *Roy Cohn/Jack Smith*. Within this context, his work is
more readily understood as theatre—and this despite his long-standing involvement with the Wooster Group, the avant-garde, New York–based performance
company. Miller, who performs in an eclectic array of venues from major regional theatres and college campuses to the steps of the Federal Building and
at ACT UP demonstrations and who is now notoriously identified as one of the
NEA Four,[61] is imagined as a performance artist. Although none of these artists
accepts these terms, the politics and economics of the theatre tend to categorize
these artists accordingly. These labels are arbitrary and not necessarily fixed
within the cultural imaginary. In other words, the links between artists and
categories are not always marked, evident, or even consistent. Rather, the poli-

tics and economics of performance along with the critical need to locate artists
within an already determined and ideologically marked rubric force the association between performer and category. In part, Kearns and Miller are positioned on the margins of the theatre because their work is more overtly autobiographical and their politics more apparent. Queer performers who work with
autobiographical material are more easily dismissed as ideological. Vawter's
work, on the other hand, is perceived as theatre since his politics are less evident
in the performance of *Roy Cohn/Jack Smith*.

And yet despite the disciplining tendencies of the national and regional
theatre industries, which establish and sustain the categories under which their
work is promoted and understood, these artists are able to exploit the systems
that attempt to contain them. Each of these performers breaks out of the representational system in performance, addressing the audience about the specific
political terms of his work. Moreover, these performers exploit the media—local
and national—generated by their performances and touring itineraries. In these
interviews and profiles, they call into question the ways we understand AIDS
and the ways that we understand theatre. Such direct addresses to the audience
and to the media about the meaning and context of their AIDS performances,
including even commentary on the hosting venue, challenge spectators to recognize the politics of AIDS and the politics of theatre. By unveiling the alleged
neutrality of AIDS research and funding, media portrayals and coverage of
AIDS, and the unmarked ideologies of other industries related to AIDS, including the theatre, these artists expose the systems that combine to construct AIDS
nationally. On and off the stage, they intervene in the dominant AIDS ideologies that assume neutrality and inevitability.

The definitions that govern our understanding of the theatre, like the definitions that govern our understanding of AIDS, are neither neutral nor inevitable. Both systems are political and arbitrary. AIDS activists, since the beginning
of the epidemic, have gone to great length and at times with great achievement
to reveal the ideological underpinnings of the systems that construct AIDS.
More to the point, AIDS activists have also been able to alter and transform
our understanding of AIDS in the process. The systems that construct AIDS,
along with being political and arbitrary, are thereby also malleable. Consider,
for example, that the very *official* definition of what constitutes AIDS itself has
changed. AIDS activists have been successful in advocating for the CDC to expand the definition of AIDS to include the opportunistic infections specific to
women with HIV. The systems that determine the meanings of AIDS, while
malleable, are also vulnerable to competing systems in terms of funds. These
economic effects, of course, are determined by the governing bodies of the na-

tion, of the state, and of the local community, and have direct impact on the material bodies of their constituents.

AIDS solo performers participate in the agitation of the industries that render AIDS intelligible to the nation. The work of Kearns, Vawter, and Miller demonstrates as much. In terms of the theatre, these solo performers call into question the politics of the categories that label their work. The economics of performance, like the economics of AIDS, conditions and disciplines bodies into a hegemonic norm that assumes neutrality and fixity. The political and ideological marks of these systems that produce AIDS and that produce theatre, if unchecked, remain veiled and thereby assume a privileged site of truth, of claims to the real. AIDS activists and AIDS performers call into question these systems, contesting the means by which these very systems produce and circulate the meanings by which AIDS and performance are understood. These interventions themselves are not always self-evident, nor are they consistent; rather, they are played out differently and occasionally covertly, and sometimes even in contradiction depending on the local politics governing and constructing the meaning and policies—including funding—of AIDS, theatre, and even AIDS theatre itself. Nor are these interventions always successful. AIDS performance is always vulnerable to the historical conditions and social contexts of both AIDS politics and performance politics. The 1994 scandal associated with Ron Athey is a final case in point.

Flesh and Blood (Part II)

Ron Athey is on stage at PS 122 in New York City, inserting long spinal needles into his head. Blood is dripping down his face. A voice-over contextualizes the moment, which is part of Athey's full-evening performance piece *Four Scenes in a Harsh Life*. Throughout the tape, Athey offers a harrowing account of drug abuse and addiction, suicide attempts, and the various factors that led him to both. It's the end of October 1994, exactly a year since I saw Vawter's *Roy Cohn/Jack Smith* at the Kitchen. Athey is performing *Four Scenes* in the United States for the first time since the now infamous performances in Minneapolis in March. Since then Athey has been catapulted from the marginal world of performance into the national cultural wars regarding the fate of the National Endowment for the Arts. The Walker Art Center, which sponsored the performances in Minneapolis, spent less than $150 to support the show. A local newspaper, the *Minneapolis Star-Tribune*, published a report—based on secondhand accounts—that sensationalized a section of the performance "The Human Printing Press," where Athey, dressed as a factory worker and wearing surgical

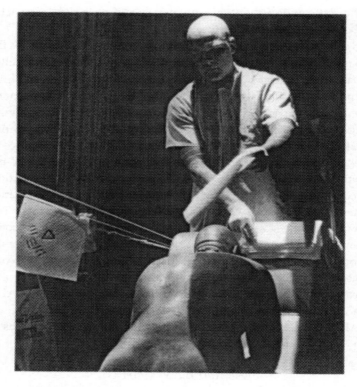

24. Ron Athey and Darryl Carlton in "Human Printing Press,"
from *Four Scenes in a Harsh Life* at PS 122, New York City,
October 1994.
© Dona Ann McAdams

gloves, carves geometrical patterns on an another performer's back (fig. 24). The
other performer, Darryl Carlton, is naked. Carlton is African American. Athey
is white. Carlton is HIV-negative. Athey is HIV-positive. The news reports focused on the fact that Athey is HIV-positive and that he exposed audiences to
blood during his performance. Here is how Athey describes the section of the
performance in his synopsis of scenes:

Scene I: Working Class Hell
[section] 2. Back to work in the factory, The Human Printing Press goes
back to Africa. Two factory workers strip Divinity Fudge [Carlton] and
strap him down. Athey carves an African scarification into his back. Athey
blots the incisions with absorbent medical paper towels and then attaches

them to clothes lines which are rigged on pulleys. The lines are pulled out above the aisles over the audience.[62]

A Minneapolis spectator feared that Athey was irresponsibly putting the audience at risk for HIV. The spectator notified the health department and the press. This local incident was then wired across the nation and Athey became yet another target of the Christian Action Network, who issued a "declaration of war."[63] Suffice it to say, Athey did not endanger his audiences in any way. The AIDS hysteria resulting from this scene obscured the full effect of Athey's, at times, intensely moving meditation on pain and despair.

The notion that Athey was putting audiences at risk was one of the many fallacies that became associated with his performances. Among the most obvious misconceptions for anyone who has seen the performance is that *Four Scenes in a Harsh Life* is a solo performance piece. Athey performs with a company of at least ten different performers, each of whom consents to the rigorous demands of Athey's modern primitive rituals: "The Blood and Pain and Exhaustion are Real," he explains.[64] Athey's performances enact rituals that are designed to at once invoke the fears of living with HIV and the spiritual healing involved with reclaiming the body. His work speaks and performs the vernacular of a subcultural world. Athey does not translate this vernacular for his audiences; rather, audiences are left to their own devices to construct meaning from the performance. Since Athey does not provide any pedagogical means for the uninitiated to enter into the world of his performance, the rituals remain hermetic and extremely vulnerable to expropriation. For instance, the beauty of Athey's self-inflicted and highly choreographed self-mutilation in the "Suicide/Tattoo Survival" section, the scene where he inserts long needles into his scalp, is lost to audiences who have no sense of the symbolic rituals of piercing, tattooing, and self-inflicted pain and who can focus in on only the material flesh and blood of the performer.

Athey, of course, is not culpable for the AIDS hysteria generated by the press and the subsequent cuts to the NEA. In fact, like other artists who have been dragged into the cultural wars, he has little to gain from this exposure. Like the NEA Four, his work is now forever linked with scandal and, more to the point, the expectation of scandal. Performing venues have since been reluctant to sponsor his work for fear of losing funds.[65] The personal turmoil of having his work stand as the pinnacle of the perverse is yet another burden he must undoubtedly bear. The spectacle of AIDS, as I have discussed, surfaces to preserve the status of the nation. The spectacle of AIDS is always framed under the auspices of morality. People with AIDS (and, by association, queer people) in this system are rendered disposable. But the spectacle of AIDS also underlies a second agenda: economics. The idea that homosexuals are being subsidized by the federal government with funds to produce work that is not only morally offensive but also threatening to the general public lies at the heart of the line of attack from both the Christian Action Network and the elected representatives in Washington advocating for the disbandment of the NEA. The link between these two cultural forces—homophobia and economics—has been the basis for the crisis at the NEA.[66] One of the results of this is that queer theatre is now understood as scandalous and dangerous. Tonight, before we can even enter into the performance space, we must all sign consent forms, ostensibly to absolve PS 122 of any responsibility for the harm that we may encounter as a result of the performance. What harm? This pre-performance ritual—oddly the only one we are asked to participate in all evening—frames the performance as both a scandal and a danger. For me, this is the most intense moment I will encounter all evening. The moment when I must examine my own complicity in this system that defines AIDS performance along such lines. Still, I sign the form and take my seat.

While much has been made of Athey's sero-status and the alleged danger to which he exposed audiences, there has been virtually no discussion of the actual flesh and blood of Darryl Carlton, the performer into whom Athey carved. Carlton is generally described as a "large, naked African-American man."[67] Discussions about his race, while foregrounded in these descriptions, have been virtually eclipsed by the fear of contaminated blood dripping on unconsenting spectators. The fact that Athey has explained that Carlton is HIV-negative seems somehow beside the point. The associative logic of this anxiety presumes Carlton's blood is Athey's blood; the blood is presumed to be the blood from an AIDS body. No concern is generated by any of the other bleeding bodies on stage, bodies that are white and whose sero-status is unmarked in performance and in the press. So how and why is this anxiety heaped upon the back of the black man? On the one hand, the hysteria around AIDS contagion is generated by the conscious fact that the blood absorbed by the medical paper towels and rigged over the audience is from Carlton's back. But on the other hand, on an unconscious level, as I will argue in the next chapter, the anxiety stems in part from the blood of the black gay man, which has been intrinsically and historically linked with a set of cultural fears ranging from miscegenation to AIDS *regardless* of sero-status. Carlton does not speak in the performance or in interviews. His voice is not part of the discussions inside or outside of the performance. Instead he remains both literally and figuratively inscribed by the performance and absorbed into the spectacle of AIDS. This racialized AIDS inscription and its circulation are never acknowledged, passing, like the imprinted towels, over our heads.

The hysteria surrounding "The Human Printing Press" points to the need for a closer analysis of the ways that cultural fantasies and anxieties about race, sexuality, and AIDS interact with one another in theatrical representation and its reception. In the next two chapters, I will address how gay men of color have used performance to intervene in the cultural politics of AIDS and gay self-representation. As we shall see, the work of both Pomo Afro Homos, a black gay performance trio who toured nationally from 1991 to 1995, and Teatro Viva!, a community-based Latino AIDS outreach theatre project still active in Los Angeles, insists upon situating questions of AIDS and sexuality in relation to those of race and ethnicity.

5

Pomo Afro Homos' *Fierce Love*

Intervening in the Cultural Politics
of Race, Sexuality, and AIDS

A T THE BEGINNING of their collaborative performance, *Fierce Love*, Pomo Afro Homos fill the stage with a cappella/gospel harmonies. The opening song, which frames the performance, immediately invokes the heterogeneity of black gay experience(s) that *Fierce Love* will bring to life:

> . . . We are numerous and varied
> flamboyant and dull
> pious, perverse
> . . . these are some of our stories
> our passions and fears
> our victories and tears
> drink them like water
> savor them like wine
> spread them like fire
> We are
> an endangered species
> But our stories must be told . . . [1]

Brian Freeman, Eric Gupton, and Djola Bernard Branner, the three performers who in 1991 cofounded the Pomo Afro Homos (postmodern, African American homosexuals), begin *Fierce Love* by demanding the recognition of multiple black gay male subject positions. The Pomos enact what Kobena Mercer, writing on marginalized or minoritized situations, has explained as speaking *from* the specificity of experiences of marginality rather than speaking *for* the entire community from which they come.[2] Pomo Afro Homos at once provide a forum for some of the experiences of black gay men while reminding audiences of all colors that the juncture of black and gay, as novelist Steven Corbin explains, need not be read only as "a major two-point score on the shit list of oppression."[3] Rather, as the Pomos demonstrate, being black and gay calls for a cultural politics that recognizes and intervenes in the dominant social inscriptions around race and sexuality. The double bind of black homophobia and queer racism can exhaust the psychic resources necessary to counter such systemic oppression. With this in mind, it becomes easy to champion the Pomo Afro Homos for simply taking the risk of asserting black gay identities in such a visible venue as the theatre. However, as I hope to demonstrate, the Pomo Afro Homos go much further than simply staging and celebrating difference. *Fierce Love* must be read as a direct intervention in the prevailing mythologies around both black and gay identities, but especially black gay identities, and as a critical practice intervening in the historically situated popular discourses on race and sexuality in contemporary U.S. culture. That these same discourses contribute to an AIDS ideology rendering black gay men invisible suggests all the more the urgency of the messages within *Fierce Love.*

In order to establish my argument for *Fierce Love* as a necessary intervention into AIDS, I will begin by calling into question some of the dominant productions in recent U.S. culture that display and proliferate anxieties about black gay bodies. Specifically, I will discuss John Guare's enormously successful play *Six Degrees of Separation* (1990) and Magic Johnson's unsettling HIV disclosure (1991). These two very different cultural occasions—a theatrical event, a celebrity news item—when examined together begin to provide the cultural and historical context for the work of the Pomo Afro Homos. *Six Degrees of Separation,* I will argue, not only depicts racist fears and anxieties but, in light of its success with critics and audiences, perpetuates certain racialized sexual discourses. The Magic Johnson incident demonstrates both the racist discourse of white America associating blackness with AIDS and the rampant homophobia prevalent among U.S. blacks. In both cases, I am interested in the production and reception of these two seemingly incongruent occasions and how they reveal certain cultural fantasies constructed to contain black gay sexuality. Pomo Afro Homos address this phenomenon by insisting that the theatre and its inherent role in offering representations be seen as a viable and necessary site for contestation. In this sense, Pomo Afro Homos join other gay men of color who have found theatre and performance a viable means of intervening in the cultural politics of race, sexuality, and AIDS.

Six Degrees of Separation and the Spectacle of Experience

By the end of John Guare's celebrated comedy *Six Degrees of Separation,* Ouisa Kittredge, the white, Upper East Side, affluent, liberal heroine of the play, is faced with what for her seems an impossible dilemma. Guare's play details the interruption of the lives of Ouisa and her husband, Flan, by a black gay man, identified only as Paul, who arrives at their doorstep one evening claiming to be the son of Sidney Poitier and a Harvard classmate of their children. Claiming to have been mugged outside their Fifth Avenue apartment, Paul succeeds in winning the confidence of the couple so much so that he is invited to spend the night. In the morning, he will join his father, who is directing the film version of *Cats* and who is scheduled to arrive the next day to begin auditions. For Ouisa, charmed by Paul's stories of their children and his supposed father, Paul's arrival offers her an opportunity to connect emotionally with another human being: "I just loved the kid so much. I wanted to reach out to him."[4]

While much of the tone of the play in these early scenes can be categorized as comic, and Ouisa as the central voice of irony, once Paul's scheme is revealed Ouisa moves from comic disengagement to tragic identification. Everyone, she has read somewhere, is "separated by only six other people. Six degrees of separation. . . . But to find the right six people" (81). For Ouisa this concept holds the key to intimacy: that despite differences, there is a fundamental humanity shared by all people. Once aware that she has been duped, Ouisa still wants to hold on to the "experience" of Paul, the revitalization that the black gay man has provided for her through his attentive and demonstrative interest in her life. Moreover, Paul's humanity must be available to her on some level even if he is neither the son of Sidney Poitier nor her children's classmate.

By the end of the play, Paul has been arrested by the police. Ouisa, not knowing Paul's true identity, now has no idea how to help him. "Why does it mean so much to you?" her husband asks (116). Transformed by her experience with Paul, Ouisa now questions the security of her liberal politics and identity. Her own epiphanic rhetorical question—"How do we *keep* the experience?"— follows her own insistence upon not turning Paul into an anecdote "to dine out on" (117). The play ends with Ouisa's own enigmatic and unarticulated scene of transformation. She imagines Paul once more, this time describing the two-sided Kandinsky painting that hangs in the Kittredge home: "The Kandinsky. It's painted on two sides. [*He glows for a moment and is gone. She considers. She smiles. The Kandinsky begins its slow revolve.*]" (120). The painting becomes the emblem of the play's leitmotif that "there are two sides to every story" (65) and announces Ouisa's own reconnection with her imagination. The conclusion offers Ouisa's epiphany as a model for its audience, or as Frank Rich writes, "a transcendent theatrical experience that is itself a lasting vision of the humane new world of which Mr. Guare and his New Yorkers so hungrily dream."[5] Rich is not alone in his appraisal of the play. Most of the play's reviews in the popular press offer similar readings and champion Guare for writing a play that captures what is described as the mood and moral dilemma in the United States at the end of the 1980s and the beginning of the 1990s.[6]

If critics (and presumably audiences) are drawn to Ouisa's situation and revel in her resolute determination to "keep the experience," it seems logical if not necessary to interrogate the role that Paul—Guare's phantasmatic construction displaced onto the character Ouisa—plays in the drama and determine how Paul's race and sexuality figure in Ouisa's and her audiences' own self-imaginings. Race is immediately and obviously marked in the play by the actors who perform the roles and further established by the textual narrative that insists on maintaining whiteness and blackness as two opposing, defining social categories. In the earliest scenes, audiences are introduced to white characters and actors who set up these differences. The story addressed to the audience by Ouisa and Flan begins a series of enactments of the events leading up to Paul's arrival in their home. The Kittredges are entertaining one of Flan's prospective clients, Geoffrey, a wealthy, white British South African who can help finance Flan's private art dealings. South African politics and race relations become the litmus test for white liberal policies and affinities, as the Kittredges delicately, and quite humorously, maneuver around Geoffrey's obvious pomposity—"One needs to stay [in South Africa] to educate the black workers and we'll know we've been successful when they kill us" (10)—in order to secure the two million dollars Flan needs to close a deal. But if Geoffrey's views of South Africa proved a challenge for the Kittredges, Paul's immediate arrival at their door puts into motion the vexed history of U.S. race relations for the white liberal politics they have been espousing all evening. Paul's seductive narrative detailing the class privileges available to him as the son of Sidney Poitier ("I don't feel American. I don't even feel Black," [30]) puts Ouisa and Flan at ease, and charms Geoffrey ("OUISA: Even Geoffrey was touched" [25]), so much so that he not only offers Flan the money, but leaves New York with the idea for a Black American Film Festival in South Africa.

Only when Ouisa discovers Paul the next morning receiving oral sex from a white male hustler is the goodwill of the previous evening retracted. The spectacle of sexuality *and* race—specifically of a black gay man—is too much for her, and she throws Paul out of their apartment. The Kittredges soon discover that they have not been the only ones who have hosted Paul. The rest of the play consists of the Kittredges—along with the other conned white, liberal socialites—attempting to reconcile their seduction by Paul's rhetoric with their own unimaginative lives, although it is Ouisa who is most concerned with understanding these events. At first, she can only come up with the glib comment that "it seems the common thread linking us all is an overwhelming need to be in the movie of *Cats*" (68), but as she continues to unpack the events of the Paul incident, she discovers that his presence has initiated a series of questions about herself, questions about her identity that can no longer be left unanswered. The black gay man thus becomes the vehicle for Ouisa to reevaluate her own beliefs and sense of self.

John Clum argues that the scene of frontal nudity dramatically stages the Kittredges' "feared unknown—a gay black stranger, an alien who brings into the Kittredge house and sexless marriage a threatening, alien sexuality."[7] Clum's reading, however, focuses on how the naked male body of the white hustler represents "not male sexuality, but gay sexuality."[8] Clum continues: "In the world of Guare's play, blackness provokes a mixture of liberal guilt and uncertainty, but gayness provokes chaos."[9] While I agree with Clum's overall reading, I want to focus more specifically on the intertwining of race and sexual politics that eludes Clum in these quotes. Gayness alone is not what "provokes chaos," but, more to the point, Paul—as a black gay man—embodies the chaos in the play. That Paul is the only nonwhite character in the play further facilitates such a reading. This chaos is construed at one point or another by all the characters in the play. He is described as "this fucking black kid crack addict," "a black fraud," continually associated with drugs, urban crime, and AIDS ("OUISA to PAUL: Are you suicidal? Do you have AIDS? Are you infected?" [98]). He is fetishized as a sexual object by Ouisa, who enjoys watching him; by Trent Conway, the young white man who teaches Paul the argot of "rich people" in exchange for Paul's body; and by Rick, the young aspiring actor from Utah, who, after his sexual encounter with Paul, commits suicide by jumping off a building. It is Paul and not the white hustler (whose sexuality is never clear) who becomes the site of white liberal anxieties. *Six Degrees* demonstrates that being both black and gay only heightens the suspicions of the white heterosexual characters who interpret blackness and gayness as doubly duplicitous and inherently associated with AIDS. Yet, in light of these various incidents, Paul is still always cast as an "experience": one that must be contained within the racialized sexual discourse of white liberalism.

While his race and sexuality are staged as a spectacle of difference, if not chaos, Paul is contained in precisely the anecdotal narratives that Ouisa sets out to avoid. Only Rick, who moved to New York with his girlfriend, shares the same profundity that Ouisa experienced with Paul. After a night of rented tuxedos and dancing at the Rainbow Room, Paul fucks Rick during a carriage ride through Central Park. Rick addresses this experience directly to the audience in the same manner that Ouisa conveys her stories: "It was the greatest night I ever had and before we got home he kissed me on the mouth and he vanished" (91). The direct audience address circumvents the inevitable filtering of narrative events via anecdote or gossip. Rick's sexuality is never an issue in the play for anyone other than himself ("I didn't come here to be *this*" [91]), although admittedly, his suicide immediately told as an anecdote in the next scene curtails any threat his homosexual activities may pose and provides a clichéd closure to his character. Indeed, all the white men who have sex with Paul—the hustler, Trent Conway, and Rick—are conveniently led offstage after their encounters with Paul, further indicating that it is black gay sexuality that poses the problem for Guare's white characters. The fact that all of Paul's sexual relations are with white men further fuels the crisis in *Six Degrees*. Black gay sexuality is constructed in the play as duplicitous, aggressive, and uncontainable, rendering white men passive, penetrable, and, as Clum suggests, "unmanned."[10]

Such a racialized sexual discourse eludes mainstream critics. The focus of the popular press centers on Ouisa and Stockard Channing's brilliant performance in the central role. Ouisa's journey is universalized not only by the production, but by critics who see in Ouisa the spiritual awakening necessary to resolve the effects of a postmodern politics of doubt and despair. Once again, Frank Rich—in a second review of the play published in the *New York Times* only two weeks after his first—leads the critical acclaim:

> What finally allows *Six Degrees of Separation* to become a touching, beautiful, sensitive work is that Mr. Guare doesn't waste time assigning the predictable political blame for all the separations that turn a city's people into what Holden Caulfield called phonies. Instead the playwright points the way—by the lustrous examples of Ouisa's redemptive spiritual journey to authenticity and his own elevated act of art—to a transcendent alternative to the inhuman urban collage. This play invades an audience's soul by forcing it to confront the same urgent question asked of its New Yorkers. If we didn't come here to be this, then who do we intend to be?[11]

Rich's notion that *Six Degrees* speaks to a specific New York milieu suggests that the play targets the specific issues of a certain constituency—mainly a white, politically liberal elite. The venue of the performance, first at the smaller Newhouse Theatre and then the Vivian Beaumont (both at New York's Lincoln Center), would support this idea.

The performance venue, the mainstream review process—in particular at the *New York Times*—along with the issues and characters of the play all contribute to the interests of a specific audience that is construed as both normative and universal by the very operations of the theatre industry. Audiences entering the theatre are asked to identify with Ouisa and share her interpretation of Paul. And since Ouisa participates with all of Guare's white characters in the racialized sexual discourse that they use to construct Paul, there is little room for audiences to question the assumptions that the play and the production offer as truths. Paul can be defined only as a spectacle of difference recast as an experience for liberal whites. As Guare's creation and Ouisa's fantasy, Paul has no identity other than the one imagined by Guare and his white characters. The ultimate irony brought forth by this process is that Paul could well be the son of Sidney Poitier, at least from the perspective of Paul's description of his supposed father: "My father, being an actor, has no real identity. . . . He has no life—he has no memory—only the scripts producers send him in the mail through his agents. That's his past" (22). *Six Degrees* inadvertently stages how white privilege can erase black agency; blacks are actors who are given social scripts produced and imagined by others. Paul's identity, like Sidney Poitier's, is never known; instead, Paul remains to the end an adventure for Ouisa offered by Guare to his audiences and, not surprisingly, ends up becoming the talk of the town.

Six Degrees is based in part on the true life story of David Hampton, a young black bisexual man who in the early 1980s posed as the son of Sidney Poitier to get inside elite and trendy New York establishments, and later into the homes of prominent New Yorkers, only to be arrested in 1983 and made to serve twenty-one months in prison.[12] The leap from Hampton's biography to Paul's case in Guare's play further demonstrates how black experience is translated into anecdote, albeit under the rubric of art. Guare's play is inspired by the events of Hampton's life to the extent that Hampton felt he was entitled to a share of its profits. Hampton sued Guare, claiming that his personality deserved the same protection as patents, copyrights, or trademarks, only to have his case dismissed by the New York Supreme Court in May 1992.[13] The processing of Hampton's experiences, reinterpreted by Guare in his construction of Paul and then presented to his central character Ouisa to offer back to audiences at Lincoln Center, sets up a series of transactions that tellingly reveal the limited discourses available within liberalism for discussing race and sexuality.[14] "There are two sides to every story," the play insists, but by offering only the one-sided perspective of white liberalism, *Six Degrees of Separation* obscures the actual experience of Paul. He remains the catalyst for whiteness to retain—at whatever cost—its centrality.

Magic and Black Gay Men

If *Six Degrees* demonstrated the limited discourses available to discuss black gay sexuality in the popular culture, Magic Johnson's announcement on November 7, 1991, that he tested positive for HIV demonstrated that the way AIDS is addressed in relation to race and sexuality is also wanting. Despite the fact that black heterosexuals joined white gays and straights in the national forum on AIDS that followed Johnson's press conference, not all sides of the story were made available in the popular press. Gay men of color, especially black gay men, were denied the opportunity to voice how Johnson's announcement might help—or hinder—the battle waged against AIDS by gay men of color on a daily basis. Instead, what was played out in the weeks immediately following Johnson's announcement exhibited the conflation invoked in the concept of "African AIDS,"[15] which erroneously associates blackness and AIDS as well as sensationalist speculations of Johnson's "real" source of transmission.

Magic Johnson's high profile immediately following his disclosure occasioned an unprecedented number of articles, editorials, radio shows, and TV discussions on AIDS, in particular, on AIDS and communities of color. Johnson, singlehandedly with his announcement, returned AIDS to the international spotlight, so much so that even then President George Bush was forced to admit that he needed to improve his AIDS record. Leaders in communities of color were also forced to state their efforts to secure AIDS services, including health care and education, and cornered to go on the record for future implementations.[16] And yet the media frenzy surrounding Johnson's disclosure barely touched upon AIDS and gay and bisexual men of color. Johnson's own assurance on "The Arsenio Hall Show" that same week that he was "far from being a homosexual" was met with cheers of heterosexist, if not homophobic, complicity.[17] Six months later, Johnson clarified his statement, explaining that he wanted "everybody to know that [HIV] wasn't just a gay disease."[18] The interview, a cover story in the gay and lesbian publication the *Advocate*, was held "to start a dialogue with the gay and lesbian community."

In an essay regarding Johnson's HIV disclosure, Douglas Crimp writes of the effects of this announcement for the gay community and the black community. Crimp acknowledges the progressive cultural politics engendered by Johnson's disclosure, but he calls attention to the homophobic and sexist discourse it perpetuates as well. While Johnson's disclosure of testing HIV-positive forced the media finally to distinguish between HIV and AIDS; to present images of HIV-positive people "living normal, productive lives"; and to take a critical stance against President George Bush, his new role as AIDS spokesperson needed to intervene in the anti-gay and misogynistic positions standard in AIDS discourse. Near the conclusion of his essay, Crimp reminds us of the grim statistics of AIDS:

We gay men who have unequally borne the burden of AIDS in the United States know that the burden has also been unequally borne by people of color. In 1992, the *majority* of new AIDS cases in the United States was reported among people of color. Blacks account for 12 percent of the population, but more than 25 percent of total reported cases of full-blown AIDS.

More than half of all women with AIDS are black. Three out of four women with AIDS are black or Hispanic. Nine out of ten children with AIDS and over half the teenagers with AIDS are black or Hispanic.[19]

Consider, too, some other statistics not foregrounded in Crimp's essay. At the time of Magic Johnson's announcement, 44 percent of all black men with AIDS cited unprotected sex with men as the source of contraction; 23 percent of all gay men with AIDS at this time were African Americans. And yet, as Charles Stewart claims, black gay and bisexual men are "one of the largest and most invisible groups affected by the AIDS epidemic."[20] Stewart, a contributing editor of *BLK*, a black lesbian and gay periodical based in Los Angeles that has consistently reported on black gay and bisexual men and AIDS, further explains how it is that, despite these disturbing figures, gay and bisexual black men are the least targeted for assistance by either the government or nonprofit agencies, pre- or post-infection. Gay community institutions, including AIDS service organizations, are often segregated, leaving black gays and bisexuals on the margins of inclusion. In order to counter the neglect by many white gay male AIDS organizations, AIDS agencies and councils addressing the specific concerns and needs of various people of color began appearing in the mid-1980s. Only one week before Magic Johnson's announcement, for example, the National Minority AIDS Council met in Los Angeles for its Annual Skills Building Conference. Over 600 people working to fight AIDS networked and exchanged information and strategies. Earlier that same month, the HIV and People of Color Conference held in Seattle brought hundreds of people of color together to form coalitions of support. Among the issues discussed in Los Angeles and in Seattle, and at like conferences across the country, was what has been awkwardly defined by HIV professionals as "nongay-identified men who have sex with men." Such men, who refuse to identify as gay or bisexual for whatever reasons, are perceived as posing a severe threat for the spread of AIDS. Mark Haile, however, explains that

> there is a construction of sexuality far more elaborate than mere "straight" or "gay," especially in the black community. When coupled with the racism that is the history of this nation, that affects every aspect of life, the end result is a field of sexual identities for black lesbian and gay men that is identical to neither the white lesbian and gay community in America, nor the framework of sexual orientation as has been studied on the African continent.[21]

Rather than dismissing this sexual continuum as a readily available grid for the denial of homosexuality, Haile insists that communities of color should begin to recognize sexual variance within a more inclusive system than the current hetero/homo binarism. While nongay-identified men who have sex with other men need to have their communities understand and support the complexity of their sexual identifications, Haile makes sure to insist that black gay and bisexual men should receive similar support. In other words, what is at issue is not the potential denial of nongay-identified men who have sex with men but rather the denial of out black and bisexual gays and lesbians by the larger African American community. It is precisely the systemic denial of black gay identity that contributes to the double bind of invisibility, what Michael Broder describes as the "twofold invisibility that black gay people face in this society, the invisibility of color, and the invisibility of sexuality."[22]

If racism within the white gay community ostracizes black gays, homophobia in the black community only contributes to this black gay invisibility. Many black gay and lesbian intellectuals and activists have been fighting this homophobia within the African American community and have written extensively on the subject. Ron Simmons, for instance, speculates that homophobia in the African American community is "not so much a fear of homosexuals but a fear that homosexuality will become pervasive in the community. Thus a homophobic person can accept a homosexual as an individual friend or family member, yet not accept homosexuality."[23] Barbara Smith offers a similar point and claims that the real issue is how "out" the individual is: "If you're a lesbian, you can have as many women as you want. If you're a gay man, you can have all the men you want. But just don't say anything about it or make it political."[24] Marlon Riggs, on the other hand, sees less tolerance:

> What lies at the heart, I believe, of black America's pervasive cultural homophobia is the desperate need for a convenient Other *within* the community, yet not truly *of* the community, an Other to which blame for the chronic identity crisis afflicting the black male psyche can be readily displaced. . . . [25]

Riggs is concerned with the proliferation throughout the 1980s and early 1990s of derogatory and inflammatory representations of black gay men in the culture produced by heterosexual blacks. He cites examples from film, television, and popular music that display the fad for "negro faggotry." Such blatant disregard for the lives of black gay men, Riggs relates, demonstrates that "negro faggotry is the rage! Black gay men are not."[26] It has been up to black gay artists, like Riggs, to counter such stereotypes with self-made representations from the African American gay community. The same holds true for issues regarding AIDS and black gay men. In fact, it is essential to recognize this rage for "negro faggotry" within the context of black gay male invisibility in order to fully recognize the intervention efforts by black gay cultural activists. U.S. popular culture in the early 1990s, from *In Living Color* to *Six Degrees of Separation*, intensified the need for the assertion of black gay and bisexual identities, especially if the fight against AIDS was to succeed. Black gay cultural activists insisted that the fight against AIDS and black gay invisibility must be fought on all fronts, including the theatre.

Fierce Love and Fierce Response

"There hasn't been anything like this in American theatre," Pomo Afro Homo Eric Gupton explains.[27] Gupton is discussing *Fierce Love*, one of the first black gay collaborations in the history of U.S. theatre to openly and unabashedly present the issues of black gay men on stage. *Fierce Love* grew out of fellow Pomo Brian Freeman's interest in developing an evening of safe-sex stories. When Freeman, Gupton, and Branner first met to discuss the project, they realized that they had a full evening of performance material that encompassed many facets of black gay life. *Fierce Love* premiered in January 1991 at Josie's Cabaret in San Francisco's Castro district; played in alternative performance spaces in Seattle, Chicago, and Los Angeles; and by the end of the year was performed at New York's Public Theater. The Pomos composed a second performance piece, *Dark Fruit*, which they toured in repertory with *Fierce Love* throughout the 1990s until the group disbanded in 1995.

Fierce Love is composed of thirteen sections or stories from black gay life. Each story stands on its own as a fully realized presentation of black gay experience and may include all three performers or any one or two. The performance is formally designed to facilitate travel and adaptability. There is no set to speak of, props are minimal, and lighting and music cues are manageable enough to accommodate different performance venues. Part of this stripped-down-to-the-basics type of theatre is undoubtedly due to limited finances; the effect, however, like much current identity-based performance, places the emphasis on narrative and the focus on the performers' bodies. But unlike solo performers, whose voice and movement can be used to signal a shift in characterization and thus display the performer's versatility, the Pomos are able to manipulate this form more readily by staging any combination of their three bodies and voices. While the Pomos also display versatility, they inevitably contest any essentialized reading of their bodies since they cannot be reduced to any one notion of "African American homosexual"; the postmodern, or pomo, is located in this free play of identity and performance. While the Pomos insist on being heard as black gay men, they offer no fixed reading of a black gay male identity. Spectators, regardless of race or sexual orientation, are asked to consider what it means to be black and gay. The Pomos perform multiple black gay identities in

25. The Pomo Afro Homos (Djola Branner, Brian Freeman, and Eric Gupton) in *Fierce Love*, San Francisco.
© Jill Posener

a variety of sketches and vignettes; they continually shift the tone of the performance, disturbing an audience's expectations both formally and thematically. Beginning with their name choice—Pomo Afro Homos—the three performers parody the very terms of reference abbreviated in the group's title—postmodern, Afro-American, homosexual. The name itself enacts the humor and parody associated with their performance.

After the short a cappella prologue announcing the multiplicity of black gay male possibilities, the first item on the Pomo agenda is to zap Blaine and Antoine, the snap queens/movie critics of television's Emmy Award–winning black comedy series *In Living Color*, perhaps the most widely circulating images of black gay men in U.S. popular culture of the early 1990s. A member of ACT-BLACK, a revolutionary organization of Pomo Afro Homos, storms the set of "Men on Mens" and threatens to out the two supposedly straight TV actors who have dropped the pretense of reviewing films and now "just look at mens" (fig. 25). ACT-BLACK demands "an end to mainstream misappropriation of Negro Faggotry" and sends the snap-happy pair into a fit of despair. Caught off guard, Blaine and Antoine respond, "Look, Eldridge, we did politics in college. . . .

Hated it!" But they find themselves in no position to deny ACT-BLACK's complaint. The activist—as a supposed member of the Pomo Afro Homos, the militant black gay–visibility group—mouths the concerns of Pomo Afro Homos, the black gay male performance trio. Black gay men, these Pomos show, will no longer allow the uninformed pilferage of black gay codes by heterosexual performers for the amusement of their equally ignorant heterosexual audiences. The fine art of the snap is specific to the context of black gay lives, and anyone who fails to recognize this context will be "read" accordingly.[28] The Pomos stage their own performance mission in this short comic scene; like the ACT-BLACK activist, their fellow Pomo Afro Homo, the performing Pomos will hold those accountable who either perpetuate black gay invisibility or participate in the cultural neglect of black gays.[29]

Once Blaine and Antoine are zapped offstage, the Pomos are able to present a series of alternative images that offer more insight into the actual experiences of black gay men. Ten vastly different scenes follow, each varying in tone, style, and point of view. Moreover, the Pomos are not afraid to stage the problematic and disturbing issues that many audience members would perhaps rather not see. "I Don't Want to Hear It!" the scene that immediately follows "Men on Mens," dramatically changes tone and stands to remind its viewers that the Pomos aren't simply onstage to replace Blaine and Antoine for the sake of audience amusement. To upset such expectations, *Fierce Love* next presents a serious and discomfiting point of view of a nongay-identified man who has sex with other men. In "I Don't Want to Hear It!" Brian Freeman plays a working-class black who rides the audience for its assumption that he is gay:

> Gay? What is that, huh? Do I look like somebody's gay to you?
> Yeah, I like to catch a little taste of the other side now and then. That don't make me nobody's punk.

This scene could easily have been delivered as a critique of internalized homophobia and a bitter rebuttal to men who, while married and straight-appearing, continue to have sex with other men. Freeman's performance, however, simultaneously poses both a serious critique and an empathetic response to this man's situation. What, if anything, we are asked to consider, can the Castro gay community offer this working-class black man? Will the support from the predominantly white gay community match the understanding he receives from the African American community? These questions, while relevant, might miss yet another point central to Freeman's performance: at no point are we actually asked to suspend our disbelief of the performance. The theatricality of Freeman's performance is foregrounded and, therefore, the performance reasserts the idea that *Fierce Love* is not about the coherence of a single black gay

26. Pomo Afro Homos performing as the "Just Us Club" in
Fierce Love, San Francisco.
© Jill Posener

experience but rather is about the proliferation of black gay identities. The performative nature of identity along with the multiplicity of black gay experience is marked by the actor in performance. At one point, the character Freeman performs confides his disgust for black gay men. Such black-on-black hate is sent up later in *Fierce Love* when we meet Peaches, Popcorn, and Pepper, three "effeminate black gay men" who, after years of suffering abuses as PBUs ("poor, black, and ugly"), form in defiance the Just Us Club (fig. 26). Freeman, who earlier performed the character in "I Don't Want to Hear It," is now performing the black gay inverse of the previous character, inflecting the prior performance of internalized homophobia and differentiation with the current performance of flamboyance and effeminacy.

The Just Us Club, with its elaborate rituals and entitlements, shows how PBUs counter the elitist tendencies of many gay men of color—"that's all them Bryant Gumbel lookin' boys," explains Pepper—who frown on black queens not necessarily interested in, or economically privileged to, middle-class ideals. Rejected by whites for being black, the PBUs find little support from other black gays. Once again, the Pomos offer wicked humor that cuts both ways. At first, Pepper, Popcorn, and Peaches seem ridiculous in their affectations and nasty "dishing"; the three performers play this scene for laughs, but the humor quickly turns when the members of the Just Us Club lay down the law and refuse to be the last invitees to the party. Since no one else will have them, they'll join forces to survive their neglected position in the underclass. In an act of solidarity, the PBUs tighten their bonds—"tighter than Oprah's weave"—and form a club all their own. In other words, we are warned, don't go calling the Just Us Club for advice or a late-night date—these girls are busy. By the end of the story, the Pomos have restored the dignity of the Just Us Club to the extent that when Pepper, Popcorn, and Peaches reclaim vogueing for all the "nellie sissies" and dance themselves off the stage, the *audience* is left with that empty feeling of exclusion.

In each of these scenes, and throughout *Fierce Love*, the Pomos continually subvert the expectations of their audiences. Spectators are at once invited to share in the exploration of black gay life and then reminded that those who are not black and gay are more likely misunderstanding much of the performance. This insistence on positioning the audience "simultaneously inside and outside the comprehension of their performance" works to code *Fierce Love* in such a way that it always remains clear that these are stories by and about, and especially but not exclusively for, black gay men.[30] "Just because the show is written for a specific community doesn't mean that other people are excluded. If they don't get certain jokes, they can ask," Brian Freeman explains in the *Advocate*.[31]

While the Pomos perform *Fierce Love* for all audiences, spectators who do not share the experience of being black and gay are asked to think through their identification with and self-positioning around the performance. One scene, "Sad Young Man," especially points to this process. In "Sad Young Man," a young black man tells of his experience growing up gay in a "Model Negro Family" in Roxbury, Massachusetts. Finding comfort in the records of Johnny Mathis and the words of the Rev. Dr. Martin Luther King, Jr., the young man grows to celebrate his identity despite the lack of support from both black heterosexuals and white gays. Freeman, who performs this monologue, punctuates his narrative with direct confrontations to the audience. "It's a black thing; you wouldn't understand," he matter-of-factly states.[32] Audience members who are not black and gay are brought into the story by the moving pseudo-autobiographical narrative of growing up gay in a black household, but Freeman has much more in mind than simply soliciting pity for his subject. "Sad Young Man," like Paul's narrative in *Six Degrees of Separation*, pulls liberal heartstrings but goes further in holding its audience complicit in such well-meaning politics. Nonblacks have much to learn about black culture and need to abolish their tokenistic practices of inclusion. Heterosexual blacks, on the other hand, have much to learn about homosexuality. The "Model Negro Family"—advocating civil rights for blacks—will need to come to terms with its many gay sons and daughters and fight for their rights as well. Freeman pulls the spectator into the narrative in effect to implicate spectatorial complicity in racism and homophobia. Black gays and lesbians, who presumably "get it," remain the ideal audience in this scene. Other gays and lesbians of color, who also must confront these paradigmatic structures of oppression, are led to consider the specificity of their own experiences. And yet, as this scene suggests, there remains a certain ambivalence regarding the place of nonwhite and nonblack gays within this black/white and gay/straight polarization throughout *Fierce Love*. While the stories in *Fierce Love* are specific to the experiences of black gay men, it remains unclear what position the performers have regarding affinities with other nonblack gays and lesbians of color. There are no specific moments in the performance that directly address either black lesbians or nonblack gays and lesbians of color. Instead, the Pomos seem to indicate that the spectatorial process—for all audiences—involves a certain self-positioning. *Fierce Love* forces viewers to locate their own positionality with the material staged. Not all black gay men, for instance, will choose to identify with—or be included within—the representations available in the performance.

Another scene that foregrounds audience positionality is more risky in that it focuses on sex. In Eric Gupton's solo scene, "Good Hands," the performer delivers a powerful erotic fantasy of two black men getting off in the back room of a predominantly white gay club. But first Gupton observes the many forms of racism directed at him by a parade of white men, all of whom signal to him that he should "take his black ass home." But then—this is after all a fantasy—a beautiful black man walks into the back room and the two black men proceed to get busy. Gupton's slow and sexy delivery first details the man's body and then provides a scene-by-scene account of their erotic play. The stranger's "good hands" bring them both to orgasm, at once eroticizing sex between two men of color and the safe sexual play they practice. Gupton catches his breath and prepares us for the monologue's final *coup de théâtre*. The stranger explains to him what is equally true for many audiences of *Fierce Love:*

> You know, the white boys get real nervous when they see the two of us in the same room together, some of the brothers do too, but I like you.

The stranger then offers a hot and safe-sex scenario that ends the scene. The stranger in the back room is nothing less than yet another Pomo Afro Homo—defined, at least in this scene, as a black gay man who cares about his brothers, eroticizes men of color, and recognizes the necessity of AIDS awareness and practice. Like "Hot, Horny, and Healthy"—AIDS activist Phil Wilson's safe-sex workshops for gay men of color (which were popular in the late 1980s and early 1990s)—Gupton's "Good Hands" educates audiences in safer sexual practices and eroticizes sex between men of color.

Of all the scenes of *Fierce Love*, "Good Hands" usually solicits the most participatory response from the audience. Shouts like "Go ahead, Eric!" or "Save me some of that loving!" move the monologue from the limits of the stage to the lively exchange between performer and spectator, blurring the boundaries between the two. Such a shared sexual fantasy points to the power of the theatre to inform its audiences of both the pleasures and the dangers coinciding in the age of AIDS. That most of these shouts come from gay men of color only reinforces the power of self-representation so seldom available in the theatre. After all, the triumph in this scene comes from Eric's encounter with a man of color in a predominantly racist environment.

Oddly, many whites sometimes respond by applauding the gay men of color in the audience who are engaging in the performance. In this regard, the spectacle on the stage is expanded to include gay men of color in the audience who are participating in the shared fantasy. The risk here, as in *Six Degrees*, is that the realities of gay men of color may be experienced by some whites as anecdotal fodder. Liberal white spectators, in this sense, get two shows for their money: an entertaining performance onstage and an equally entertaining sideshow from the gay men of color in the audience. And yet this risk of appropriation is worth taking since the gay men of color—regardless of the potential for white voyeurism—have shared in a powerful transaction of support. Eric, the performing pomo, has bonded with a sexy pomo-afro-homo in the back room of a gay club, and gay men of color in the audience have bonded with Eric, a sexy pomo-afro-homo, in the spotlight of a darkened stage.

In a later scene, Djola Bernard Branner presents the other side of the AIDS reality. "Silently into the Night" recounts the frightening ordeal of a black man coping with the death of his friend Aman. The by now familiar devastation of AIDS is bypassed to focus on the maddening funeral service taken over by the homophobic relatives who arrive to discredit the dead. The preacher—"Six foot one and every inch as Christian as Aman was queer. If you knew Aman you know that was some serious faith"—annihilates the gay friends with his gay-bashing rhetoric. Aman's friends learn that ritual mourning takes many forms; they leave the family service defeated. Recognizing that Aman's relatives seemed more upset about his gayness than his death, the friends organize another memorial service, one that honors Aman's life and celebrates the community of gays and lesbians who knew and loved him.

Fierce Love ends with a utopian vision brought on by a disillusioned black queer nationalist and the good advice of James Baldwin. In "Toward a Black Queer Rhythm Nation," a young black gay activist humorously journeys through urban gay life in search of a cause. Feeling oppressed by Queer Nation, he finds himself at "old clone night" at the Stud. At the bar, he hears the musical refrain of the opening prologue to *Fierce Love*'s "We Are." The voices signal the arrival of another black gay man—"we'd seen each other before but never spoke"—who hears the same voices calling. Together, they leave and head off to the Box, a dance club popular among San Francisco's queers of color. But on this night it has "snowed"; the club, the white boys, the DJ, and the music are all "tired." Once again they hear the melody of "We Are" and notice the only other black gay man on the dance floor. Suddenly, their world is transformed from the tired predictability of the "monochromatic crowd" into a glorious fantasy sequence of black gay visibility:

> BERNARD: I looked up at the DJ booth and saw Sylvester push that white girl out of the way.
> ERIC: Willi Smith and Patrick Kelly were up onstage, modeling the fiercest drag I'd ever seen.
> KID: And James Baldwin was behind the bar, pouring free drinks for himself and everybody else. . . . James says, "My dear young boy, you are a Black Queer growing up in America. I think you've hit the jackpot! Work it, my dear. Work it!"

Inspired by the lives of black gay men who have died of AIDS and Baldwin's insight, the three men leave the club together not for a *ménage à trois* but for a "totally transgressive" act—sharing their various experiences through conversation.

Much of the power of this scene is in its evocation of a black gay male history signaled by Sylvester, Kelly, Smith, and Baldwin. That three of these men died of AIDS at the height of their careers further suggests that the younger generation, represented by Kid, holds the responsibility for remembering their names and contributions. For black gay men in the audience (and others) not familiar with Willi Smith's pioneering achievements in men's fashion, the Pomos insist that they learn.[33] The Pomos recirculate the names of the dead to remind the living of the legacy of black gay male achievement. By putting the lives of black gay men in a context—in particular, the effects of AIDS—the Pomos offer their black gay spectators an unprecedented opportunity in the theatre to respond to the magical refrain of the "We Are" prologue and join them in the process of performing all their lives. The fantasy of returning the dead to speak to the living is usurped only by the final powerful image of black gay men who are alive today speaking amongst themselves. Such fierce love is what the Pomos are all about.

While *Fierce Love* was nearly unanimously praised in reviews in gay and lesbian publications, alternative newspapers, and the straight establishment press—many of whom eagerly dub the show a "must see"—it was virtually ignored by the black press. Moreover, the Pomo Afro Homos were turned down by the 1991 National Black Theatre Festival in North Carolina, further limiting the larger African American community's opportunities to view their show. "I think the struggle for us in the next decade is coming out at home," Brian Freeman admits.[34] Before any change in black gay invisibility is to be realized at "home," black heterosexuals need to hear the difficult questions that the Pomos ask in their performances.

The challenge is still there for white gay audiences as well. There is always the possibility that white gays and lesbians and well-meaning straight audiences will fall into the "Ouisa syndrome"—recasting the experiences of black gay men in order to placate their own liberal political views. Like Ouisa in *Six Degrees*, audiences might respond in the old imperialistic enterprise of cultural tourism or inclusionist tokenism. Spectators are well advised to forego Ouisa's self-obsessing indulgence, where the encounter with difference is perceived as an "experience": a spectacle consumed at the expense of the black gay man. Such a racialized sexual discourse, commodifying and reinterpreting black gay sexuality, is at the heart of Guare's play and, more pertinently, of much of the discourse around AIDS and people of color. In *Six Degrees*, the phantasmatic circulation of this racialized sexual discourse that passed from Guare to Ouisa to Lincoln Center audiences rendered Paul's case nothing more than an anecdote of the lived experiences of David Hampton. In AIDS discourse around issues of people of color, as the Magic Johnson incident revealed, blackness and homosexuality are set against each other, obliterating the experiences of those living at the intersection of the two. Gay men of color who have died of AIDS, who are living with AIDS, and who are struggling to survive amid AIDS have long engaged in a fight against this reality. When the Pomos claim that "we are an endangered species but our stories must be told," they are not simply asking to be included within a multicultural paradigm of canonicity. Instead, the Pomos are using the theatre as a means to initiate communication and debate; "we need to be able to argue with the white gay community, amongst ourselves and with the larger society," insists Freeman.[35] In *Fierce Love*, the Pomos perform the multiplicity of black gay experience through parody and humor and not heavy-handed polemics. They foreground the theatricality of identity through the proliferation of contradictory characters, vignettes, and tones. Black gay identity is therefore never stabilized through the individualizing performatives characteristic to autobiography or confession. With *Fierce Love*, the Pomos contest the coherency of the identity-based term "black gay man" even as they demonstrate its necessity.

Events throughout the 1990s demonstrated how direct artistic interventions against prevalent racist and homophobic myths found themselves recontextualized to serve the agenda of the growing fundamentalist right. In the early months of 1992, for example, Marlon Riggs became a target of the New Right extremists when his award-winning film *Tongues Untied* was used in an anti-National Endowment for the Arts ad produced by columnist Pat Buchanan in his campaign for the U.S. presidency. In an editorial in the *New York Times*, Riggs blames the Buchanan campaign for scapegoating and maligning gays and lesbians of color. In the mudslinging match between Buchanan and Bush, Riggs writes, "gay and lesbian Americans, particularly those of color, have again become the mud."[36] Given such a cultural climate, critics championing works by gay and lesbian artists of color need to reconsider the ways in which these works are discussed. In this sense, I join Kobena Mercer, who has called for a critical discourse that historicizes the social forces that produce racial and sexual rhetorics of marginality.[37] For it is both within—and against—these forces that the work of the Pomo Afro Homos reaches its deepest historical significance.

I want to end this study of the Pomo Afro Homos and their production of *Fierce Love* with a brief discussion of their second full-evening show, *Dark Fruit*. I introduce these comments to demonstrate all the more forcefully the kind of cultural work the Pomos practice through performance. I also want to point out how both pieces need to be historicized. *Fierce Love* premiered in early 1991, Magic Johnson announced his HIV-status later that year in November, and *Dark Fruit* premiered as a work-in-progress one month later.[38] The Magic Johnson incident, it needs to be noted, occurs between these two pieces. Productions of *Fierce Love* and *Dark Fruit* were performed from 1991 to 1995. *Fierce Love*, as this chapter argues, intervened in the cultural politics of the early 1990s, which governed our understanding of race, sexuality, and AIDS. With *Fierce Love* the Pomo Afro Homos made visible the multiplicity of black gay identities and contested the notion of any totalizing experience of being black and gay. *Dark Fruit* continues this mission, although it confronts more immediately the rising rates of AIDS fatalities among black gay men. The performance, which is similar in format to *Fierce Love*, begins with the scene "Aunties in America: Epiphanies 'n' Roaches!" a parody of contemporary theatre's representation of black gay men, and concludes with "Chocolate City USA," an angry challenge to the systemic forces that sustain AIDS in the black gay community. This frame puts forward the direct link the Pomos forge between theatre and AIDS and the simultaneous (and related) intervention the Pomos perform in our understanding of both of these specific (and related) cultural formations. *Dark Fruit* begins as the three Pomos simulate a meeting of three black characters of the mainstream stage: Jacob from *La Cage Aux Folles*, Belize from *Angels in America*, and Paul from *Six Degrees of Separation*. The scene begins with Belize performing his role while Jacob and Paul watch on. Each character complains of the constraints placed upon him by the production and links his role with a history of black stereotypes in American drama. The opening scene puts pressure on spectators to place the Pomos' performance, in this skit and in those that will follow, in the context of contemporary theatre. In this sense, *Dark Fruit* begins where *Fierce Love* ends—in the contested space of performance. Performance is therefore both the site of contestation and the very means of intervention. The scene calls attention to the representations of black gay men on the popular stage and the limited roles available for black actors in the commercial theatre. "But what we gonna do? Quit?" asks Belize.[39] The scene ends with the three performers yanking off their minstrel headrags in defiance, setting the tone for the rest of the performance of *Dark Fruit*.

At the conclusion of the performance, after having performed various characters and roles, the Pomo Afro Homos take to the stage and, for the first time, appear to be performing themselves. They take turn reading letters addressing AIDS and black gay men that they have written and directed to various influential forces ranging from AIDS service providers to black churches, and to gay political leaders such as Larry Kramer and black cultural icons such as Magic Johnson. Each of these letters admonishes the cultural disregard for black gay men that these institutions and individuals practice. The sequence concludes with a reading of Dave Frechette's poem "Non, Je Ne Regrette Rien," first published in *Brother to Brother*. Frechette, an African American gay male who died of AIDS complications, is introduced by the Pomos in an effort to publicize what Kobena Mercer describes as the "field of desires that have inspired the creativity of black lesbian and gay community-building practices"[40] and in order to memorialize Frechette by bringing forth and reviving his words. The immediate confrontational performance of the readings of these texts, inspired by

Magic Johnson's HIV disclosure and the media events this news engendered, concludes with the Pomos reading in their "natural voices" the following demands:

> Dear America,
> We need equal access to drugs and treatments
> We need the love and support of our own community
> We need *our* voice to be heard
> But—
> What we don't need—
> What we really don't need—is another motherfucking hero!
> Sing girl
> [*Tina Turner's* "We Don't Need Another Hero" *plays. Letters go everywhere in a cascade. The basketball pounds the floor like a hammer. Fade to black.*][41]

This scene, which concludes *Dark Fruit*, is the only moment when the Pomos seem to speak for all black gay men, a decisive rejection of the careful anti-essentializing project that characterizes and describes the skits composing their two full-evening productions. It is also the most pronounced moment, when the performers seem to step out of "character." Unmediated by the veil of theatricality, the Pomos stage the drama of AIDS for black gay men in the performative provocation of realness. This shift in tactics is, to its own degree, a postmodern political maneuver.

The invocation of realness, that is, of performing the seemingly authentic self, when viewed within the context of the larger social sphere from which the Pomo Afro Homos must operate, suggests that the performative intervention will always be negotiated under and around the constraints of the larger political forces at play in history. In this particular moment, in the wake of Magic Johnson's disclosure of HIV, the Pomos indulge the impulse of identity politics, not so much to promote it as their preferred political stance, but rather to remind other black gay men and whomever else is in their audience that the voice of difference is theirs alone to establish. In this final image of *Dark Fruit*, the Pomos stage essentialism and the unified black gay voice as a performative option which is always available and sometimes even politically efficacious for black gay men. Such a seeming contradiction of the performance politics of their earlier work only emphasizes the complications gay men of color must maneuver when they set out to intervene in the always shifting cultural politics of race, sexuality, and AIDS. Part of the force of this last moment in *Dark Fruit* derives from the fact that, by this moment in their career, the Pomos had achieved national success and widespread name recognition within the world of performance. While the Pomos were able to intervene in the construction of black gay identity on a national level, other performers working on AIDS, race, and performance have focused on the specific issues of their local context.

The next chapter, while exploring the intersection of AIDS, race, and performance, shifts the ground of analysis from the national context of the Pomos to the local one of community-based theater in Los Angeles. More specifically, it discusses how Latino AIDS activists have used performance to articulate their distinct experiences of the epidemic in Los Angeles, the city with the largest Spanish-speaking population in the United States. The chapter surveys some of the specific challenges AIDS poses to Chicanos and Latinos and discusses some of the community-based activism that has emerged to address these issues. Performance, as we shall see, has been historically a means for Latinos to engage social and political concerns. As a result, performance has consistently proven to be a successful organizing tactic for their community survival. Latino AIDS activists and performers build upon this impressive tradition, fighting all the while the various misperceptions of AIDS and biases against homosexuality held by their communities.

6

Teatro Viva!

Latino Performance and the
Politics of AIDS in Los Angeles

T HE PATRIARCH OF a dysfunctional Latino family living in the barrio is scan-
dalized that his son has brought home the neighborhood's two crossdressers. "My son's a homo!" he cries, waving a pistol. The crossdressers retali-
ate by biting the man's arm and announcing that they both have SIDA (AIDS).
The father, horrified at the thought of contagion, shoots. This scene appears as
a segment of "Doña Flora's Family," one of the eleven skits in *S.O.S.*, written,
directed, and performed by Culture Clash, an immensely popular Latino comedy theatre troupe.[1] Such a pathological, melodramatic, indeed ridiculous scene
provides an entrance to a chapter that will begin to locate the discourses by and
about Latino gay men in contemporary U.S. theatre. My aim here is to provide
a critical methodology that at once contextualizes various contemporary Latino
performances that discuss AIDS and chronicles the important and often neglected work of Latino gay men in the theatre.[2] The chapter focuses on Latino
performances from the early 1990s in Los Angeles.[3] In the years between 1990
and 1992, Latinos enlivened the already diverse Los Angeles theatre and performance scene.[4] And while Latinos have always participated in the region's
theatre history, it was only in these years that AIDS was addressed in Latino
and Chicano theatre.[5] These performances suggest not only the ways that AIDS
was understood among Latinos in this period, but they also demonstrate the
ways that Latinos themselves intervened in, and actively shaped, that understanding.

S.O.S. premiered in the summer of 1992 at the Japanese American Cultural
and Community Center (JACCC) in the heart of Little Tokyo in downtown Los
Angeles as part of the Celebrate California Series, which promotes "multicultural diversity through the arts."[6] Tickets for the three-day run, including an
added matinee at the 800-seat capacity theatre, immediately sold out. Upon ar-
riving at JACCC, it became clear that Culture Clash's appearance was much
more than a night at the theatre for most of the Latinos in attendance. Parents

brought along their children. Long-standing community leaders were present alongside Chicano youth involved in street activist politics. For all appearances, it seemed a family affair; an in-house Latino assemblage but with an open invitation addressed to all people disturbed by the recent events in Los Angeles.[7] After all, we were gathering in Little Tokyo, not East Los Angeles. The idea of Culture Clash at JACCC seemed to be the type of gesture necessary to continue the "healing" of Los Angeles; a bicultural occasion when two communities—the Asian American and the Latino—could begin to understand each other a little better, in this case through the theatre. In the statement printed in the performance program, Culture Clash foregrounds the political nature of their work: "How can we ignore the quincentennial, the Rodney King case, AIDS, the NEA censorship and the election of yet another Republican? Time for an 'S.O.S.,' a signal of distress."

Culture Clash further called attention to the political potential of the event by offering their Saturday night performance as a fundraiser for the Latino activist organization PODER, the Pro-Active Organization Dedicated to the Empowerment of Raza. "Comedy for these urgent times," the *S.O.S.* publicity promo promised, and "necessary funds for the needs of the Latino community of Los Angeles," according to PODER activists who spoke to us before the performance. Given the multitude of problems facing many Latinos in Los Angeles—deportation, economic exploitation, gang warfare, inadequate health care—such an evening held the possibility of offering at least some relief for those able to afford the ten-dollar tickets. In "S.O.S. Rap," an early and particularly effective scene, one of the performers catalogues a litany of these social ills, repeatedly returning to the hard refrain, "todo tiene que cambiar" (everything must change). In *S.O.S.*, as in all of their work, Culture Clash sets out to denaturalize Anglo superiority and reclaim Latino culture and history from the perspective of *la raza*. Their primary method to achieve this goal is through humor, parody, and social satire.

Throughout *S.O.S.*, Culture Clash proceeded to critique many of the institutions and hegemonic processes that oppress Chicanos and Latinos, but as the scene in "Doña Flora's Family" demonstrates, they fell short of imagining Latino gays and lesbians as part of the social utopia posited in their performance. Imagined gays were attacked in one scene, raped in another ("American Me Tail"[8]), and lesbians, as usual, were not to be found. AIDS was presented as a threat posed by gays and women to unsettle the family and *la raza*. In another scene, "Angel's Flight," one of the performers positioned underneath a tapestry of "La Virgin de Guadalupe" explains to the men in the audience that they must use condoms to protect themselves from AIDS. But as the iconography of the scene too obviously suggests, men invoke the Madonna to protect them from the whore. Women in Chicano culture, as Cherríe Moraga has argued, are continually placed within this rigid Madonna/whore binary system.[9] In a gesture that immediately recalled Panamanian artist and activist Rubén Blades's appearance in the 1987 PBS video *AIDS: Changing the Rules* where Blades, talking directly to straight men, put a condom on a banana, the performer in "Angel's Flight" places a condom on an ear of corn. Douglas Crimp's complaint against the condom and the banana scene of 1987 still rings true in this context: "evidently condoms have now become too closely associated with gay men for straight men to talk straight about them."[10] In their efforts to preserve *la raza* from the oppression of centuries of Anglo domination, Culture Clash imagines in *S.O.S.* a Chicano social usurpation. Their new LA, however, fails to address the social networks—including the theatre—that oppress many Latinos outside the subject position of the straight Chicano male. If the performance, by nature of its stage venue at JACCC, is to some degree an attempt to form coalitions with other people of color, the ideal spectator is still assumed to be a heterosexual male.

In many ways, Culture Clash's performances can be best understood as participating in a long history of Chicano and Latino theatre practices and conventions originating in the United States as early as the 1840s. According to Latino theatre historian Nicolás Kanellos, this theatrical tradition has demonstrated "the ability [of Latinos] to create art even under the most trying of circumstances, social and cultural cohesiveness and national pride in the face of racial and class pressures, [and] cultural continuity and adaptability in a foreign land."[11] Culture Clash comes out of a theatrical trajectory that recalls both the energy of the Mexican *carpa* (traveling circus) of the 1890s and the political activism of El Teatro Campesino in the 1960s.

Much of the work of Culture Clash bears the influence of Luis Valdez, founder of El Teatro Campesino, who believed that the theatre should play a vital role in the awakening of the Chicano social consciousness. Like Valdez, Culture Clash insists that the theatre must remain oppositional to the exploitative practices of the dominant Anglo culture. And like El Teatro Campesino, Culture Clash posits a type of cultural nationalism with all of its inherent contradictions and problems. If, on the one hand, cultural nationalism fosters a sense of cultural pride, it also conflates all Chicano experience into a unified Chicano subject. In short, by failing to account for the differences among Latinos, Culture Clash inadvertently performs the very limits of the identity politics it invokes.[12]

Chicana feminist cultural-critic Yvonne Yarbro-Bejarano has written on the female subject in Chicano theatre and the ways by which the representational systems of Chicano theatre privilege heterosexual men. Yarbro-Bejarano argues that it is precisely the operations of cultural nationalism in Chicano theatre that have led to the uncritical "reinscription of the heterosexual hierachization of male/female relationships."[13] Yarbro-Bejarano's work on demystifying the conventions of Chicano theatre not only exposes the sexist ideology normalized in the materials of production, but also serves as a critical model to interrogate its homophobic tendencies as well.

Starting in the late 1970s, Chicanas in the theatre began organizing and networking, resulting in all-women *teatros* and a series of plays that explored women's issues. Moreover, after years of struggle, Chicanas have gained entry in traditionally male-centered venues and collectives. Chicana lesbian playwright Cherríe Moraga, for example, presents the strongest critique of patriarchal and heterosexist attitudes.[14] Her plays, as Yarbro-Bejarano argues, demonstrate how female sexuality is constructed and contained within the mythical model of La Malinche, Cortés's supposed mistress and translator. La Malinche serves as a "signifier of betrayal, through which the historical experience of domination is spoken in the language of sexuality."[15] The insistence of the *chingón/chingada* dynamic (fucker/fucked; active/passive) remains perhaps the most prevalent sociosexual system in Chicano and Latino culture. Emerging from the experience of colonization, the *chingón/chingada* dynamic locks women into subordinate roles, inscribes inflexible definitions of masculinity and femininity, and on a larger scale, becomes the surveillance test of true nationalism. Whoever is penetrated, in other words, is immediately interpreted by dominant Latino culture as passive. Passivity, within this system, is understood to mean open to sexual betrayal and therefore a threat to the nation.

The scenes in *S.O.S.* where anal rape is staged as male humiliation and punishment (for example, in "American Me Tail") or where homosexuality is introduced only to be annihilated (in "Doña Flora's Family") point as much to this kind of cultural nationalism where the assertion of male power mitigates male anxiety regarding the loss of power in a culture of domination as they do to the homophobic and sexist enterprise that constructs passivity as threatening and degrading. Rather than deconstructing the *chingón/chingada* polarization, Culture Clash participates in the continual reinscription of a binary sociosexual system that insists on fixed gender roles and rigid, socially constructed meanings for sex acts. Chicano power, as staged by Culture Clash in *S.O.S.*, remains in the hands of impenetrable men who exercise their privilege in continual displays of phallic domination; a sociomasturbatory flaunting meant to eroticize these representations of power in an unending exhibition of seduction.

Despite the fact that Chicana and Latina feminists have gone to great lengths to critique the representations of women in the theatre, many plays produced in the early 1990s continued to offer problematic if not degrading depictions of women. (The women actors who appeared in Culture Clash's three productions up to this point—*The Mission, Bowl of Beings,* and *S.O.S.*—never speak.[16]) And yet the fact that more plays by Latinas were beginning to be included in national theatre festivals and that feminist concerns were beginning to be voiced in conventional theatre forums offers a good indication of their success.[17] While women in various areas of the theatre slowly gained some degree of recognition, Latino gay male playwrights continued to be denied a place on the stage. One early exception, as Yarbro-Bejarano notes, was Edgar Poma's play about a Chicano gay man coming out to his family. Poma's *Reunion,* produced in 1981, "broke a fifteen-year silence on homosexuality within the Chicano theatre movement."[18] Yarbro-Bejarano's explanation of the play's reception is worth quoting in full:

> [*Reunion*] was performed to large community audiences at the Cultural Center in the heart of San Francisco's Mission District. Performances were followed by lengthy, lively discussions. The exclusion of a performance of this play during the TENAZ [National Teatros de Aztlán] Eleventh Festival in the fall of 1981 revealed the depth of resistance to considering the Chicano theatre movement an appropriate vehicle for the exploration of questions of sexuality. This attitude was further demonstrated during the Festival by the virtual boycott of a workshop on *Reunion* and the heated arguments by Latin-Americans and Chicanos alike against a resolution condemning sexism and homophobia during the general assembly. Dialogue has recently been reopened within the Chicano community by a production of *Reunion* in June 1986 in Tucson, Arizona, by Teatro Chicano, a member group of TENAZ headed by a woman, Silviana Wood.[19]

The problems encountered with productions of *Reunion* are typical of the resistance to gay issues in contemporary Chicano and Latino cultural discourse. Performances that foreground the perspective of gay men—as was the case with women previously—have been viewed historically as incongruent with the larger political movement. Gay issues, as in most communities of color, are often understood by the reigning heterosexist ideology of cultural nationalism to be symptomatic of white domination. For Latinos, since Catholicism rules as the religion of the majority and the church remains an infallible institution, homosexuality is knowable only as unnatural and therefore unacceptable. The combined rhetoric of cultural nationalism and Catholic dogma eradicates any identity based on homosexuality.

Even among progressive straight activists and cultural theorists who work out of the Chicano movement, homosexuality is not an issue comfortably discussed. In the recent ground-breaking anthology *Criticism in the Borderlands:*

Studies in Chicano Literature, Culture, and Ideology, for example, the editors, Hector Calderón and José David Saldívar—two of the leading Chicano critics in the United States—announce that their project "should offer an important cultural perspective absent to an international scholarly community."[20] Essays address a broad sampling of issues, but not one of the fifteen essays is authored by a self-identified gay or lesbian. Moreover, the few essays that discuss gay and lesbian writers fail to address the ways in which sexuality informs both their work and its reception.[21] This process of neglect inevitably produces a normalized conception of heterosexuality—or heterosexism—that is never critically challenged; homosexuality remains taboo.

Current counter-hegemonic critical interventions such as *Criticism in the Borderlands,* which set forth the agenda for the issues open to discussion for cultural theorists generally fail to provide a forum for gay and lesbian concerns. AIDS, moreover, is never mentioned in the essays, a serious omission, given that Latinos—and heterosexual Latinos in particular—constitute one of the largest growing groups of people affected by HIV and AIDS. By the end of 1991, for example, Latinos accounted for a total of 10,276—or 28 percent—of the cumulative AIDS cases in New York City alone. Thirty-three percent of the cumulative NYC AIDS cases among women were Latinas; 27 percent of cases among men were Latino. Intravenous drug use continues to be the leading mode of HIV transmission: Latino men at 54 percent, Latinas at 60 percent.[22] Nationally, according to the Centers for Disease Control, Latinos accounted for 16.5 percent of people diagnosed with AIDS. While the majority of Latinos with AIDS in the early 1990s were gay or bisexual men, women and intravenous drug users represented an increasing proportion of AIDS cases.[23] AIDS, like *Latino* and *Hispanic,* the very terms progressive critics interrogate, is a cultural construct. As Douglas Crimp argues,

> AIDS does not exist apart from the practices that conceptualize it, represent it, and respond to it. We know AIDS only in and through those practices. This assertion does not contest the existence of viruses, antibodies, infections, or transmission routes. Least of all does it contest the reality of illness, suffering, and death. What it *does* contest is the notion that there is an underlying reality of AIDS, upon which are constructed the representations, or the culture, or the politics of AIDS. If we recognize that AIDS exists only in and through these constructions, then hopefully we can also recognize the imperative to know them, analyze them, and wrest control of them.[24]

For Latinos, this imperative to know, analyze, and wrest control of the constructions of AIDS is of primary importance. In the early 1990s, "Hispanics" were the second-fastest growing AIDS population in the United States (African Americans were the first). Rates of HIV infection, seroconversion, and fatality among Latinos will continue to accelerate unless the Latino community directly addresses and intervenes in this crisis.[25] "Maintaining the silence is to cede terrain," write Ana Maria Alonso and Maria Teresa Koreck, "is to let dominant discourses define the politics of ethnicity, disease, sexuality, and morality."[26] Rather than maintaining the silence, Latino critical theorists and cultural workers can intervene in this process.

In the introduction to their anthology, Hector Calderón and José David Saldívar write: "*Criticism in the Borderlands* is an invitation, we hope, for readers—(Pan-)Americanists, cultural studies critics, feminists, historians, and anti-racists—to remap the borderlands of theory and theorists."[27] But if, as Calderón and Saldívar argue, studies of U.S. culture that fail to consider the centuries of Mexican-mestizo presence "will of necessity be incomplete,"[28] they will need to recognize that Latino cultural studies that fail to incorporate a critical analysis of sexuality or the effects of AIDS in Chicano and/or Latino cultures will be not merely "incomplete" but, as Eve Sedgwick succinctly states, "damaged."[29]

There is no question in my mind that the work of Culture Clash and the individual and collective work of the cultural theorists in *Criticism in the Borderlands* are necessary, indeed welcome, interventions in an Anglo culture of domination and exploitation. However, these same sites of intervention—theatre and theory—must also be interrogated in such a way that denaturalizes the assumptions and destabilizes the privileges set forth in each. Progressive cultural theorists and activists need to recognize and counter the racist and homophobic practices that oppress all Latinos. If the diverse and heterogeneous Latino populations in the United States are to successfully fight AIDS in their communities, then *todo*—not just Anglo domination—"tiene que cambiar."

The groundwork for an interrogation of AIDS in the Latino population was laid in February 1988, when various Latinos—gay, bisexual, and straight; health care providers, activists, and educators—met in Los Angeles for a National Strategy Symposium on Latinos and AIDS. This symposium, the first ever of its kind, was held in order to discuss and actualize a national AIDS policy and programmatic agenda specific to the needs of Latinos. As Lourdes Arguelles writes in the preface to the published proceedings of the conference, the HIV/AIDS epidemic in communities of color in the United States remained largely misunderstood, even by as late as 1987:

These misunderstandings, coupled with well-known historical factors having to do with the relative political powerlessness of the various communities in question, were leading to policy and programming decisions which were less than optimal in controlling the epidemic and in servicing those people of color infected.[30]

AIDS challenges Latino communities already burdened with an excess of morbidity and mortality, with inadequate resources such as access to education and health care, who suffer language oppression and a discriminatory U.S. legal system of deportation, and who all the while maintain stigmatizing views of sexual acts. The conference in L.A. set out to implement methods to counter these burdens but it also set out to empower community-based Latino AIDS projects, which for the most part, had not received adequate funding.

But perhaps the most significant accomplishment of the conference was the increased visibility and communal commitment of Latinos fighting AIDS—nationally and locally. Up until this time, most of the existing programs aimed at educating and informing the Latino community have had their sources outside the Latino community or have been headed by persons unfamiliar with Latino culture; its bicultural process; and the social, spiritual, and economic realities of the Latino community. The result has been inappropriate and inadequate educational materials and programs; inattentive, if not racist, disregard for indigenous or alternative health-care beliefs and practices; and the exclusion of Latinos and other people of color, including women, from clinical drug trials. The leadership demonstrated at the 1988 conference was as effective at forming an AIDS coalition among Latinos as ACT UP (AIDS Coalition to Unleash Power) had proven in 1987. The proliferation of AIDS organizations specific to communities of color, such as the Minority AIDS Project, Milagros, and Cara a Cara, to name only a few, have helped enormously in the fight against AIDS despite the continual struggle to maintain adequate funding for their programs and services. While many of these organizations work with clients who are gay or bisexual, services specific to gay men of color remain seriously underfunded given the grave statistics of AIDS cases among gay men of color. Moreover, in Latino communities, gay or bisexual men must confront a relentlessly homophobic ideology. As Latina AIDS activist Alice Villalobos explained in 1990:

> one of the most difficult and heartbreaking aspects of [Latino gay or bisexual men with HIV or AIDS] is that they are usually forced to live within the homophobic Latino/a community because of poverty and oppression. Not only are they rejected by their own people, but they also have to deal with a white, Anglo culture that categorizes them as second-class citizens merely because of the color of their skin.[31]

Villalobos writes as a member of ACT UP/Los Angeles in a newsletter that at the time was informing and educating primarily non-Latinos about the issues facing Latino gay men with AIDS in Los Angeles County. Los Angeles County includes the largest Latino population in the United States. Non-Latino AIDS activists and straight Latinos must both be educated continually about the specific experiences of gay or bisexual Latinos. Latino gay men fighting AIDS must find support from two very different and often opposing communities. "White AIDS agencies aren't sensitized about monolingual, non-documented seropositives who fear being deported," explains Juan Ledesma, former director of the East L.A. AIDS Hotline and now with AIDS Health Care Foundation. Arturo Olivias, former executive director of Cara a Cara Latino AIDS Project adds, "My community doesn't acknowledge that there's such a thing as a Latino man who has sex with men."[32] Latino AIDS activists have realized that the fight against AIDS is interrelated with a continuing struggle against racism, classism, sexism, and homophobia, the very issues that have enabled AIDS to infiltrate communities of color so extensively in the first place.

In Los Angeles, local Latino gay and lesbian artists and activists have attempted through performance to counter the pervasive ideologies that facilitate the spread of AIDS among Latinos. In part, this effort is due to VIVA!, a gay and lesbian arts organization founded in 1988 that serves both as a support network for local Latino artists and a coalition advocating for Latino gay, lesbian and AIDS visibility in other venues. Doug Sadownick reports, for example, that when Highways Performance Space in Santa Monica first opened in 1988, the inaugural events staged—a Cinco de Mayo marathon put on by the Border Arts Workshop—were assailed by VIVA! for failing to discuss gay and lesbian issues. One month later, VIVA! was angered again when Highways sponsored a lesbian and gay performance festival that lacked Latino representation. After VIVA! brought attention to the issue, Latinos were added to the schedule.[33] Like other gays and lesbians of color, politicized Latinos find that in order to ensure that their concerns be addressed they must consciously work within and around various hegemonic systems.

Latino gays and lesbians in theatre perform their art and activism from the multiple positions that inform their Latino gay/lesbian identities. Their performances enact the "oppositional consciousness" that Chicana lesbian Chela Sandoval has theorized as a tactic utilized by marginalized people to resist hegemonic inscription:

> The differential mode of oppositional consciousness depends upon the ability to read the current situation of power and of self-consciously choosing and adopting the ideological form best suited to push against its configurations, a survival skill well known to oppressed peoples.[34]

Sandoval argues against a political identity reduced to a single or fixed perception by dominant culture and the identity politics engendered by such configurations. Rather, oppositional consciousness accommodates a tactical privileging of one component of identity without disturbing the notion of identity as a dynamic process. While Sandoval writes specifically within the context of U.S. Third World feminism, oppositional consciousness, as she explains, "is also a form of consciousness in resistance well utilized among subordinated subjects under various conditions of domination and subordination."[35] As I hope to make clear, Latino gay performers can be best understood in light of Sandoval's theory. Moreover, as Sandoval's theory begins to suggest, one of the benefits of the differential mode of oppositional consciousness is the possibility of forging links with others experiencing social marginality. With Sandoval's theory in mind, I will argue how in one localized (albeit enormous) social space—Los Angeles—counter-hegemonic coalitions based on a model of affinity politics are materializing through performance. I draw my examples from the performances of Latino gay and lesbian artists working in Los Angeles, in particular, Luis Alfaro's solo and collaborative works. These Latino performers offer a much needed voice in the work of what Antonio Gramsci has called the "historical bloc of organic intellectuals," the counter-hegemonic practices of subordinate groups working as a coalition or "bloc" against existing power relations. In this sense, these performers participate in a cultural and artistic process that George Lipsitz has outlined in his insightful reading of popular music in East Los Angeles. Lipsitz is interested in tracing the ways that Chicano artists produce music that is "accessible from both inside and outside the community" and in placing this work within its sociopolitical context. If, as Lipsitz argues, the music of Chicanos "reflects a quite conscious cultural politics that seeks inclusion in the American mainstream by transforming it," Latino gay performers must also work against the grain of the Latino heterosexist mainstream in order to dismantle it as well.[36] Latino gay performers often must maneuver between Latino conventions on the one hand, and dominant white gay traditions on the other. In terms of the theatre, their work may involve an interreferential allusion to the already parodic and satirical models of Culture Clash, thus furthering and enhancing the intertextual dialogues within Latino theatre, or may suggest an affinity with politicized white gay male performers in Southern California, such as Tim Miller or Michael Kearns, all the while expressing the oppositional consciousness first articulated by U.S. Third World feminists.

Such a varied and deliberate tactic goes one step further than the bifocality that Lipsitz argues for popular music in East Los Angeles. Lipsitz reads the cultural performances of Chicano musicians through anthropologist Michael M. J. Fischer's concept of bifocality or reciprocity of perspectives. Bifocality, Lipsitz writes, is a process of self-respect: "prevented from defining themselves because of pervasive discrimination and prejudice, but unwilling to leave the work of

HIGHWAYS PERFORMANCE SPACE PRESENTS

DOWNTOWN

AN EVENING OF POETRY IN PERFORMANCE

27. *Downtown* promotional postcard for the 1990 production at Highways Performance Space, Santa Monica.
Luis Alfaro and Tom Dennison, courtesy of Luis Alfaro

definition to others, [Chicano musicians] adopted a bifocal perspective that acknowledged but did not accept the majority culture's image of Chicanos."[37] Sandoval's theory of oppositional consciousness provides the basis for the explication of how Latino gay performers must adjust through a *multi*focality in order to resist the stereotypes imposed by dominant heterosexist ideologies. This multifocal perspective is keenly attuned to the multiple sites of their discrimination stemming from their ethnicity, sexuality, class background, HIV status, or gender.

Luis Alfaro's performance work is a case in point. In his solo piece, *Downtown*, Alfaro—a Chicano playwright, performer, and community activist—performs various characters who live in the Pico-Union district, the heavily populated and impoverished Latino neighborhood in downtown Los Angeles, where he grew up (fig. 27).[38] *Downtown* is a nonlinear montage of multicharacter monologue, movement, autobiography, and sound. In *Downtown*, Alfaro investigates the rhythms of his neighborhood reconfiguring Los Angeles from his working-class Latino background and his gay identity. Alfaro scrutinizes Los Angeles by laying bare the glorification of the city and the glamorization of its people fabricated by Hollywood and offered for mass consumption by the entertainment industry. He provides snapshots of his neighborhood and family—from skyscrapers and alleys, undocumented workers and the 18th Street Gang, to local junkies and his tias Ofelia, Tita, and Romie—that suggest the formation of his politicized identity. But rather than offering a historical chronicle of his own political trajectory, Alfaro stages these stories as unrelated vignettes linked only as indelible memories of a vast urban and psychic landscape.

No comfortable claims are made for and about a Latino gay male identity in *Downtown*; instead Alfaro stages the multiple and often contradictory configurations that construct the possibility for the oppositional consciousness that emerges from a self-conscious and self-articulated Latino gay male perspective. Like Culture Clash, Alfaro draws from Latino culture, but he diffuses the centrality of his ethnicity by cultivating a deliberately gay perspective. From his marginality he offers a cultural politics that foregrounds ethnicity or sexuality depending on his point of emphasis at any given moment in time. As a result of this oppositional consciousness, Alfaro destabilizes the privileged status that his ethnicity or sexuality may hold as the constitutive force of his identity.

Downtown begins with Alfaro situated against a scrim onto which drive-by film shots of downtown Los Angeles street corners are projected; Petula Clark's classic pop hymn "Downtown" provides the soundtrack. The interplay between Petula Clark's escapist view of urban life and the harsh black and white images of downtown LA sets the tone for Alfaro's bittersweet relationship to the city. Alfaro first positions himself as part of this landscape by joining the nameless pedestrians projected upon the scrim. He then breaks the illusion by stepping out of the image to speak of the experience. Alfaro at once invokes the crisis of modernity—Walter Benjamin's reading of Baudelaire being "jostled by the crowd"—and the oral tradition of the epic poet composing and reciting the myths of an era. Such lofty posturing—flaneur and bard—is given a camp poignancy and a postmodern twist with Petula Clark's resounding "you can forget all your troubles, forget all your cares, so go downtown" refrain. Alfaro's man about town—Latino, gay, and poor—can't escape the omnipresence of the pop culture that infuses the neighborhood. In his performance, Alfaro will manipulate such realities by appropriation, commenting all the while on both the process of creating art and on the equally trying challenge of fashioning an identity.

With the ominous and always scrutinizing sounds and lights of a police helicopter hovering over the neighborhood in the background, Alfaro begins his first monologue, "On a Street Corner," with reminiscences of formative occasions from his childhood. He offers headlines:

A woman got slugged.
A man got slapped.
A clown threw toys.
A drunk staggered.
An earthquake shook.[39]

which are then further abbreviated to simple gestures first spoken and then performed on his own body: "A Slap. A Slug. A Shove. A Kick. A Kiss." Initially sounding like non sequiturs, these gestures will be recontextualized throughout the performance and serve as the leitmotifs of the piece, physical reminders of the battles Latinos face daily. While the LAPD surveillance helicopters patrol the neighborhood, a plastic rotating Virgin Mary doll from Tijuana surveys the Alfaro household—"she would turn and bless all sides of the room." The Virgin Mary doll becomes a symbol of kinship, a token from the homeland that comforts and distracts from the urban hardships of downtown LA, the reminder of the family mantra ingrained in the young boy's consciousness: "You see, blood is thicker than water, family is greater than friends, and the Virgin Mary watches over all of us." At one point, ten-year-old Luis offers the doll to his ailing Tia Ofelia, who has breast cancer, in order to drive away *La Bruja Maldita*, who was "slowly eating at her insides." When the boy innocently asks to see her chest, Tia Ofelia slaps him so hard on the face that even he could feel *La Bruja Maldita* eating away at his heart. Soon after his tia dies and is buried, the Crips firebomb the 18th Street Gang, living underneath her old apartment. Rummaging through the charred remains of the apartment building, he finds what's left of the rotating Virgin Mary, now useless and empty of its meaning.

Alfaro tells the story of the Virgin Mary in order to call into question the cultural belief systems of his Latino and Catholic family. This scene offers a poignant and deeply affectionate send-up of the assumptions impoverished Latinos maintain in order to endure the hardships of everyday life—inadequate health care, gang warfare, and an LAPD that essentially quarantines their neighborhoods through its aggressive surveillance. Alfaro, while critical of this system of exploitation vis-à-vis the church and the state, cannot deny the power of its influence. He ends this section with the familiar iconography of the neighborhood, expanding the connotations of his background to accommodate his emerging sexual identification:

When I was eighteen, I met this guy with a rotating Virgin Mary. He bought it in Mexico, so, of course, I fell in love. His skin was white. He ate broccoli and spoke like actors on a TV series. It was my first love and like the *Bruja Maldita*, he pounded on my heart. He taught me many things; how to kiss like the French, lick an earlobe and dance in the dark. He was every "Brady Bunch"/"Partridge Family" episode rolled into one. He gave me his shirt and I told him about the fields in Delano, picking cherries one summer and my summer in Mexico. Once my grandmother sent me a crate of grapes. We took off our clothes, smashed them all over our bodies and ate them off each other. When he left, the *Bruja Maldita's* hand replaced his in my heart and she pounded on me. And she laughed like Mexican mothers at a clothes line. And I covered my tears with a smile that was like the veils at Immaculate Conception. But my sorrow was so strong that relatives nearby would say, "*Ay Mijo*, don't you see? Blood is thicker than water, family is greater than friends, and the Virgin Mary watches over all of us." (*Blackout*).

The conflicting interpretations of the signification of the iconography—for the Latino the Virgin Mary as a sign of kinship, for the white gay man a sign of kitsch; for the Latino the "Brady Bunch" as a sign of normalized family structures, for the white gay man a popular entertainment—set off the imbalance that will eventually bring back the pounding of the *Bruja Maldita* against the young man's heart. In "Virgin Mary" Alfaro demonstrates the forces that shape the construction of his Latino gay male identity. The performer, over a decade later, offers this construction to his audience in order to demonstrate the tensions that give shape to his desire—"A Slap. A Shrug. A Kiss." The scene ends without resolution, only with the melancholy recognition of his desire and its problematic reception in two conflicting social fields of power: the kinship systems of his Latino family and of an imagined gay community.[40]

In subsequent scenes, Alfaro includes fictionalized portraits of various characters from the neighborhood that extend beyond his immediate family. He inhabits the voices and movements of Latinos in the barrio, people he encounters on the street who give him a sense of himself and who inform the performance of the desperate economic conditions of the neighborhood. In these scenes, he foregrounds different aspects of the urban Latino experience and gives voice to the underrepresented thousands who populate LA's downtown. While these portraits contribute to the overall social milieu of *Downtown*, their main purpose is to convey to his audience his political consciousness. Alfaro imagines the emotional psyches of his characters and offers these poetic constructions to the audience as his points of connection with the people in his neighborhood; these are moments of both epiphany and affinity. In these moments, *Downtown* can be understood in light of Ramon Saldívar's theory of how Chicano narrative functions as an "aesthetically and ideologically memorial to and partial reconstitution of the forgotten history of a people's oppression and struggles."[41] In the section titled "Lupe," for example, Alfaro opens by describ-

28. Luis Alfaro performing "Lupe" in *Downtown*, 1990.
Courtesy of Luis Alfaro

ing his venture through the sweatshops where undocumented Latina women labor for less than minimum wage, working twelve-hour shifts on a six-day week. He spots Lupe, who has a face "brown like my father's" and who "paid a *coyote* $150 to smuggle her across the border." He shifts from his performance persona to the voice of Lupe. To mark the transition he puts on a dress (fig. 28). We meet Lupe as she's about to go out on the town on a Saturday night. Lupe's downtown—full of cumbias, *Bohemias*, and street corner lunatics—begins as a temporary refuge from the buzz of the sewing machines of the sweatshops.

With her boyfriend she finds romance, but the promise of downtown—"you can forget all your troubles, forget all your cares, so go downtown"—is haunted by the distant sound of the machines "singing to me to come down to the other side of downtown and punch in, punch in, punch in." With fingers bleeding, sirens sounding, and the helicopter always overhead, Lupe fights to hang on to the romance of the city and the bargain of the border. Alfaro ends this portrait with her resounding, albeit temporary, triumph: "Tonight they can all be on fire. Because tonight there is no job. Tonight there is no stitch. No needle, no fabric, no pattern, no nothing. Because tonight is Saturday night and my dress is too tight and my name is Lupe (*blackout*)."

The "Lupe" section concludes with Alfaro still in character. The identification process of the Latino gay man with the young undocumented worker suggests an intracultural affinity that recognizes both class oppression and gender specificity. Alfaro's performance of Lupe is staged neither as the omniscient privilege of the creative agent's insight which escapes the character, nor as "classic" drag, where the male temporarily puts on a dress in an imagined transgression which by the end only reinforces gender binarism.[42] Instead, Alfaro's performance of Lupe seems to reveal more about his own persona and his choices of affinity. Lupe is neither mocked nor parodied. Lupe's oppression and her defiance are presented as interrelated to his own. Such is the tactic of performative oppositional consciousness. In "Lupe" Alfaro plays against preconceived notions of drag as gay performance in order to highlight the experiences shared by Latinos in the barrio.[43] His performance can be interpreted as a political tactic which challenges the alienation of the oppressed by demonstrating the affinities between and among people living in the barrio. The performance moves beyond the autobiographical performance of an individual subject and enacts instead a collective cultural unity based on the recognition of a shared but distinct oppression. The multifocalities of the performer and the character—the specificity of class, gender, sexuality, and ethnicity—join in performance to build the coalition necessary to counter hegemonic configurations of oppression that insist on the conflation of differences.

In "Federal Building," Alfaro describes his involvement in the March 1, 1990, artist chain-gang protest regarding censorship and the crisis at the National Endowment for the Arts. Over seventy artists and their supporters marched from the County Museum of Art to the downtown Federal Building, where civil disobedience turned into performance pieces staged en route. Artists dressed as criminals carried huge images of banned artists and engaged spectators to read quotations about freedom of speech (fig. 29). Guerrilla theatre vignettes, bilingual performances, and press conferences contributed to the militant defense of artistic freedom that resulted in twenty-seven arrests.

29. Federal Building Protest, Los Angeles, 1990. Luis Alfaro, holding the D. H. Lawrence image, joins members of ACT UP/LA and over seventy artists protesting censorship of the arts and demanding more federal funding for AIDS.
© Dylan Tran

For Alfaro the Federal Building—"the big beautiful marble structure on Los Angeles Street"—is an emblem of his relationship with the city that dates back to his early years when his father would drive the family by the halls of justice "looking for distant Mexican relatives with phony passports ready for a life in Our Lady Queen of the Angels." Like the helicopter that opens and closes *Downtown*, the Federal Building is omnipresent: always visible and always threatening to reveal its power. Like the rotating Virgin Mary doll, the building is a symbol of surveillance:

> We have a long history together, this *ruca* and I. She has watched me grow up and play on her steps. Watched me low ride in front of her. Watched me spit at her face at an immigration demonstration that I don't understand but comprehend enough to know that my dad can go back any time, just never when he wants to.

The personal context of the building resurfaces for Alfaro when he returns to protest with artists and members of ACT UP/LA, shouting in both English and Spanish such chants as "Art is not a crime," "Alto a la censura," and "AIDS funding now." Unlike some of the other protesters, Alfaro has been here before. The downtown Federal building has always been for him a microcosmic icon of his relationship with the city; a place where the notion of home shifts to and from a sense of belonging or displacement. The specific circumstances articulated in the first half of the "Federal Building," where long-standing Latino issues such as immigration and deportation were introduced as evidence of nationalist muscle, now resurface as HIV issues with the discriminatory policies and procedures of the INS. And while the performer's ethnicity was the initial political identity foregrounded, by this point in "Federal Building" Alfaro's political tactic is to foreground his sexuality. By the end of this section, however, Alfaro demonstrates how both facets of his identity—sexuality and ethnicity—are enmeshed in his desire for, and denial by, the downtown Federal Building and the home that it has symbolically represented:

> I didn't get arrested because my government wants to control the content of art, or because a Republican congressman from Orange County thinks AIDS activists are a "dying breed." I got arrested because [former] Mayor Sam Yorty told me we were all the mayor. Because a black and white can stop you anywhere, any time, for whatever reason. Because big marble buildings stare down with a *chale* stare. Because I've never owned anything in my life—much less a city. (*blackout*)

In "Federal Building" Alfaro demonstrates how AIDS issues for people of color cannot be understood without an analysis of race and class. Although he joins the others in the spirit and mission of the protest, his personal investment in the Federal Building extends beyond the specifics of the moment and involves the complex contextual history of his relation to Los Angeles as a Latino gay man.[44] And yet, Alfaro's arrest *does* result from his protest against censorship and AIDS bigotry and not this personal backdrop. The arresting officer who "puts handcuffs on me while hundreds of people blow whistles and yell 'shame, shame, shame' " has no idea why Alfaro is there, only that he is "trespassing on government property." The personal agenda articulated in performance is unavailable to "the man in the helmet and plastic gloves." For the arresting officer Alfaro is only one more protester. But for the spectator, manipulated by the performative tactics of oppositional consciousness, Alfaro's political identity is more complex. The oppositional consciousness model that forms the basis of this performance—the continual dynamic shift in focus from Latino to gay, for example—at its most successful, challenges the spectator to recognize differences rather than collapsing them. The operative dynamic of oppositional consciousness in Alfaro's performance suggests the possible affinities between performer and audience while simultaneously forcing the spectator to consider the specificity of their own subject positions.

In "Federal Building" Alfaro demonstrates how his multifocal identity and politics of oppositional consciousness work in the best interests of coalition movements. The demonstrators all chant various causes and concerns—anti-censorship, AIDS, queer visibility and rights—in both English and Spanish. That Alfaro's performance in "Federal Building" is then about a performance, or more specifically an activist performance, suggests the deeply interdependent nature of his politics and his art. In reclaiming and recontextualizing downtown Los Angeles, Alfaro participates in the counter-hegemonic practice of both self-individualization and community formation. *Downtown* ends with Alfaro reciting (and enacting through gesture) a litany of epiphanic moments that encapsulate the characters introduced throughout the performance; each moment is prefaced by "one strong shove":

> One strong shove and the LAPD lets me know who is in charge . . .
> One strong shove and my fingers are bleeding . . .
> One strong shove and the sound of a helicopter or ambulance in the middle of the
>   night lets me know I'm alive.
> One strong shove and a helicopter light has found me in downtown.
> (*Alfaro gestures shoves in silence. Blackout.*)

Caught once again in the glare of surveillance, Alfaro disappears into the darkness of the stage. The theatre then becomes the site of refuge, a place where identity can be explored or contested, created and shared. The theatre remains, however, a site of contestation, a place where queer Latinos, who have historically been marginalized, can intervene in the ideological systems which render them invisible or disposable. His work is, as Jan Breslauer explains in describing Los Angeles performance art, "a theatre of liberation."[45]

As with many other plays and performances by gay men of color, AIDS issues in *Downtown* are thoroughly connected with the prevailing issues of class and race bias. AIDS is experienced as one component in a complex system of exploitation and oppression. Through performance Alfaro stages affinities across boundaries of racial and gender difference in order to foreground the "historical bloc" necessary to intervene in the hegemonic scripts of dominant culture. While the material within Alfaro's performances displays many of Chela Sandoval's ideas, the productions of his performance begin to materialize Sandoval's theory toward a cogent model for political praxis. Although *Downtown* is usually produced as a solo artist evening, Alfaro has performed the piece in various group shows, ranging from *True Lies*,[46] director David Schweizer's full-scale production of three separate solo performance pieces at the Los Angeles Theatre Center, to stripped-down versions at Chicano or gay and lesbian art festivals in the Los Angeles area. In these settings, Alfaro's work is often received as either the gay piece or the Latino piece, or in the case of the LATC production, the gay and Latino piece. From this perspective, Alfaro's performance risks the appropriation of mainstream production, where either the work may be interpreted as an exercise in multiculturalism and therefore carries the burden of representation, or where his presence may be singled out as the performance of difference and therefore normalizes the assumptions inherent in the other performances staged.[47] While such risks are real and have their own specific ramifications depending upon the production and the audience, the design of *Downtown* nonetheless allows Alfaro to contextualize difference *and* point toward a politics of affinity even in these settings.[48]

The same weekend that Culture Clash premiered *S.O.S.* in downtown Los Angeles, Alfaro joined two other Los Angeles–based Latino performers, Monica Palacios and Alberto "Beto" Araiza, to premiere their collaboration *Deep in the Crotch of My Latino Psyche* at the Fourth Annual Gay and Lesbian Performance Festival at Highways (fig. 30). Palacios, a self-described "Latin Lezbo Comic" with a solo show of the same name, is a veteran of both comedy clubs and alternative performance venues. Her work is specific to her experience as a Chicana lesbian, but she sets out to refute the rigid sexual scripts expected of all women in Latino culture.[49] Araiza—an actor, playwright, and director—has toured his solo show *Meat My Beat* throughout North America and Europe. *Meat My Beat* chronicles Araiza's travels through urban gay male culture and ad-

30. Piñata, Luis Alfaro, Beto Araiza, and Monica Palacios in *Deep in the Crotch of My Latino Psyche*, Highways Performance Space, Santa Monica, 1992.
Photo by Becky Villaseñor courtesy of Alfaro, Araiza, and Palacios

dresses his experiences of living with HIV. Together in *Deep in the Crotch of My Latino Psyche*, they begin to negotiate through performance a Latino gay and lesbian politics.

In scenarios that vary from stand-up, melodrama, satire, and personal testimony, the three performers critique the institutions of both Latino culture and mainstream gay communities. As "Latino homos without a home" in either world, they take to the stage to carve out a niche and claim their rights. They contest the idea of a monolithic Latino gay experience by underlining the vast differences among them, from their own performance styles to their HIV status. *Deep in the Crotch of My Latino Psyche* closely resembles *S.O.S.* in style; short skits that may involve all three performers, solos, or combinations of two. But unlike Culture Clash, these performers insist on rupturing the gender binarism of the *chingón/chingada* polarity and critiquing Latino homophobia and the silence around AIDS.

Deep in the Crotch of My Latino Psyche, as its title indicates, is a humorous and provocative exploration of Latino lesbian and gay sexuality. Their promotional slogan "Comedy, Drama, Pathos, and Piñatas!" further accentuates the humor. The performance, however, also seriously engages a number of political issues. Palacios, for example, contributes a solo, "Tom Boy Piece," which addresses her coming-out process. Araiza includes two sections on AIDS and HIV in the Latino community, "HIVato" and "Safos." Araiza's solo sections participate in the larger cultural project expanding the theatrical representations of people with HIV and AIDS to include Chicanos. Cultural critic Alberto Sandoval's concern with the paucity of staged AIDS work by Latinos resonates for Araiza, who explicitly positions himself as HIV-positive in performance. Araiza's two solo sections are quasi-autobiographical monologues about living with HIV in the barrio. Alfaro also focuses his monologues on the experience of survival; however, he addresses it from a different angle. He offers a number of solos, including a lyrical AIDS memorial, "Where Are My Heroes? Where Are My Saints?" which, in its meditation on his experience of being gay and Latino in the public sphere, references the loss of a community besieged by AIDS. This dialectic between loss and survival now informs what it means for him to be Latino, gay, and presumably uninfected. In "Isolation"—the most effective piece of the performance—the three actors, with only their upper torsos lit, sit on stools and face the audience as an ominous voice-over interrogates them at length about their personal lives. The performers must raise their hands in silence to answer the interviewer's questions, which range in tone and intensity from "Have you ever lied about your nationality?" and "Have you lost a lover to AIDS?" to "Do you prefer flour to corn tortillas?" and "Have you ever put on make-up while driving your car?"[50] By the end of this scene, composed of nearly fifty questions, spectators—whether Latino or non-Latino, gay or non-gay—cannot possibly consider Latino gay and lesbian sexuality within a comfortable categorization. Latino gay identities are presented as dynamic and contradictory. The material production of performance, stripped down here to its most basic, demystifies the performance process and facilitates the effective representation of both the silence around homosexuality in Latino culture and the real and living bodies of Latino queers. The interactions among these very different Latino performers in *Deep in the Crotch of My Latino Psyche* demonstrate Chela Sandoval's claim that "self-conscious agents of differential consciousness recognize one another as allies, country women and men of the same psychic terrain."[51]

Alfaro, Araiza, and Palacios, three of the driving forces behind VIVA!, have collaborated on various "behind the scenes" efforts to gain visibility for Latino gays and lesbians. *Deep in the Crotch of My Latino Psyche* is but one of the many tactics that demonstrate the inseparable nature of their art and activism. Perhaps their most impressive collaboration so far has been the AIDS Intervention

31. Refugio Guevera, Frank Castorena, and Ron Sandoval from Teatro VIVA!, a Latino
AIDS educational theatre project, Los Angeles, 1993.
Photo by Becky Villaseñor courtesy of VIVA

Theatre project Teatro VIVA!, an AIDS outreach program that provided bilingual prevention information in both traditional (community centers and theatres) and nontraditional sites (parks, bars, community fairs and bazaars, art
galleries, and private homes). Funded in the early 1990s with a $50,000 grant
from the United States Conference of Mayors, Teatro VIVA! presented short
skits on such HIV/AIDS issues as transmission, prevention, safer sex negotiation skills, popular misconceptions about AIDS, daily considerations of people
with HIV and AIDS, and local community resources. The main component of
the program was its bilingual mobile teatro presentations, performed in agitprop minimalist style, allowing for flexibility in response to the varying aspects
of each venue. These teatros, presented by three performers, Refugio Guevera,
Ron Sandoval, and Frank Castorena (also known to some as the Divas from
VIVA), were then followed by a question-and-answer period which allowed for
more detailed discussions about AIDS (fig. 31). Araiza, the project director for
the first grant, reported that over 5,000 individuals—including nearly 2,000 self-
identified gay and bisexual Latinos—viewed the Teatro VIVA! AIDS Outreach
Project. Forty presentations were given within Los Angeles County between

July 1991 and April 1992. The following is an example of a Teatro VIVA skit written by Guillermo Reyes:

MARIO: Good morning, this is AIDS radio.

PANICO: Radio SIDA.

MARIO: I'm Mario Simpatico.

PANICO: I'm Panico Alerto . . . don't touch that dial, it might be contagious.

MARIO: And I'm here to counter Panico's fears and self-loathing with rational and positive attitudes toward our sexuality.

PANICO: You're a celibate, what do you know?

MARIO: Moving on . . . here's Judy Calabasas with the morning intimacy report.

JUDY: Good morning, Panico. Good morning, Mario. Pretty busy out there on Motel 101. An early morning condom shortage alert has been issued and the California Patrol is rushing in with more supplies. Out on the West Hollywood fast lane, watch out for a huge spill of Nonoxynol 9, which has brought certain forms of intercourse to a standstill . . . all folks are urged to avoid substitute jellies without water-based lotions as condoms might tear and rupture. Watch out for stalled sexual urges out on uninformed communities where AIDS hysteria and self-defeating attitudes prevent proper information to be disseminated. If you're out driving on the road to Nirvana, be on the lookout for sexual compulsives known to stop motorists and throw safe-sex guidelines out the window. Keep guidelines near you at all times to guard off the lawlessness of compulsion. This report has been brought to you by the future . . . helping you get there safely.

PANICO: Thank you, Judy. This is Panico Alerto, spreading fear and disinformation.

MARIO: And this is Mario Simpatico, countering lies and disinformation with healthy attitudes toward sexuality. . . . [52]

Such interventions demonstrate that Latino gay men can begin to unsettle the muscle of cultural nationalism and homophobia that have combined with other social factors to render Latino gay men powerless. Latina lesbians have already proven their power by organizing first and foremost as Latina lesbians and by forming coalitions with other women who respect the issues specific to their survival. With the supportive and reciprocal alliances between Latina lesbians and Latino gay men available through VIVA! the possibilities for future political work seem endless.

The proven success of Teatro VIVA!, while localized in Los Angeles to help combat AIDS among Latino gay and bisexual men, hints that the political landscape is changing. Consider that Teatro VIVA! was refunded in 1993 by the County of Los Angeles AIDS Program Office through the gay men of color consortium, with Palacios and Alfaro serving as codirectors. Consider as well that at the time of this grant, 6,510 people were confirmed with AIDS in Los Angeles County. Nationally, by 1993, Latinos accounted for 29 percent, nearly one-third, of all cases reported to the Centers for Disease Control.[53]

Beginning in 1991, Teatro VIVA! set out to provide Los Angeles Latinos life-saving HIV-prevention information through the combined methods of AIDS educational performance and Chicano agitprop theatre, two historically distinct traditions. The theatre, of course, is only one of the many sites of contestation in the fight against AIDS and performance, only one of the many means possible to counter AIDS and its mystifications in dominant culture. But performance, as this book argues, holds the capacity to articulate resistance and generate social change. The work of Alfaro, Palacios, and Araiza—individually and in collaboration, in the theatre and on the streets—provides one model for Latinos and our supporters to engage at once in the tactics of oppositional consciousness and in the coalition building available through an affinity politics. The name Teatro VIVA! translates in the most pragmatic and descriptive sense as "VIVA's theatre," the theatre component of the Latino gay and lesbian arts organization VIVA! However, I employ "teatro viva" here in the literal sense of "theatre" and the imperative modality of the present subjunctive of the verb "to live" to convey, quite simply, an acclamation for theatre and life.

The concept of the local can, of course, be defined in multiform ways. In this chapter, I have addressed the local as an effect of a specific urban and ethnic community. In the next chapter, I locate the local not in geographic or ethnic terms but in personal and temporal ones. More specifically, I take a single performance of Tony Kushner's *Angels in America* (a performance which I attended) and speculate on the political interventions into AIDS made available to audiences of the play on the eve of the 1992 U.S. presidential elections.

7

November 1, 1992

AIDS/*Angels in America*

We must speak for hope as long as it doesn't
mean suppressing the nature of the danger.
—Raymond Williams, *Resources of Hope*[1]

November 1, 1992

It's Sunday, November 1, 1992, and I am in Los Angeles at the Mark Taper Forum for the opening marathon performances of *Millennium Approaches* and *Perestroika*, the two plays that comprise Tony Kushner's *Angels in America: A Gay Fantasia on National Themes*. I am with four friends. We are all quite thrilled. We are five gay men of the theatre at the theatre: Jim Pickett is a playwright, Matthew Silverstein is a director, Tim Miller is a solo performer, Michael Callen is a singer, and I am a professor. We are five gay men who have lived to be thirty-years old and beyond, an accomplishment we never lose sight of these days. We have anticipated today's marathon for some time now. It's an arrival of sorts, although we aren't sure precisely what it is that we will experience today. What we do know is this: we are about to partake in a full-day-and-evening marathon. *Angels in America* is a two-part work that held its world premiere in San Francisco at the Eureka Theatre in May 1991. At the Eureka, Part I, *Millennium Approaches*, was presented in a fully staged form, and Part II, the then incomplete draft of *Perestroika*, was presented in a staged reading as a work-in-progress. The Mark Taper production will be the first time *Perestroika* will be fully staged and the first time both parts of *Angels in America* will be seen together as a complete and fully staged work performed in marathon and in repertory. We have brought along water, fruit, candy, medications, and cigarettes. Some of these things we will be sharing, but not all of us smoke, nor do we all have AIDS. The plays have been previewing in repertory for the past weeks and the buzz is big and loud.

We arrive at the Taper in clusters. Matthew, Michael, and I are the first ones to arrive a little before noon. While we are waiting for the others, Michael shows us his foot, which is bloated and discolored; he's undergoing chemo treatment for his lesions. Michael has been living with AIDS for over a decade and, for all practical purposes, has had a concurrent career as a longtime survivor. He is one of the founders of the People with AIDS Coalition, has published books and essays on surviving AIDS, and has spoken about AIDS everywhere from daytime talk shows to the United States Congress. He is one of the people I most respect in the world. We wonder out loud how comfortable he will be sitting in the theatre for such a long time. We've been told that the plays can last over seven hours. We speculate on Clinton's chances of beating Bush out of the White House. The elections are on Tuesday. None of us feels we can endure four more years of a Republican administration's lousy record on AIDS and other pressing social issues. It's not clear who will win, but some of us have hope. Tim and Jim show up next. We all exchange hugs and kisses and display the goods that we have brought along for the marathon. It's a gorgeous day in Los Angeles.

Once inside the theatre and before the house lights dim completely, actor Kathleen Chalfant takes to the stage crossdressed as Rabbi Isidor Chemelwitz and begins the first scene of *Millennium Approaches*. Rabbi Chemelwitz is presiding over the funeral of Sarah Ironson. Sarah Ironson is, according to the rabbi, "not a person but a whole kind of person."[2] Like the old rabbi himself, she was a Jewish immigrant who "carried the old world on her back across the ocean" and who now, in October 1985, the month in which the play's action commences, is dead. "You can never make that crossing that she made, for such great Voyages in this world do not any more exist. . . . Pretty soon . . . all the old will be dead (10–11)," the rabbi prophesies. It's an exhilarating moment in the play. Chalfant's perfectly complex reading of the scene at once satirizes the grandiosity of the speech while at the same time dares us to imagine our own lives in such terms.

Angels in America opens with an exit, a ceremonial closure for Sarah Ironson. The rabbi, aware of his own mortality and perhaps because of this, insists upon performing a ritual to render her life-history official; he sets out to inform Sarah Ironson's clan of her remarkable journey, one that he mundanely demonstrates was typical. Now that she is dead, the rabbi must also offer a type of tribute to her life—despite his having minimal contact with her. ("She preferred silence," he offers; "So I do not know her and yet I know her" [10].) He introduces one of Kushner's central themes of the play, the idea of the journey, and contextualizes the dead woman's life within the concepts of history and community. The rabbi's invocation of Sarah's journey (and, by extension, his own) announces *Angels in America* as a play concerned with the problematic concept of an official history. Fearing his pending extinction, the rabbi admonishes his listeners to take note of the spectacular realities of their unrecorded lives.

Kushner's ambitious and remarkably successful play invites audiences, particularly gay male audiences, to identify throughout the play with these moments. Recall that *Angels in America* is subtitled a "*gay* fantasia on national themes." Kushner sets out to exploit this fact by offering gay men in the midst of plague an occasion to continue to interrogate what it means to be part of a community in these difficult times. His project, as rendered in the cultural practices of the theatre, demands that as gay men we persevere in locating and claiming our agency in the constructions of our histories. Kushner insists that we recognize that the procedures of our lives in response to AIDS not only matter (the matter of traditional AIDS plays) but that these procedures also hold insight and concern into the current U.S. political landscape—again, subtitled a "gay fantasia on *national* themes." *Angels in America* calls into question the concept of an official history. The play asks us to make distinctions between official and lived history, to notice what is documented and to bring forth into the public sphere what is not. In this sense, Kushner puts pressure on the naturalization process embedded in official history. Theatre histories, as I have argued in the introduction, also involve questions of official documentation.

The history of *Angels in America* especially calls attention to this process, particularly around the notion of theatrical origin. *Angels in America* was commissioned in 1987 by Oskar Eustis, who, at the time, was the artistic director of the Eureka Theatre in San Francisco. The first reading of *Angels in America* took place in November 1988 at the New York Theatre Workshop. When Eustis accepted a position as resident director at the Mark Taper Forum, Gordon Davidson, the Taper's artistic head, struck a deal with the Eureka Theater: "the Taper would develop the play on its own, but the Eureka would stage the world premiere."[3] At the Taper *Angels* broke into two parts. In the spring of 1990, a workshop production of *Millennium Approaches* was staged. One year later, *Angels in America* held its world premiere at the Eureka. Part I, *Millennium Approaches*, was presented in a fully staged form and accompanied by a staged reading of a draft of *Perestroika* as a work-in-progress. On November 1, 1992, the Taper was set to host the Los Angeles opening of *Millennium Approaches* and *Perestroika*, the first official performances of the complete, fully staged *Angels in America*. Even though *Perestroika* received its first fully staged production at the Mark Taper Forum, the Taper—because of contractual obligations to the Eureka Theatre—was not able to claim a world premiere for *Perestroika*. The idea of an opening and a premiere, as this brief production history suggests, is in some ways misleading. By the time the complete *Angels In America* was presented at the Taper, thousands of people had already experienced some version of either or both parts.

The opening of *Angels in America* scheduled for November 1, 1992, was actually postponed. For various reasons, the plays were withheld for review by critics for a week.[4] Thus the accounts of *Angels in America* in the popular press— in the *New York Times*, the *Los Angeles Times*, *Time*, and *Newsweek*, for example— were based upon the performances beginning on November 8, 1992, the week *after* the national elections. The performances of November 1, 1992—which were followed by a reception and party attended by the playwright, actors, director, and artistic staff of *Angels*; the management and staff of the Mark Taper; various other playwrights, actors, and artists; and the many friends of all these people— escaped the critical process of review. Despite the opening festivities, these performances on the eve of the elections were not entered into theatre history as official. One could argue, perhaps, that this postponement was yet another tactic to call attention to the demands of production, a Brechtian estrangement-effect extending beyond performance and production to include historical reception. Given Tony Kushner's admitted admiration for Brecht, such an assertion is not without its relevance. A postponement in the theatre, such as this one, cannot help underscoring the material conditions of theatre production. As such, the informal and unofficial opening of *Angels* on November 1, 1992, became then a rehearsal for the official press opening of November 8, 1992. So what then of November 1, 1992, other than its Brechtian *gestus*?

The eve of the national elections held profound promise for lesbians and gay men and all people involved in the fight against AIDS. As of October 31, 1992—the day before the originally scheduled opening of the Taper's production of *Angels in America*—245,621 cases of AIDS had been reported in the United States alone.[5] These people, needless to say, were all diagnosed with AIDS during the Reagan and Bush administrations. In the one week between November 1 and November 8—the week between the opening night and the official press opening of *Angels in America*—an estimate of nearly 1,000 people in the United States would be diagnosed with AIDS; "terror as usual," as Michael Taussig would have it.[6] Over 171,890 people had officially died of AIDS-related causes in the United States alone by the time of Bill Clinton's January 1993 presidential inauguration.[7] Such numbers, or rather the deaths of so many people with AIDS, underscored the high stakes of the election; electing Bill Clinton, if nothing else, would put into relief the utter despair of twelve years of government neglect.

AIDS, up through 1992, emerged and was determined by the regulatory schemas of the U.S. sociopolitical institutions whose effects, in Judith Butler's phrasing, "produce and vanquish bodies that matter."[8] Butler's insistence upon making intelligible the cultural forms that produce and vanquish bodies that matter speaks directly to the work of AIDS activists in the United States who relentlessly pursued the presidential candidates during the earliest days of the primaries—"AIDS is a primary issue!"—and who tirelessly pressed Clinton and Bush to address AIDS from a national platform. Fueled by the reprehensible politics of the 1992 Republican convention and inspired by Clinton's gestures toward lesbian and gay people, those of us engaged in the fight against AIDS saw the 1992 election as a potential turning point in U.S. cultural politics surrounding AIDS. Revising the cultural psyche around AIDS has always been one of the foundational missions of AIDS activists, from the earliest efforts of people with AIDS to redress the notion of "AIDS victim" to more current efforts to reposition AIDS centrally in the political sphere.[9] In these attempts to revise the cultural psyche, when people with AIDS and their supporters contest the regimes of power sustaining AIDS, hope emerges as a political means to bring about social change. In this context, to watch *Angels in America* on the eve of the 1992 presidential elections was to participate in a public ritual of hope.

On one level this hope materialized through our identification with Prior Walter's journey with AIDS, from his fear and despair in *Millennium Approaches* to his new-found power in *Perestroika*. And on the eve of the elections, the hope of *Perestroika*, rekindled in the play through love and kinship, announced a shift from the utopic to the possible. On another level, the expulsion of evil in *Perestroika*, thematized by the death of Roy Cohn and the ritual forgiveness and banishment initiated and performed by Belize, Cohn's nurse and Prior's best friend; along with Louis Ironson, Sarah's grandson and Prior's ex-lover; and the ghost of Ethel Rosenberg, Roy Cohn's most famous casualty, enacted a ritual for us in the audience as well. "A particular evil can be at once experienced and lived through," Raymond Williams explains in *Modern Tragedy*, an insight that informs the place of Cohn in the plays and of the Republican administrations in all our lives.[10] The recital of Kaddish by Belize, Louis, and the ghost of Ethel Rosenberg for Cohn's spirit signaled an end to an era that, while in the play occurs in early 1986, took on new symbolic meaning when performed on November 1, 1992. In the play, the scene of Roy Cohn's death and the Kaddish prayer that follows is pivotal; it moves the play from the despair and paralysis of Part I to the hope and agency of Part II. The scene brings the characters and their audiences to the recognition of evil, as embodied by Cohn, "as actual and indeed negotiable."[11]

That Roy Cohn, who as a key figure of the regulatory regime instrumental in producing the bodies that matter and vanquishing those which don't, would himself die an AIDS death is a Foucauldian irony, but also a tragic one too. "A

queen can forgive her vanquished foe," Belize instructs in *Perestroika*, a reminder
in the play of the AIDS activist claim that all people with AIDS are innocent.[12]
From Belize's perspective, Cohn, no matter how execrable, cannot be "blamed"
for his own illness. Such rituals of atonement and forgiveness can only be politically efficacious when accompanied by a recognition of the negotiable structures of evil. (This is not to say we disavow our anger: the scene of the Kaddish
prayer for Roy Cohn, while entrenched in feelings of love and forgiveness, ends
with Louis and Ethel Rosenberg both exclaiming, "You sonofabitch.") Political
agency, as Raymond Williams explains, emerges from a new system of feelings
and ideas motivated by a shift in the social structures of oppression. The potential for such change, emanating from the lived experiences of people in the public world, is what escaped the official theatre historiography of *Angels in America*. For many of us at the Mark Taper Forum on November 1, 1992—the eve of
the presidential election—a new system of feelings seemed possible.

History and Tragedy

The paradox of Roy Cohn as evil and innocent (in terms of AIDS) and the
ritual of banishment and forgiveness enacted by Belize, Louis, and Ethel Rosenberg begin to explain the sense of tragedy that structures *Angels in America*. For
Raymond Williams, the recognition of evil as something other than transcendent and absolute was necessary in order for a culture to begin to understand
the tragic experience of its time. In part, this recognition is achieved through
the contextualization of the historical process, what Williams celebrated in
Brecht's mature work, and would acknowledge the forces that both construct
and resist evil. "There is no evil which men have created which other men
have not struggled to end," Williams insists.[13] We see this struggle performed
in *Angels in America* by most of the characters in Part II. Such a struggle is set
up in the play as a dialectic not between the two characters with AIDS, Roy
Cohn and Prior, who are both white, but between Roy Cohn and Belize, Prior's
black gay friend and former lover and Roy Cohn's personal nurse (fig. 32). Cohn
and Belize, more dramatically than any other coupling in the play, embody the
most extreme positions around gay politics and identity. Despite our investments in following Prior's and Cohn's personal journeys with AIDS, it is
not helpful ultimately to read *Angels in America* as a type of binarism around
these two characters with AIDS; that is, to read the plays as a dialectical tension
between two competing ideologies based upon their individual responses to
AIDS. In other words, *Angels in America* is not a work about individual heroism.
Instead, these characters, along with the others in the play, demonstrate what
Raymond Williams would call a "new structure of feeling" based upon the col-

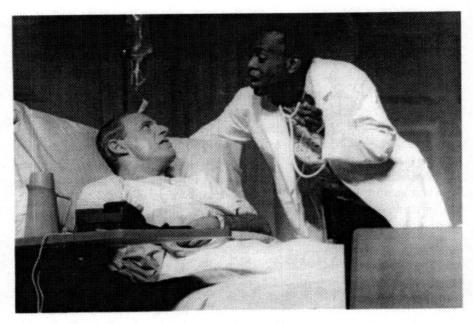

32. Ron Leibman as Roy Cohn and K. Todd Freeman as Belize in Tony Kushner's
Angels in America, Part 2: Perestroika, Mark Taper Forum, Los Angeles, 1992.
Photo by Jay Thompson courtesy of the Mark Taper Forum

lective experiences of people attempting to live through a specific historical era;
in our case, the age of AIDS.[14] Belize is the catalyst for this new ideology, and
his relationship with both Prior and Cohn its practice. Kushner's dramaturgy
is based upon this premise of a new structure of feeling which in turn, derives
from the philosophy of Walter Benjamin—the prior Walter to Kushner's Prior
Walter—who claims that the "state of emergency" in which we live is "not the
exception but the rule."[15]

With no cure or vaccine, and only minimal and often questionable treatments available—and this continually pounded into consciousness by the relentless pronouncements of medical experts and government agencies—the
devastating realities of AIDS proliferate and are sustained. In fact, rates of HIV
in communities of color, among women in particular; in populations of adoles-
cents, especially among gay and bisexual males of all races and ethnicities; and
in once HIV-negative gay men over thirty-five, largely in urban settings con-
tinue(d) to grow at rapid and uncontrolled rates. For people with HIV and
AIDS, Walter Benjamin's maxim on the "stage of emergency" makes explicit the
continual tease of possible innovative treatments and drugs around the corner,

across the border, and any day now. Such promises are exacerbated by the idea of progress, what Benjamin, in the "Ninth Thesis on the Philosophy of History," invokes through the metaphor of the angel of history. For Benjamin, progress is a misnomer for catastrophe.[16] Benjamin's angel of history, who "would like to stay, awaken the dead, and make whole what has been smashed" (257), spectacularly arrives to Prior in his bedroom at the end of *Millennium Approaches*. The dramatic arrival of the angel accents the investments of both Prior Walter and the audience in the teleology of angelology, one which quickly diminishes in *Perestroika* when it becomes clear that the angel can only witness the "pile of debris grow skyward" (258). Prior's angel, like Benjamin's angel, we learn in *Perestroika*, is unable to stop "the singular catastrophe which keeps piling wreckage upon wreckage" (257).

For Walter Benjamin the opportunity to "blast open the continuum of history" could materialize from an awareness of the present, what he calls the "time of the now" (263). *Millennium Approaches* ends with the angel of history appearing to Prior suspended in time and space. Dramaturgically the angel signals both the official processes of history which Benjamin rebukes *and* the theatricality which Kushner advocates.[17] Remember, however, that the angel is not the only apparition to appear to these characters. The prior Priors awaken from the dead to prepare Prior Walter for his journey and to foretell the arrival of the angel who will guide him. (Like the rabbi in the opening scene, Prior's ancestral namesakes also function as historiographers, informing him rather campily of his cultural heritage.) And while Prior suffers these dementia-like hallucinations, Roy Cohn—as the other person with AIDS in the play—experiences an arrival of an angel in America all his own. It is Ethel Rosenberg, after all, whose pronouncements in Part I cite Walter Benjamin's philosophy of historical materialism: "History is about to crack wide open. Millennium approaches" (112). Such a performative citation at once situates her against the angel who appears to Prior. In this sense, her utterance enacts a self-referential gloss for the play itself; it is Ethel Rosenberg, and not the angel, who names what Benjamin calls "a revolutionary chance in the fight for the oppressed past" (263) and situates Kushner's play as an articulation of this fight in light of AIDS. The dialectical relationship between an established "ideology of containment," articulated throughout *Angels in America*, and a continuous "ideology of a long revolution," already in place in *Millennium Approaches*, both shapes Kushner's drama and suggests the new structure of feelings emerging in the late 1980s and early 1990s.[18]

Tony Kushner, of course, is not the first to articulate such concerns or such a mission, nor does he position himself as such. AIDS activists have tirelessly fought to revise the cultural psyche around AIDS and often against the grain of popular sentiments even within the lesbian and gay movement. Nor is he the first to do so in the theatre. The driving force behind performances and plays about AIDS may be neither rage nor remembrance, as some critics argue, but the attempt to intervene in a dominant AIDS ideology as it takes shape and is sustained instead.[19] In *Angels in America* this intervention works dramaturgically on a number of fronts. We see this new structure of feeling emerge in the two plays themselves, primarily around concepts of kinship and community. But Kushner's plays open up the microstructures of the characters' interactions in order to comment on the macrostructures of social institutions, political philosophies, and competing historiographies. Both the micro- and the macrostructures, he insists, inform each other. Rather than positioning private and public systems of experience as discrete and unrelated, Kushner makes explicit how the two interact in order to sustain or challenge dominant ideologies.[20] This is announced most grandly in Kushner's naming of Part II, *Perestroika*. The citation of a key word of Gorbachev's reform plans for the former Soviet Union gestures both toward the new structures of feeling resulting in part from the end of the cold war and Gorbachev's new social agendas, which were explained in his 1987 international bestseller, *Perestroika*, and toward Kushner's own politics of dialectical materialism.[21] Despite such contexts, Kushner's title needs to be read as a metaphor for change that refers with some irony to its original deployment, rather than as model for U.S. cultural and political structures.

Thus the focus on national themes—justice, democracy, freedom—which are debated in a series of locations ranging from the halls of justice to the bedroom, coffeeshops to hospital rooms, and, most bizarrely, in Antarctica by Harper and Mr. Lies, her imaginary friend, is the concern of nearly all of the characters in the play. The pervasive refusal in the United States to see the political operations inevitable in private life is manifest in *Millennium Approaches* through the interactions between these characters who often fail to see, even as they speak of their failures, how politics informs their every action. Part I begins in the height of the Reagan years—1985—and charts the "trickle-down effects of self-interest as Kushner's characters ruthlessly pursue their sexual and public destinies."[22] Kushner insists on putting pressure upon this individualism and in the process indicts the ideology of Reaganism in all its forms. But rather than only naming names, *Angels in America* demonstrates the effects of an internalized oppression produced by the elements and feelings of the dominating center. Such a phenomenon, where one internalizes the very system of oppression that one is fighting against, is identifiable in many of the characters in *Millennium Approaches*—think of Louis's long exegesis on democracy in America but also Harper's private self-doubtings—and, by extension, of many gay people in America. The force of internalized homophobia, where lesbians and gay men, for various reasons, accept the terms of the regulatory regimes policing sexual desires and censor themselves accordingly, is also of concern in the play. Joe Pitt, the closeted Mormon law clerk who struggles with his sexual identity in Part I and who, Louis learns in Part II, has written some of the most vehement legal briefs against lesbians and gays, is representative of this type of internalized oppression. But it is Roy Cohn who is, of course, the apotheosis of the closeted man.[23] Such tensions are the state of affairs throughout *Millennium Approaches;* individualism breeds isolation, the structure of feelings of a dominating center prevails, and an angel and the ghost of Ethel Rosenberg prophetically appear to the characters with AIDS. *Perestroika,* Part II, sets out not only to restructure many of these social arrangements, but to offer hope in the new kinship alliances—ones that challenge if not refute the heteronormativity of prevailing social practices[24]—that conclude the play. As Una Chaudhuri explains, "*Perestroika* is, above all, a going beyond, a trying out, an experiment with the politics of possibility."[25]

Critics in the mainstream press reviewing the Los Angeles production—the post-election *Angels* opening of November 8, 1992—have focused their responses around the macrolevel commentary of Kushner's play, rightfully celebrating Kushner's ability to locate gay themes and AIDS issues within a national political sphere. Kushner's ability to historicize the system of feelings under Reaganism, his contextualization "in which the modern march of gay people out of the closet is likened to the courageous migrations of turn-of-the-century Jews to America, and of 19th-century Mormons across the plains,"[26] and his portrait of Roy Cohn's philosophy of power all position *Angels in America* against more seemingly provincial meditations of AIDS that foreground the actual feelings of people involved in the fight against AIDS: fear, anger, despair, rage. But it is precisely this system of feelings—as they are played out in the public arena vis-à-vis the "theatrical rage"[27] of people engaged in the fight against AIDS, and as they emanate from within as we live amid AIDS—that informs the political dimensions of the play and of our times. This representation of the interplay between the structures of feelings sanctioned by the dominating center and the acts of intervention which suggest new structures of feelings emerging from people engaged in the fight against AIDS lies at the heart of *Angels in America.* To focus on only one element of this historical process misses the point. In *Angels in America,* Kushner sets out to examine this system of feelings in order to expand the field. Among the sentiments he (re)circulates for our responses to AIDS is hope.

On the microlevel, hope springs from the restructuring of the various misalliances so apparent in Part I. In Part I, various competing kinship ideologies are given voice and seen in seeming disrepair. Conventional familial relations based on the regulatory practices of heterosexuality—husbands and wives, mothers and sons—and the alternative family structures of lesbian and gay people—lovers, mentors, and friends—are all performed as exercises in dysfunction. Louis gives voice to this state of disrepair. He is at the Hall of Justice in Brooklyn with Joe Pitt and wonders aloud, "What's it like to be the child of the Zeitgeist?"

> LOUIS (*looking away*):
> Nowadays. No connections. No responsibilities.
> All of us . . . falling through the cracks that separate what we owe to our
> selves and . . . and what we owe to love. (71)

The ideology of containment which breeds isolation trickles down into the very interactions of our lives. The personal relations of people in family, in community, and in society are fraught with political tensions unaccounted for and disavowed. "Children of the new morning, criminal minds," Louis names us. "Selfish and greedy and loveless and blind. Reagan's children." He continues, helplessly vulnerable and thoroughly implicated, "You're scared. So am I. Everybody is in the land of the free. God help us all" (74).

We see this fear and hear its articulation as characters confirm their insecurities, their anxieties, and their loneliness. Such feelings are most apparent in the split scenes between Louis and Prior and between Harper and Joe; these domestic failures are the misalliances characteristic of Shaw. Already in Part I, we see a move toward restructuring in the threshhold of revelation sequence (act 1, scene 7). Harper and Prior connect, if only for a moment of mutual support; the same can be said of Joe and Louis, whose sexual relationship is based upon mutual isolation. Other attempts at restructuring are also negotiated and staged in the split scene between Cohn and Joe and between Louis and the leatherman in Central Park. Cohn's desire to mentor Joe and Joe's admiration of Cohn are based upon the privileges of power and should be read as such. But it would be unfortunate to dismiss too quickly Cohn's concept of patriarchal bonding however misogynistic its practice: for Cohn, as an older closeted homosexual, mentoring is as much a form of kinship as it is a type of initiation into the fold. (The point to be made here is quite simply that Cohn is not very good at mentoring.)

All of these characters operate in isolation in Part I. Of all the relationships presented in Part I, only the friendship between Belize and Prior endures unequivocally:

> BELIZE: Whatever happens, baby, I will be here for you.
> PRIOR: Je t'aime.
> BELIZE: Je t'aime. (61)

In *Perestroika*, it is the love between these two men, manifest in friendship, that extends into a model for a new structure of feeling based on a reimagined notion of kinship and community.[28] Thus the significance of Belize as a gay man of color becomes more clear. Belize signifies (and citationally refers to) the contributions of people of color in the history of the modern lesbian and gay movement.[29] In this sense, he carries the burden of representation. On the one hand, it needs to be stated that of all the major characters, Belize seems to lack an interiority. We mainly see him in relation to the other characters, who are all white, never quite getting a sense of his inner life or outer journey. And yet, on the other hand, Belize is the political and ethical center of the plays. If he carries the burden of race, along with the burden of representing the political intervention in the system of feelings produced by the dominating center, Kushner's representation is not at all off the mark of the lived experience of lesbian and gay people of color in the lesbian and gay movement including—and particularly, in relation to—AIDS politics. Thus the emotional strength Belize and Prior offer to each other as support becomes the basis for a network of alliances that moves the play from the paralysis and misalliances in *Millennium Approaches* to the change and community of *Perestroika*. By the end of the play, in the tableau of the epilogue, this new kinship structure—one not based on heteronormative reproductive family structures—is displayed; it consists of Prior, Belize, Louis, and Hannah Pitt (fig. 33). Their journey, like our own through AIDS, involves loss, pain, and suffering. At critical points throughout their journeys, each of the characters has had to face up to his or her own complicity in dysfunctional personal, communal, and social alliances.[30] For Prior, this involves an extensive working through and subsequent rejection of the teleology of angelology and a restructuring of his relationship with Louis; for Belize, it involves a confirmation of the powers of love in the midst of racial hatred and oppression; for Hannah Pitt, it involves a deliberate divorce from the orthodoxy of heteronormativity; and for Louis, the journey transforms his positivist concept of history into a more direct responsibility toward the "time of the now." These are only some of the practices and feelings these characters bring forth into community. When they combine and interact with the familiar structures of feelings of fear, anger, despair, and rage, the processes of hope begin to emerge once again. Love and hope amid the tragic, *Perestroika* instructs, structure and maintain community. In *Perestroika*, it is a sense of community which provides the foundation for "more life." The reproductive dictums of heteronormativity are rejected for a queer politics invested in sustaining life.

    And yet as the past twelve years have demonstrated, hope can be cultivated and maintained by the regulatory regimes of power in order to placate people with AIDS and other AIDS activists. The dominating center's construction and circulation of hope is too closely related to a politics of deferral. Various socio-

33. Kathleen Chalfant as Hannah Pitt, Stephen Spinella as Prior Walter, K. Todd
Freeman As Belize, and Joe Mantello as Louis, in Tony Kushner's *Angels in America,
Part 2: Perestroika*, Mark Taper Forum, Los Angeles, 1992.
Photo by Jay Thompson courtesy of the Mark Taper Forum

political institutions which compose the network of a dominating center—especially during the Reagan and Bush years—cultivate hope insidiously in order to postpone responsibility and direct action; the transference of government responsibility to community-based service organizations, for example, positions hope and compassion in the domain of the private sector and fails to account for the systemic disenfranchisement of the various overlapping communities affected by AIDS.[31] "Scientific research, health care, and education are the *responsibility and purpose* of government and not of so-called 'private initiative,' an ideological term that excuses and perpetuates the state's irresponsibility," writes Douglas Crimp in his introduction to *AIDS: Cultural Analysis/Cultural Activism*.[32]

Such a system sanctions compassion under the condition of altruism and constructs this altruism exclusively within the private domain. Unfortunately, this model reinvigorates a binarism between those who care and those who need care. Those who need care are disciplined under this system to hope for care. Care under this altruism is constructed as emotional support at the expense of more direct accesses to health care. To position people with AIDS and their loved ones to hope for compassion limits the possibilities of agency and comes perilously close to reproducing the morphology of the "victim." This has been the traditional complaint AIDS activists involved in more overt forms of direct action have lodged against those who work in more conventional AIDS service organizations. The efforts of ACT UP, for example, especially in its formative years, made explicit this need to revise the cultural psyche around people with AIDS and AIDS volunteerism. While there was, and continues to be, a profound need for emotional and practical support for people with AIDS, ACT UP insisted that the cultural tendency to construct hope as a hope for compassion was not only not inadequate but also suspiciously positioned people with AIDS as the object of social tolerance. From *Millennium Approaches*:

> LOUIS: . . . What AIDS shows us is the limits of tolerance, that it's not enough to be tolerated, because when the shit hits the fan you find out how much tolerance is worth. Nothing. And underneath all the tolerance is intense, passionate hatred. (90)

And from *Perestroika*:

> PRIOR: I have always depended on the kindness of strangers.
> HANNAH PITT: Well, that's a stupid thing to do. (141)

The hope for new and more efficacious drug treatments at reasonable cost, inclusion of all people to clinical trials, more effective education and prevention methods, and a more aggressive assault against AIDS from the institutions of the dominating center was elided in the cultural production of the hope for compassion. Hope, as it circulated in the Reagan and Bush years under the realm of compassion and altruism, was simply not enough. Nor could hope be maintained without more direct interventions against AIDS. To rely on the kindness of strangers, as Hannah Pitt so glibly retorts, succumbs to a system of feeling where hope and compassion are produced arbitrarily and without consistency; they remain optional sentiments leisurely offered to people with AIDS in the spirit of tolerance, a symptomatic effect of a politics of containment where people with AIDS are defined as expendable others.

While the dominating center produces a system of feeling that constructs hope in relation to an arbitrary compassion based on variable degrees of tolerance, it also recirculates hope within the logic of what science historian Allan Brandt terms "the magic bullet." Brandt's discussion of the magic bullet, in his illuminating social history of venereal disease in the United States, calls into question the prevailing paradigm of the scientific and medical approach to disease:

> Perhaps more than any other single theme, twentieth-century medicine has been characterized by the search for "magic bullets"—specific treatments to root out and destroy infecting microorganisms. This biomedical model has come to define the role and nature of the medical enterprise. In this paradigm, individuals become infected with a parasite that causes dysfunction of some sort; disease is defined as a deviation from a biological norm. Social conditions, environmental phenomena, and other variables are generally discounted as causes of disease. The physician dispenses "magic bullets" that restore the patient to health.[33]

The cultural investment in the magic-bullet approach relies on an association between disease and individual behavior. Such a conflation occludes "social and external determinants" of disease and health; invariably, as Brandt explains, "behavior—bad behavior at that—is seen as the cause of disease" (202). The cultural production of hope for the magic bullet—as it relates to AIDS—is played out in multiple and contradictory ways. The magic-bullet approach (re)positions people with HIV and AIDS to see illness through the lens of moral rectitude; that is, as the result of behavior and not contact with a pathogen, thus to hope for a magic bullet is to hope not only for a medical cure but also and inevitably—under these conditions—to hope for a cure for social abnormality. This unfortunate circularity is sustained by the biomedical paradigm that has historically failed to unpack the social constructions of disease, but it also permeates the cultural psyche around AIDS as well: consider the popularity of Louise Hay, Marianne Williamson, and other psychoimmunologists among people with AIDS. Inevitably, the hope for the magic bullet feeds into a structure of feeling of despair; the teleology of scientific progress based upon the magic bullet sets up a narrative which is not a viable one. Since magic bullets never materialize, magic-bullet narratives enact a deferral not unlike the deferral that circulates compassion as arbitrary tolerance; each can only produce disappointment. Hope, under these conditions, is always invoked and inevitably diminished. The ultimate irony is that this very hope ends up producing despair.

And yet magic-bullet models of response to AIDS based upon the naive premise of a single medical or social intervention proliferate in contradiction in our society. They materialize in constructions of occasions of scientific research as *the* breakthrough knowledge; in notions of Clinton, operable throughout the elections, as the single agent of change; and even in fantasies of Tony Kushner as the savior of American theatre and Broadway. (Bruce Weber captures this phenomenon around *Angels in America* when he sums up the sentiments of many: "If this show doesn't make it, what will?"[34]) Admittedly, many of us at the Taper on November 1, 1992, invested to some degree in these magic-bullet narratives. Our friend Michael was very excited over a breakthrough shark-cartilage treatment that cleared his extensive pulmonary KS;[35] Clinton delivered a major speech on AIDS in New Jersey only a week before and was holding steady in the national polls; and Kushner's plays were receiving an unprecedented amount of media attention for a play subtitled, after all, *A Gay Fantasia on National Themes*. On November 1, 1992, we were five friends in the theatre participating in the production of hope.

Theatrical Occasions and the Production of Hope

"The theatrical occasion," Eric Bentley writes, "is a supreme instance of confusion."[36] For Bentley, the intimacy of the theatre sets up ambiguous relations between spectators, actors, and roles. "Who, at the theatre, is related how to whom?" (180) he wonders. The "brief romance" between spectators, actors, and roles generates a certain type of unregulated love that leaves Bentley asking, "Where in the auditorium does the amorous outpouring actually land?" (181). Such "promiscuous"—his word—experiences of desire and identification unsettle the comfortable securities of knowing who we are. (The history of theatre criticism is based on this ontological crisis and produces, in the process, the competing discourses of pleasure and anti-theatricality.[37]) These desires and identifications between and among spectators, actors, and roles produce the confusion inherent in the theatrical occasion. These "confusions" may produce hope (for companionship, for the love of the "leading lady") if only, at times, to transform hope into despair (feeling "crowded," learning that the actor is not her role).[38]

These scenarios of confusion, however, are not the only options. Various cultural theorists have posited a different perspective on performance that allows for a rearticulation of hope. Anthropologist Victor Turner, for example, extends performance to include the social dramas performed and witnessed in any given cultural instance. For Turner, hope is possible in the ritual processes of culture. The performance of resolution—the always temporary and fragile outcome of any social drama—allows members of a community to take stock of an event momentarily until the ritual process begins once again. Such a continuous play of conflict and resolution and conflict and resolution is less about Hegelian dialectics than about the performative process of rituals. Social rituals generate hope for the participants, Turner claims, because "they show them-selves and others what they are doing or have done."[39] The performance of our lives in these social dramas constructs our subjectivities and our social roles, and this ritual process is what constitutes the survival of a community.

Richard Schechner, whose work is deeply indebted to Turner, locates hope in the transformations available through theatre. Transformations in theatre, he argues, occur in three different places and at three different levels: "(1) in the drama, that is, in the story; (2) in the performers whose special task it is to undergo a temporary rearrangement of their body/mind, what I call a 'trans-portation'; (3) in the audience where changes may be either temporary (enter-tainment) or permanent (ritual)."[40] Schechner distinguishes between aesthetic drama and social drama on the basis of the "performance of the transformation effected" (171). In aesthetic dramas—*Angels in America*, for example—the audi-ence and the performers are separated:

> This separateness of the audience is the hallmark of aesthetic drama. In social drama all present are participants, though some are more decisively involved than others. In aesthetic drama everyone in the theater is a par-ticipant in the *performance*, while only those playing roles in the drama are participants in the *drama* nested within the performance. The perfor-mance as distinct from the drama is social, and it is at the level of per-formance that aesthetic and social drama converge. The function of aes-thetic drama is *to do for the consciousness of the audience what social drama does for its participants*: providing a place for, and means of, transforma-tion. (171)

Schechner's ideas on the theatre's availability to actualize alternative con-sciousness through the process of transformation extends Turner's notion of the continual play of social dramas as ritual process. Performance, according to Schechner, is an agent for the invention of new realities and these new realities are made available through transformation. Of course, this does not ensure that they will indeed materialize.

All live performances, because of their nonreproductive qualities, inevita-bly and invariably produce a type of mourning. A live performance event can never be repeated or reproduced; its life exists only within the confines of its playing time. This is what Peggy Phelan explains as the "ontology of perfor-mance":

> Performance's only life is in the present. Performance cannot be saved, re-corded, documented, or otherwise participate in the circulation of repre-sentations *of* representations: once it does so, it becomes something other than performance. To the degree that performance attempts to enter the

economy of reproduction it betrays and lessens the promise of its own ontology. Performance's being . . . becomes itself through disappearance.[41]

Spectators may mourn the loss of performance and make efforts to reproduce
the experience through memory, conversation, and even consumption.[42] For
Phelan, hope is regenerated by our continual desire to re-create, revisit, and/ or
remember. Such a circular process—mourning the loss of the performance/ hoping to remember the performance—is both recognized and disavowed through
the practices of theatre historians in our attempts to document performance.
Our writing about the performance that can never be repeated comes from our
experience of loss and accents it accordingly. We hope to remember. For performances about AIDS, these ruminations raise serious concerns: why reenact
a scenario that (re)produces loss? what happens to the possibilities of performance to resolve and transform in the midst of such loss? The deluge of mourning
in the specific cases of performances around AIDS is both immediate and debilitating. In the theatre we witness the performance that will never survive. In
the time that we take to go to the theatre and witness the performance that will
never survive, more people will die. (Our friend Philip Juwig died during the
November 1, 1992, performance of *Angels in America*.) Now we must mourn for
not only our lost friends but also the lost performances which may have represented them.

Theatre audiences are collectives, congregations of people gathered together to participate in performance.[43] The experience of performance, as
Bentley suggests, may well be a lonely occasion experienced in confusion with
others. But it doesn't need to remain so. Throughout the five intermissions in
the marathon production, we stretched, peed, cruised (is this where the "amorous outpouring" has landed?), smoked our cigarettes, took our medications,
and rubbed each other's backs. "Intermission," Schechner reminds us, "confirms the existence of the 'gathering,' a group assembled specifically to attend
this particular theatrical event" (174). Intermission disrupts the fantasy of realness embedded in representation; it breaks the spell of isolation and reorientates
the spectator into the social. It also, as our activities suggest, confirms the materiality of our bodies.

To participate in the marathon performances of a play as demanding as
Angels in America, as spectator or actor, is to participate in a ritual of endurance
(and also one of commitment: the marathon performances run the length of a
conventional workday and cost more than what many people earn for a day of
labor). The ritual of endurance makes explicit the material body. The explicit
representation of some of the signatures of AIDS that Prior Walter experiences
throughout *Angels in America*—the visible lesions, the shit and blood of Prior's

illness, the night sweats, the effects of treatments—asks us to focus on, if not actually identify with, Prior's body and the actor who plays him. The representation of Prior's endurance of AIDS staged in excess in *Angels* works in part to invoke the compassion of liberalism, the standard deployment of hope through compassion. But in the representation of endurance, a feeling of endurance resonates outside the field of representation and extends into material production. The body of the spectator enduring the length of the performance and the physical demands of theatregoing—reaching the theatre, walking to our seats, finding comfort in our setting, needing to stretch, feeling hunger—identifies metaphorically with the bodies of actors onstage performing the roles. Certainly if we are fatigued, hungry, or restless in the leisure activities of our watching, the actors, who are the most visible laborers of the performance, must be as well. Spectators must endure the labor of actors and the technical crew who must endure the demands of the workplace. So while we register the effects of AIDS on Prior Walter's body, we also register the effects of the labor of this representation on the actor who plays him. Our identification is therefore as much with the actor as it is with the representation. The ritual of endurance is made explicit through this free-floating identification process; at intermission we honor our endurance, acknowledge the endurance of the actors and technical team, and rally behind the endurance represented onstage. During intermission material bodies temporarily disengage from the body in representation, if only to return once again into the ritual of endurance we call performance.

Thus as the drama nested within the performance of the aesthetic drama begins to articulate a new system of feelings for the social dramas of our lives, the actual experience of the aesthetic drama in the social space of the theatre is realized through the body. The convergence of the physical experience of watching a performance of *Angels in America* with the feelings produced by *Angels in America* transforms a ritual of endurance into a ritual of hope. The collective experience of endurance—of the actors, the technical artists, and the audience—suggests the miraculous possibilities of community. In other words, we live through the representation of AIDS. We mourn the loss of the performance that cannot be repeated and celebrate our participation in a ritual of endurance that we have passed through. It is here, at this juncture of mourning and endurance, that despair meets hope. We need this hope as we step back into the social reality of AIDS: the "terror as usual" that we face outside of the theatre. The performance ends, and the mourning for the performance that will never survive begins. Grief deepens. We leave the theatre and turning to each other may ask: do you remember? Already resigned to the loss of the performance. In isolation we wonder: will we remember the performance that cannot be repeated and that will never survive?

The theatre insists on gathering a congregation to witness the performance that will never survive. We are asked to bring our bodies to participate in a ritual of endurance that may transform us. The possibility of such a transformation moves the ritual of endurance toward a ritual of hope. This hope is aware of the need to relocate our isolated and fading memories—of lost friends, of lost performances—into the contested public sphere. This hope recognizes evil as actual and indeed negotiable. This hope comes from the restructuring of love and kinship in the midst of tragedy. This hope does not disavow; rather it is informed by mourning and rage. And so we offer each other—along with our mourning and our rage—our hope and our love. Once again, from *Millennium Approaches*:

> BELIZE: Whatever happens, baby, I will be here for you.
> PRIOR: Je t'aime.
> BELIZE: Je t'aime.

Once again, *Perestroika*; we restructure. On the eve of elections we consider the feelings that determine our agency: grief, rage, hope, and love. We bring our memories of twelve years of living with AIDS into the contested public sphere; once again, perestroika. We parade the bodies of loved ones through the rain to the New York Bush/Quayle campaign headquarters.[44] We raise our voices in the streets of Oregon and Colorado. We cast our votes for Clinton. We cast our votes—"an action illuminated by a tragic consciousness"[45]—and play our part in a national ritual performed in the social drama of our lives. We return again and again to the space of performance. There are degrees of agency amid tragedy.

November 1993

How much can happen in a year![46]
—Charles Ludlam, *Camille*

It's November 1993 and I am back with my friends in Los Angeles, visiting from the East Coast. How much can happen in a year: a year ago on November 1, 1992—the eve of the national elections—I was in Los Angeles with my friends Jim, Matthew, Michael, and Tim, attending the opening marathon performances of *Angels in America*. Michael's shark-cartilage treatment got him through a bad bout of KS, but he's still very ill; there is no effective treatment for him right now. Clinton won the election, but his policies on AIDS, while an obvious improvement from the nightmare of Reagan and Bush, are still negligible; he has no forceful agenda on AIDS as of yet. Tony Kushner, who won the Pulitzer this year for *Millennium Approaches*, is set to open *Perestroika* this month

34. Michael Kearns in Charles Ludlam's *Camille,* Highways
Performance Space, Santa Monica, 1993.
Richard Armas

on Broadway; however, it is unlikely that he will save Broadway. And so we
wonder: how much can happen in a year?

It's November 1993 and I am in Los Angeles visiting with my friends.
Matthew and I are, once again, at the theatre. We are watching another of
our friends, Michael Kearns—whose lover, Philip Juwig, died of complications
due to AIDS on November 1, 1992—perform the lead in the revival of Charles
Ludlam's *Camille.* The play has been running for weeks at Highways Performance Space, and Michael's performance is simply thrilling (fig. 34). In a press
statement, Michael explains his reasons for staging the play: "Ludlam, Camille,
and I are sisters under the skin."[47] Michael, who is HIV-positive—the first
Hollywood actor to be public about his status—and asymptomatic, has been
producing AIDS performances since the early 1980s. In 1985, he founded along

with Jim Pickett—a playwright and director who now has full-blown AIDS—
Artists Confronting AIDS. Their work has been produced throughout Southern
California for over a decade, but that's another story that I will tell.[48] *Camille* at
Highways is the latest Artists Confronting AIDS production.

Matthew is taking a break from caring for our friend Michael Callen, whose
health is very fragile. How much can happen in a year: today Michael Callen
barely can walk and Jim Pickett is lucky to be up and about for more than a
couple of hours a day. Still, they continue to sing and to write plays. Michael
Kearns, who spent November 1, 1992, not in the theatre but at his dying lover's
side, is now onstage every night at Highways performing the lead in Charles
Ludlam's *Camille*. We return again and again to the space of performance.

Matthew and I met at Highways at Tim's gay male performance workshops.
Years ago, we etched the names of the dead on the floor of the Highways art
gallery in a ritual for World AIDS Day. In this space we have told stories, made
friends, built community. Tonight we walk through the gallery memorial on our
way to our seats.

In the morning, Matthew and I drive to Glendale to visit with Michael
Kearns and to see Jim, Michael's roommate. Jim is a playwright and director
who cofounded with Michael Kearns Artists Confronting AIDS. Jim isn't feeling very well right now. He has been out of the hospital for a few days, but he
is still extremely tired. Mornings are his best time, he explains; a reminder that
he cannot visit with us for too long. Jim is telling us the story of his romance
with David, a man who is HIV-negative and with whom he is now involved.
He also tells us of his treatment options, minimal choices, each with severe set-
backs. He weaves in and out of these narratives as Matthew and I take turns
pouring coffee and updating him on our own lives. Stay negative, he asks of us.
Michael Kearns is off with his friend Bruce, who is visiting from Sydney. Bruce,
one of the founders of ACT UP/Sydney, has full-blown AIDS and is taking time,
while he still can, to visit his friends in the United States. These are the times
that we live in. This is the way we live now, still.

It's November 1993 and I am in Los Angeles with my friend Jim. I am a
professor and he is a playwright. A year ago, we were at the theatre; today, we
are in his bedroom and he is giving me his unpublished papers. He hands me
scripts, videos, photos, and reviews of his performances of the past ten years.
These are documents of the performances that cannot be repeated, the performances that may not survive. I will take them home and write about his work.
They will join a pile of scripts that grows skyward in my room.

Michael Kearns returns. We offer each other a big warm embrace. He gives
me *his* unpublished papers: scripts, videos, photos, and reviews of his performances of the past ten years. These, too, are documents of the performances that

cannot be repeated, the performances that may not survive. I will take them home and write about his work, and they will join the same growing pile.

How much can happen in a year: a year ago at the theatre, now in the homes of those we love. The ritual of endurance continues to play out in the performance of our lives. Millennium approaches.

Once the inevitabilities are challenged, we begin gathering our resources for a journey of hope.[49] Perestroika.

This is not an ending; our friends know this. We are on a journey of hope. We vow to remember our dead and care for our ill. We offer each other our mourning, our rage, and our love. We know that these feelings are still not enough, but they provide us a foundation for hope. And we must speak for hope, as long as it doesn't mean suppressing the nature of the danger.[50]

8

Negative Energies

HIV-Negatives and the Problem of Seroconversion

IN THIS LAST chapter, I want to focus on an issue which has thus far gone un-addressed: HIV-negatives and the problem of seroconversion. The hope that was marked by the events of 1992 shifted, as I have suggested in the last section of the previous chapter, by 1993. This shift brought forth a series of challenges for gay men in the 1990s, including a reconsideration of HIV-prevention efforts and a more forceful attempt to reduce the rising rates of seroconversion in gay communities. The immediate challenge was how and where to address the problem of seroconversion among gay men in this time of aggravated crisis, when medical and scientific communities, ever since the 1993 International AIDS conference in Berlin, kept telling us that AIDS would not be resolved in our lifetimes, *regardless* of our status; the political climate in the local, regional, and national spheres kept shifting to the right, and the already limited funding for AIDS research, care, and prevention faced continual drastic cuts; direct action groups like ACT UP were considered no longer politically efficacious or viable; gay men increasingly engaged in unprotected sex and HIV-negative gay men seroconverted at alarming rates; HIV-positive gay men, asymptomatic for over a decade, developed symptoms and opportunistic infections while longterm survivors died; the gay community's response was a fractured and divisive HIV-prevention politics that perpetuated the anxieties between HIV-negative and HIV-positive gay men, and even efforts by prevention activists to reimagine gay political and sexual culture were cast in doubt and through despair. In order to understand seroconversion we need to understand seronegativity—seronegatives, after all, are the ones who seroconvert.[1] And in order to understand seronegativity, it becomes necessary to interrogate the ways that seronegativity has been understood historically and to speculate on the effects of this understanding on HIV-negative gay men.

One of the primary means by which identities are understood is through representation and language. Given this claim, the critical necessity is to chart the representational and discursive systems that render seronegativity intelligible in both the dominant culture and in gay subculture. Among the questions we need to ask ourselves are: how is seronegativity referenced in the visual and performing arts? in print and visual media? in political and social vernaculars? In other words, what are the ways that HIV-negative gay men are represented and talked about in public culture? What images and discourses circulate nationally—for whom and to what effect? And what is the relationship between the ways that dominant culture and queer subculture perceive seronegativity? In terms of the theatre, the recent proliferation of successful gay plays such as Paul Rudnick's *Jeffrey* (1993) and Terrence McNally's *Love! Valour! Compassion!* (1994), while not about the experience of HIV-negativity per se, revolve around characters who are implicitly understood to be uninfected. Why is HIV-negativity simultaneously suggested and covered over in contemporary gay culture and, more specifically, in recent gay theatrical productions? In answering this question, we need to contextualize historically the discourses for the uninfected both in the theatre and in gay culture.

Seronegativity has remained an unmarked category, the unexamined term in the HIV-negative/HIV-positive binarism. "HIV-negative" has not been adequately addressed by AIDS activists, and therefore the category has been vulnerable to a series of inscriptions by both dominant culture and queer culture. For uninfected gay men, these markings remained uncontested and, as a result, normalized as the experience of all HIV-negatives. The origins of this problem can be traced back to the introduction of the HIV antibody test in 1985.[2] Previously, gay men not diagnosed with AIDS had no way of knowing our relationship to AIDS other than through symptoms associated with the early stages of AIDS, what was then termed AIDS Related Complex (ARC), or through our own conjectures. The reactionary politics of homophobic and/or AIDS-phobic public figures in the mid-1980s who advocated for quarantines, mandatory testing, and legislation designed to discriminate against people testing HIV-positive or diagnosed with AIDS, accentuated the separatist politics already in place within and among gay men. Once armed with HIV-negative test results, many gay men defined themselves in opposition to, and at the expense of, gay men testing positive. One of the first means by which HIV-negative gay men defined themselves *as* HIV-negative gay men was through the formation of HIV-positive gay men as other.

Progressive and radical activists provisionally advocating for, or at times hesitantly endorsing, anonymous testing in some ways exacerbated the problem by inadvertently introducing the concept of the secret.[3] Out to eliminate the possibility of discrimination directed toward HIV-positives, progressive activists advised gay men to keep our test results private. The closet constructed to contain discrimination, and the accompanying skepticism among progressive activists for any type of systemic surveillance of gay men's sexual or health profile, engendered a progressive political response to HIV testing which discouraged HIV-negative gay men from constructing an identity around negative test results. The belief hidden behind this response questioned the possibility of HIV-negative gay men announcing their serostatus in public without perpetuating a reactionary politics to AIDS. To announce one's seronegativity was constructed as insensitive, politically suspect, and ultimately as complicit in maintaining a binary between HIV-negatives and HIV-positives, a divisive gesture understood to be at the expense of people living with HIV.

The introduction of the HIV antibody test also put forward the myth that to test HIV-negative is to be immune to HIV. Some gay men who tested negative assumed incorrectly that they were naturally immune to HIV and therefore could continue the very sexual practices that put them at risk for HIV in the first place.[4] Walt Odets, the Bay Area clinical psychologist who theorizes the effects of AIDS on HIV-negative gay men, explains that the availability of the HIV test soon became "much more than a way to screen the blood supply and determine the 'antibody status' of an individual. Today the fact of HIV antibody status stands as a laboratory marker with unprecedented psychological, interpersonal, and social significance."[5] The HIV antibody test launched a cultural binarism between HIV-negatives and HIV-positives and introduced the idea of having a "status." Binary systems rely on an interdependent relationship between the two terms in opposition. Cultural theorist David Savran explains that "despite the fact that each term of each [binary] opposition is strictly dependent on the other and, indeed, is produced by its other, these relations are not symmetrical. Binary oppositions are always hierarchical—especially when the fact of hierarchy is repressed."[6] In the HIV-negative/HIV-positive opposition, HIV-negative is rendered not only as the preferred position but, given its relation to HIV, the moral one as well. Indeed, as William Johnston, author of *HIV-Negative: How the Uninfected Are Affected by AIDS,* explains, *HIV status* is a term itself laden with ideological meanings. "In one sense," Johnston writes, "the word 'status' implies a rigid social or moral hierarchy, like caste.... HIV-negative status is portrayed as better than—rather than merely different from—HIV-positive status. In another sense, the word 'status' implies a state of being that is mutable, like a status report."[7] Odets, while concurring with Johnston's ideas, problematizes the use of the term *status* when he writes that "in daily life antibody status is usually tacitly acknowledged as an important difference between positive and negative [gay] men, even when we do not quite know what it means—

either medically or humanly."[8] That we are not quite sure "what it means" suggests that, to some degree, we (and others) can put forth interpretations on these very specific clinical terms: *HIV-negative*, *HIV-positive*, and *HIV-status*.

The effects of these competing, and sometimes contradictory, meanings of the term *HIV status*, understood as signifying certain unarticulated social positions for gay men, have been historically divisive. The very term *HIV status* engenders the complex psychosocial responses to the specific results of the HIV antibody test among gay men. Simon Watney agrees with this idea when he claims that "[i]t is not sufficiently recognised that HIV antibody testing involves ways of thinking about ourselves, and one another, that have the profoundest implications for everyone."[9] While the goal of activists was to protect HIV-positives from potential discrimination, one of the ironic and unfortunate results of obfuscating gay men's specific serostatus was the emergence of an imagined social binary opposition between those who tested HIV-negative and those who tested HIV-positive, even if this binary did not enter fully into public culture and debate. Despite the efforts to shelter HIV-positives from public discriminations, the social practice of privatizing the serostatus of all gay men allowed for the social binary and its moral underpinnings to take shape in the subaltern world of gay male culture.

The political situation of the mid-1980s necessitated the obscuring of gay men's HIV status; the fear of personal, institutional, and systemic discrimination was a reality then as it is still.[10] Progressive gay men, regardless of status, combined energies to fight the discriminatory policies and practices of the institutions and individuals invested in sustaining AIDS. Such a political practice by progressive gay men was in direct response to the dominant culture's construction of AIDS, which positioned all gay men as inherently diseased and subsequently as a threat to the family. Within this cultural logic, the heterosexual family unit stood as the iconic emblem of the national interest; therefore defending the national investment in the morality of the family became the foundational logic of a conservative and dominant AIDS ideology. The force of this logic disciplined many gay men to internalize it, setting up the conditions for an unconscious belief that for gay men, AIDS is inevitable. Walt Odets explains how this idea of AIDS as inevitable is one of the pressing factors contributing to seroconversion:

When HIV infection seems inevitable, many men derive comfort from contracting it *now* and thus eliminating anxiety about *when.* . . . A sense of inevitability about contracting HIV is evidenced in a variety of forms. It expresses itself in depression, in a sense of hopelessness, in feeling out of control about one's life, in anxiety, in the belief that one actually *has* HIV when this is not the case, in careless exposure to HIV, in the abandonment of any effort to protect oneself from HIV, and, on occasion, in the deliberate pursuit of HIV infection. Inevitability is also expressed in HIV-negative men who visualize no future for themselves and live as if they had none. Such men often live in a gloomy, unconscious assumption of a short life that pursues fulfillment of its own prophecy.[11]

Odets argues that the culture of AIDS—from HIV testing to AIDS education campaigns—inadvertently contributes to this unconscious belief that eventually all gay men will seroconvert. Concerned with the emotional health of HIV-negative gay men, Odets points out the underlying homophobic and moralizing rhetoric of the very prevention programs that are meant to save gay men's lives.[12] The power of this pervasive logic of inevitable seroconversion—not *if* but *when*—is set forth both by reactionary political forces and by AIDS prevention programs, which, while different in intent and in experience, converge in the individual and cultural psyches of HIV-negative gay men as a primary means of understanding and experiencing seronegativity. The cultural logic of inevitability, in other words, begins to define what it means to be HIV-negative. Within this system, HIV negativity is considered a tentative status or a temporal condition located on a trajectory leading to eventual seroconversion.

Within dominant culture and the culture of AIDS, HIV-negative gay men also entered into public recognition through AIDS work either as employees or volunteers of AIDS service organizations. Cast within the realm of altruism, HIV-negative gay men affiliated with ASOs were still construed within the logic of inevitability. Dominant culture imagined HIV-negative gay men doing AIDS work as HIV-positive through a logic of association. HIV-negative gay male volunteers, driven by both compassion for people with AIDS and a politics of communal resistance in the face of oppression, were conflated with AIDS and circulated in dominant culture as prodigal sons, gay men striving to redeem ourselves as moral and righteous before our inevitable collapse, the good sons of the nation relieving the government of any social responsibility. The grassroots organizing of early lesbian and gay community-based AIDS activism, which was based less on the model of compassionate volunteerism and more on the model of political resistance, was replaced in the cultural imaginary as nonprofit altruism, the result of cuts in federal funding under the presidency of Ronald Reagan. Rather than focusing on the collective resistance of people infected and affected by HIV, dominant culture individuated AIDS and thus, as Cindy Patton observes, inscribed "a rigid role structure which constructed 'victims,' 'experts,' and 'volunteers' as the *dramatis personae* in its story of AIDS."[13] HIV-negative gay men working from the position of "volunteer" were some-

times absorbed under the rubric of "victim," a cultural forecasting of the projected conversion of roles for gay men fighting the epidemic. Within the gay
community, post-HIV testing volunteerism was founded on the political model
of pre-HIV testing, that is, as a community-driven and community-organized
response to AIDS. If earlier community organizing did not have the means to
differentiate activists on the basis of their HIV status, later community-based
AIDS organizing did, but chose not to make much of it. HIV-negative gay
men failed to politicize their AIDS involvement *as* the politicized work of HIV-
negative gay men; the result of this failure led HIV-negative gay men to see
themselves as singular entities in the growing AIDS service industries rather
than as communal participants in a tactic of shared political resistance.[14]

While dominant culture positioned HIV-negative gay male volunteers
within a trope of redemption, the culture of AIDS activism made room for negative gay male ASO volunteers to enter into public AIDS discourse as responsible
and compassionate. The formation of the HIV-negative gay man as caregiver
was evident in independent gay film, gay literature, and gay politics throughout
the mid-1980s. Caregiving, a valued and necessary contribution in the fight
against AIDS,[15] emerged as the primary means for HIV-negative gay men to
identify as HIV-negative gay men in a manner valorized by the culture of
AIDS. And yet even within this system, HIV-negative gay men did not mark
their serostatus. The unexamined social roles of HIV-negative gay men—*as*
HIV-negative gay men—as AIDS volunteers and caregivers unwittingly domes-
ticated the origins of political communal resistance from which these social
practices emerged. Before the HIV-antibody test, AIDS volunteerism and
caregiving were understood within lesbian and gay culture as a direct form of
AIDS activism, a product of the long-standing community-based resistance to
social oppression. Volunteerism, as Cindy Patton observes, which began at
"grassroots organizations in which unpaid labor was seen as a contribution to
community self-determination and liberation," shifted by 1986 to "an accept-
able vehicle for the New Altruism promoted by Reaganism."[16]

With the arrival of ACT UP in 1987, HIV-negative gay men participated in
a public culture that reimagined AIDS activism and challenged, among other
things, the trope of the volunteer. ACT UP intervened in the logic of inevitability and the trope of the good son by agitating the forces of power sustaining
AIDS. AIDS was not inevitable, ACT UP demonstrated, but negotiable and pre-
ventable. Yet HIV-negative gay men in ACT UP rarely spoke publicly about their
seronegativity or about the issues specific to HIV-negative gay men. Instead
they subscribed to the Diamanda Galás ethos that "we are all HIV-positive."
Galás, an internationally acclaimed performing artist whose work has addressed AIDS since the mid-1980s, put forth the idea that "we are all HIV-posi-

tive" as a means to show political solidarity with people living with HIV. Galás directly challenged the formation of an identity politics based on seronegativity: "These days when you hear people say, 'I am HIV negative,' what it generally means is, 'I am separate from this epidemic, I am separate from this political situation.' "[17] Galás's political identification with "HIV-positive" put pressure upon all people to join the fight against AIDS regardless of their HIV status. Her idea gained national currency as the political mantra of HIV-negatives involved in AIDS activism. Such a politics, while effective at establishing a united front to fight for treatment and access, and for galvanizing a community to fight discrimination and abjection, nonetheless falsifies the experiences of HIV-negative gay men. HIV-negative gay men, regardless of our political identifications with HIV-positives and people with AIDS, are not HIV-positive.

Conversely, the cultural disregard of the specific experiences of HIV-negative gay men's relationship to AIDS results from the falsification of the experiences of people with HIV and AIDS. Shifting from the status of victim to hero, at least within the culture of AIDS, people with HIV and AIDS are often fetishized throughout culture as having access to certain truth claims unavailable to the uninfected. The bravery of the person with AIDS was introduced in representation and discourse partly to empower people living with HIV but also as a public service to assuage the uncertainties and anxieties of the "worried well," an epithet for HIV-negatives and the untested introduced in the early years of the epidemic, and the "general public at large," a designation which has yet to lose its cultural grip for the majoritarian AIDS-phobic culture unwilling to grant people with AIDS and queers any entitlement to the social. Gregg Bordowitz, an independent videographer living with AIDS, explains how within dominant culture, the person with AIDS is constructed as either victim or hero to appease and service the needs of the uninfected:

> For example, if the PWA is now being brave, for whom is he being brave? That's a question which preoccupies me. I see the AIDS hero as a close cousin of the AIDS villain or the AIDS victim of the early eighties. Ten years ago the figure of the PWA was a scapegoat and a figure of horror.[18]

Rarely is a person with AIDS entitled to participate in public culture to address and speak to other people with AIDS. Bordowitz sees this situation, what he calls the "specular relation of the PWA as other" (106), as the central problem of most AIDS representations. The distortion of the experiences of people with AIDS—as victim, as hero—primarily serves the interests of the uninfected. The distortion of the experiences of HIV-negatives—as "we are all HIV-positive"— while designed to serve the interests of the infected, ends up obscuring the specific experiences of people living with HIV and the specific experiences of those who are not. So for whom does this performative utterance ultimately operate and to what effect? As a public stance of communal identification and solidarity, the HIV-negative's political insistence that "we are all HIV-positive" intervenes in the potential divisions between HIV-negatives and HIV-positives and puts pressure on HIV-negatives to get involved in AIDS activism "as if your life depended on it." But the phrase also plays into the majoritarian hysteria of associative contagion, on the one hand, and the conflation of HIV with gay men on the other. When spoken by HIV-negative gay men, the phrase invests in an unconscious logic that presumes seroconversion. Unlike the earlier AIDS activist acts of surrogacy and identification—the public performatives of the lesbian and gay community between 1982 and 1984 and before the HIV-antibody test—where people unsure of their own relationship to AIDS publicly performed an identification with people who had died of AIDS, the new activist identification with HIV-positives, now that HIV status is knowable, contributes to the idea that gay male life is intrinsically linked with "being positive." Politically, it runs the risk of locating HIV-negative gay male experience not merely in solidarity with people with AIDS, but rather as symbiotically dependent on people with AIDS. In other words, HIV-negatives are imaginable only if linked inextricably with a person with AIDS.

Such was the case throughout the late 1980s and early 1990s when HIV-negative gay men entered public representation as "AIDS widows" and as partners in "magnetic" relationships. The terms *AIDS widow* and *magnetic relationship* are gay male vernaculars for the surviving partner of a person who has died from AIDS complications and for couples where one partner is HIV-positive and the other is HIV-negative.[19] In both the medias and art forms of the dominant culture and of the gay subculture, HIV-negative gay men were marked as HIV-negative in direct relation to someone who was either HIV-positive or who had died from AIDS complications. Brought into public culture on the coattails of the person with HIV or AIDS, the HIV-negative gay man was identified as HIV-negative only through his relationship to someone on the other side of the HIV binary pole. Public culture licensed HIV-negative gay men to speak and be heard as HIV-negative gay men based on these relationships, a perpetuation which fetishized the person with AIDS as having the authentic experience of AIDS.

But what if you weren't an AIDS widow or involved with someone HIV-positive? HIV-negative gay men could speak as HIV-negative gay men if they adhered to two primary discourses: quantitative and qualitative. The quantitative discourse allows the HIV-negative gay man to identify as such when he prefaces his identification with a catalogue of the number of friends buried and friends ill. According to the logic of this discourse, the more AIDS fatalities accumulated the more legitimate the HIV-negative's voice. Often this quantitative discourse is accompanied by, or leads to, the qualitative discourse which proceeds to account for the poor quality of the HIV-negative gay man's life in the midst of AIDS. The qualitative discourse has its origins in survivor's guilt, but it goes further: life is now meaningless and empty. Survivor's guilt involves a series of questions, emotions, and practices based on the information that one has tested HIV-negative. William Johnston explains how HIV-negative gay men who exposed themselves to the same risks that infected others often wonder why they were spared from HIV when so many others were not:

> Often [HIV-negative gay men] attempt to explain why they have survived, attributing their survival to simple luck or natural immunity to HIV. Still others, troubled at having survived, take on an unrelenting commitment to AIDS work as a way of atoning for their survival, or of punishing themselves for having survived. Finally, many men seek to tell stories about the epidemic's impact on their lives as a way of "witnessing the epidemic."[20]

The combination of these complex emotions with the unending deaths of people from AIDS puts forward the idea that life is no longer worth living—who wants to be the only one to survive? Moreover, who wants to survive if, as Odets observes, "[i]t is an aspect of survivor guilt that one feels so profoundly identified with the dying that surviving *is* betraying?"[21] Guilt and betrayal, according to these accounts, are the emotional means by which many HIV-negative gay men begin to understand their HIV status. The public circulation of these two limited discourses—quantitative and qualitative—participates in the distortion of HIV-negative gay men's lives. Although many of us are AIDS widows or partners in magnetic relationships, and many of us have buried countless friends and care for many who are ill, and although we may also suffer severe bouts of depression and anxiety regarding our lives given the context of AIDS, these are not our only experiences of AIDS. Rather these are the experiences which are culturally acknowledged and their circulation begins to construe what it means to be HIV-negative.

How might the public discourses available for HIV-negative gay men have something to do with the rising rates of seroconversion? All of the ways HIV-negatives have been represented in public culture are extremely depressing and, consequently, offer little incentive to imagine a life worth living. One effect of this situation is that HIV-negative gay men have begun to overidentify with the new culture of HIV-positives; another effect is the occasional fantasy of seroconversion.[22] While the culture of HIV-positives—which includes periodicals, 'zines, films, documentaries, support groups, and socials—is a direct result of the PWA self-empowerment movement founded in 1983, it is also often constructed by dominant medias as *the* experience of gay life in the 1990s. If earlier conflations of AIDS and homosexuality were based on the logic of inevitability, that is, homosexuality and AIDS were not only associative but interchangeable, the current variation on this theme anchors gay men's ontology in a narrative of sequential "coming out" occasions—as gay, as positive—into a culture of positivity. In this sense, the sociocultural support systems of, by, and for HIV-positive gay men become urban gay culture. This translation of the support structures of HIV-positive gay men, from a subcultural process within the larger lesbian and gay culture to the majoritarian understanding of what gay life is in the 1990s, domesticates the political necessity of seropositive gay men who must create and sustain social and institutional structures for their survival. Moreover, the conflation of positive culture with gay male culture ignores the specific needs of HIV-negative gay men in the midst of AIDS. Given these conditions, as Odets points out, HIV-negative gay men sometimes embark on fantasies of seroconversion. In response to a culture that systematically denies their identity and experience, some HIV-negative gay men assume that seroconversion will bring meaning to their lives, and attention and love.

HIV-negative gay men's desire to test positive results from the anxiety associated with the logic of inevitability, but it is also motivated by the desire to be seen and heard. The current proliferation of HIV-negative gay men's unprotected sex stories is symptomatic of these interrelated (but not interdependent) desires.[23] HIV-negative gay men can now enter into the public sphere as HIV-negative gay men through confessional discourse. Despite the many stories HIV-negative gay men have to tell about our experiences as HIV-negative gay men, the unprotected sex confession seems to be the preferred narrative of our times. Although the unprotected sex story holds the capacity to inaugurate important discussions concerning sexual practices and desires, the circulation of these stories in public culture demonstrates the limits of the ways in which seronegativity is currently rendered intelligible. Now we can add confession to the list of the discourses which public culture allows HIV-negative gay men to be heard and unprotected sex to the list of practices public culture links with seronegativity. If the latest means of being HIV-negative entails a story of unprotected sex, then the category of HIV-negative is rendered all the more vulnerable. Within this logic, seronegativity can be understood and located only in a trajectory that will lead to seroconversion, to AIDS, and ultimately to an AIDS-related death. In other words, seronegativity is assumed as a condition which leads to AIDS.

HIV-negative did not exist as a medical category before the HIV-antibody test was introduced in the spring of 1985. How then did playwrights and performers represent the uninfected? At the same time that HIV-antibody testing became available, the two most celebrated early AIDS plays, *The Normal Heart* and *As Is*, premiered in New York City. These plays, and the other AIDS plays and performances of the early 1980s, of course, were not able to stage representations of HIV-negatives, but playwrights were able to provide an insight into the ways AIDS was imagined by gay men not diagnosed with AIDS. Previous to 1985, playwrights and performers staged representations of the worried well or the assumed infected. In plays such as *Warren*, *As Is*, and *The Normal Heart*, characters with AIDS—often based on actual people—are placed within a narrative trajectory that ends in an AIDS-related death. This dramatic pattern became so prevalent that it soon emerged as the structuring convention of AIDS drama. And yet if the primary AIDS narrative in these plays follows the character with AIDS toward his death, what can be said of the other gay male characters in these plays who interact with the character with AIDS? Early AIDS plays written in a linear narrative with realist conventions end in the death of the character with AIDS and often with the revelation of a new person with AIDS among the supporting characters. The question of who's next, familiar to gay audiences haunted by the reality of the nearly arbitrary disclosure of someone else's newly announced diagnosis, was reflected in early AIDS plays. The logic of inevitability, based on the disturbing possibility that you could be the next to be diagnosed with AIDS, which many gay men experienced before the HIV-antibody test's availability, was mirrored in the theatre.[24] Among gay male characters, the passing of the AIDS baton in early 1980s plays was meant to rupture the individuation of AIDS resulting from the closely monitored trajectory of the primary character with AIDS that these plays charted. These plays implied that AIDS was not a singular occasion, but instead a communal crisis unresolved by the death of the protagonist. Before the end of Rebecca Ranson's 1984 play *Warren*, a scene at the hospital between two secondary characters, Warren's stepmother, Helen, and Warren's leather friend, Sam, attempts to make this point:

HELEN: And all these rooms have men with AIDS?
SAM: There are a lot more hospitals in the city with more men and there are people like Joe [Sam's lover, who also has AIDS and is being cared for at home] and there are more who are showing symptoms of AIDS and outpatients at the clinic.
HELEN: Now, is everybody Warren slept with going to get AIDS?
SAM: No. At least not as far as anybody knows yet. Some people seem to be more susceptible.
HELEN: So you might get it from Joe or you might not?
SAM: Looks that way.
HELEN: Are you afraid?
SAM: I'd be stupid not to be.[25]

Sam's lover, Joe, whose AIDS diagnosis is revealed in the middle of the play, dies—as Warren does—by the end of the play. Warren's lover, Kelly, is unable to visit Warren in the hospital because "he's getting a cold." The questionable health of Sam and Kelly is meant to reflect the possibility of their own potential AIDS condition.[26]

In Larry Kramer's *The Normal Heart*, there is no central protagonist with AIDS. Instead various gay men with AIDS are observed, referred to, and acknowledged. The play begins with main character Ned Weeks waiting along with two friends, Craig and Mickey, for a meeting with Dr. Emma Brookner. Immediately, the two friends are diagnosed with AIDS—"EMMA to NED: Your two friends I've just diagnosed? One of the them will be dead. Maybe both of them."[27]—and the roll call of the infected who will die throughout the duration of the years (1981 to 1984) documented in the play begins:

> (DAVID *comes out of* EMMA's *office. There are highly visible purple lesions on his face. He wears a long-sleeved shirt. He goes to get his jacket, which he's left on one of his chairs.*)
> DAVID: Whoever's next can go in.
> CRAIG: Wish me luck.
> MICKEY: (*Hugging* CRAIG.) Good luck.
> (CRAIG *hugs him, then* NED, *and goes into* EMMA's *office.*)
> DAVID: They keep getting bigger and bigger and they don't go away. (*To* NED.) I sold you a ceramic pig once at Maison France on Bleeker Street. My name is David.
> NED: Yes, I remember. Somebody I was friends with then collects pigs and you had the biggest pig I'd ever seen outside of a real pig.
> DAVID: I'm her twenty-eighth case and sixteen of them are dead. (*He leaves.*) (32)

While people with AIDS, such as David, are introduced briefly throughout the play only to die AIDS-related deaths, it is not until Ned Weeks's lover, Felix, is diagnosed with AIDS in act 2, scene 10 that AIDS affects a major character. And while Felix dies by the end of the play, one of the other major characters, Bruce Niles, is left unsure of his own health, upping the ante on the suspense of AIDS in the play:

> BRUCE: Ned, Albert is dead.
> NED: Oh, no.
> BRUCE: What's today?
> NED: Wednesday.
> BRUCE: He's been dead a week.

NED: I didn't know he was so close.

BRUCE: No one did. He wouldn't tell anyone. Do you know why? Because of me. Because he knows I'm so scared I'm some sort of carrier. This makes three people I've been with who are dead. I went to Emma and I begged her: please test me somehow, please tell me if I'm giving this to people. And she said she couldn't, there isn't any way they can find out anything because they still don't know what they're looking for. (105)

The scene takes place in February 1983, well over a year before the availability of the HIV-antibody test. The suspense of not knowing—if one was a "carrier," infected, and at risk for succumbing to AIDS—produces an anxiety, as Bruce articulates, based on the uncertainty of AIDS. The dramatic tension of daily life and theatrical representation is formulated around the need to know one's relation to AIDS and on the unavailability of obtaining that knowledge at the time. The strength of this cultural suspense—who's next? could it be me?—sets up an identificatory relationship between dramatic character and theatrical spectator. Early AIDS drama staged the reality that it could be you, that it could be anyone, enhancing the anxiety and sense of inevitability already experienced by gay men in daily life. That there was no way of knowing whether or not one was infected before 1985 only exacerbated this anxiety. Early AIDS plays represented the worried well and the presumed infected as potential people with AIDS.

The random announcement in these early plays of other characters either showing AIDS-related symptoms or receiving an AIDS diagnosis, while based on the lived experience of gay men at the time, nonetheless participated in the formation of an AIDS diagnosis or symptom as a dramatic device. The strength of this formation carries into post-HIV-antibody-test plays. In the plays and performances written in the years following the availability of HIV testing, testing HIV-positive joins the standard dramatic devices established by early AIDS plays. The fact that so many AIDS plays in the early to mid-1980s relied on either the death of the AIDS protagonist, the revelation of a new character with AIDS, or someone testing HIV-positive to achieve their dramatic conclusion contributes to the idea of inevitability. These plays intensify the fear of AIDS for their audiences. That so many of these plays also rely on the dramatic conventions of realist theatre suggests that the formal structure of tragedy, which these plays generally adhere to, participates in the logic of inevitability.

AIDS as it was imagined and experienced in the early to mid-1980s was a "tragedy." But, as Raymond Williams has taught us, *tragedy* is a term with multiple meanings and ideological implications depending on the context and traditions in which it is produced. Williams's project, written in the early 1960s and published in 1966, sets out to distinguish between the dramatic tradition of tragedy and what he describes as "the forms and pressures of our own tragic experience":

> To examine the tragic tradition, that is to say, is not necessarily to expound a single body of work and thinking, or to trace variations within an assumed totality. It is to look, critically and historically, at works and ideas which have certain evident links, and which are associated in our minds by a single and powerful word. It is, above all, to see these works and ideas in their immediate contexts, as well as in their historical continuity, and to examine their place and function in relation to other works and ideas, and to the variety of actual experience.[28]

AIDS plays which rely on conventional concepts of dramatic tragedy present AIDS as a totalizing and inescapable condition, a condition with little or no agency to fight the powers contributing to the epidemic and with little or no hope for those affected. When there is no agency and no hope, there can only be victims and despair. Williams asks us to recognize that tragedy is neither a condition nor an inevitability. AIDS, while a condition, is not inevitable. And yet AIDS plays insist on perpetuating what director Peter Adair, in the introduction to his 1990 documentary of people with HIV, *Absolutely Positive*, puts forward when he claims that testing HIV-positive is a "good story." The idea that testing HIV-positive or living with AIDS is a good story—or, in theatrical terms, a good drama—implies that testing HIV-negative is not. An HIV-negative disclosure is not imagined as dramatic.[29] Only if—not if but when?—the HIV-negative seroconverts is the HIV-negative the subject of the drama. To test HIV-negative and to remain seronegative is, of course, not the subject of a tragedy. Thus, perhaps, it is understandable that HIV-negatives who present themselves as such, and who remain so, do not appear as central characters in the majority of AIDS plays structured within the formal confines of conventional tragedy.

Seronegativity is rarely presented explicitly in AIDS plays. Even in plays where characters question or reveal their HIV serostatus, seronegativity is positioned outside the drama of the play. Instead, the dramatic tension revolves around either HIV-antibody testing or the disclosure of an unexpected HIV infection. In the 1989 revised version of Terrence McNally's play *The Lisbon Traviata*, for example, the question of HIV-antibody testing, which is not included in the initial 1985 version, becomes a means for the protagonist Stephen to manipulate his soon-to-be ex-lover into remaining in their relationship. Mike, who still lives with Stephen, has started a new relationship with Paul.

> STEPHEN: I worry about you. Has he been tested?
> MIKE: Yes. We both have. Have you?[30]

Mike reverses the power dynamic of Stephen's question, which is meant to imply that Paul is a threat to Mike's health, first by responding that he and Paul
have both been tested and then by redirecting the question back to Stephen. He
never reveals to Stephen the test results and, by extension, the audience is unsure of Mike's and Paul's serostatus. Seronegativity, if we are meant to believe
through this exchange that Mike and Paul are HIV-negative, remains unmarked. The accusatory directness of their questioning—"Has he been tested?"
"Have you?"—suggests that HIV testing will determine more than the presence
of antibodies to HIV. Testing is introduced as a means to discredit or call into
question the moral fiber of a gay man's character. In *The Lisbon Traviata*, the dramatic tension is located in the force of the very questioning of serostatus and
not in the actual results of HIV-antibody testing.

In Harvey Fierstein's *On Tidy Endings*, the final one-act play in his trilogy
Safe Sex (1987), Arthur, a gay widow who recently buried his lover, competes
with Marion, the man's former wife, for the various entitlements that come
with being the surviving "spouse." At the play's conclusion, it's revealed that
Marion, and not Arthur, has tested HIV-positive:

MARION: I keep meaning to ask you; how are you?
ARTHUR (*At first puzzled and then*): Oh, you mean my health? Fine. No, I'm
fine. I've been tested, and nothing. We were very careful. We took many
precautions. Collin used to make jokes about how we should invest in rub-
ber futures.
MARION: I'll bet.
ARTHUR (*Stops what he's doing*): It never occurred to me until now. How
about you?
MARION (*Not stopping*): Well, we never had sex after he got sick.
ARTHUR: But before?
MARION (*Stopping but not looking up*): I have the antibodies in my blood.
No signs that it will develop into anything else. And it's been five years,
so my chances are pretty good that I'm just a carrier.
ARTHUR: I'm so sorry. Collin never told me.
MARION: He didn't know. In fact, other than my husband and the doctors,
you're the only one I've told.[31]

Arthur's announcement that he is HIV-negative is immediately upstaged by
Marion's disclosure that she is HIV-positive. The play ends with this exchange
of information and nothing else. There are no discussions of what it means to
be a gay man who is HIV-negative and how he can remain so, or of what it
means to be an HIV-positive woman and how she can find treatment and support. HIV-antibody test results are the end point of the drama, a dramatic device
that signals a reversal of fortune.

AIDS plays and performances, as I have argued throughout this book, participate in the formation of our larger understanding of AIDS. In this sense, they are capable of introducing and formulating certain pedagogical interventions that can help us begin to resolve AIDS. In terms of HIV prevention, AIDS plays and performances historically have left the question of HIV-negativity and seroconversion unexplored. In part, this may have to do with the conventional formal design of AIDS plays, which tend to be tragedies, and with the cultural constraint of viewing AIDS as essentially tragic. AIDS plays and performances avoid the challenge of representing HIV-negatives and addressing seronegativity, and focus instead on the alleged "good story" or "good drama" of people living with HIV and AIDS. One effect of this phenomenon in the theatre is the inadvertent replication of AIDS as inevitable: when AIDS plays exclusively focus on presenting and representing a variation on the same "good drama" of the person living with, or dying from, AIDS, the theatre unwittingly duplicates AIDS culture's neglect of the problem of seroconversion among HIV-negative gay men. AIDS theatre, while not responsible for educating its audiences about specific issues regarding AIDS, should still be examined from a critical standpoint in terms of the implications of its representations. Moreover, plays and performances about AIDS participate in the formation of AIDS ideologies, which have direct impact on the lives of their audiences. The fact that AIDS plays and performances do not address seronegativity is not an indictment of these plays; rather this fact is symptomatic of a larger cultural process in which the theatre is complicit. One way to approach this problem of representation is to focus on the relationship between dramatic form and its audience. Most AIDS plays attempt to universalize AIDS; playwrights and performers want to reach as wide an audience as possible in order to raise the issue of AIDS as a general concern for everyone. The irony here is that in the attempt to reach mainstream audiences, and for playwrights "mainstream" audiences almost always means uninfected audiences, the specific psychosocial issues of HIV-negative gay men are not addressed. Plays which neglect to differentiate the issues specific to the various relationships of their audiences to AIDS confuse the identifications between the spectator and the representation.[32]

The failure of AIDS activists and educators since 1985 to establish primary-prevention efforts specific to HIV-negative gay men was symptomatic of a larger political need to address the lives of the new category for those who were infected but not diagnosed with AIDS: "HIV-positive." Furthermore, the sociopolitical effects of this inadvertent neglect of HIV-negatives, extended beyond the specific practices of HIV prevention and into gay male culture. Undifferentiated AIDS pedagogies fail to acknowledge and address the differences between HIV-negatives, HIV-positives, and people with AIDS. Undifferentiated primary HIV-prevention efforts for uninfected gay men fail to mark HIV-negatives as the only outcome population. This missed opportunity to mark seronegativity within the address of primary-prevention campaigns has contributed to the rising rates of seroconversion among this outcome population. AIDS plays, although not necessarily designed as sites of HIV-prevention pedagogies, nonetheless participate in the ways that AIDS is understood. The circulation of AIDS plays—locally, regionally, and nationally; before HIV-antibody testing and since; through theatrical production, through publication—contributes to this understanding. In the theatre, the limited understanding of "HIV-negative" produces a paradox between representation and reception. Most AIDS plays written by gay men about contemporary gay life, although they fail to mark and explore the psychosocial issues of HIV-negative gay men, direct their representations to an assumed HIV-negative audience. In the attempt to universalize AIDS issues and speak to virtually everyone, contemporary AIDS plays—like undifferentiated HIV-prevention campaigns—produce confused identifications for its uninfected audiences. HIV-negative gay male spectators are directed to identify with the character with AIDS in order, as I have argued throughout this book, to forge political alliances with people living with HIV. The fact that AIDS plays produce few if any representations of HIV-negative characters contributes to the possibility of over-identifying with people with HIV. This over-identification puts into motion the disregard of the issues specific to HIV-negative gay men. It also, on an unconscious level, helps maintain the fallacy that for gay men AIDS is inevitable.

AIDS plays, of course, are not necessarily intended as a site for primary HIV-prevention, nor should they be expected to establish HIV-prevention efforts. Nonetheless the circulation of these plays provides a location where AIDS pedagogies—both intended and inadvertent—are produced. In this sense, AIDS plays and performances are often understood—both consciously and unconsciously—as conveying AIDS pedagogies even when they do not intend to do so. AIDS plays and performances *do* teach us *something* about AIDS, and these lessons convey certain ideological meanings and biases.

AIDS plays and performances generally do not differentiate their audiences by the spectator's HIV-status, nor am I suggesting that they should.[33] However, in calling attention to the undifferentiated address of AIDS plays, I want to point out the ramifications of this practice, especially as it concerns HIV-negative gay male audiences. I base my claim that AIDS plays and performances tend to address assumed uninfected audiences on the fact that there are very few plays and productions directed specifically to people living with HIV and AIDS. Even within performances by and about people with AIDS, the primary pedagogical effect of these productions is to instruct audiences on what it is like to live with HIV or AIDS. For people living with HIV or AIDS, the implied pedagogical address of these productions relays the important message that people with HIV or AIDS can still work, that HIV is not a "death sentence." This message, however, is never targeted only for people living with HIV; in fact, the message is directed toward all of its audience members. Although these productions are undifferentiated in terms of audience address, one of their most effective interventions is that they specify the representation of people living with HIV and AIDS as such. The aim of deliberate discursive markings such as "HIV-positive" and "person with AIDS" is to provide the spectator with a more expansive understanding of what it means to be living with HIV or AIDS. As of yet, no specific discursive marking for "HIV-negative" exists within these productions.

Consider Paul Rudnick's successful comedy *Jeffrey*, which was first produced at New York City's WPA Theatre in 1993. Jeffrey, according to Rudnick's stage directions, "is in his thirties, attractive, and well put-together. He is an innocent; he is outgoing and optimistic, cheerful despite all odds. Jeffrey believes that life should be wonderful."[34] The play opens with a condom breaking, the first of many frustrations in a humorous scene which satirizes gay male safer-sex negotiations, negotiations which lead Jeffrey to declare sexual abstinence: "No sex!" (7). The following scenes introduce various supporting characters who depict urban gay life in the midst of AIDS and who serve to remind the audience that Jeffrey's decision to abstain from sex is not a representative practice of the gay community. Jeffrey's "no sex" declaration sets up the initial dramatic tension. Can Jeffrey—who confesses in the first of his many direct addresses to the audience: "You know those articles, the ones all those right wingers use? The ones that talk about gay men who've had over five thousand sexual partners? Well compared to me, they're shut-ins" (7)—succeed in sexual abstinence? The scenes and characters provide the laugh track and the framework for a traditionally plotted romantic comedy, one so successful that Frank Rich, writing in the *New York Times*, proclaimed the play as "the funniest play of this season and maybe last season, too."[35] Among these characters is Steve, "a good-looking, extremely sexual man in his thirties" (8), whom Jeffrey first meets at the gym. Steve challenges Jeffrey's decision to abstain from sex and proceeds to court him. After meeting up with Steve at the home of Sterling and Darius, a couple who know them both, Jeffrey finally agrees to a date with Steve. In an effort at honesty, Steve announces to Jeffrey that he is HIV-positive:

STEVE: And Jeffrey?
JEFFREY: Yes?
STEVE: I just . . . okay, just so are there no surprises . . .

JEFFREY: Uh-huh.
STEVE: I'm HIV-positive.
JEFFREY (*after a beat*): Um, okay, right.
STEVE: Does that make a difference?
JEFFREY: No. No. Of course not.
STERLING (*dismissing any doubt*): Please.
DARIUS: HIV-positive men are the hottest.
STEVE: I mean—I'd understand. I'd be hurt and disappointed, but—I just wanted to be clear.
JEFFREY: No really, it's fine—I mean, come on, it's the nineties, right? (33)

Steve's announcement, the dramatic device of the HIV-positive disclosure standard in AIDS plays, sets up the dramatic tension of the play: AIDS as love's obstacle. What will Jeffrey do? Jeffrey, who's already sworn off sex, remains steadfast. He cancels the date, retreats from his gay friends, and decides to leave New York City to return to Wisconsin.

Although Jeffrey never announces his serostatus, we are led to believe that he is HIV-negative. Critics, too, assume Jeffrey's HIV-negativity: "Interestingly," Michael Feingold remarks in the *Village Voice*, "[Jeffrey] never seems to worry that his promiscuous past may have already infected him."[36] Promiscuity, Feingold should remember, has nothing to do with HIV transmission; unprotected sex, however, does.[37] Still, Feingold's comment is worth consideration. Although Jeffrey "never seems to worry" that he is infected, his decision to abstain from sex is a familiar strategy for those who *plan* to get tested or retested. Many gay men stop having sex for a three- to six-month period before testing (the supposed interval between infection and the presence of the HIV antibody in the bloodstream) in order to ensure the accuracy of their test results. If Jeffrey is one of these men who are unsure of their serostatus, he keeps this uncertainty to himself. Many HIV-negative gay men also choose to abstain from sex once they become aware of their serostatus in order to preserve it, a process which William Johnston terms "revirginization."[38] Jeffrey, an "innocent," may believe himself a revirgin. Jeffrey never confides either of these positions, so why then is he assumed by spectators to be HIV-negative? In part, spectators may assume Jeffrey is uninfected because HIV-negative gay men generally present themselves publicly as unmarked. In dramatic representation an unspecified serostatus signals that the character is untested or seronegative. Characters who are HIV-positive or living with AIDS, on the other hand, are identified as such. *Jeffrey* seems to follow this pattern. The fact that Jeffrey never marks his serostatus suggests that he doesn't need to do so; in this sense, seronegativity is presented as a position of privilege. HIV-negative status functions similarly to what José Muñoz, in addressing the racial politics of the 1995 film version of

Jeffrey, terms the "normative imprint."[39] According to Muñoz, the normative imprint of whiteness is an image of "ideality and normativity" that remains unexamined in cultural representation even as it is positioned in relation to a racialized other. If white men are exempt from identifying as such, so
HIV-negative gay men are exempt from explicitly identifying or being so
identified in relation to HIV. This option is typically not available to gay men
living with HIV.

Jeffrey never justifies his decision to renounce sex, nor does he raise any
concerns about his health. Jeffrey's only problem, so far as the play is concerned, would seem to be his anxiety around sex. Jeffrey's decision to cancel
the date with Steve, for example, is based on a type of fear which he is unable
to specify. In yet another address to the audience, he asks: "Okay, what am I so
afraid of? Him getting sick? me getting sick?" (39). Jeffrey refuses to date Steve
because he is HIV-positive: "I just—couldn't deal with it. Not right now" (46).
Steve continues to court Jeffrey, offering Jeffrey a complete profile of his health
record. Jeffrey, who's sexually attracted to Steve, still refuses to kiss him. The
HIV-positive character is burdened with the responsibility of full disclosure,
while the presumed HIV-negative character is able to maintain a silence around
his own relation to HIV. Jeffrey even seems to assume that he is uninfected and
this despite the broken condom scene which opens the play. In fact, no one in
the play ever questions Jeffrey's status. Rudnick's supporting characters are not
concerned with Jeffrey's serostatus; they prefer to question the choices Jeffrey
makes and respond to him accordingly. Throughout the play, safer sex is introduced as the primary means to prevent the transmission of HIV. Jeffrey, however, sees HIV as the obstacle to his happiness and safe sex as too complicated
for him to negotiate. Thus he chooses to abandon sex entirely. Jeffrey's inability
to engage safe sex as a viable option is perceived by his friends, prospective
sexual partners, and love interests as his major problem. For them, and everyone
else in the play, HIV status is not necessarily the issue—unsafe sex is the issue.
In this sense, whether Jeffrey is HIV-negative, HIV-positive, or untested is beside the point. Safer sex, as his friends and acquaintances demonstrate, is a collective endeavor undertaken and supported by his community. Safer sex is presented as the normative ideology of the play's gay community. Jeffrey, not the
others, is the one who is outside of this social belief structure.

Jeffrey's confusion around the issue of safer sex results in his decision to
abstain from sex entirely and remove himself from gay culture and community.
His confusion activates the spectator's confusion. Jeffrey is presented as a sort
of gay Everyman, a regular, good-natured guy who is unable to cope with the
reality of HIV. His direct addresses to the audience assume a certain complicity on the part of the spectator—we are encouraged to identify with Jeffrey and

sympathize with his dilemma. But Jeffrey's unmarked HIV status complicates this identification. If Jeffrey is HIV-negative, is the ideal spectator also HIV-negative? And if the ideal spectator is assumed to be HIV-negative, what then does *Jeffrey* say to gay men who are HIV-positive? The undifferentiated address—who does Jeffrey represent and to whom is Rudnick speaking?—allows for the play, like its central character, to abstain from certain risks of its own, specifically the risk of alienating spectators with HIV. The undifferentiated address, moreover, proves confusing both to spectators who are HIV-negative and to those who are HIV-positive.[40] Such a muddled attempt to establish a universalized spectatorial position ends up bringing forth the question of serostatus introduced but unresolved in the play. In one scene, a mock fashion show of AIDS-wear, Steve raises the question of Jeffrey's serostatus: "What will today's sassy and sophisticated HIV-positive male be wearing this spring, to tempt the elusive, *possibly negative* waitperson?" (59, my emphasis). Steve's provocation unsettles the audience's presumption that Jeffrey is HIV-negative. Jeffrey doesn't clarify Steve's comment, leading Steve to decide for himself that Jeffrey must be HIV-negative. Moreover, spectators are now forced, like Steve, to consider Jeffrey's serostatus. Steve, in other words, forces the issue.

Steve, the HIV-positive character, carries the burden of responsibility for raising and exploring the relations between HIV and sex, between HIV status and gay community, and for demonstrating how gay men have formulated identities based on their HIV-test results.[41] From this perspective, Steve is the pedagogical center of the play. Steve's efforts, however, are not enough to convince Jeffrey to live his life fully. That task is shared by Darius, the endearing chorus member of *Cats*, who, after his AIDS-related death, returns to offer Jeffrey and the audience the play's moral:

> DARIUS: Jeffrey, I'm dead. You're not.
> JEFFREY: I know that.
> DARIUS: You do? Prove it.
> JEFFREY: What do you mean?
> DARIUS: Go dancing. Go to a show. Make trouble. Make out. Hate AIDS, Jeffrey. Not life. (84)

The play ends with Jeffrey following Darius's advice. Jeffrey decides to be with Steve. The HIV-positive gay man and the spirit of the person with AIDS teach Jeffrey about life's pleasures. Jeffrey, on the other hand, teaches no one.

The play concludes with Jeffrey's new-found commitment to life and love. The final image of *Jeffrey* is of Jeffrey and Steve on top of the Empire State Building tossing a balloon (fig. 35). Earlier, in a hilarious scene between Jeffrey and a lustful priest, the image of people tossing a balloon and trying to keep it from

35. John Michael Higgins as Jeffrey and Tom Hewitt as Steve in Paul Rudnick's *Jeffrey*,
WPA Theater production, New York City, 1993.
Martha Swope © Time Inc.

touching the ground is introduced to signify, according to the priest, "the very
best in all of us" (69). In the final scene, the balloon, and the effort to keep it
afloat, still contains its original meaning, but it now suggests the prophylactic
between them. The balloon stands in for the condom, broken in the play's first
scene, the negotiated risk Jeffrey is now willing to assume.

Jeffrey's failure to explore HIV negativity is absorbed by the play's final im-
age, which announces the formation of a serodiscordant couple. And yet,
within this magnetic relationship, only one identity—HIV-positive—is marked.
HIV-negative, Jeffrey's assumed status, remains the unexplored term in the
HIV-negative/HIV-positive binarism. *Jeffrey* seems to want to speak to HIV-
negative gay men, to teach the Jeffreys in the gay community to "Hate AIDS,
Jeffrey. Not life." The play's message, however, is undifferentiated—who is
Jeffrey?—and universalized—Jeffrey is everyone—and because of this, the play
ends up leaving the specific issues of HIV-negatives on hold. We never know
Jeffrey or his issues except on the most superficial of terms. Rather than pre-
senting Jeffrey as being negative and negotiating his life accordingly, Rudnick

obscures the content and practices of being negative, of how to go about being (and remaining) negative. Rudnick's universal message, along with his jubilant depiction of gay men's spirit and wit, intervenes in the logic of AIDS as tragic. "It's easy to write about despair. It's tough to present optimism realistically and appealingly. I think it's a worthwhile goal to help people find genuine pleasure without feeling like fools," he explained to *Time* magazine.[42] *Jeffrey* accomplishes this goal. Rudnick notably taps into comedy's ability to temporarily resolve social tension through laughter and through the always temporary social renewal made possible by love's fulfillment. In this sense, the dramatic form of romantic comedy provides Rudnick the theatrical means to best achieve his "worthwhile goal."

Jeffrey concludes with the image of love's triumph, a happy ending. Northrop Frye, who has written extensively on comedy, explains that

> [h]appy endings do not impress us as true, but as desirable, and they are brought about by manipulation. The watcher of death and tragedy has nothing to do but sit and wait for the inevitable end; but something gets born at the end of comedy, and the watcher of birth is a member of a busy society. (170)[43]

Jeffrey's watchers of birth are, no doubt, members of a busy society desiring a joyful life in the midst of AIDS. Rudnick successfully manipulates his audiences to laugh at AIDS, and his efforts here serve to remind gay men of our resilience throughout these harrowing times.[44] Rudnick, however, is unable to bring forth comedy's potential to accommodate the specific issues of HIV-negative gay men. Still, Rudnick's failure should not be individuated as his failure alone. The inability to address HIV negativity explicitly is symptomatic of a larger process of neglect endemic to gay culture. The cultural neglect is predicated, as I have argued, in part by the idea that to announce one's HIV-negative serostatus is to differentiate politically from people living with HIV and AIDS. Rudnick's undeveloped exploration of Jeffrey's issues as a presumably HIV-negative gay man raises questions regarding the theatre's ability to present this discourse: is this problem in *Jeffrey* related to the play's undifferentiated address or to the limits of the comic form? Perhaps, as Northrop Frye argues, the hero of a comedy, a genre which traditionally favors the renewal of community over the triumph of the individual, is a catalyst whose primary purpose is to help the play's society renew its values. In this sense, comedy does not set out to address the issues of the hero, but rather the issues of the society in which the hero lives.

In Rudnick's play, Jeffrey is the comic hero. Since it is Jeffrey who seems most out of sync with the social norms governing the world of the play, it is therefore Jeffrey's social reformation that brings about the happy ending. The happy ending, moreover, informs the desired world of the play's society and of the larger culture which produces the play. The hero is part of this world, although his social role is unrealized until the play's conclusion. Thus, as Northrop Frye explains,

> [t]he successful hero is so often left undeveloped: his real life begins at the end of the play, and we have to believe him to be potentially a more interesting character than he appears to be. (169)

Romantic comedy, as Frye reminds us, is a dramatic form which insists on the rejuvenation of the comic society. If tragedy has been unable to accommodate the issues specific to HIV-negative gay men, perhaps comedy, with its insistence on social renewal and survival, will. But comedy's promise of a happy ending is often conditioned by a conservative gesture toward conformity emblematized by the insistence on marriage. For gay men resistant to the domesticating impulse of marriage, comedy's fetishization of the couple poses yet another series of concerns, mainly what Paul Morrison suggests as "the end of pleasure."[45] The idea that survival is linked with a kind of bourgeois couplehood has been the subject of radical critique and debate since the early 1980s. *Jeffrey* absorbs this tension through its ending, offering no comment on the radical departure of the conventional romantic pairing, which in traditional comedy is the young and healthy heterosexual couple who signify both reproduction and the regeneration of the community. The play closes and forestalls the question of Jeffrey's future. The HIV-negative gay man's future is secured in love's resolution even if the members of this relationship are serodiscordant. Perhaps, as Frye argues, this is because Jeffrey's "real life" begins at the end of the play.[46] In those as yet to be staged moments of Jeffrey's promised future, his development as an interesting and insightful HIV-negative gay man may potentially emerge. In other words, Jeffrey's assumed seronegativity is not a sign, as he initially imagines, that he has escaped AIDS. Staying negative is itself a lifelong struggle. Perhaps, in this case, it is the limit of the comic form that withholds the discussion of Jeffrey's performance as HIV-negative as an ongoing process. The exploration of this process of being negative was the promise of Rudnick's *Jeffrey*, although its realization remains unfulfilled by the play's end. Jeffrey still needs to negotiate for himself a way of being negative which acknowledges the difficult challenges of remaining uninfected. In other words, we have to believe the HIV-negative gay male—and in Rudnick's play, he is Jeffrey—to be potentially a more interesting person than he appears to be.

HIV-negative gay men are prominent in Terrence McNally's 1995 Tony Award–winning drama, *Love! Valour! Compassion!* Unlike *Jeffrey*, there are no se-

36. Original Broadway cast of Terrence McNally's *Love! Valour! Compassion!* (left to right) John Glover, Randy Becker, Justin Kirk, Anthony Heald, John Benjamin Hickey, (at bottom) Nathan Lane and Stephen Bogardus, Walter Kerr Theatre, New York City, 1995.
Martha Swope © Time Inc.

rodiscordant couples in the four sets of lovers in the play, nor is McNally interested in exploring the comic hero's journey into the social. Instead *Love! Valour! Compassion!* dramatizes the social world as it already is understood. Seronegativity is not the topic of *Love! Valour! Compassion!* Still, the prominence of HIV-negative gay men, even if, for the most part, they are inconspicuous as HIV-negative gay men, provides a glimpse into the ways that HIV-negative gay men interact with one another and with gay men living with HIV. McNally's play portrays eight gay men, most from New York City, who gather one summer for the major holiday weekends—Memorial Day, the Fourth of July, and Labor Day—at the upstate New York summer home of Gregory, a successful choreographer and dancer (fig. 36). The play has been compared to the major works of Chekhov and to Mart Crowley's 1965 play *The Boys in the Band*,[47] but its comic structure, multiple lovers, and invocation of the pastoral seem more in line with Shakespeare's romantic comedies, especially *As You Like It*. (The play even includes a Jacques figure, John Jeckyll: the malcontent who is left unpaired at the play's end.) Like most comedies, *Love! Valour! Compassion!* is a play about generational relations and struggles, romantic love and sexual desire, and the expressive needs of individuals for the communal. And like most plays that address gay issues, characters with AIDS are central in the drama. In an interesting romantic turn, the only two characters with AIDS become lovers. Buzz, a thirty-something musical-comedy fanatic and GMHC volunteer who is forever looking for a boyfriend, finds one in James, a British costume designer in his late forties who is visiting his twin brother, John. Their courtship and romance, while a reminder to audiences that people with AIDS can have fulfilling sexual and emotional lives, suggests implicitly that the world of *Love! Valour! Compassion!* supports seroconcordant relationships. In fact, all of the relationships in the play are structured around a shared HIV status. Among the other couples, all presumably HIV-negative, are Gregory, a forty-three-year-old choreographer, and Bobby, his blind lover who is in his early twenties; John, who arrives each holiday weekend with Ramon, an up-and-coming Puerto-Rican dancer in his early twenties and the only nonwhite; and Arthur and Perry, two men in their "late thirties/early forties" who have been together for fourteen years. Among these latter couples, only Arthur and Perry discuss being uninfected. And while Arthur, an accountant, and Perry, a lawyer, are sometimes teased for their domestic predictabilities, they provide much of the emotional structure and continuity for the others nonetheless. In other words, the HIV-negative couple, while not necessarily "interesting," are appreciated as important and beloved members of a kinship circle composed of more artistically creative and sexually adventurous friends.

In the play's most explicit scene addressing the distinct experiences between HIV-negatives and people living with HIV, two sets of couples are canoeing separately on the lake. In one canoe, Arthur and Perry question their survival. In the other canoe, Buzz and James contend with health matters. The image of these seroconcordant couples—an HIV-negative pair, an HIV-positive pair—canoeing on the lake becomes a metaphor for these men's relationship to AIDS. Although they are "paddling" through the same waters, they are not in the same boat. Their experiences of AIDS—as HIV-negative gay men; as gay men living with HIV—bring forth separate issues and specific concerns. While Buzz and James must deal with the often random physical effects of their compromised immune systems, Arthur and Perry discuss the emotional effects of AIDS on the uninfected. By focusing on Arthur and Perry, McNally puts forward the idea that the HIV-negative couple's experience of AIDS may also be "a good story":

PERRY: How did we manage?
ARTHUR: Depends on who you slept with.
PERRY: Fourteen years. I haven't been perfect. Just lucky.
ARTHUR: I've been perfect.
PERRY: Sure you have!
ARTHUR: Do you ever feel guilty?
PERRY: No, grateful. Why, do you?
ARTHUR: It used to be nearly all the time. No, first I was just scared. Then the guilt. Massive at first. Why not me? That lingers, more than the fear. We've never really talked about this. Paddle.
PERRY: I'm paddling.
ARTHUR: Every time I look at Buzz, even when he's driving me crazy, or now James, I have to think, I have to say to myself, "Sooner or later, that man, that human being, is not going to be standing there washing the dishes or tying his shoelace."
PERRY: None of us is. Are. Is. Are?
ARTHUR: I don't know. Are. You're right. It's no comfort, but you're right.
PERRY: Will be. None of us will be.
ARTHUR: Paddle, I said.
PERRY: Why not, not you?
ARTHUR: That's a good question. I wish I could answer it.[48]

Various complex emotions are introduced, displaying the range of contradictory and at times even competing feelings—luck, guilt, gratitude, fear—HIV-negatives often experience. Although Arthur and Perry never say they are HIV-negative, their conversation leaves little doubt. The HIV-negative couple is represented in this scene neither in competition with the couple with HIV nor to set up the couple with HIV as more dramatic.[49] Instead, the scene stages the two couples as undergoing a shared but distinct experience.[50] Still it is peculiar that in a play about the lives and kinship structures of eight urban gay men, where the concerns of people living with HIV are explicitly accommodated, the HIV-negative couple must retreat, from a summer house already troped as pastoral, in order to give voice to their experiences of AIDS *as* uninfected gay men. Their conversation occurs outside the walls of Gregory's home and in the private "green world" of the lake, unheard by any of the other characters. Moreover, it seems implausible that Arthur and Perry, two gay men whose fourteen-year relationship began before AIDS, have never had such a conversation—"We've never really talked about this." The scene highlights the silence around HIV negativity and the resulting survivor's guilt that accompanies this silence:

ARTHUR: . . . He gets sick, I don't. Why is that? I think we should both go together. Is that gay solidarity or a death wish?
PERRY: Don't talk like that.

ARTHUR: I will always feel guilty in some private part of me that I don't let anyone see but you, and not even you all of it; I will always feel like a bystander at the genocide of who we are.
PERRY: You're not a bystander.
ARTHUR: If you didn't save the human race you're a bystander.
PERRY: That's crazy. You sound like Buzz.
ARTHUR: That's how I feel.
PERRY: You're not a bystander. (122)

By the end of the lake scene, the two couples (now back on land) regroup in the kinship network of the house. Once back at the house, Arthur and Perry resume the banal discourse that characterizes the majority of their conversations and those of the group. The issue is never reintroduced. Despite the various symposia throughout the play, where the characters debate a wide range of topics, very little of substance is shared verbally between these men. In these Chekhovian moments, where silences and miscommunications punctuate the extended conversations, McNally foregrounds the need for these eight gay men to forge intimacy. In this sense, the mood of the play, while uproariously funny thanks to Buzz's campy quick-wittedness, borders on the tragicomic. Communication and connection is an effort in *Love! Valour! Compassion!* and this effort—sometimes successful and sometimes not—is what is communicated to the audience of the play.

If the characters are occasionally incapable or unwilling to sustain connection with one another, they are determined to do so with the spectator. The most immediate verbal communications of *Love! Valour! Compassion!* are directed to the audience. Throughout the play, characters will break the fourth wall to narrate the events as they are occurring or to express their inner feelings. Unlike *Jeffrey*, where only the title character has this direct address to the audience and thereby manipulates the spectator's identification, most of the characters of *Love! Valour! Compassion!* shift in and out of commenting on the action of the play. One potential result of this strategy is that audience members are provided with both a more expansive identificatory continuum in which to locate themselves *and* a sense of the communal commitments that these characters enact for one another. HIV negativity, however, is never the subject of these dramatic asides. Nor is HIV negativity and the possibility of seroconversion the subject of any of the conversations among the men in the house.

Love! Valour! Compassion! presents three generations of gay men—gay men in their twenties, thirties, and forties—and stages the various relationships—lovers, friends, collaborators—between them. Some of these relationships are intragenerational. Perry and Arthur, for example, are generational peers, as are the two youngest, Ramon and Bobby, who are in their early twenties. But only

Perry and Arthur seem interchangeable. Every other relationship, romantic or otherwise, is marked by difference—age, ethnicity, serostatus—and those differences promote much of the drama in the play. Perry and Arthur, affluent and professional, white HIV-negative gay men, bear the mark of privilege in the play. Their interchangeability, moreover, seems necessitated. In many ways, their similarity, rather than obscuring their identity, actually pushes it forward. Unlike the other gay men in the play, Arthur and Perry become representative of a generational norm which the other characters are positioned against. "We're role models," Perry says to James after explaining that he's been with Arthur for fourteen years, "It's very stressful" (84). Perry's self-reflective comment, while somewhat ironic, seems to refer to the position he and Arthur inadvertently hold as partners in a long-term relationship, a concept already laden with various moral values—fidelity, commitment, maturity—that they rehearse for each other and the others throughout the play. But since they also represent a generational norm and are presented as self-identifying uninfected gay men, this notion of the role model takes on an added embedded meaning. As older uninfected gay men who have lived through fourteen years of AIDS and all that this entails, Arthur and Perry are positioned uniquely to role-model for a younger generation of gay men determined to remain uninfected. Unfortunately, they do not do so. Arthur and Perry are barely capable of discussing their seronegativity among themselves—"We've never really talked about this"—let alone introducing the topic to others. Their occasional encounters with the younger gay men are awkward and strained. There is no "role-modeling" on remaining uninfected on their behalf. In fact, the older generation of uninfected gay men—Arthur, Perry, Gregory, and John—have little to offer the younger generation—Bobby and Ramon—on their experiences of AIDS, nor do they even seem all that interested in this possibility. During one symposium, Perry observes how the older gay men have taken over the conversation—"The younger generation hasn't put in their two cents worth, I notice" (53).

Bobby and Ramon, as representatives of a generation who have come out into a gay public world already informed by AIDS, are the counterparts to Arthur and Perry, gay men who have had to adjust to the reality and threat of AIDS. Unlike Arthur and Perry, who embody—as white, affluent, healthy, and able-bodied—the position of unmarked privilege, Bobby and Ramon bear the marks of difference. Bobby's blindness and Ramon's ethnicity already situate them outside the governing norms of the play, as does their age. Within the kinship structures of the play and the formal conventions of the comedy, they represent the social future of the play's world. This idea of a future, endemic to comedy, is much more problematic in light of AIDS. Bobby and Ramon, as uninfected younger gay men, suggest not simply a future but a certain kind of

future. Younger HIV-negative gay men often feel as if they must remain uninfected for the future of the gay community. Thus, as William Johnston explains,
"[HIV-negative gay men] viewed staying uninfected not only as a personal responsibility but as a communal one" (229).[51] This is the case for most uninfected
gay men regardless of their age. Younger gay men, however, are often viewed
because of their age as potentially seeing the end of AIDS within their lifetimes.
In this sense, Bobby and Ramon, like Jeffrey, are largely symbolic. McNally does
not explore the social meaning of their affair or Bobby and Ramon's own sense
of it. Instead, their affair is presented in terms of its effect on the others in the
house.[52] Bobby and Ramon, whose initial sexual liaison opens the play, never
return to center stage again. Only in the final scene of act 1, an exhaustive post-
dinner group debate, when the other older gay men finally leave the dining
room table, do Bobby and Ramon share the stage again. Their conversation,
however, is not audible. The spectator only hears Buzz narrate that "Bobby and
Ramon sat quietly talking across the deserted dining table—empty glasses and
soiled napkins between them" (62). The first act ends with this image of the two
younger gay men at the table, their concerns unheard. They too must be potentially more interesting than they appear to be.

I raise this issue of role-modeling and its effects on younger HIV-negative
gay men in order to pursue a line of questioning that unveils the ideological
effects of the play's pedagogy around HIV and AIDS. Uninfected gay men of
all ages experience confused identifications with HIV. For older gay men, like
Arthur and Perry (whose personal history with the epidemic spans over a decade), sexually active before AIDS and before knowing their HIV-antibody test
results, the confused identification begins with the possibility of having been
infected and not knowing so. Once aware of their status, they experience survivor's guilt. Younger gay men, like Bobby and Ramon, come out into a public
world already informed by AIDS. Gay identity and gay community are already
linked with AIDS, because of this, as Walt Odets explains, "younger men . . .
may experience confused identifications with HIV." Odets is concerned with the
possible disenfranchisement of younger HIV-negative gay men from gay communities because of this confused identification—that AIDS is inevitable, that
HIV-positive culture is gay culture—and the relationship between these feelings and thoughts with the rising rates of seroconversion:

> Thus for younger men, *some* confused identifications with AIDS and vir-
> tually all feelings of disenfranchisement for being uninfected are a prod-
> uct of undifferentiated education and the community values that support
> it. It is crucial that younger men—*every one of whom enters the gay community
> in an uninfected condition*—not be exposed to these influences. At the present

time, we are using publicly funded and generated education to acculturate young gay men into psychological confusions that exacerbate the transmission of HIV.[53]

Both of the younger men in *Love! Valour! Compassion!* already feel a certain disenfranchisement from the world of the play: Bobby, because he is blind; Ramon, because he is Latino. These differences, which the other HIV-negative gay men tend to either obscure or reduce them to, inform the younger men's identities.[54] Gregory is the shared link between the play's two generations. He is Bobby's lover and Ramon's mentor. Gregory, we might say, is at the center of the play's pedagogical politics. He teaches Buzz tennis, his guests the *Pas de Cygnes* from *Swan Lake*, and Ramon his newest dance. And it is only Gregory, in the play's most overt moment of generational legacy, who offers something both personal and tangible to the gay men in their twenties. Gregory's decision to give his newest work to Ramon to dance at its world premiere becomes the moment of passage in which the creative legacy of one generation is handed on to the next. Dance, perhaps the most elusive of the performing arts in terms of documentation, becomes the site for intergenerational connection. It stands in as a reminder that queer people, unlike heterosexuals, do not have the larger institutional or ideological structures which secure community from one generation to the next. But Gregory's decision to offer Ramon his new choreography also symbolizes the fact that queer culture passes from one generation to another despite the constraints under which queer people exist.

In terms of HIV and AIDS, Bobby and Ramon's potential disenfranchisement from the gay community is unclear since neither they nor any of the other HIV-negatives ever discuss their serostatus and its emotional effects publicly. This failure to address seronegativity, HIV transmission, and the means to remain uninfected ultimately becomes one of the HIV and AIDS ideologies circulating in the play. The inability of an older generation of uninfected gay men to mentor a younger generation of gay men who might want role models for remaining uninfected further confuses the play's purported interest in this very notion of mentoring and teaching expressed by Arthur, Perry, and Gregory. This confusion is only heightened by the ambiguity of the play's conclusion.

McNally ends *Love! Valour! Compassion!* with each character speaking to the audience and fastforwarding to their death. The couples with marked serostatus speak first: Arthur and Perry live long lives and die quiet deaths; Buzz dies sooner than the others and "sooner than I thought, even"; James commits suicide (137). The circumstances of the characters' deaths are shaped by their HIV status. Those with a marked serostatus die deaths that confirm that HIV status; those with unmarked serostatus—who, at the time of the play, are presumably

HIV-negative—die deaths whose relation to HIV remains unclear. Ramon dies in a plane crash, although we aren't told when in his life this crash will occur. Bobby doesn't want to know about his death or doesn't want to tell. The deaths of the younger generation continue the concealment of their HIV status. In other words, there is no suggestion that they seroconverted and no suggestion that their deaths are unrelated to AIDS. John's and Gregory's deaths are similarly unmarked. The conflation of all these deaths replaces the primacy of the notion that for gay men AIDS is inevitable with the cliché that death is inevitable. By the end of the play, the reality of AIDS is eclipsed by the banality of death. No one—regardless of HIV-status—can escape death, or as Perry explained to Arthur in the canoe, "none of us will be." Tragedy and comedy converge; HIV-positive and HIV-negative become undifferentiated means to the same end. After forecasting their deaths, the eight gay men move offstage. The play's final image of the group shows the eight gay men undressing, moving toward the water, and finally swimming in the lake. This scene references the earlier canoe scene, where HIV-positives and HIV-negatives paddled the waters in separate canoes. Now back in these same waters, the eight gay men—naked and together—bath in the light of the full moon. Only now, and only for the moment, there is nothing between them. The pastoral world of the summer house, where men retreat to renew the bonds which form the social structures of communal life, is located at the rear of the stage, outside the reach of the audience. During this moment, John reappears alone frontstage and provides the play's epilogue, Perry's one-word response to nearly everything ["PERRY: I don't say 'anyway' when I'm cornered, I say it when I'm overcome"]: "Anyway." Perry's clumsy maneuver to shift the focus of the conversation becomes McNally's means to end the play.

Cornered or overcome? In *Love! Valour! Compassion!* McNally considers the way that gay men structure life under the constraints of AIDS. The tragic impulse which accompanies AIDS theatre is indulged in the suddenness of Buzz's death and in the abruptness of James's suicide. But comedy's impulse to focus on life and renewal is foregrounded in the long lives of Arthur and Perry and in the image of the men bathing in the lake. Gregory outlives everyone, including Bobby and Ramon, the younger generation, who signify the future. The death of the young suggests that there will be no future. Gregory's closing remarks confirm this idea. In the scene forecasting their deaths, Gregory reveals to Bobby that after their relationship, "there was no one else. Not even close. You were the last" (138). In dramatic literature, the death of the young registers the death of the community. If this is so, what then is left? Only the discourse of witnessing, which Gregory must perform alone: "I. Um. Bury every one of you. Um. It got. Um. Awfully lonely out here" (139). Once again, McNally indulges the impulse of tragedy. In *Love! Valour! Compassion!* tragedy's ubiquity is a given—as is HIV and AIDS. There is no hope except through temporary excursions into the troped world of the pastoral, of comedy. If tragedy is the genre of the infected and comedy the genre of the uninfected, then the hybrid genre of the play's structure—tragicomedy—is what allows McNally to deal with both HIV-negatives and HIV-positives. In other words, although McNally chooses to present only seroconcordant couplings in his play, the formal structure of *Love! Valour! Compassion!* supports genre discordance.[55] The actor double-cast as John/James stands as the emblem of this structure. As the central embodiment of the play's binary structures, the actor must perform HIV-positive and HIV-negative, good brother and bad brother, comedy and tragedy. In doing so, the actor calls into question the rigidity of the binary and brings to light the theatre's capacity to comment upon them. And yet despite such formal and representational innovations, the play leaves little room for the exploration of a restructured public world, a world where HIV-negatives and HIV-positives combine energies to bring the very lessons of the pastoral world back home.

In the year and a half between *Jeffrey* and *Love! Valour! Compassion!* a shift in the theatre's representations of HIV-negative gay men begins to emerge. The move from unmarked status to marked status signals a discursive opening where seronegativity can be more forcefully addressed. Consider, for example, Chay Yew's play *A Language of Their Own,* which was produced at the Public Theater in New York in 1995. *A Language of Their Own* begins with the breakup of Ming and Oscar, a gay Asian American couple who have lived together for four years in Boston. While their relationship has always been fraught with tensions, it is Oscar's recent HIV-positive test results which launch the breakup. It is also Oscar who initiates the discussion regarding their separation:

OSCAR: You know, this is not easy to say.
MING: Please, get on with it.
OSCAR: It's not working out. We've become two very different people.
MING: You just don't become different people overnight.
OSCAR: What I'm trying to say is that things haven't quite been the same.
MING: Let's not start this—
OSCAR: Especially—
MING: You always—
OSCAR: Since the test.
MING: The test. You always bring it up.
OSCAR: It's the truth.
MING: It's not true.
OSCAR: Of course, it's true. He has a life ahead of him, and my days have suddenly become numbered.[56]

Oscar leaves Ming, in part because Oscar doesn't want to saddle Ming with his illness. Oscar, however, does not immediately tell Ming his feelings. The final line in the dialogue quoted here is directed to the audience. At first, Oscar assumes Ming is HIV-negative, but soon he begins to question Ming's status and pushes Ming, who is reluctant, to get tested. Throughout these scenes, Ming's serostatus is unmarked. For a few more scenes, the question of Ming's serostatus becomes the subject of the play, an issue which forces the spectator to invest in the resolution of this information. Yew structures the beginning of the play in such a way that we are led to believe Ming's serostatus will matter and inform the rest of the plot. Before the end of act 1, Ming gets tested and finds out that he is HIV-negative. The information that Ming is HIV-negative pushes the couple further apart, although they do not communicate this to each other. Instead, the characters directly address the audience:

> MING: I suddenly felt free. Like I've been given wings. To fly.
> OSCAR: I am happy for him. I am. Yet I feel a little left behind. A little betrayed.
> MING: Then it got uncomfortable.
> OSCAR: We got uncomfortable.
> MING: We had nothing to say to each other.
> OSCAR: If we did, the word that lingered at the tip of our tongues was AIDS.
> MING: If we didn't, we thought it. Loudly.
> OSCAR: We stopped having sex. With each other.
> MING: All of a sudden, I couldn't bear his touch.
> OSCAR: We began spending strenuous hours in the apartment in our own different worlds.[57]

Ming and Oscar do split up. By the end of act 1, they are already in new relationships which pose their own distinct set of problems (fig. 37). (Ming gets involved with Robert, a white gay man, and moves with him to Los Angeles; Oscar meets Daniel, a young Filipino AIDS activist.) Ming and Oscar are no longer speaking to each other. But along with the fact that the play is the first mainstream production to focus on gay Asian Americans, what distinguishes *A Language of Their Own* from other plays that address AIDS is that Ming's struggle remains central to the unfolding of the drama. Unlike other AIDS plays, where the HIV-negative character is seen only in support of the character who is HIV-positive or who has AIDS, or where HIV test results resolve the drama of the play, *A Language of Their Own* focuses on the life of both the HIV-positive character and the HIV-negative character. Even after they split up as a couple, Oscar and Ming remain the dual focus of the plot. Yew does not prioritize one

37. Francis Jue as Oscar and Alec Mapa as Daniel (foreground) with David Drake as Robert and B. D. Wong as Ming (background) in Chay Yew's *A Language of Their Own*, Public Theater, New York City, 1995.
© Michal Daniel

character over the other. Ming's relationship with Robert becomes as much the focus of the drama as Oscar's relationship with Daniel. These relationships, Yew demonstrates, have a language of their own. Even within these new relationships, all four characters develop a complex identity that defies simple categorizations based on serostatus, ethnicity, or race. Yew goes to great length to show how the three Asian American characters are not only distinct from but often at odds with each other. *A Language of Their Own* does not dwell on Ming's serostatus, but by marking the character as HIV-negative and by keeping the character at the heart of the play even after he is no longer involved with the HIV-positive character, the play gestures toward a recognition of negativity as a dramatic process worth exploring in its own right.

While *A Language of Their Own* raises the dramatic possibilities of HIV negativity, it does not explore them in great depth. Ming is marked as negative, but the specificity of his experience as such is not highlighted by the play. One place where an investigation of HIV negativity has been pursued more explicitly, however, is solo performance. Since solo performance, especially community-based solo performance, allows for the autobiographical impulse, HIV-negative gay men may find their AIDS stories welcome in this format. In the published introduction to his award-winning solo performance *The Night Larry Kramer Kissed Me* (1992), David Drake writes of being HIV-negative and his involvement in AIDS activism.[58] While Drake's performance doesn't reference his sero-status—the piece is only partially autobiographical—in his introduction to the published script he explains:

> The naming and claiming of the truth of my oppression is how I came to realize that although I wasn't living with HIV in my blood, I was living with it in my life.[59]

The Night Larry Kramer Kissed Me is a document of AIDS activism and a tribute to AIDS theatre. Drake's commitment to AIDS activism is performed as a generational norm, as representative of a community; in fact, he opens the play to other actors who perform the piece across the world.

In *Naked Breath* (1994), solo performer Tim Miller places the issue of HIV negativity at the center of his performance. Miller, who identifies as HIV-negative in the performance, tells two stories in the performance, and in the process, provides a discursive space for HIV-negatives to address the specificity of their experience of the AIDS pandemic. The stories are framed by a communal ritual where the performer breathes in the energy circulating within the performance space. *Naked Breath* also includes recorded songs from Michael Callen's *Legacy*. The simplicity of *Naked Breath*'s structure—two stories of love and about life (one from the past and one in the present) joined together by a ritual bathing of the performer's body—position the spectator to focus on Miller's narrative (fig. 38). The effect, as Miller explains at the end of the performance, is to encourage people to tell their own stories. In this sense, *Naked Breath* performs a pedagogical intervention in its very structure. Miller asks gay men to find their own stories and bring these stories into the public world. Not all of these stories will be familiar, nor will these stories always follow convention. Miller himself, for example, refuses to allow the impulse of tragedy to override the story of his relationship with Andrew, a "boyfriend" who is HIV-positive. On hearing a voice in his head insisting that "something bad happen to these guys," Miller removes his story from its potential absorption into the history of AIDS representation as tragic and the idea that AIDS makes good drama: "Sorry. Nothing so dramatic. Nothing so tragic. For now. For tonight. For now, Andrew and I became friends."[60] The stripped-down theatricality of *Naked Breath* enables Miller to shift the focus from the theatrical and dramatic conventions associated with

38. The ritual washing scene in Tim Miller's *Naked Breath*, PS
122, New York City, 1994.
© Dona Ann McAdams

AIDS performance to a more direct community-based and community-specific social performative.

The first story, "Good with Wood," recounts Miller's early years in New York City and provides Miller the opportunity to historicize his personal relationship to AIDS. After a series of odd jobs, he becomes a carpenter—"a maker of beds"— meets the performer John Berndt, and they become lovers. Miller suffers a minor accident at work and goes to the emergency room, leaving a trail of blood behind him. He calls Berndt from the hospital to bring him home. The first story ends with Miller and Berndt walking on East Sixth Street to Berndt's apartment in May of 1981, before the onslaught of AIDS, which "will sweep away John" (20 A). Miller, looking to the East River, catches a glimpse of the "deluge about to come." Once in the apartment, "John puts me in the bathtub in the kitchen and washes the blood from the body." The second story begins with Miller back on East Sixth Street, "twelve years into the plague," on his way to a performance workshop he is leading and where he will meet Andrew, a workshop participant. That night Andrew and Tim begin a sexual romance; in the morning they share an "AIDS tune-in." In a direct address to the audience, Miller explains how he negotiates this process:

> Now, I don't know about you, but if I'm indeed ever gonna have this conversation I usually wait and have this talk after we've had sex a coupla times. This is not unusual, I think. Show of hands. See.

Miller continues, offering audiences a near histrionic rant on his need to believe in safe sex. Like Jeffrey, Miller's performance persona conveys an anxiety around sex and HIV that borders on the debilitating and, because of its excessiveness, on the comic. Unlike Jeffrey, however, Miller wants to believe in safe sex. And while Jeffrey refrains from the sexual, Miller embraces it:

> I believe in safe sex and its principles. I structure my understanding of the world around its precepts. I have that faith. I must believe. As I must believe in gravity, photosynthesis, friction, the forgiveness of sins, and the oxygen in the air I breathe. I believe in safe sex because it allows me to get up in the morning, make breakfast and not have a nervous breakdown. I do believe in safe sex. I do. I do. I do. I do. I do believe in safe sex . . . so help me God. (28)

I want to quote extensively from *Naked Breath* because it is the first and most fully staged account of HIV-negativity. Miller's first-person monologue constructs a public intimacy where the issues of HIV-negative gay men can begin to be heard and addressed. The primary pedagogical intervention of *Naked Breath* is that it can serve as one possible model for HIV-negative gay men to express these issues. Miller continues:

> So, since we've been careful. Respectful of each other. This is a perfectly responsible time if we even need to have the discussion. It came up. As it often does.
>
> I said, "It's so intense to be here lying in bed on East Sixth Street. My boy-friend, John, who I told you about who died of AIDS, lived down the street on this side."
> He held me. Said something sweet. We breathed together for a bit. He told me, "My ex-boyfriend back in California is pretty sick right now. I worry about him a lot."
> We held this close between us too.
> I asked him, "How are you in all of this AIDS stuff?"
> Andrew said, "I'm positive. Just found out a little while ago. How about you?"
> I said, "I'm negative. Last time I checked."
>
> Well. The cards were on the table. A full house. The cameras zoom in for the close shot. Everything going real slow. The winter morning light blar-ing thru the windows onto our bodies. Burning away the bullshit. Now this is a powerful moment, isn't it? It was like a strange bird had flown into the room. Perched there at the end of the futon. A bird that could be very fierce or very beautiful. It was up to us. (29)

Andrew's disclosure of his HIV-positive status, one of the conventional dra-matic devices of AIDS theatre, brings forth the suspense and shock which ac-companies the utterance "I'm positive." Andrew undercuts this overdetermined individuation of his serostatus by asking Tim about his serostatus. Miller's dis-closure—"I'm negative"—heightens the dramatic tension in the performance—"Now this is a powerful moment, isn't it?"—as it unsettles the notion that only HIV-positives have a social identity to HIV. The dramatic tension is now di-rected to what these two serodiscordant gay men will do with this informa-tion—"It was up to us." They decide to make love—"even better this time." Miller's individuated story—one HIV-negative gay man's point of view—be-gins as a firsthand, deeply subjective, and localized account of his experience of HIV. From this personal tale, Miller universalizes the encounter and then moves on to immediately implicate the audience:

> This is how it is. This is *our* life and we live and breathe now. These two men. These two people. You or you or you. Us.

Through his experience with Andrew, Miller opens up *Naked Breath* to address the world of his spectators. In the process, he comments on the nature of the story and his own uncertainty of its meaning:

> I knew something special had happened. . . . Now I don't think this has to be made into a big deal. I'm not even sure what any of this information means. But to say it means nothing is a lie. A big lie. And I'm tired of lying. . . .

Miller then restates to his audience what he first told to Andrew. His direct, undifferentiated address to the spectator—is he speaking to HIV-negatives? HIV-positives?—now invites each of these two spectatorial positions to negotiate a relationship with him based on this HIV-negative public disclosure: "I'm negative. It scares me to say that here to you." The first announcement of his serostatus occurs with Andrew in the private space of Andrew's home. And while Miller tells the audience of this disclosure in the public realm of the theatre, the story primarily concerns the one-on-one dynamics between HIV-negative and HIV-positive gay men. In other words, HIV-negativity is announced in relation to an HIV-positive and, more to the point, isolated in this one encounter. In order to not rarefy his relationship to Andrew, Miller proceeds to catalogue a number of other HIV-positive gay men he's had sex with—"I have been to this place before. With other men in my life." The intent of this story is to advocate against a practice of sexual apartheid, although by framing his seronegativity within a serodiscordant relationship, Miller inadvertently suggests that having sex with an HIV-negative gay man is not as good a "story." The second time Miller reveals that he is HIV-negative, the statement is addressed to the audience. This statement moves *Naked Breath* from being a performance which addresses personal and romantic magnetic relations to being a performance about coming out as HIV-negative in the public world.

Miller explains that with *Naked Breath* he intended to "make a leap into a topic that carries a lot of tension in my community of queer men: sexual intimacy between HIV-negative and HIV-positive men. . . . It became clear to me that my own deepest need to claim sexual connection in the face of the AIDS crisis was a necessary subject both for me and my tribe. This called the piece forward."[61] *Naked Breath* sets out to speak to an undifferentiated gay male spectator. The performance, however, calls for HIV-negative gay men to bring their emotional responses to the AIDS crisis into the public sphere. Miller demonstrates that this public assertion need not be at the expense of people with HIV. Speaking out as an HIV-negative gay man involved in serodiscordant relationships, Miller opens up the possibility of representing the support that both HIV-negative and HIV-positive gay men should have in maintaining a sexual life.

And yet what distinguishes this story from other stories of magnetic relationships is that Miller's identity as HIV-negative is not determined by his relationship with someone who is HIV-positive. The second pronouncement of his seronegativity is not stated within the context of a personal relationship but instead is announced as a public performative. By marking his HIV-negative serostatus in this way, Miller invites other HIV-negative gay male spectators to come out as HIV-negative and begin to tell their various stories. The proliferation of these stories will open up our understanding of what it means to be HIV-negative.

HIV-negative gay men have only recently been the topic of gay theatre and performance. As this brief historical trajectory demonstrates, gay male playwrights and performers have been reluctant to explore the issues of HIV-negative gay men in the theatre for a number of reasons. Some of these reasons, I have argued, are based upon a progressive political concern to focus attention on the distinct needs and experiences of gay men living with HIV and a desire to avoid a divisive politics between HIV-negative and HIV-positive gay men. Other reasons are based upon dramatic conventions and generic constraints. Tragedy and comedy each pose specific challenges to gay playwrights interested in portraying HIV-negative characters. Solo performance faces its own constraints, including, in particular, the limited referential field of the solo performer's body. Solo performers run the risk of having their work individuated, interpreted as the rarefied experience of the sole body onstage. Despite these limitations, gay playwrights and performers have begun the necessary task of exploring seronegativity in their work. These recent attempts to mark seronegativity in theatrical representation have opened up a new set of questions and possibilities for gay men. Perhaps the most pressing question raised by these recent explorations is whether or not to mark seronegativity as such. In other words, what are the effects—political, artistic, psychological—of naming HIV-negativity? And relatedly, what are the effects—political, artistic, psychological—of leaving HIV-negativity unmarked?

Gay men have accepted the logic of the binary and as a result have sustained the force of the HIV-negative/HIV-positive division. Gay men often imagine, and at times even enforce, the idea that the HIV-negative/HIV-positive system is homologous to other social binarisms based on identity factors such as race, gender, and sexuality. In these binaries—white/black, male/female, heterosexual/homosexual—one of the terms of the binary assumes a dominant position—white, male, heterosexual—and that term circulates as unmarked. Within the specific logic of these social binarisms, one of the terms must emerge as unmarked, as the alleged norm. In this regard, unmarked translates as normative, marked as deviant. Feminists, anti-racists, and queer theorists, along with the activism behind these intellectual movements, have gone to great lengths to denaturalize the cultural logic that positions unmarked categories as normative. "Whiteness," "masculinity," and "heterosexuality" have thus emerged as sites of contestation and denaturalization. These various cultural theorists have demonstrated new ways of seeing the terms of these binaries. Moreover, feminists, anti-racists, and queer theorists have unsettled the myth that these binary systems work in culture as monolithic structures.

AIDS cultural theorists have consistently argued against the monolithic structure which has forced *HIV-negative* and *HIV-positive* into a simple binary. This important project has been played out primarily in critiques of the systems of power—government, science, media, for example—which promote the concept of a general population vs. an abject population. Dominant culture, as various AIDS theorists have argued, presumes itself HIV-negative; the threat of HIV is imagined through the cultural abject: homosexuals, intravenous drug users, prostitutes, and people of color. In this system, all gay men regardless of our status are implicated as embodiments of HIV. The either/or logic of the HIV-antibody test—either one has HIV antibodies in the bloodstream or one does not—allows for only two test results: HIV-negative or HIV-positive.[62] Within dominant culture, these test results were molded into a binary structure. The binary established around *HIV-negative* and *HIV-positive* positioned *HIV-positive* as the abject term. The unmarked term—*HIV-negative*—has assumed the position of power, the status of natural.[63]

In general, HIV-negative gay men do not set out to oppress HIV-positive gay men. But insofar as HIV-negative gay men have accepted the structure and language of the HIV-positive/HIV-negative binary, we have accepted the power accompanying the logic of HIV-negative as the natural status. The fact that these characteristics accompany the logic of the binary—normative, abject; natural, unnatural—functions as an oppressive force for infected gay men. By marking seronegativity, HIV-negative gay men begin the process of denaturalizing HIV-negative as the natural condition. The effect of this denaturalization will remind us that HIV-negative is itself an "unnatural" act, that HIV-negative is a process of being associated with a medical procedure and not the assumed normative status.[64] The logic of the HIV-antibody test sets up the assumed binary between *HIV-positive* and *HIV-negative*, but these test results only reinforce the binary between its related terms—*infected* and *uninfected*—through the official language of biomedical science. In other words, the terms *HIV-positive* and *HIV-negative*, although related to the terms *infected* and *uninfected* are neither interchangeable nor coterminous. By marking seronegativity as a constructed category and by contextualizing HIV-negative within a larger more official ideological system concerning HIV and AIDS, we can begin to unpack what it means to be HIV-negative. And by marking seronegativity in this way, we may actually help to keep those who live under the "category" of HIV-negative alive. Since we have not adequately addressed what it means to be HIV-negative or what it means to be uninfected, we have allowed the force of the binary to take shape and the two terms *HIV-negative* and *uninfected* to be conflated. For infected men, the effects of this binary have led to the establishment of necessary social and political structures of support, under the rubric of *HIV-positive* or *person with AIDS*. For uninfected gay men, the effects of this binary system have primarily perpetuated our anxieties about, and perhaps even our desires for, seroconversion. But this need not remain the case. This enterprise of denaturalizing *HIV-negative* will demand that we address our experience as either uninfected or HIV-negative gay men in public culture, small groups, and among our friends. These discussions, moreover, will need to address the ways that we are imagined and constructed in dominant culture, including the actual HIV-negative/ HIV-positive binary system that makes our status intelligible in the first place.

Gay men living with HIV have already demonstrated to the world the possibilities of this practice by revising the cultural psyche around our understanding of what it means to be positive or living with AIDS. It's time now for uninfected gay men to begin to intervene in the limited understanding of what it means to be HIV-negative. The current means we have of understanding seronegativity do not adequately reflect the actual lived experiences of uninfected gay men. Representations and discourse, of course, do not transmit HIV, but they do transmit meanings, and these meanings have their effect on our understanding of who and what we are and, to a great extent, what we do. The first step in intervening in the systems which make us intelligible to ourselves and to others is to interrogate the means by which uninfected men are understood and heard in public culture. The challenge set before us is to construct a public culture for all of us—infected and uninfected—in which we can love one another and survive.

Afterword

Rent's Due

> There is an excitement we haven't seen in a long time. We've
> opened a new chapter in AIDS research. But it's not the final chapter,
> and we have a long way to go before the book is closed.[1]
> —Dr. Martin T. Schechter, co-chair of the
> 11th International AIDS Conference

THE NEWS FROM the Eleventh International AIDS Conference held in Vancouver, British Columbia, during the summer of 1996 caused Dr. Martin Schechter, one of the conference co-chairs, to announce that the world was "at a crossroads in the history of the HIV epidemic . . . we are beginning to see glimmers of hope."[2] Reports that a handful of new and recently approved drugs by the FDA, known as protease inhibitors, when combined with other, older drug therapies, reduced the progression of HIV in people infected with the virus, shifted the mood from the disappointment and despair of the previous conferences in Berlin and Yokohama to a new sense of optimism in Vancouver.[3] At the time of the Vancouver conference, which is to say at the time of this writing, over twenty-one million people throughout the world have contracted HIV, over four and a half million people have AIDS, and over four million have died. The *Los Angeles Times* reports that the most recent available data documents between 650,000 and 900,000 people in the United States infected with HIV, and that over 350,000 have died of AIDS.[4] Given such astounding figures, the findings that new drug therapies are proving efficacious in treating AIDS were greeted with great enthusiasm as well as profound relief. Reports in the popular press, including lesbian and gay publications, heralded the news from Vancouver as a breakthrough moment in the history of AIDS. AIDS was beginning to be discussed as a chronic but manageable and treatable condition. Still, as Lawrence Altman reported in the *New York Times*, almost exactly fifteen years after his infamous "Rare Cancer Seen in 41 Homosexuals" article, optimism surrounding these new studies was neither unanimously felt nor unequivocally experienced:

> Experts' enthusiasm is restrained by many caveats, like the still short duration of the trials, the small number of patients in them, the practical difficulty of the drug regimen, and the enormous cost of the drugs and the accompanying tests. . . . Health officials are also concerned that if patients fail to follow the difficult drug treatment schedule, the emergence of resistant strains of virus may be encouraged. . . . [5]

While the various caveats Altman includes in his report have raised degrees of skepticism among AIDS scientists and activists over the potential of these new drugs, by far the most serious concern has to do with the extraordinary expense of these drug therapies. The average cost of combination drug therapies is estimated at about $16,000 per year.[6] The prohibitive price of the drugs limits their access to the few who can afford them or who are involved in the clinical trials. Eric Sawyer, an AIDS activist from New York City, voiced this concern when he stated that "people with AIDS need access to treatments, not false hope," and joined various others who demanded drug companies to make these new treatment options available to people outside of the clinical trials, especially to those in developing countries.[7] The conference slogan "One World—One Hope" was quickly transformed to "Third World—No Hope" and "One World—One Hype" by activists at Vancouver.[8] For people in the United States, Larry Kramer has already pointed out that, in terms of treatment options, "the fate of people with HIV varies widely, depending on the insurance company or the state of residence."[9] According to Gary Rose, of the AIDS Action Council in Washington, D.C., only 29 percent of HIV-positive people in the United States have private health insurance; Medicaid provides coverage for an additional 56 percent, although many states limit patients to a monthly allotment of only three prescriptions.[10] The news from the Vancouver conference led to an immediate paradox: although there now seems to be a potentially efficacious AIDS treatment, few people with HIV can afford it.

The news from the Vancouver conference not only shifts the biomedical understanding of AIDS but also, as David Dunlap suggests, "seemed to certify a profound transformation in the social nature of the epidemic."[11] People with HIV and AIDS, for example, now may live beyond their previous short-term expectations, a potential that for many is as confusing as it is heartening.[12] The uninfected are also readjusting to the news of these new combination drug therapies; Dunlap explains how "many of those at risk for HIV began balancing two critical and apparently conflicting messages: that their sexual conduct was still a life-and-death matter but that AIDS was becoming a manageable, even treatable, condition."[13] It is precisely this conflicting message that Gabriel Rotello, a conservative AIDS activist, worries will lead to an increase in sero-conversions. Citing the so-called "second wave" of infection among gay men, Rotello asks: "If the potential for death hasn't been enough to compel people to practice safe sex, what might happen when that threat seems eased?"[14] Rotello answers his question with the following "nightmarish scenario":

> As the new drugs become the therapy of choice, many individuals may not be able to maintain the strict regimen and will develop multiple-drug-resistant HIV. At the same time, governments throughout the world may relax prevention efforts, while many people, rejoicing that the AIDS epidemic seems to be contained, drift back to a life style of unprotected sex with multiple partners. The drug-resistant strains could easily enter these newly reconstituted viral highways, and we might end up with a super-epidemic that stymies even the strongest drugs.

Rotello's scenario is indeed "nightmarish," not only because of its hyperbolic rhetoric of AIDS as "super-epidemic," but also because it restages people with HIV and AIDS in the moralistic realm of blame and gay men, in general, within the all too familiar trope of irresponsibility. What Rotello does not address is the fact that by 1995 gay communities and AIDS service organizations were aggressively reinvigorating prevention efforts to combat the rising rates of sero-conversion. HIV-negative support groups, town meetings between HIV-positives and HIV-negatives, differentiated prevention campaigns, and a nascent consciousness around the distinct psychosocial concerns of the uninfected and the infected initiated the difficult task of disentangling the immediate and, at one point, inevitable association between gay men and AIDS *among* gay men. While these efforts are relatively recent and their actual long-term effect still uncertain, it needs to be stated that a community-based movement has already emerged to confront the transforming social landscape of AIDS. While the news from Vancouver included reports of increased unprotected sex and infection rates among young gay men, it also reported considerable interventions in the epidemic in communities which had established new prevention efforts specifically directed toward them.[15]

The 1996 Vancouver conference raises important and troubling issues concerning the relationship between hope and access—access to treatment, health insurance, and prevention efforts. As the epigraph to this chapter insists, the book on AIDS is far from closed; Vancouver, according to Dr. Schechter, opens a new chapter, but alas not the final one. I, on the other hand, have already written my last chapter, a response, in part, to the last two International AIDS Conferences, which were characterized by a mood of pessimism and despair. Despite the specific constraints gay men have faced in light of the shifting medical, political, and social landscape of AIDS, they have resiliently intervened in this process, defining and redefining AIDS in turn. *Acts of Intervention* pays tribute to the accomplishments gay men have achieved through a wide range of performances. The generative sentiment of these performances, and thus of the book, has been hope.

Act of Intervention has sought to highlight the shifting relationship between these three associated social processes: theatre, AIDS, and hope. As I write, we stand once again on the eve of a presidential election. Four years ago, only a few days before the 1992 elections, I went with some friends to the opening night performances of the world premiere of *Angels in America* at the Mark Taper Forum in Los Angeles. Four years later, Michael Callen and Jim Pickett, two of these theatre companions, are dead.[16] The hope that characterized our lives at that time, and which we brought with us to the theatre and which *Angels in America* symbolized for us on that day, has been tempered by skepticism and sadness. Who now has access to hope? The reports from Vancouver that a handful of new community-generated prevention efforts are proving to be successful interventions in reducing the rates of seroconversion among young gay men is indeed a sign of hope. The results of the clinical trials involving protease inhibitors promise even more hope. The combination of new prevention campaigns and treatment options radically alters the reality of AIDS and sets the potential for eradicating AIDS once and for all, or so we hope. The key to all this hope is access. Access is the issue. Access, according to Benjamin Schatz, the executive director of the Gay and Lesbian Medical Association, "only becomes an issue when there are drugs that provide some hope."[17] But access remains an issue when the majority of people who would benefit from these drugs cannot afford them.

Given the context of Vancouver, I find it ironic yet significant that the most talked about theatrical occasion of 1996 is a musical about a community of artists and activists living in New York City's East Village, most of whom are HIV-positive and facing eviction. *Rent*, Jonathan Larson's musical, which won the 1996 Pulitzer Prize for Drama and the 1996 Tony Award for best musical, highlights the systemic inequities I have been discussing so far. Both *Rent*'s book and its own circulation as a marketed commodity for mass-cultural consumption call attention to this central problem of access and its relationship to material economies of power and control. There are various stories told in *Rent* and, ever since Jonathan Larson died unexpectedly of an aortic aneurysm hours after *Rent*'s final dress rehearsal for production run at the New York Theatre Workshop, various stories told about it. AIDS factors into these stories, but as *POZ*, a periodical devoted to reporting and reflecting the issues of people who are HIV-positive, argues "in the resulting media frenzy over the death of Larson and the rebirth of musical theatre, AIDS has been overlooked."[18]

POZ's concern that AIDS has been overlooked is surprising since, as the feature points out, *Rent* contains more characters with HIV than "earlier Broadway hits that *were* perceived as 'AIDS plays.'"[19] *Rent* reflects the demographics hardest hit by HIV: gay men, women of color, IV drug users, Latinos, and African Americans. Four of the main characters of *Rent* are HIV-positive, including the heterosexual lovers, Mimi and Roger, who are the musical's two lead roles. Mimi is Latina and an intravenous drug user. Roger, who is white, is a musician and former junkie. (At the beginning of *Rent* we are told that April, his previous girlfriend, left a note on a mirror informing him that they both had AIDS and then slit her wrists.) The other two characters who are HIV-positive are gay men of color. Collins, who is black, meets Angel, a Latino drag queen, and they become lovers. Angel dies in act 2. Mimi will also die but only for a moment. (She miraculously comes back to life once Roger serenades her in *Rent*'s finale.) The other characters with major plot lines in *Rent* include Maureen and Joanne, an interracial lesbian couple, and Mark, a straight white guy, who is Roger's roommate. (There are no HIV-negative gay men represented.) All of these characters become entangled in a community effort to protest, and then sabotage, their landlord's plan to get rid of a tent city in the empty lot adjacent to their building.[20] Most of these characters are poor, although even here their economic realities vary.[21] Although AIDS does not drive the plot of *Rent*, AIDS informs and helps to shape it. As we shall see, *Rent* contains scenes of an AIDS support group meeting and an AIDS memorial, standard conventions of traditional AIDS theatre.

The fact that the musical represents four people with HIV led *POZ* to enthuse that "by facing AIDS as yet another of life's uncertainties, *Rent*'s HIV-positive pairings love each other with a sexual passion that not only turns on Broadway audiences, but brings them to their feet" (56). In the photo feature on the actors who play these roles, shot by the award-winning AIDS photographer Carolyn Jones, *POZ* speculates that perhaps the reason AIDS is overlooked is that "[i]n *Rent* AIDS isn't a metaphor for the end of the century, the end of the world, the end of anything. AIDS just is. It's not pitied, it's not pampered, and it's not ignored" (56). Even as *POZ* claims that "AIDS has been overlooked" it seems to contradict this statement by then claiming that "it's not ignored." The tension between these two statements suggests the complex relationship between AIDS and *Rent*. I want to pursue the question *POZ* has posed concerning this relationship because I find its answer crucial for our understanding of AIDS in this specific historical moment. As *POZ* illustrates, *Rent* includes an unprecedented number of representations of people with HIV. AIDS is also constantly referenced throughout the musical's plot. Furthermore, AIDS is even an element behind the actual idea for *Rent*. Larson, who was heterosexual and HIV-negative, stated that he was inspired to represent AIDS after "a number of my friends, men and women, were finding out they were HIV-positive. I was devastated, and needed to do something."[22] Larson, who was already collaborating on an update of Puccini's *La Boheme* with playwright Billy Aronson, felt that the Puccini opera could serve as his vehicle. "I decided to ask Billy if he would let me continue by myself, and he was very cool about it," Larson explained.[23] In terms of *Rent*'s representation of HIV-positive characters, its narrative and structural content, and even its genesis, the topic of AIDS seems hard to avoid. In fact, AIDS saturates *Rent*.

The idea that AIDS has been overlooked seems even more paradoxical given that nearly every review of, or feature about, *Rent* mentions AIDS. *Newsweek*, for example, put two of the actors from *Rent* who portray HIV-positive characters on the cover of its May 13, 1996, issue (fig. 39). The cover photo shows Adam Pascal and Daphne Rubin-Vega, the two talented actors who portray Roger and Mimi, in an embrace above the caption, "*Rent* Strikes: A Sexy Hit for the '90s Electrifies Broadway."[24] While this cover image gives no indication that these attractive singers represent an HIV-positive couple, the accompanying story begins with an immediate reference to AIDS:

> There's a scene in the new musical *Rent* that may be the quintessential romantic moment of the '90s. Roger, a struggling rock musician, and Mimi, a junkie who's a dancer at an S/M club, are having a lovers' quarrel when their beepers go off and each takes out a bottle of pills. It's the signal for an "AZT break," and suddenly they realize that they're both HIV-positive. Clinch. Love duet. If you don't think this is romantic, consider that Jonathan Larson's sensational musical is inspired by Puccini's opera *La Boheme*, in which the lovers Mimi and Rodolfo are tragically separated by her death from tuberculosis. Different age, different plague.[25]

The surprisingly casual tone of this passage, and its reduction of AIDS to a soundbite—"Different age, different plague"—not only confirms the association between AIDS and *Rent* but actually insists upon it. How then is it possible to claim that AIDS has been overlooked when the play consistently references AIDS and the national press insists upon associating AIDS with *Rent*? The reason AIDS has been overlooked is linked precisely with the fact that AIDS is omnipresent in *Rent*. AIDS is so ubiquitous in *Rent* that it is no longer even dramatic. *Newsweek*'s smug observation that the "AZT break" may be "the quintessential romantic moment of the '90s" demonstrates a variation on what Douglas

EXCLUSIVE: RALPH REED'S NEW CHRISTIAN AGENDA

New~~~~eek

'Rent' Strikes

A Sexy Hit for the '90s Electrifies Broadway

39. Adam Pascal and Daphne Rubin-Vega from the cast of *Rent* on the cover of *Newsweek*, May 13, 1996.
Photo © Barron Clairborne; © 1996 *Newsweek*, Inc. All Rights Reserved. Reprinted by permission.

Crimp described, already by 1990, as "the normalization of AIDS." Crimp is referring to a specific set of indifferences which he associates with the Bush administration:

> If, for the first eight years of the epidemic—the terms of Ronald Reagan's presidency—indifference took the form of callously ignoring the crisis, under George Bush, AIDS was "normalized" as just one item on a long list of supposedly intractable social problems. How often do we hear the

list recited?—poverty, crime, drugs, homelessness, and AIDS. AIDS is no longer an emergency. It's merely a permanent disaster.[26]

This exact list is introduced in *Rent* within its first few minutes. Despite the musical's sympathetic portrayal of characters who must live with and through these social problems, AIDS in *Rent* is normalized to such a degree it can't help but be, if not overlooked, at least, unexamined. As the *Newsweek* cover story exemplifies, the same process is true for discussions about *Rent* in the popular press. In this sense, I would adjust and update Crimp's account of the normalization of AIDS, which is based upon government indifference, to what I would call the banalization of AIDS. The banalization of AIDS is also based upon a type of indifference; however, it is an indifference that is no longer confined to the government, but endemic to the culture at large. In this scenario, AIDS is no big deal. "AIDS just is." The banality of AIDS strips the epidemic of its political and personal emergency; it shifts the drama inherent in all experiences of AIDS, regardless of status, from the deadly serious to the almost trivial. AIDS is represented as trend, as fashion, as style.

In *Rent*, the characters wear mismatched funky clothes, play electric guitar, experiment with video, and take AZT. At the end of act 1, in "La Vie Boheme," one of the musical's highlights, the ensemble sings of this life (fig. 40):

> To riding your bike, midday past the three piece suits
> To fruits, to no absolutes
> To Absolut, to choice, to the *Village Voice*, to any passing fad
> To being an us, for once
> Instead of a them
> La Vie Boheme . . .
> To sodomy, it's between God and me
> To S & M
> La Vie Boheme . . .
> To faggots, lezzies, dykes, and crossdressers, too
> To me, and you, and you, and you, and you
> To people living with, living with, living with, not dying from disease
> Let he among us without sin be the first to condemn
> La Vie Boheme.[27]

The defiant and exuberant celebration of difference that lies at the heart of this scene positions AIDS as part of the style of downtown life, absorbed in "la vie boheme" as any other passing fad. (The cliché "only the good die young" is visible on Roger's leather jacket.) Even the heartfelt communal articulation of AIDS activism in the middle of this scene—"Actual Reality—ACT UP—Fight AIDS"—appears at the end of a long list of absurd performances that parody

40. Original cast of Jonathan Larson's *Rent*, led by Anthony Rapp as Mark (far right) with arms raised, performing "La Vie Boheme," Nederlander Theatre, New York City, 1996.
© Carol Rosegg/Joan Marcus

the community's individual artistic identities. While this "impromptu salon" includes its own self-referential critique in these moments, AIDS activism is nonetheless diluted even as it is being paradoxically evoked and performed. Such hyper-romanticizations of marginalization and ironic performances of AIDS activism resurface in accounts of the musical, as *Newsweek*'s introductory frame of *Rent* attests; one reviewer even went so far as to write that "some of the adorable bohemians in *Rent* are HIV-positive,"[28] a comment that had its camp equivalent in the *Advocate*, which joked that the musical "at first plays like the *Mickey Mouse Club* with syringes."[29]

There is nothing romantic about taking AZT. Even Larson's HIV-positive characters recognize their vulnerability in these moments. Consider that Roger and Mimi's AZT break appears in a song entitled "I Should Tell You," a song which is as much about the anxiety associated with HIV disclosure as it is about the fear of unrequited love. Still the scene stages the daily regimens of AIDS treatment as a kind of hip ritual of the initiated, like sharing your works or receiving holy communion. (In this same scene, Angel and Collins will place their pills into each other's mouths.) While this scene, like the larger scene of "La Vie Boheme" which frames it, imagines AIDS as mainly a function of bohemia, two other scenes, of an HIV-positive support group meeting and an AIDS memorial service for Angel, foreground AIDS in a manner that suggests that the banalization of AIDS is something that this community depicted in *Rent* may also resist.

In "Life Support," for example, Angel and Collins attend an HIV-positive support group meeting. They join other random characters who are HIV-positive in a musical ballad which showcases members from the ensemble who do not play leading roles. One by one, these HIV-positive characters voice their fears—"Will I lose my dignity? Will someone care?"—as they affirm their resolution to live their lives to the fullest—"No day but today."[30] In a later scene, "I'll Cover You," the love song between the two HIV-positive gay men in act 1 becomes, at Angel's memorial in act 2, the community's statement of support to Angel's surviving partner, Collins. At first, when Angel and Collins sing "I'll Cover You," the song confirms their commitment to one another:

COLLINS:
So with a thousand sweet kisses
I'll cover you
With a thousand sweet kisses
I'll cover you
When you're worn out and tired
When your heart has expired
BOTH:
Oh lover, I'll cover you

ANGEL:
If you're cold
and you're lonely

You've got one nickel only
With a thousand sweet kisses
I'll cover you

Upbeat and joyous, "I'll Cover You" is the first love song performed in *Rent* (fig. 41). When the song is reprised in act 2, after Angel's death, Collins sings alone accompanied only by a piano. As the rest of the band gradually begins to play the song's full score, Joanne, the African American lesbian character, steps in to sing Angel's part. Joanne's performance initially registers as a moment of memorialization, a paradoxical yet meaningful tribute to the impossibility of surrogacy. But as she is joined by the rest of the company, Joanne's response to Collins becomes the community's own; the song functions as a poignant demonstration of the community's determination to renew itself even as it must take stock of its devastating losses.[31]

These scenes, which I found extremely moving, complicate the AIDS poli-

41. Wilson Jermaine Heredia as Angel and Jesse L. Martin as Collins performing "I'll Cover You" from Jonathan Larson's *Rent*, directed by Michael Greif, Nederlander Theatre, New York City, 1996.
© Carol Rosegg/Joan Marcus

tics of *Rent*. They create a tension between the banalization of AIDS and the communal energy available to resist it. And yet despite the important symbolic function these scenes enact, "Life Support" and "I'll Cover You" may unwittingly add to this idea that AIDS has been overlooked. In 1996, audiences may have become so familiar with the conventions of AIDS theatre that they remain just that—conventions, part of a recognizable formula. In this sense, the banalization of AIDS may extend even to AIDS theatre.[32]

Michael Greif, the openly gay director of *Rent*, emphasizes throughout these scenes the significance of community as a force to confront AIDS indifference. Greif's direction showcases the ensemble; even in these scenes which may appear formulaic for AIDS theatre, Greif's staging suggests that whatever resistance to the banalization of AIDS we might find will originate in the community itself. The importance of staging a representation of a community in *Rent* emerges from the artistic process of production, itself a communal endeavor.[33] Jim Nicola, the artistic director of the New York Theatre Workshop, the East Village theatre which developed *Rent*, explains how this materialized in the musical:

> Like *La Boheme*, [*Rent*] centered on Roger and Mimi surrounded by subplots. We thought it would be more interesting—and democratic—to see the struggle of community. Mimi and Roger are still the main lovers, but we brought the other love stories up front. The challenge was to make a community of people the protagonist of the play. . . . *Rent* would not have emerged without the seeds in this soil. The sense of a community-of-artists as a healing force is *our* theme. And it became the play's theme.[34]

The discourse of community, as Nicola emphasizes, is central to *Rent*. Furthermore, this notion of community—as it is thematized in the play, staged in the production, and revealed through the artistic process—informs the projections of critics and commentators who claim that *Rent* is the "most original American musical to come along this decade"[35] and the completion of "a marvelously fortuitous trilogy that started with *Hair* and went on to *A Chorus Line*."[36] Critics nearly unanimously agree that *Rent*, like *Hair* and *A Chorus Line* before it, exemplifies the specific cultural moment in which we now live. All three of these musicals, according to *Newsweek*, "deal with 'marginal' Americans: the flower children of the '6os, the gypsy dancers who sweat and smile on Broadway, and now the young people who follow the often quixotic dream of art in a chilling time for soul and body."[37] Since *Rent* originated at and was first presented by an East Village theatre, its representation of "marginal Americans"—and I would add AIDS—is imagined as authentic. "*Rent*," proclaims a headline in the *New York Times*, "has the nerve to be true to its times."[38]

This theme of community and its relation to our contemporary cultural moment, as it is has been constructed in the popular press, suggests that the symbolic representation onstage is an authentic replication of a recognizable world which, nonetheless, remains unfamiliar to those outside its immediate constituency. Representation provides access to this world. (The producers of *Rent* literally capitalize on this idea by transforming the Nederlander Theater into a theme park version of the East Village, complete with a café, distressed walls, a corridor which doubles as an exhibition space for East Village artists, and beads adorning the door frames.) The representation enables the spectator to believe that *Rent* approximates, on some level, the real. But what happens for those people who are the imagined constituency of the musical's symbolic commu-

nity? Margo Jefferson begins her review of *Rent* with this very concern and immediately asks what *Rent* may mean or do for those whom the musical sets out
to represent and address:

> It's odd to have joined the generations that talk about what "the young"
> are doing, saying and going through these days, and how that is reflected
> in art and entertainment. When *Hair*, the countercultural antiwar musical,
> opened in the late '60s, I was pleased but a little patronizing as well: you
> always are when you're part of a subculture that suddenly goes mass cul-
> ture. So I wonder what today's counterculture young think when they see
> themselves or a facsimile of themselves on stage in *Rent*, the rock opera of
> the '90s? What do they think of this portrait of avant-garde experiment
> and rock-bottom desperation on the Lower East Side of New York?[39]

I am not sure if Jefferson's question can be answered at this point mainly because *Rent*'s implied community hasn't really had access to it. *Rent*'s initial run
at the 150-seat New York Theater Workshop, part of its subscription series, sold
out soon after Larson's death and created a demand for tickets which the theater
could not satisfy even by extending the limited run. Ticket prices for the extended run actually jumped from thirty dollars to forty-five dollars. The Broadway production, which opened soon after at the 1,206-seat Nederlander Theater,
continues to be an extremely difficult ticket to obtain. It is also expensive. *Rent*
plays to advance-sale full-houses who pay up to seventy dollars per ticket.[40] In
order to encourage lower-income theatregoers, *Rent*'s producers have followed
the lead of the Public Theater, which sets aside a limited number of day-of-sale
tickets for their Broadway productions at twenty dollars. Thirty-four seats, the
entire two front rows of the orchestra, go on sale two hours before every performance of *Rent*, but as anyone who has attempted to buy these tickets already
knows, the line forms hours in advance.[41] All of this is to say that there exists
a certain discrepancy between the community represented in *Rent* and those
who can actually afford to see it. The producers' voluntary attempt to resolve
this issue, while significant, still mainly accentuates the systemic inequities that
come with the economic structure of the commercial theatre industry. Access
remains a problem.[42]

Rent's other attempt to intervene in the business-as-usual of Broadway theatre yet again calls attention to this problem of access. In an innovative effort
to cast future productions of *Rent*—including, along with the New York replace-
ments, the Boston, Los Angeles, and Toronto casts—the Bernard Talsey casting
agency held open auditions. *Rent*'s open call for "raw singers who truly have a
quality for street life, can move well, and have a good time onstage" brought
close to three thousand hopeful actors to New York for the chance to audition

for the fifteen roles and four understudy spots that comprise the *Rent* ensemble. People from all over the country arrived at the audition site, some as early as 4:00 A.M., to register for a ten-second spot before a talent scout—what casting agents refer to as a "type out"—which would determine whether or not they would then proceed to sing sixteen bars of any song. While many of these actors were seasoned veterans of the audition circuit, others who came had little or no experience with this process. The open call indicated that anyone, not just equity or professional actors, could audition. This unusual casting method was designed to provide "authentic" bohemians—who may not have agents, read *Variety*, or have money to even see *Rent*—access to the audition process.[43]

The open audition and the twenty-dollar day-of-performance tickets create a space for hope, albeit a limited one: there are only 34 seats and only 15 roles. *Rent*'s effort to intervene in the institutional structures which determine people's access to the theatre, whether as spectators or actors, puts this hope into circulation. The circulation of this hope competes and collides with the frustration generated by the systemic inequities which led one to hope in the first place. The paradox of *Rent* therefore echoes the paradox of Vancouver. Both point to the limits of access even as they provide the continual promise of hope. In both cases, access is determined either by economics or by the structural conditions which only allow a limited number of people to participate in clinical trials or theatre ensembles. I realize that by linking AIDS and *Rent* through this question of access, I run the risk of contributing to the notion of the banalization of AIDS that I have just described. Of course I would not suggest that the hope for affordable and effective treatment is analogous to the hope for a ticket to, or a part in, *Rent*. What I do want to point out, however, is that even though hope and access are in a closer and more promising alliance than they have ever been before, certain systemic inequities must still be challenged or, at the very least, pointed out. We still need to interrogate the various discourses of AIDS in circulation, including these discussions of hope and access, and place them within their complex historical and political context. Nor is it enough to simply deconstruct *Rent* without pointing to the successful interventions it so often performs. *Rent* may have "the nerve to be true to its times," but more than anything else in our theatre right now, *Rent* has become a vehicle for what the times tell us about AIDS.

Consider that the cast of *Rent* performed at the opening night of the 1996 Democratic National Convention in Chicago (fig. 42). The idea that a song from an AIDS performance has now become linked with the very political systems that AIDS performance has historically set out to confront is not without its irony. Certainly, the contradiction between the inclusion of *Rent* within the spectacle of presidential politics and the political reality of the people which *Rent*

42. C-SPAN coverage of Taye Diggs, Daphne Rubin-Vega, Kristen Lee Kelly, and Rodney Hicks from the original cast of *Rent* singing "Seasons of Love" at the Democratic National Convention, Chicago, 1996.
Author's photo

represents is unavoidable. *Rent's* performance at the convention is a vivid reminder of how AIDS performance can be absorbed and redefined by other, more powerful systems who use it to serve their own interests, whether that interest is in denying voice and visibility to the communities represented in *Rent* (no person with AIDS addressed the delegates during the prime-time televised convention programming) or whether the interest is in benignly entertaining the convention delegates with a musical number from a popular Broadway show.[44] But to make this critique is to overlook another point. Popular culture is not just a means of cooptation and mass manipulation. Popular culture may inspire meanings that exceed or contradict the process of commodification. Might, for example, the performance of *Rent* at the Democratic Convention suggest the possibility of a more participatory political process? When *Rent* first opened earlier this spring, Frank Rich wrote that

> at so divisive a time in our country's culture, *Rent* shows signs of revealing a large, untapped appetite for something better. It's too early to tell.

What is certain is that Jonathan Larson's brief life belies the size of his spirit. In the staying power of his songs, he lingers, refusing to let anyone who hears his voice abandon hope.[45]

At the convention, the cast sang "Seasons of Love," which opens act 2 of *Rent*. In performances of the full production of *Rent*, the ensemble forms a line at the front of the stage and sings the gospel-inflected song:

Five hundred twenty-five thousand
Six hundred minutes
How do you measure the life
Of a woman or a man?

In truths that she learned
Or in times that he cried
In bridges he burned
Or the way that she died.

It's time now—to sing out
Tho the story never ends
Let's celebrate
Remember a year in the life of friends
Remember the love . . .
Measure in love
Measure, measure your life in love.

The fifteen actors seem to break temporarily the theatre's fourth wall. The actors, in costume but not necessarily in character, sing of love's capacity to bring meaning to the ephemerality of life. While this theme may seem hopelessly sentimental, it continues, in the age of AIDS, to carry meaning. The song becomes one of the musical's refrains, reprised at key moments which slightly shift the song's meaning to adjust to the context of its performance. In these moments, the ensemble functions as a chorus, commenting and interpreting the representation onstage.

The inclusion of "Seasons of Love" at the Democratic National Convention can only loosely be described as an AIDS performance since it was never explicitly framed as such on the convention stage in Chicago. Nevertheless, I was moved to hear the *Rent* company pay tribute to the song's composer and to their collective efforts to make their message of hope and love accessible to a larger public world. When they sang that "it's time now—to sing out, tho the story never ends, let's celebrate, remember a year in the life of friends, remember the love," I couldn't help but join them, pausing to celebrate the lives of my own friends, especially those who have died. I thought of the people whose work I have written about in these pages and of so many other people who have participated in the collective efforts of AIDS performance and activism.

If discussions of *Rent* are to insist upon associations with AIDS, then these discussions will need to address the ways *Rent* not only represents AIDS but also, and more urgently, shapes our responses to it. Placing *Rent* in the specific historical and sociopolitical context of AIDS is not simply an occasion for critique or celebration; rather, it is an opportunity for us to locate sites of intervention where we can confront AIDS, even as the meanings and practices around AIDS continue to evolve and transform. This focus is what has been missing from accounts of the musical despite this being *Rent*'s due.

Rent's due is also that of AIDS performance. What's due is a recognition of the historical achievement of AIDS performance—from the earliest candlelight vigils and benefits to the most recent Broadway productions—in helping us confront AIDS. These cultural events provide the means for memorializing the dead, mobilizing the living, and sustaining hope and survival. Equally as important, AIDS theatre and performance create new ways of imagining community in the face of crisis. If we are now to resist the banalization of AIDS, and if we are to continue the cultural work necessary so that we do not abandon hope, we will need to draw upon the historical legacy of AIDS performance and activism. When we do so, we both recover a record of our past and seek to secure the future of our communities. These efforts, as I hope my book has demonstrated, are the acts of intervention that we must continue to produce in the ongoing struggles against AIDS.

Notes

Introduction

1. While nearly all studies of AIDS in culture include this caveat, I still find Thomas Yingling's explication of this notion the most provocative meditation on this subject. See his essay, "AIDS in America: Postmodern Governance, Identity, and Experience," in *Inside/Out: Lesbian Theories/Gay Theories*, ed. Diana Fuss (New York: Routledge, 1991).

2. See Peggy Phelan, *Unmarked* (New York: Routledge, 1994), who writes about the need to find a way to remember the "undocumentable" art of performers: "writing records the memory of the image of the future that will not be—the one I will never see. (They are dying and they have taken that future with them.) I am writing in that blank about that disappearance" (31). Phelan's comments on the nature of performance, or what she calls "the ontology of performance" ("Performance's being . . . becomes itself through disappearance" [146].) resonate throughout my own project; I am especially indebted to her final chapter and afterword. See also her "Reciting the Citation of Others, or, a Second Introduction," in *Acting Out: Feminist Performances*, ed. Lynda Hart and Peggy Phelan (Ann Arbor: U of Michigan P, 1993). But see also Sue-Ellen Case's critique of Phelan in "Performing Lesbian in the Space of Technology: Part I," *Theatre Journal* 47 (1995): 1–18. Bert States also questions Phelan's concept of performance and disappearance in his essay "Performance and Metaphor," *Theatre Journal* 48 (1996): 1–26.

3. Raymond Williams, *Keywords: A Vocabulary of Culture and Society*, revised edition. (New York: Oxford UP, 1976, 1983).

4. Jan Zita Grover, "AIDS: Keywords," in *AIDS: Cultural Analysis/Cultural Activism*, ed. Douglas Crimp (Cambridge, Mass: MIT P, 1987), 18. But see also her "AIDS, Keywords, and Cultural Work" along with the discussion following her essay in *Cultural Studies*, ed. Lawrence Grossberg, Cary Nelson, and Paula Treichler (New York: Routledge, 1992), 227–39.

5. Throughout this book I will occasionally examine other keywords related to my project. In chapter 4, I examine the following words: *performance art, performance*, and *theatre*. In chapter 8, I examine the terms *HIV-positive* and *HIV-negative*.

6. Thomas Postlewait explains the problems of such evidence in his essay "Historiography and the Theatrical Event: A Primer with Twelve Cruxes," *Theatre Journal* 43 (1991): 157–78.

7. Bruce A. McConachie, "Historicizing the Relations of Theatrical Production," in *Critical Theory and Performance*, ed. Janelle G. Reinelt and Joseph R. Roach (Ann Arbor: U of Michigan P, 1992), 176.

8. Grover, "AIDS: Keywords," 19.

9. One needs only to remember that, even with the official adaptation of AIDS by the CDC in 1982, the definition of AIDS—opportunistic infections, T-cell count, et al.—has been the subject of debate. Only in 1993 did some of the opportunistic infections specific to women with HIV officially register an AIDS diagnosis. Consider too that someone with a T-cell count of under 200 and with no opportunistic infections was not diagnosed with AIDS until that same year.

10. Douglas Crimp makes this point in "How to Have Promiscuity in an Epidemic." See especially 249–50 and footnote 11. In *AIDS: Cultural Analysis/Cultural Activism*.

11. Cindy Patton, *Inventing AIDS* (New York: Routledge, 1990), 1.

12. Michael Callen, *Surviving AIDS* (New York: Harper Collins, 1990), 6.

13. Yingling, "AIDS in America," 292.

14. Bruce A. McConachie outlines this positivist approach with three points: "(1) The belief that only objective truths can be counted as knowledge; (2) The assumption that only facts, dispassionately observed, can provide the basis for significant truth; and (3) A commitment to a "theory free," inductive process of arranging the facts so that they yield objective explanation. Armed with this method, the positivist investigator believes he can describe 'how it was' and explain 'how it happened.' " "Towards a Postpositivist Theatre History," *Theatre Journal* 37 (1985): 467.

15. Many of these performances were events experienced at gay bars, emerging alternative arts organizations, and early AIDS benefits. See chapters 1 and 2.

16. There is much scholarship to be done here. I want to point to some projects already in process, many addressing gay performances which I do not discuss in this book. John Bell's work on Reza Abdoh is among the best work currently available; readers should see the special issue of *TDR: A Journal of Performance Studies* devoted to Abdoh's theatre. Various dissertations are currently focused on AIDS and performance, and I look forward to them. Brad Boney (University of Texas–Austin) is writing on the AIDS plays of 1993; Joe E. Jeffries (NYU) is writing an impressive study of Ethyl Eichenberger; Robert Sember (NYU) is writing on the work of David Wojnarowicz; David Gere (UC–Riverside) is focusing on AIDS and dance; readers interested in updates on dissertations should see Philip G. Hill's annual "Doctoral Projects in Process in Theatre Arts," published in the May issue of *Theatre Journal*.

17 See Cindy Patton in *Inventing AIDS* where she argues how AIDS shifted from homosexual to queer.

18. Simon Watney, "The Spectacle of AIDS," in *Practices of Freedom: Selected Writings on HIV/AIDS* (Durham: Duke UP), 52.

19. Douglas Crimp, "How to Have Promiscuity in an Epidemic," 250. Crimp's comments here are directed against Randy Shilts and Larry Kramer, who, in *And the Band Played On* and *The Normal Heart* respectively, display a "negative view of gay politics and sexuality" (246). The final clause of the sentence, which I replaced with ellipses, actually reads: "and that the response to AIDS would depend in very large measure on the very gay movement Shilts and Kramer decry."

20. Paula Treichler, "AIDS, Homophobia, and Biomedical Discourse: An Epidemic of Signification," in *AIDS: Cultural Analysis/Cultural Activism*, ed. Douglas Crimp (Cambridge: MIT P, 1987), 31–70.

21. See the work of Douglas Crimp, Simon Watney, Jan Zita Grover, and Cindy Patton cited in the bibliography.

22. I have written on this topic with Tim Miller. See our collaboration, "Preaching to the Converted," *Theatre Journal* 44: 2 (1995): 1–18.

23. Dolan writes exclusively on feminist performance; I have substituted "progressive" for "feminist" in order to make my point. See *The Feminist Critic as Spectator* (Ann Arbor: U of Michigan P, 1988), 120–21. Dolan, whose work is a model of critical generosity, explains the complicated relation between the feminist critic and feminist cultural production: "Precarious feminist theatre and performance groups need favorable documentation of their work to persuade funding organizations and audiences to continue their support. The feminist critic who writes frankly of a feminist production's problems risks a certain ostracism from the creative community. In the spirit of progress, however, it seems necessary to point out the limitations of even the most well-intentioned feminist work . . . and to institute a dialogue that resonates beyond the confines of an insular feminist community" (120).

24. The bibliography in this area is voluminous. Janelle Reinelt provides a brief and invaluable assessment of feminist performance theory in "Feminism(s): Introduction," in *Critical Theory and Performance*, ed. Janelle G. Reinelt and Joseph Roach (Ann Arbor: U of Michigan P, 1992), 223–25. But see also Jill Dolan's important discussion of the debates among feminist per-

formance theorists in *Presence and Desire: Essays on Gender, Sexuality, Performance* (Ann Arbor: U of Michigan P, 1993).

25. Kate Davy, "Fe/male Impersonation: The Discourse of Camp," in *Critical Theory and Performance*, 231–32. But see also her essay "Constructing the Spectator: Reception, Context, and Address in Lesbian Performance," *Performing Arts Journal* 29 (1986): 43–52.

26. On the influence of the women's health care movement to AIDS activism, see Cindy Patton's *Sex and Germs: The Politics of AIDS* (Boston: South End P, 1985).

27. Cornel West, "The New Cultural Politics of Difference," in *Out There: Marginalization and Contemporary Cultures*, ed. Russell Ferguson, Martha Gever, Trinh T. Minh-ha, and Cornel West (Cambridge, MA: MIT P, 1990), 19–20.

28. Cornel West, *Race Matters* (New York: Vintage Books, 1993), 23.

29. Paul Monette, "Sleeping Under a Tree," in *Last Watch of the Night* (New York: Harcourt Brace, 1994), 261.

1. Acts of Intervention

1. Benedict Anderson, *Imagined Communities*. For Anderson, newspapers and their readers perform a "profound fictiveness," which, in commodity-based industrial capitalism, allows for the mass ceremony of "creating that remarkable confidence of community in anonymity which is the hallmark of modern nations" (36).

2. Lawrence Altman, "Rare Cancer Seen in 41 Homosexuals," *New York Times*, July 3, 1983, A20. All quotes are drawn from this report.

3. And yet it needs to be noted that immune-suppression-related opportunistic infections such as Kaposi's sarcoma and pneumocystis pneumonia were being diagnosed and detected in a number of people "outside the homosexual community." See Crimp's discussion of "junkie fever" in *AIDS: Cultural Analysis/Cultural Activism* and Shilts's documentation of cases across the globe in *And the Band Played On*.

4. Simon Watney, *Policing Desire*, 23.

5. These two modes of implication fit into what Cindy Patton describes in *Sex and Germs* as the two primary myths of interpreting AIDS medical research discourse. The first, informed by "overload theories," is based on the idea that gay men irresponsibly overindulge and overload the body's immune system and thus "get the diseases they deserve" (7). The second theory, the "Russian roulette theory," assumes that gay men, stereotyped as promiscuous and perverted, will eventually come into contact with a deadly germ.

6. For Anderson, calendrical coincidences are secular simultaneities, direct links to the "birth of the imagined community" (24). Anderson bases his ideas on Walter Benjamin's notion of "homogenous, empty time" developed in *Illuminations*. Anderson writes: "What has come to take the place of the mediaeval conception of simultaneity-along-time is, to borrow again from Benjamin, an idea of the 'homogenous, empty time,' in which simultaneity is, as it were, transverse, cross-time, marked not by prefiguring and fulfillment, but by temporal coincidence, and measured by clock and calendar" (24).

7. By 1983, forty theatres had joined Gay Theatre Alliance, the newly established organization for gay and lesbian theatre.

8. For early accounts of lesbian and gay theatre and performance, see Shewey, *Out Front*; Hoffman's introduction to *Gay Plays*; and Stefan Brecht, *Queer Theatre*. Keep in mind that until 1967, New York state law prohibited the onstage presentation of homosexuality.

9. Don Shewey, introduction to *Out Front*, xi.

10. "Lifestyle journalism" on people with AIDS and their loved ones and the social rituals we practice has been consistently underrepresented by the popular media. Rock Hudson's death in 1985 changed the media's response considerably. See the writings of Treichler, Patton, Watney, and Crimp, among others.

11. And yet here I am compelled to unsettle my own point concerning the social role of the artist. Many of the political workers in the lesbian and gay movement and in the AIDS activist community continue to see performance *as* entertainment and not in collaboration with intervention. Performers are often invited to various political meetings, conferences, and even "actions" precisely to entertain the "activists." While there is nothing inherently wrong with the idea of art as entertainment and, in particular, the entertaining of activists, these systems fail to recognize the role of the artist as a cultural worker and activist. In this way, many non-artist activists themselves perpetuate the notion of art's inability to save lives. Rather than exploiting the arts' availability to intervene in AIDS myths, activists inadvertently end up exploiting the artists instead.

12. Consider, for the context, that various performers and others involved in the theatre galvanized behind some of the other political issues and organizations of the early 1980s, such as Cispes and U.S. policies in El Salvador and the debates about the nuclear freeze. By 1984, for example, Artists Call Against U.S. Intervention in Central America—a coalition of visual and performing artists protesting U.S. military presence in Central America—had expanded to twenty-five cities across the country. As for issues specific to the lesbian and gay community, consider that on September 5, 1982, Jerry Herman (*Hello Dolly* and *Mame*) and Tommy Tune (*Nine* and *Cloud 9*) presented a star-filled performance hosted by Harvey Fierstein for Senior Action in a Gay Environment (SAGE). "Broadway Salutes SAGE" raised over $18,000. The SAGE fundraiser was reported in *Michael's Thing* 12:39 (September 27, 1982): 34–35. The Artists Call Against U.S. Intervention in Central America was reported in the *New York Native*, January 16, 1984.

13. See also Cindy Patton, *Fatal Advice: How Safe-Sex Education Went Wrong* (Durham: Duke UP, 1996), for a discussion of what she calls the 1981 to 1983 "information campaigns."

14. Larry Kramer, *Reports from the Holocaust*, 13.

15. Ibid., 14.

16. Randy Shilts, *And the Band Played On*, 92.

17. Kramer, *Reports from the Holocaust*, 15.

18. Ibid.

19. The Gay Men's Health Crisis Committee reported these facts in "Thanks to You We're a Hit!" a letter published in the *New York Native*.

20. All quotes from Popham's speech are from the published script in the *New York Native*.

21. From the advertisement in the *New York Native*, June 7, 1982, 22; the following issue (June 21, 1982) of the *Native* announced the *Dreamgirls* cast appearance (45).

22. Reported in the *New York Native*.

23. Gay Men's Health Crisis Committee acknowledged these early fundraising efforts in letters published in the *New York Native* and *Christopher Street*; see also Michael Shepherd's review of the benefit at Don't Tell Mama.

24. Reported in the *New York Native*, March 28, 1983, 48. See also James Saslow's coverage of the event in the *Advocate*, June 23, 1983, 14.

25. See John Wallace's review of the benefit, which includes Martin's statement.

26. Reported in the *Bay Area Reporter*, July 22, 1982.

27. Charles Morris, *San Francisco Sentinel*, November 11, 1982, 4. But see also Allen White's earlier piece in the *Bay Area Reporter*, "KS Foundation Needs More Support"

28. As advertised in *Frontiers*, December 9, 1982, unnumbered classified pullout section. Leo Ford hoped to raise over $2,000 for the KS Foundation with his sculpture. See Allen White's profile of Ford, "Cover Story: Leo Ford," and KARR's "Porn Corner" in the September 9, 1982 *Bay Area Reporter* for further information.

29. Four other unnamed contestants also raised money for the KS Foundation. The CMC fundraising efforts are reported in Karl Stewart's November 18, 1982 *Bay Area Reporter* column.

30. Quoted in Karl Stewart's "My Knights in Leather," *Bay Area Reporter*, December 23, 1982, 29.

31. Reported by Paul-Francis Hartman; see also Stephen Kulieke's reportage of the benefit in the August 18, 1983, issue of the *Advocate*.

32. Shilts, 331.

33. The Los Angeles fundraiser was covered by the *Bay Area Reporter* and the *Advocate*; see Scott P. Anderson. I should state that the Hollywood Bowl event was not the first effort in Los Angeles to raise money for AIDS research and care. The first Los Angeles fundraisers were held in November and December 1982 for the recently established L.A. chapter of the Kaposi's Sarcoma Foundation. Among the earliest fundraisers were a pledge drive by the Valley Business Association, which raised over $2,000, and a December 4, 1982, supper/tea dance at a private home in Bel-Air. These efforts are reported in *Frontiers*, November 25, 1982, 9. The L.A. chapter of the KS Foundation evolved into the AIDS Project Los Angeles.

34. Quoted in Allen White, *Bay Area Reporter*, September 8, 1983, 1.

35. Ervin Munro, the acting Executive Director of AIDS Project Los Angeles, is quoted in Allen White, *Bay Area Reporter*, September 1, 1983, 17.

36. Quoted in White, *Bay Area Reporter*, September 8, 1983, 1.

37. The events I discuss do not by any means exhaust the list of benefits and fundraisers throughout the country in these early years. My goal here is to document some of the range of activities across the country. Each of these events entails a performance or series of performances and adds to my point that performance served as a primary means to assemble people in local public spheres—the space of performance—to join in the fight against AIDS.

38. As reported by Albert Williams in *Gay Life*, November 25, 1982, 20.

39. See Albert Williams, *Gay Life*, December 25, 1982, 13.

40. Reported by Jim Marks in the *Washington Blade*, April 15, 1983, 17.

41. AIDS information was provided by AID Atlanta; however, it needs to be stated that in 1983 AIDS information was primarily addressed to gay men and not lesbians.

42. Reported in the March 17, 1983, issue of the *Advocate*, 8.

43. Kramer, *Reports from the Holocaust*, 66.

44. Seymour Kleinberg, "Dreadful Night," 42.

45. Shilts, 282.

46. Kramer, *Reports from the Holocaust*, 66.

47. Andrew Holleran, "The Spectacle at the Bottom of the Shaft," 19.

48. I use the anthropological terms *exogamy* and *endogamy* metaphorically to describe "in-group" and "out-group" rituals fully aware of their specific anthropological meanings: *exogamous* refers to cultures who expect members to marry outside of the group, *endogamous* refers to cultures who expect members to marry within the group. I borrow the terms to link them with the concepts of kinship and community and their contestation and negotiation in the midst of AIDS. I do not intend my use of the terms to converge with the concept of risk groups and the idea or, more particularly, the cultural logic of containment suggested by their usual employment in dominant AIDS ideologies. This is not to suggest that fundraisers are not contestatory; the problems with the Hollywood Bowl benefit make clear how AIDS fundraisers must always be held accountable for their actions.

49. This is of course true for the most basic of memorial services—the obituary—where it is often the case that sexuality and cause of death are occluded. Significantly, obituaries even obscure the very kinship structure of the deceased. Remember that the *New York Times* did not acknowledge lovers or "companions" until the late 1980s.

50. I should add that AIDS memorial services are also cultural instances when the deceased are narrativized into history. Thus, the person with AIDS is, many times, heroicized, desexualized, and/or spoken of in saintly terms depending upon the nature and location of the service.

51. See Kath Weston, *Families We Choose: Lesbians, Gays, Kinship*.

52. Ibid., 186.

53. Reported by Paul Lorch in the *Bay Area Reporter*, December 23, 1982, 15.

54. These issues are still, of course, relevant. The *Bay Area Reporter* published Richard Herbaugh's suicide in 1982. On the very day I first drafted this section, I read in the *Bay Area Reporter* of another twenty-nine-year-old gay man who committed suicide. After learning he had tested HIV-positive, Alex Rankin jumped to his death from the Golden Gate Bridge on March 27, 1994. See Rankin's obituary in the *Bay Area Reporter*, April 14, 1994, 20.

55. Cowley was thirty-two years old at the time of his death. His contributions to popular dance music are evident in the body of music produced by Megatone Records, which he co-owned with Marty Blecman, including Sylvester's "Disco Heat," "Mighty Real," and "Do You Want to Funk"; Paul Parker's "Right on Target," and his own 1981 hit "Menergy." His albums include *Megatron Man* (1981) and *Mind Warp* (1982). A private memorial service for Cowley's biological family was held in Buffalo, NY. Allen White's coverage of Cowley's death and memorial are published in *Voice*, November 19, 1982, 4 and *Voice*, December 3, 1982, 18.

56. Konstantin Berlandt, "Cowley Services at MCC," 10.

57. This process of self-production stems out of the people-with-AIDS self-empowerment movement where treatment options, health care, and other means of support are direct results of the choices of the person with AIDS. On this notion see "PWA Coalition Portfolio," in *AIDS: Cultural Analysis/Cultural Activism*, ed. Crimp, and Michael Callen's *Surviving AIDS*.

58. A private traditional funeral service was observed in Washington by Howell's biological family.

59. Konstantin Berlandt, "Gay Victim Dances over Death," *Bay Area Reporter*, November 11, 1982, 10.

60. Personal communication (phone interview) with Robert Perkins, April 25, 1994; subsequent quotes are from this phone interview. I am indebted to Perkins for his generosity in sharing with me his memories and for helping me find a videotape of *Ritual*. See also Allen White's "A Celebration of Life."

61. Crowd estimations are always contested. The San Francisco march, for example, was estimated at anywhere between 6,000 to 10,000, and the New York City march anywhere between the police count of 6,000 and the organizers' count of 9,000; these numbers are from the coverage of the marches in the *Advocate*, June 9, 1983, 8.

62. Quoted in Steven C. Arvanette, "Thousands in Vigil Demand Millions for AIDS," *New York Native*, May 23, 1983, 9.

63. Ibid.

64. Bobbi Campbell, letter to the editor, *Christopher Street*, December 1983, 6.

65. On this idea, see Douglas Crimp's "Mourning and Militancy."

66. Printed in *Out in Texas*, April 28, 1983, 10.

67. Reported by Ogden Robertson in the *Advocate*, June 9, 1983, 8.

68. *Newsweek*, April 18, 1983, 76.

69. Reported by Chris Helm in the *Advocate*, June 9, 1983, 8.

70. Quoted by Arvanette in the *New York Native*, May 23, 1983, 10.

71. Reported by Peter Freiberg in the *Advocate*, June 9, 1983, 8.

72. Cecchi's speech was published in the *New York Native*, May 23, 1983, 10.

73. Reported by Gary Schweikhart and Stephen Kulieke in the *Advocate*, June 9, 1983, 8.

74. Reported by Larry Bush in the *Advocate*, June 9, 1983, 8.

75. Reported in the *Advocate*, July 7, 1983, 11.

76. Ibid.

77. Quoted in the *New York Native*, July 4, 1983, 12. For a discussion on the media coverage of Ramsauer, see Jan Zita Grover ("Visible Lesions") and Simon Watney (*Policing Desire*), who both make the claim that people with AIDS with less visible markings of AIDS were turned away for Ramsauer's more grossly disfiguring KS lesions in order to sensationalize AIDS. The 1983 Denver Health Conference, which Vachon spoke about at the memorial, provided the opportunity for a bicoastal caucus of people with AIDS to meet and vote for the self-identifying and self-empowering "people with AIDS" as the preferred phrase to describe themselves

78. I thank Cindy Patton for explaining to me the politics behind this early AIDS protest and for helping me recreate the event itself. I am especially indebted to Lee Snider for opening up his archives for this project and generously permitting me to reprint his indispensable photos of the memorial service.

79. George Charles Guarino, letter to the editor, *Washington Blade*, July 1, 1983, 21.

80. Vernon W. Palmer III, "The Life You Save Could Be Your Own," *Washington Blade*, October 7, 1983.

81. Clint Hockenberry and Carlene Carter, "Being 'AIDSed Out': This Is Not the Time," *Washington Blade*, October 7, 1983, 10.

82. Quoted in Janice Irvine, "National AIDS Vigil: Coming at Low Time?" *Gay Community News*, October 7, 1983, 1.

83. National AIDS Vigil poster; published on the back page of *Washington Blade*, September 30, 1983.

84. For coverage of these events, see Jim Marks, "Brouhaha Erupts over AIDS Office Location," *Washington Blade*, July 22, 1983, 5.

85. The disappointment in the numbers supporting the vigil in D.C. was consistent with the response across the country. In San Francisco, one of the fifteen cities to hold local vigils, several hundred people participated in the event, a disturbingly low turnout for a city with two AIDS deaths per week.

86. Quoted in and reported by Dave Walter, "AIDS Vigil Brings High Emotion, but Low Turnout," *Washington Blade*, October 14, 1983, 11. Virginia Apuzzo, the executive director of the National Gay Task Force, however, offered a different point of view. In the same article, she suggests that the community's commitment should not be registered by a single demonstration.

87. Reported by Dave Walter, "AIDS Vigil, Black Conference This Weekend," *Washington Blade*, October 7, 1983, 1.

88. Ibid.

89. Ibid.

90. Reported (unsigned) in "AIDS Vigil Low in Turnout," *Bay Area Reporter*, October 13, 1983, 10. All quotes of the San Francisco vigil are pulled from this unsigned article.

91. Reported in Steve Martz, " 'I Don't Want to Die of Red Tape,' " *Washington Blade*, August 5, 1983, 1, 10.

92. Reported by Dave Walter, "AIDS Vigil Brings High Emotion, But Low Turnout," *Washington Blade*, October 14, 1983, 11. One of the participants in the Iowa AIDS vigil, a lesbian who attended the vigil with her lover and whose face was inadvertently shown on television, was harassed considerably. See Dave Walter, "Rough Day for Iowa Woman," *Washington Blade*, October 14, 1983, 1+.

93. Douglas Crimp, "Introduction" in *AIDS: Cultural Analysis/Cultural Activism*, 7.

94. See also Nina Felshin's introduction to *But Is It Art? The Spirit of Art as Activism* (Seattle: Bay Press, 1995), where she argues that "activist art, in both forms and methods, is process—rather than object—oriented, and it usually takes place in public sites rather than within the context of art-world venues" (10).

95. Sue-Ellen Case, *Feminism and Theatre*.

96. David Savran, *Communists, Cowboys, and Queers*, 11.

97. Jill Dolan, *The Feminist Spectator as Critic*, 14.

98. Elin Diamond, "Mimesis, Mimicry, and the 'True Real,' " 365.

2. *One* and Counting

1. Artists Involved with Death and Survival, *The AIDS Show*, 41.

2. Quoted in Michael Kearns, "Gay Dramatists Pen New Works Responding to 'Age of AIDS,' " *Advocate* January 22, 1985, 25.

3. The play had only two performances at Company—a gay bar located on Halsted Street in the heart of Chicago's gay neighborhood—a 4:00 P.M. matinee and an 8:00 P.M. evening show on August 14, 1983; see Albert Williams, "Human Element Explored in *One*," *Gay Life*, August 11, 1983, 1. The performances at Company raised almost $500; see Lawrence Bommer, Review of *One*, *Gay Life*, August 23, 1983, 8.

4. Readers wishing to learn more of Ranson's work, including her 1988 AIDS play, *Higher Ground*, and more about Atlanta's response to AIDS should consult William Alexander's essay "Clearing Space: AIDS Theatre in Atlanta," *Drama Review*.

5. Kearns, "Gay Dramatists," 25.

6. This figure was reported in Michael Kearns, "Gay Dramatists." Hagedorn donated all profits to the sponsoring AIDS organization.

7. Joseph provides an excellent survey of AIDS plays produced by Theatre Rhinoceros. Not only does she offer an insightful reading of the representational politics of their production, she also provides a useful historical context for the shifting AIDS ideologies these plays engendered. The other AIDS plays in the four-play cycle are *Unfinished Business* (1985), *Life of the Party* (1986), and *Quisbies* (1988). See Joseph's essay "Constucting Gay Identity and Community: The AIDS Plays of Theatre Rhinoceros" for a discussion of these plays.

8. These essays first appeared in the *New York Native* and are reprinted in Larry Kramer, *Reports from the Holocaust: The Making of an AIDS Activist*.

9. Unbeknownst to Hagedorn, perfomances such as *Ritual: The Journey of the Soul* preceded Hagedorn's play. See my discussion of *Ritual* in chapter 1.

10. Jeff Hagedorn, *One*. Unpublished and unpaginated manuscript (copyright 1983), 12. All quotes from *One* are from this version.

11. Bommer, review of *One*, 52.

12. Kearns, "Gay Dramatists," 25.

13. Ibid.

14. I want to stress that I am not intending to critique Hagedorn's play for failing to explore the relationship between AIDS and race. Instead I want to point out how the play—as an inaugural representation in AIDS theatre—participated in a larger cultural phenomenon in the early 1980s that put forward the image of the gay white man as both the dominant representation of the "gay man" and, subsequently, the "gay man with AIDS." I discuss this process and its effects on gay men of color in chapters 5 and 6.

15. Personal communication, August 5, 1995.

16. All quotes from *Warren* are from Rebecca Ranson's unpublished manucript, 1984.

17. Quoted in Phillip Padgen, "*Warren*: A Moving Tribute to a Friend," *Advocate*, January 7, 1986, 72.

18. Quoted in Kearns, "Gay Dramatists," 24.

19. Quoted in Padgen, "*Warren*: A Moving Tribute to a Friend," 72.

20. Ibid

21. Ibid.

22. Unsigned article, "Cast Members Talk about *Warren*," *The News: A Publication of the Atlanta Gay Center*, January 3, 1985, 2.

23. See Larry Vittoriano, "*Warren*: A Moving Look at Tragedy of AIDS," *Au Courant*, June 10, 1985, 10.

24. Quoted in Kearns, "Gay Dramatists," 24.

25. Rebecca Ranson was also invited to participate as one of ten lesbian and gay community representatives in a CDC-sponsored conference on AIDS in 1984.

26. All quotes from *Warren* are from Rebecca Ranson's manuscript.

27. See Eric MacDonald's essay on Theatre Rhino in *Drama Review* 33:1 (Spring 1989), where he writes that "rather than presenting a morbid view of death, the project set out to create an event which would be empowering and enlightening to gay audiences, as well as

appealing to heterosexuals" (89). MacDonald's essay provides the documentation of the origins of the *A.I.D.S. Show*.

28. These characters are developed in Doug Holsclaw's play, *The Life of the Party*, which premiered at Theatre Rhino in 1986.

29. Artists Involved with Death and Survival, *The A.I.D.S. Show*, 89.

30. Quoted in Samir Hachem, review of *A.I.D.S. Show* Documentary, *Advocate* July 8, 1986, 37.

31. Quoted in Ray O'Loughlin, "Gay Culture," *Advocate*, December 11, 1984, 55.

32. Robert Chesley, *Hard Acts/Stiff Parts*, 10.

33. Jeffrey Matson, review of *Night Sweat*, *New York Native*, July 2, 1984, 51.

34. I should add that this departure from realism and overtly political theatre is characteristic of Chesley's dramaturgy. Moreover, Chesley's style has not always alienated gay audiences. *Stray Dog Story*, produced in New York by the Meridian in 1983, was widely praised by critics and audiences.

35. Tish Dace, review of *Night Sweat*, *Advocate*, July 10, 1984, 46.

36. Kramer details these debates in *Reports from the Holocaust*.

37. Dace, review of *Night Sweat*, 46.

38. Matson, review of *Night Sweat*, 50.

39. Part of the confusion around *Night Sweat* had to do with Chesley's overt critique of gay capitalism and its *effects* on urban gay men. Chesley adds to this confusion in his deliberately ambiguous ending. By the end of the play it is not clear if the hero survives (rescued by a gay activist) or if he dies.

40. Chesley had to wait until 1986 for one of his plays, *Jerker, or the Helping Hand: A Pornographic Elegy with Redeeming Social Value and a Hymn to the Queer Men of San Francisco in Twenty Telephone Calls, Many of Them Dirty*, to fully converge with the political and social needs of gay men. Don Shewey makes this point in the Introduction to *Out Front*. See also John Clum's discussion of *Jerker* in *Acting Gay*.

41. I was unable to get a script of Holt's play. I base my description of the plot on the few secondary materials written about it.

42. Stuart Timmons, "Playwright Stephen Holt: Haunted by Life's Ironies, Fever of Unknown Origin," *Advocate*, December 9, 1986, 53.

43. Ibid.

44. Ibid., 54.

45. Ibid.

46. Theater for the New City had previously staged gay plays, however, including earlier work by Stephen Holt.

47. Remember that *Torch Song Trilogy* was developed off off Broadway at La Mama and produced by the Glines, a gay theatre company.

48. William M. Hoffman, "As It Was," in *As Is*, xiii.

49. Kramer, *Reports from the Holocaust*, 73.

50. The bibliography on these two plays is extensive. See John Clum, *Acting Gay*, and *AIDS: The Literary Response*, ed. Emmanuel S. Nelson, for a bibliography.

51. Hoffman, *As Is*, 94–95.

52. John Clum, *Acting Gay*, 70–71. Clum argues that this final scene of sexual reintegration affirms Rich and Saul's commitment. I would go further and argue that this scene, while certainly commenting on their relationship, demonstrates more explicitly their sexual desire for each other. In this sense, Saul's "I'll take you as is" is as much a comment on unconditional love as it is a comment on unconditional desire.

53. Quoted in "Fast Forward: People, Places and Things," *Advocate* October 15, 1985, 33–34.

54. Ibid.

55. Hoffman, *As Is*, xiii.

56. Blurbs from these reviews are cited on the back cover of the Vintage paperback edition of the play.

57. Jan Zita Grover, "Visable Lesions: Images of the PWA in America," in *Fluid Exchanges: Artists and Critics in the AIDS Crisis,*" ed. James Miller (Toronto: U of Toronto P, 1992), 35.

58. "Fast Forward: People, Places and Things," 33.

59. Kramer, *Reports from the Holocaust,* 32.

60. Kramer, *The Normal Heart,* 57. All quotes from the play are from this edition.

61. David Bergman, *Gaiety Transfigured: Gay Self-Representation in American Literature* (Madison: U of Wisconsin P, 1991), 126–27.

62. Mark Gevisser, "Gay Theater Today," *Theater,* 49.

63. See Joseph Allan Boone, *Tradition Counter Tradition. Love and the Form of Fiction.*

64. Douglas Crimp, "How to Have Promiscuity in an Epidemic," 248.

65. Raymond Williams, *Modern Tragedy,* 87.

66. Critiques against Kramer's writings and politics begin as early as the controversy surrounding his 1978 novel *Faggots* and become increasingly pronounced with the emergence of AIDS. Kramer's conservative sexual politics and his moralistic condemnation of gay men's so-called "promiscuity" have been contested by gay figures throughout the 1980s. See David Bergman's discussion of this history in *Gaiety Transfigured.*

67. For a discussion of feminist theatre and realism, see Janelle G. Reinelt, "Feminist Theory and the Problems of Performance"; as it concerns lesbian representation, see Jill Dolan, "Lesbian Subjectivity in Realism."

68. Stuart Marshall, "Picturing Deviancy," 21.

69. I base my discussion of the Madison production on my own experience as a volunteer educator and fundraiser for this event.

70. Quoted in Rick Harding, "Springfield's Shame," *Advocate,* December 19, 1989, 8–9.

71. Ibid.

72. Quoted in William Alexander, "Clearing Space," 122.

73. D. S. Lawson, "Rage and Remembrance: The AIDS Plays," 140.

74. Ibid.

75. Joel Shatzky, "AIDS Enters the American Theatre: *As Is* and *The Normal Heart,*" 131.

76. Quoted in Michael Denneny, "AIDS Writing and the Creation of a Gay Culture," 44–45.

77. Ibid., 46.

78. James W. Jones, "The Sick Homosexual," 119.

79. Don Shewey, "Introduction: *Out Front,*" xxiv.

80. Ibid., 82.

81. Joseph Cady, "AIDS on the National Stage," 26.

82. Ibid., 25–26.

83. John Clum, *Acting Gay,* 82. Clum retracts this claim in the second edition of his book published in 1994, which includes a new chapter on *Angels in America,* Larry Kramer's *The Destiny of Me,* and various other plays While his efforts to revise are welcome, his analysis of these plays fails to consider the ways that AIDS activism and the theatre interact in direct engagement. Nonetheless, Clum's added chapter provides a helpful glimpse of the 1993 New York theatre.

84. Eric Rofes, "A Healing Performance: Immunity Mandala—A Community Ritual," *Gay Community News,* October 29, 1983, 14.

85. Ibid.

86. Ibid.

87. Ibid.

88. Alisa Solomon, "AIDS Crusaders ACT UP a Storm," 40.

89. Ibid., 121.

90. Artists Confronting AIDS, unpublished mission statement.

91. See Michael Kearns's introduction to his book, *T-Cells and Sympathy: Monologues in the Age of AIDS* (Portsmouth, NH: Heinemann, 1995) for a discussion of these early plays.

92. Personal interview, November 1993.

93. Ibid.

94. *Newsweek* published an article on Helenclare Cox and her son, Andrew Hiatt. See Jean Seligmann with Michael Reese, "A Family Gives Refuge to a Son Who Has AIDS," *Newsweek*, August 12, 1985, 24.

95. Artists Confronting AIDS, *AIDS/US*, unpublished and unpaginated performance script.

96. Arlene Goldbard, "Postscripts to the Past," 23. For an excellent introduction to the community-arts-practice movement, see the special issue of *High Performance* 64 (Winter 1993). The community-arts-practice movement in the United States has a long, involved history always associated with specific agendas for progressive social change. In this sense, in no way should community arts performance be confused with what is popularly understood as "community theatre"—the ubiquitous and denigrated practice of staging productions of Americana in churches, high schools, and dinner theatres across the United States. While there is some immediate overlap in the idea of community and the performance of its values, beliefs, and customs, "community theatre" homogenizes particular localities through its reiterative citationality of a limited set of social scripts and mainly from the arsenal of the American musical.

97. Quoted in Richard Owen Geer, "Of the People, By the People and For the People," 31. According to Alternate Roots (Regional Organization of Theatres South), the most prominent community-arts organization in the United States, community can be defined in one of three ways: by location (neighborhoods, towns), spirit (beliefs or values; Catholics, gays, and Trekkies, are Geer's examples), or tradition (groups constituted around shared activities and maintained over time through these activities). I am indebted to Geer's discussion, which I quote throughout this note.

98. Cindy Patton, "Safe Sex and the Pornagraphic Vernacular," 32.

99. Michael Warner, introduction to *Fear of a Queer Planet*, xxv–xxvi.

100. Don Shirley, review of *AIDS/US, Los Angeles Times*, May 31, 1986, C11.

101. Jacki Horwitz, review of *AIDS/US, Daily News*, April 11, 1986.

102. Michael Lassell, *LA Weekly*, April 11, 1986, 42.

103. Artists Confronting AIDS, *AIDS/US*; unpublished and unpaginated performance script.

104. Personal interview, November 1994.

105. Catherine Saalfield, "On the Make: Activist Video Collectives," 27.

106. But see also Saalfied's discussion of other activist video collectives such as House of Color, a collective of lesbians and gays of color whose main focus, according to Saalfield, "is not necessarily the interaction of their work with a viewing audience" (23). See also her collaborative essay written with Ray Navarro, "Shocking the Pink: Race and Gender on the ACT UP Frontlines," in *Inside/Out: Lesbian Theories, Gay Theories*, ed. Diana Fuss (New York: Routledge, 1991).

107. Judith Butler, "Critically Queer," 23.

108. Artists Confronting AIDS, *AIDS/US/Women*, unpublished and unpaginated performance script.

109. Quoted in Daryl H. Miller, "Understanding Takes the Stage," *Daily News*, July 1, 1990, 20.

3. "It's My Party and I'll Die If I Want To!"

1. Robert Patrick, *Pouf Positive*, in *Untold Decades: Seven Comedies of Gay Romance* (New York: St. Martin's P, 1988), 212.

2. For Larry Kramer's manifesto on AIDS activism, see *Reports from the Holocaust: The*

Making of an AIDS Activist (New York: St. Martin's P, 1989). On the theatrics of ACT UP, see Doug Sadownick, "ACT UP Makes a Spectacle of AIDS," *High Performance* 13:1 (1990): 26–31.

3. See David Bergman's introductory essay to his anthology *Camp Grounds: Style and Homosexuality* (Amherst: U of Massachusetts P, 1994), for a discussion of camp's vexed role in gay and lesbian history.

4. For a critical reading of classic realist plays and AIDS activism, see David Román, "Performing All Our Lives: AIDS, Performance, Community," in *Critical Theory and Performance*, ed. Janelle Reinelt and Joseph Roach (Ann Arbor: U of Michigan P, 1992). See also the excellent analysis of the limits of classic realist forms from a cultural materialist methodology in Catherine Belsey, *Critical Practice* (New York: Methuen, 1980), and Jill Dolan, *The Feminist Spectator as Critic* (Ann Arbor: U of Michigan P, 1988).

5. For comprehensive discussions of these issues, see Simon Watney, *Policing Desire: AIDS, Pornography, and the Media*, second edition (Minneapolis: U of Minnesota P, 1989); Cindy Patton, *Inventing AIDS* (New York: Routledge, 1990); and *AIDS: Cultural Analysis/Cultural Activism*, ed. Douglas Crimp (Cambridge, MA: MIT Press, 1988).

6. Terrence McNally, *The Lisbon Traviata*, in *Three Plays by Terrence McNally* (New York: Plume, 1990), 85. All quotes are from this edition.

7. Catherine Clément, *Opera, or the Undoing of Women*, trans. Betsy Wing (Minneapolis: U of Minnesota P, 1988), 5.

8. McNally, quoted in Scott Rosenberg, "Playwright Dreams of the Road," *San Francisco Examiner*, October 21, 1990.

9. Terrence McNally, *Three Plays*, 87. An earlier version of the play is available in *Out Front: Contemporary Gay and Lesbian Plays*, ed. Don Shewey (New York: Grove P, 1988). Sam Abel has documented the mainstream critical response to these different versions of McNally's play in his unpublished essay "The Power of Death: The Politics of Genre, Sexuality, and Opera in *The Lisbon Traviata*."

10. Clément, *Opera, or the Undoing of Women*, 10.

11. Gayle Rubin, "The Traffic in Women: Notes on the 'Political Economy' of Sex," in *Toward an Anthropology of Women*, ed. Rayna Reiter (New York: Monthly Review, 1975), 157–210; Luce Irigaray *This Sex Which Is Not One*, trans. Catherine Porter (Ithaca: Cornell UP, 1985); and Eve Kosofsky Sedgwick, *Between Men: English Literature and Male Homosocial Desire* (New York: Columbia UP, 1985); but see also Karen Newman, "Directing Traffic: Subjects, Objects, and the Politics of Exchange," *differences* 2 (1990): 41–54.

12. Eve Kosofsky Sedgwick, "Across Gender, Across Sexuality: Willa Cather and Others," *South Atlantic Quarterly* 88 (1989): 57. Mitchell Morris applies many of Sedgwick's ideas to his insightful reading of *The Lisbon Traviata*. See Mitchell Morris, "Reading as an Opera Queen," in *Musicology and Difference: Gender and Sexuality in Music Scholarship*, ed. Ruth A. Solie (Berkeley: U of California P, 1993). Morris's writing led me back to the Sedgwick essay, but see also her *Epistemology of the Closet* (Berkeley: U of California P, 1990).

13. See, however, Steven Drukman, "Gay-Gazing at *The Lisbon Traviata*, or: How Are Things in *Tosca, Norma*?" *Theatre Topics* 5:1 (1995): 23–34, for a different point of view on this process of identification and reception.

14. Morris, "Reading as an Opera Queen," 186.

15. Wayne Koestenbaum, *The Queen's Throat. Opera, Homosexuality, and the Mystery of Desire* (New York: Poseidon P, 1993), 29.

16. See, however, the work of Carolyn Abbate, a feminist musicologist who refutes Clément's argument. For Abbate, the female singer usurps or, at the very least, calls into question the authoritative control of the male composer or librettist. Since opera is a performed genre, "No single (and, in opera, all-knowing) composer's voice sings what we hear." "Opera; or, The Envoicing of Women," in *Musicology and Difference*, 235.

17. Allan Bérubé, *Coming Out Under Fire: The History of Gay Men and Women in World War Two* (New York: Plume Books, 1990), 86. See also Esther Newton, *Mother Camp: Female Impersonators in America* (Chicago: U of Chicago P, 1979); Sue-Ellen Case, "Toward a Butch-Femme

Aesthetic," in *Making a Spectacle: Feminist Essays on Contemporary Women's Theatre*, ed. Lynda Hart (Ann Arbor: U of Michigan P, 1989); and the chapter entitled "Uses of Camp" in Andrew Ross, *No Respect: Intellectuals & Popular Culture* (New York: Routledge, 1989).

18. Quoted in Ken Dickman, "Lypsinka: The Real Voice of a Show Biz Phenomenon," *San Francisco Sentinel*, July 18, 1991, 19.

19. Ibid.

20. Ibid.

21. See, for instance, Michael Bronski, *Culture Clash: The Makings of a Gay Sensibility* (Boston: South End P, 1984), who unravels some of the investments gay men hold for opera and diva-identification.

22. On the camp components of *I Could Go on Singing*, see Richard Dyer, *Heavenly Bodies: Film Stars and Society* (New York: St. Martin's P), 1986.

23. On the formal designs of female impersonation and lip-synching, see Esther Newton, *Mother Camp: Female Impersonators in America*.

24. *I Could Go on Lip-Synching* program note, Callboard Theatre in Los Angeles, California; Spring 1991 run. For me, the irony of actually seeing the show in Hollywood only adds, as Lypsinka would argue (that is, if she were talking), to "the legend of Lypsinka."

25. On this concept, see Mark Thompson, "Children of Paradise: A Brief History of Queens," in *Gay Spirit: Myth and Meaning*, ed. Mark Thompson (New York: St. Martin's P, 1987), 49–68.

26. Bérubé, *Coming Out Under Fire*, 86–87.

27. I need to point out here that lesbians and gay men have different relations to camp and drag, and different responses to gay male camp and drag. For a discussion of these differences, see Kate Davy, "Fe/Male Impersonation: The Discourse of Camp."

28. Mark Gevisser, "Gay Theater Today," *Theater* 21:3 (1990): 46–51.

29. Quoted in Jeffrey Hilbert, "The Politics of Drag," *Advocate*, April 23, 1991, 42.

30. Ibid., 44.

31. Douglas Crimp with Adam Rolston, *AIDS Demo Graphics* (Seattle: Bay P, 1990), 17. Crimp and Rolston document ACT UP New York's participation in *Nine Days of Protest*. I use their text as the base for my synopsis.

32. There was also a women's graphic for the Read My Lips campaign. One image was pulled from a photo of a lesbian couple in a 1920s Broadway play and showed the two women yearning with desire but not kissing. After objections from women activists who claimed this image only perpetuated the invisibility of lesbian sexuality, Gran Fury offered the image of two women of color kissing. See Crimp with Rolston, 53.

33. Richard Meyer, "This Is to Enrage You: Gran Fury and the Graphic of AIDS Activism," in *But Is It Art? The Spirit of Art and Activism*, ed. Nina Felting (Seattle: Bay Press, 1995), 60.

34. Ross, *No Respect*, 151.

35. Many of these "apolitical" entertainers—including John Epperson—have generously participated in various benefits for gay and lesbian and/or AIDS organizations.

36. Glines is quoted in Michael Sommers, "Beyond Off-Broadway: Just What Is the State of Gay Theatre?" *Genre* (Summer, 1991): 31.

37. From the promotional postcard for the production at Highways Performance Space.

38. *AIDS! The Musical!* ran at Highways (130-seat capacity) on the following dates: August 1–4 and 8–11, 1991. Performances were sold out during the entire run.

39. *AIDS! The Musical!* press release for Highways Performance Space production.

40. All quotes from *AIDS! The Musical!* are from the, at the time of production, unpublished script (book/lyrics by Wendell Jones and David Stanley), copyright 1991. I am grateful to David Stanley for offering me a copy of their script for the purpose of this essay. *AIDS! The Musical!* has since been revised for publication in *Sharing the Delirium: Second Generation AIDS Plays and Performances*, ed. Therese Jones (Portsmouth, NH: Heinemann, 1994). All quotes from *AIDS! The Musical!* are from the authors' 1991 unpaginated performance script.

41. Wendell Jones and David Stanley, "Authors' Notes," in *Sharing the Delirium*, 208.

42. Jill Dolan, *The Feminist Spectator as Critic*, 107. But see also the work of Elin Diamond, Janelle Reinelt, and Sue-Ellen Case among others. Their essays have been published in various journals since the mid-1980s; see Dolan's *Presence and Desire* for a bibliography and discussion of the field. On Brecht's concept of epic theatre, see Bertolt Brecht, *Brecht on Theatre*, trans. John Willett (New York: Hill and Wang, 1964).

43. See Patton's *Last Served? Gendering the HIV Pandemic* (London: Taylor and Francis, 1994), 3.

44. On this issue, see The ACT UP/NY Women & AIDS Book Group, *Women, AIDS, & Activism* (Boston: South End P, 1990). In the early 1990s, AIDS activists successfully advocated for the expansion of the Center of Disease Control's definition of AIDS to include the opportunistic infections specific to women, inclusion of women (and people of color) in clinical drug trials, and research specific to women's health and health care.

45. Gay audiences, of course, might also dismiss some of these production choices. I discuss this possibility in "Preaching to the Converted," an essay co-written with Tim Miller. Although I do not engage *AIDS! The Musical!* in the essay, the ideas there are applicable. No matter how intent the production team behind *AIDS! The Musical!* is on providing an "in-house" representation, they cannot control the spectator's interpretation or investment in the production. They can, however, go to great effort to manipulate the spectator's response; from this perspective, the Sodomy Players, most involved with ACT UP/LA, transported many of their activist tactics to the theatrical process.

46. Robert Koehler, review of *AIDS! The Musical!* in the *Los Angeles Times*, August 7, 1991, F9. All subsequent quotes are from this review.

47. Robert Patrick, *Pouf Positive*, in *Untold Decades*, 129.

4. Solo Performance and the Body on Stage

1. Ron Vawter died of AIDS complications in 1994.

2. Marvin Carlson provides an excellent overview of these debates in *Performance: A Critical Introduction* (New York: Routledge, 1996).

3. C. Carr, *On Edge*, xiv.

4. Roselee Goldberg, *Performance Art: From Futurism to Present*, rev. ed. (New York: Harry N. Abrams, 1988), 9.

5. See Goldberg's documentation of early performance artists and their social commentary, as well as Sue-Ellen Case's survey of women and performance art in chapter 3 of *Feminism and Theatre* (New York: Methuen, 1988), 56–61.

6. This departure from a strict compliance arguing for performance arts' "location" as a visual art is especially evident in the 1980s. See Linda Frye Burnham's essay "High Performance, Performance Art, and Me," *Drama Review* 30:2 (1986): 15–51, for the history of the performance art movement and its continual contradictions and internal debates.

7. See Goldberg, *Performance Art*, for this history.

8. Jackie Apple, "Performance Art Is Dead! Long Live Performance Art!" *High Performance* (Summer 1994): 58–59.

9. See Guillermo Gómez-Peña, "The Multi-Cultural Paradigm," in *Warrior for Gringostroika* (St. Paul, MN: Graywolf Press, 1993).

10. Once again, see Guillermo Gómez-Peña's essay and Linda Frye Burnham, "Getting on the Highways: Taking Responsibility for the Culture in the '90s," *Journal of Dramatic Theory and Criticism* Fall (1990): 264–277.

11. On this topic see my collaboration with Tim Miller, "Preaching to the Converted," *Theatre Journal* 47:2 (1995): 169–188.

12. See Goldberg for a discussion of these artists.

13. For the history of *High Performance* and of performance art, see Linda Frye Burnham, "High Performance, Performance Art, and Me."

14. Ellen Zweig, "The Best Kept Secret," *American Book Review* (August-September 1994): 14.

15. Performance art and grassroots performance converged in New York City in the late 1970s and early 1980s. In *On Edge*, C. Carr explains how performance art in the East Village, a major location of performance art in the 1980s, went unnoticed outside of its immediate constituency of artists, enthusiastic supporters, and neighborhood clubgoers. The East Village emerged as a haven for various types of performances which, as Carr documents, not only defied categorization but also, and more important, the need for categorization. Since no one outside of the immediate neighborhood cared about this work at the time, performers were free to call themselves solo performers, performance artists, dancers, or any other term. The categories, despite their specific contexts, were able to be used interchangeably precisely because there was no one from the established culture who insisted on policing these terms. While the East Village was perhaps the most active location for performance in the early 1980s, it was not the only site of proliferation.

16. Carr, *On Edge*.

17. Jeanie Forte raises many of these concerns in her article "Women's Performance Art: Feminism and Post-Modernism," in *Performing Feminisms*, ed. Sue-Ellen Case (Baltimore: Johns Hopkins UP, 1990), 251–269. See especially her discussion of Karen Finley, p. 268.

18. Forte, "Women's Performance Art," 268.

19. See my discussion of this phenomenon in chapter 3 and in Mark Gevisser, "Gay Theater Today," *Theater* 21 (1990): 46–51.

20. Philip Auslander, "Going with the Flow: Performance Art and Mass Culture," *Drama Review* (1989): 119–136. See also Jon Erickson, "Appropriation and Transgression in Contemporary American Performance: The Wooster Group, Holly Hughes, and Karen Finley," *Theatre Journal* 42:2 (1990): 225–236.

21. Margot Mifflin, "Performance Art: What Is It and Where Is It Going?" *Art News* (April 1992): 89.

22. Jackie Apple, "Notes on Teaching Performing Art," *Performing Arts Journal* 50/51 (1995): 121.

23. See, for example, Josette Feral, "Performance and Theatricality: The Subject Demystified," *Modern Drama* 25 (1982): 170–81.

24. Simon Watney, "The Spectacle of AIDS," in *Practices of Freedom: Selected Writings on HIV/AIDS* (Durham: Duke UP, 1994), 52.

25. Ibid.

26. Ibid., 53.

27. Ibid., 59.

28. Phelan, *Unmarked*, 150.

29. Many of these earliest theatre pieces were solo performances which, to varying degrees, addressed AIDS. Jeff Hagedorn's *One*, a monologue performed from the perspective of a person with AIDS, premiered in Chicago in the fall of 1983; Dan Turner's comic monologue *Pearls of Wisdom* opened for four performances in San Francisco in February of 1983; and Bill Barksdale's *Nightmare of the Son: My Shadow Land* ran through December of that year at San Francisco's Studio Eremos at Project Artaud. Turner's monologue—a fifteen-minute portrayal of Adlai Stevenson's great aunt, whom Turner knew from his childhood days in Indiana—is not about AIDS, however. According to Turner, in an interview in the *Bay Area Reporter*, the short monologue "was inspired by my recent health crisis with AIDS" (unsigned interview, *Bay Area Reporter*, February 3, 1983, 22). Barksdale's solo centers on the emotional impact of his caring for a friend with AIDS and includes a short hand-puppet skit, based on the deathbed scene of *La Traviata*, in which the person with AIDS, like Violetta, is dying and the friend, like her lover, is unwilling to recognize the truth. Dan Turner reviewed Barksdale's performance; see his "The Ultimate Disconnection," *Bay Area Reporter*, December 15, 1983, 26. In New York City, dancer and performer John Bernd was one of the pioneer gay artists in the East Village

scene and one of the first to go public with his diagnosis. Throughout the early 1980s, Bernd set out to establish what he described as a "second generation of gay culture," (quoted in Terry Helbing, "A Boom Time for Theater," *Advocate*, January 21, 1982, 54). Ethyl Eichenberger's unique brand of drag performance was already, according to Robert Chesley, referencing AIDS as early as 1983. See Chesley's profile of Eichenberger in *Advocate*, July 7, 1983, 52. The point here is that gay male performers began addressing AIDS in various ways and to varying degrees in 1983. Some of these representations set out to explicitly address AIDS, while others could be understood to contain an implied, but nevertheless deliberate, response to AIDS.

30. Michael Kearns, *Intimacies/More Intimacies*, 237.

31. Kearns, *T-Cells and Sympathy: Monologues in the Age of AIDS*, xiii.

32. Kearns, *Intimacies/More Intimacies*, 268–69.

33. Kearns, personal interview.

34. See Richard Meyer, "Rock Hudson's Body," in *Inside/Out: Lesbian Theories, Gay Theories*, ed. Diana Fuss, for a discussion of Rock Hudson, the closet, and AIDS.

35. Rob Hecht, "An Odd Blessing: An Interview with Michael Kearns," *Spectrum* 34 (1992): 58.

36. Hecht, "An Odd Blessing," 59.

37. All quotes from *Rock* are based on the May 30, 1992, performances at Sushi in San Diego.

38. In 1996, a documentary film on the final performances of *Intimacies* premiered at the Los Angeles lesbian and gay film festival.

39. Richard Schechner, "Ron Vawter—For the Record: An Interview with Richard Schechner," *Drama Review* 37: 3 (1993): 27.

40. See Schechner's interview with Ron Vawter in *Drama Review* for the specific details of this process.

41. See C. Carr and Stefan Brecht for more on Jack Smith.

42. As quoted by C. Carr in "Life's Rich Pageant," *LA Weekly*, August 7, 1992, 39.

43. Patrick Pacheco, "Self-Hate Crimes," *Los Angeles Times/Calendar*, August 2, 1992, 72.

44. Ibid., 8.

45. This is especially noteworthy considering Cohn's postmortem popularity in film, performance, and theatre. On this topic, see Stephen J. Bottom, "Re-staging Roy: Citizen Cohn and the Search for Xanadu," *Theatre Journal* 48:2 (1996): 157–184. I return to Roy Cohn in my discussion of *Angels in America* in chapter 7. However, comparisons of these representations of Cohn fall outside my immediate interests and project.

46. Bottoms, "Re-staging Roy," 175. Bottoms goes on to argue that this reading is possible if one considers that Vawter went from the military to the Wooster Group. For Bottoms, this idea becomes more pronounced in the Jack Smith section. He writes, "Yet in recreating one of Smith's bizarre pieces of performance art, Vawter is also, in a sense, performing a version of his post-military, Wooster-ized self" (177).

47. Jim Leverett, "Ron Vawter," *Village Voice*, May 3, 1994, 96.

48. Schechner, "Ron Vawter—For the Record," 26.

49. Ibid., 25.

50. This is especially true of work emerging from specific community-based AIDS activist roots such as ACT UP. In the late 1980s, for example, testing was a contestable site of political debate. See chapter 8 for a discussion on how "HIV-negative" remains unmarked.

51. See the final chapter, on HIV-negative gay men, in which I discuss this issue at length.

52. All quotes from *Sex/Love/Stories* are from the author's performance text.

53. I am reminded here of Richard Dyer's observations on gay male pornography, specifically his claim that the narratives of conventional gay porn position the viewer to anticipate orgasm. See "Coming to Terms," in *Out There: Marginalization and Contemporary Cultures*, ed. Russell Ferguson, Martha Gever, Trinh T. Minh-ha, and Cornel West (Cambridge: MIT P, 1990), 289–98. My reading of Miller's "get hard" segment does not by any means imply that the piece

is "pornographic" but rather suggests that Miller manipulates the spectator into the narrative of gay porn only to reposition the spectator from orgasmic anticipation to political action. Furthermore, I am not suggesting that all gay male spectators share this same arousal but, following Dyer's lead, allow for the powerful, culturally determined configurations of gay male sexual desire that permeate much of contemporary urban gay culture. On this issue see Leo Bersani, "Is the Rectum a Grave?" in *AIDS: Cultural Analysis/Cultural Activism,* ed. Douglas Crimp (Cambridge: MIT Press), 1987.

54. See chapter 2, especially my discussion of *The Normal Heart.*

55. Luis Alfaro describes his own experience at this event in "Federal Building," in his solo performance, *Downtown.* See my discussion of Alfaro's performance in chapter 6.

56. Here Miller seems to undertake what Judith Butler advocates in her brilliant reading of the Helms amendment and its own implication as a site of homosexual pornography. In "The Force of Fantasy: Feminism, Mapplethorpe, and Discursive Excess," *differences* 2:2 (1990): 105–125, she writes: "My recommendation is not to solve this crisis of identity politics [who and what wields the power to define the homosexual real] but to proliferate and intensify this crisis . . . the task is . . . to affirm identity categories as a site of inevitable rifting, in which the phantasmatic fails to preempt the linguistic prerogative of the real" (121).

57. Tim Miller, *My Queer Body,* in *Sharing the Delirium: Second Generation AIDS Plays,* ed. Therese Jones (Portsmouth, NH: Heinemann Press, 1994); 318.

58. Ibid., 322.

59. Ibid., 326.

60. See my essay "Performing All Our Lives: AIDS, Performance, Community," in *Critical Theory and Performance,* for a discussion of Miller's performance workshops.

61. In the summer of 1990, John Frohnmeyer, then chairperson of the National Endowment for the Arts, rescinded the peer-reviewed grant recommendations for Tim Miller and three other solo performers, Karen Finley, John Fleck, and Holly Hughes.

62. Ron Athey, "Casebook: *Four Scenes in a Harsh Life,*" *Theatre Forum* 6 (Winter/Spring 1995): 62–63.

63. These events have been well documented in the popular press. See William Harris, "Demonized and Struggling with His Demons," *New York Times,* October 23, 1994, H31; Jeff Spurier, "Blood of a Poet," *Details* (February 1995): 106+; and Ben Brantley, "A Little Infamy Goes a Long Way," *New York Times,* October 29, 1994, B13.

64. Quoted from the text of promotional postcard for *Four Scenes in a Harsh Life* at PS 122 in New York City, October 27–30, 1994.

65. Athey explained to the *Village Voice* that "[a]fter Minneapolis, the alternative spaces got scared to deal with me." Guy Trebay, "Ron Athey's Slice of Life," *Village Voice,* November 1, 1994, 38.

66. See Peggy Phelan, "Money Talks" and "Money Talks Again," and Alisa Solomon, "Art Attacks."

67. Jeff Spurrier, "Blood of a Poet," 109.

5. Pomo Afro Homos' *Fierce Love*

1. *Fierce Love: Stories from Black Gay Life,* Brian Freeman with additional material by Eric Gupton and Bernard Branner, unpublished manuscript. All subsequent quotes are drawn from the performance script the Pomos used at the time. Thanks to Brian Freeman for sharing the performance script with me. I base my analysis of *Fierce Love* on this text and the various performances I attended in San Francisco, Santa Monica, and Seattle between March 1991 and January 1992. *Fierce Love* was published in 1996. See *Colored Contradictions: An Anthology of Contemporary African-American Plays* (New York: Plume, 1996).

2. Kobena Mercer, "Skin Head Sex Thing: Racial Difference and the Homoerotic Imaginary," in *How Do I Look? Queer Film and Video,* ed. Bad-Object Choices (Seattle: Bay P, 1991), 204.

3. Steven Corbin, "The Fire Baptism," *Frontiers*, June 19, 1992, 78.

4. John Guare, *Six Degrees of Separation* (New York: Vintage Books, 1990), 31. All further quotes are from this edition.

5. Frank Rich, review of John Guare's *Six Degrees of Separation*, *New York Times*, June 15, 1990, C1.

6. See for instance: Jack Kroll, *Newsweek*, June 25, 1990; John Beaufort, *Christian Science Monitor*, June 26, 1990; David Patrick Stearns, *USA Today*, June 19, 1990; Melanie Kirkpatrick, *Wall Street Journal*, June 25, 1990; and David Richards, *Washington Post*, July 12, 1990.

7. John Clum, *Acting Gay: Male Homosexuality in Modern Drama* (New York: Columbia UP, 1992), 19.

8. Ibid., 21.

9. Ibid., 22.

10. Ibid.

11. Frank Rich, "A Guidebook to the Soul of a City in Confusion," *New York Times*, July 1, 1990, C1+.

12. See, for example, Alex Witchel, "The Life of Fakery and Delusion in John Guare's *Six Degrees*," *New York Times*, June 21, 1990, C17; Alex Witchel, "Impersonator Wants to Portray Still Others, This Time, Onstage," *New York Times*, July 31, 1990, C3; and Joyce Walder's profile of David Hampton in *People*, March 18, 1991, 99–100.

13. Imprisoned first in the New York state prison system and then later as Paul in the New York City theatre, David Hampton announced after seeing *Six Degrees* that he would pursue, like Sidney Poitier, a career in acting.

14. Moreover, it points to the limited roles for black men in plays written and produced by whites. Both James McDaniel and Courtney Vance, two of the most esteemed black actors in the United States, played the role of Paul during the New York run. In London, where the play opened at the Royal Court Theatre in June 1992, Paul was played by Adrian Lester. I base my analysis on performances I viewed in New York and London with Vance and Lester cast as Paul.

15. On the concept of African AIDS as opposed to AIDS in Africa, see Cindy Patton's *Inventing AIDS* and Simon Watney's "Missionary Positions: AIDS, 'Africa,' and Race," *differences* 1:1 (1989): 83–100.

16. See, for example, Clarence Page, "Deathly Silence: Black Leaders and AIDS," *New Republic*, December 2, 1991, 15–18, and a follow-up discussion in Lindsey Gruson, "Black Politicians Discover AIDS," *New York Times*, March 9, 1992, A7.

17. There is a double irony in this limited scheme; on the one hand, when asserting a heterosexual identity, AIDS is disassociated from gay men and the usual media conflation of AIDS and homosexuality, yet on the other hand, Magic Johnson is immediately reconfigured in racial terms and the conflation of Africa and AIDS. Within this binary system Johnson must fall into one of these misconceptions. Most problematic, those who are of African descent and homosexual are either rendered invisible or, if seen at all, must be rendered as obscene.

18. *Advocate*, April 21, 1992, 36. Some gay and lesbian activists have complained that the cover photo of Johnson obscures the full masthead, which reads "The National Gay and Lesbian Newsmagazine."

19. Douglas Crimp, "Accommodating Magic," in *Media Spectacles*, eds. Marjorie Garber, Jann Matlock, and Rebecca Walkowitz (New York: Routledge, 1993), 262.

20. Charles Stewart, "Double Jeopardy: Black, Gay, (and invisible)," *New Republic*, December 2, 1991, 13–15.

21. Mark Haile, " 'It Can Happen to Anybody. Even Me, Magic Johnson.' " *BLK* 3:9 (1991): 20–25.

22. Michael Broder, "High Risk, Low Priority: Society Turns a Double Blind Eye on AIDS in the Black Community," *BLK* 3:7 (1991): 7–14.

23. Ron Simmons, "Some Thoughts on the Challenges Facing Black Intellectuals," in

Brother to Brother: New Writings by Black Gay Men, ed. Essex Hemphill (Boston: Alyson Publications: 1991), 211.

24. Jewelle Gomez and Barbara Smith, "Taking the Home out of Homophobia: Black Lesbians Look in Their Own Backyards," *Outlook* 8 (1990): 32–37.

25. Marlon Riggs, "Black Macho Revisited: Reflections of a Snap Queen," *Brother to Brother: New Writings by Black Gay Men*, 254.

26. Marlon Riggs, "Black Macho Revisited," 254.

27. Alan E. Miller, "Young, Gifted, and Fierce," *BLK* 3:8 (1991): 9–13.

28. For a detailed education on the art of the snap, see *Tongues Untied* by Marlon Riggs, 1990.

29. If heterosexual blacks are shown to misappropriate the snap, white gay men are exposed for coopting the symbols of African American history. In "Red Bandanas" the Pomos angrily reclaim the red bandanas whose currency in gay male circles as a sexual code undermines its legacy and significance for African Americans. When worn in the right hip pocket, the red bandana means "fuck me," but the pomos wear the red bandana around the neck which means "I am remembering my granddad who owned it before I did."

30. Amy Robinson, review of Pomo Afro Homos' *Fierce Love, Theatre Journal* 44:2 (1992): 225–227.

31. David Perry, "Black, Fierce, and Funny: New Performance Group Crafts Stories of Black Gay Life," *Advocate*, July 2, 1991, 86–87.

32. This scene is also one of the funniest in performance. Freeman's repetition of the phrase points out the degrees of limitations of various nonblack gay male spectators' subject positions through humor.

33. Willi Smith, who revolutionized the commercial fashion industry with his Willi Wear line—"I don't design clothes for the Queen but for the people who wave at her as she passes by"—was 39 when he died of AIDS in April 1987; Patrick Kelly, yet another exceptional fashion designer, died of AIDS in January 1990; and Sylvester, the grand diva of disco for well over ten years, died of AIDS in 1988.

34. Laura Jamison, "Queer Like Me," *Village Voice*, October 8, 1991, 101–102.

35. Barbara Beebe, "Pomo Afro Homos: Brian Freeman Talks about *Dark Fruit* and the State of the Black Gay Community," *B&G* 3:3 (1992): 11–14.

36. Marlon Riggs, "Meet the New Willie Horton," *New York Times*, March 6, 1992, A19.

37. See Kobena Mercer, and also Alisa Solomon's insightful essay "Art Attack: What Do Plato and Pat Buchanan Have in Common?" *American Theatre* 9 (1992): 19–24.

38. The skit of the three black gay characters on Broadway was added for the Pomos' performance of *Dark Fruit* at the Serious Fun Festival at NYC's Lincoln Center during the summer of 1993.

39. Pomo Afro Homos, *Dark Fruit*, in *Staging Gay Lives: An Anthology of Contemporary Gay Theater*, ed. John Clum (Boulder: Westview P, 1996), 325.

40. Kobena Mercer, *Welcome to the Jungle: New Positions in Black Cultural Studies* (New York: Routledge, 1994), 30.

41. Pomo Afro Homos, *Dark Fruit*, 343.

6. Teatro Viva!

1. Culture Clash. *S.O.S.* Performed at the Japan American Theatre, Los Angeles. July 9–11, 1992.

2. I want to stress that there are necessary distinctions between AIDS-phobia, homophobia, and misogyny; that these same discrete and dynamic terms, however, are often conflated in people's understandings and responses to AIDS; and that the practice of viewing the terms as interchangeable, in this case when discussing AIDS, is itself symptomatic of the very conditions that the terms describe.

3. The topic of this chapter is specifically local (Los Angeles) and temporal (1992). I have written elsewhere on the representations of Latinos and AIDS in mainstream production. See my collaboration with Alberto Sandoval, "Caught in the Web: Latinidad, AIDS, and Allegory in *Kiss of the Spider Woman, the Musical,*" *American Literature* 67:3 (September 1995): 553–585.

4. See Jorge Huerta, who makes the point that the production of *August 29*, which premiered in 1990 at the Los Angeles Theatre Center (LATC), was "perhaps the most significant Chicano production of the 1980s." Huerta's essay is important: he provides a valuable genealogy of Chicano and Latino theatre, focusing his discussion on Southern California. Huerta argues that "[u]ntil the 1980s Chicano theatre in this country could only be found in the Chicano communities that had spawned their own *teatros,* playwrights, directors, and actors." His essay goes on to document and discuss the more recent practice of staging Chicano plays by mainstream theaters. His essay "Looking for the Magic: Chicanos in the Mainstream" can be found in *Negotiating Performance: Gender, Sexuality, and Theatricality in Latin/o America,* eds. Diana Taylor and Juan Villegas (Durham: Duke UP, 1994).

5. Alberto Sandoval, who has collected numerous Chicano and Latino plays dealing with AIDS, points out the diversity of this work: "Playwrights stage the personal, social, political dimensions of the crisis in a variety of forms within a theatrical spectrum from workshops, street theatre, protest plays, agit-prop, documentary, and popular theatre to conventional models of theatrical genres and staging" (64). Sandoval, "Staging AIDS: What's Latinos Got to Do with It?" in *Negotiating Performance.* See also Sandoval's essay "So Far from National Stages, So Close to Home: An Inventory of Latino Theater on AIDS," in the special issue of *Ollantay* (Summer/Fall 1994): 54–72.

6. Press release.

7. Including not only the Rodney King verdict and the riots that resulted, but also the racist rhetoric that characterized much of the popular media's coverage of these events. For artists' responses to the LA riots, see the special edition of *High Performance,* "The Verdict and the Violence" (Summer 1992).

8. "American Me Tail" is a clever takeoff on *American Me,* a 1992 film about Latino prisoners, and *An American Tale,* a Disney Studios animated film. The core of the skit involves the power relations within competing factions in a prison negotiated, predictably enough, through male rape.

9. See Cherríe Moraga, *Loving in the War Years* (Boston: South End P, 1983) and Tomás Almaguer. "Chicano Men. A Cartography of Homosexual Identity and Behavior," *differences* 3:2 (1991): 75–100.

10. Douglas Crimp, "How to Have Promiscuity during an Epidemic," *AIDS: Cultural Analysis/Cultural Activism,* ed. Crimp (Cambridge: MIT P, 1987), 255.

11. Nicolás Kanellos, *A History of Hispanic Theatre in the United States. Origins to 1940* (Austin: U of Texas P, 1990), xv.

12. Perhaps the most obvious failure of identity politics in the performance emerges from the interchangeable Chicano/Latino terminology. *Chicano* refers to a very specific set of political identifications among Mexican Americans; *Latino,* like *Chicano,* is a term of self-identification that differentiates from the more official and imposed term *Hispanic.* See Ana Maria Alonso and Maria Teresa Koreck, "Silences: 'Hispanics,' AIDS, and Sexual Practices," *differences* 1:1 (1989): 101–124, for a detailed account of these terms in relation to AIDS.

13. Yvonne Yarbro-Bejarano, "The Female Subject in Chicano Theatre," in *Performing Feminisms: Feminist Critical Theory and Theatre,* ed. Sue-Ellen Case (Baltimore: Johns Hopkins UP, 1990), 132.

14. See for instance her trilogy of plays, *Giving Up the Ghost, Shadow of a Man,* and *Heroes and Saints,* along with Yarbro-Bejarano's discussion of them in her essays.

15. Yarbro-Bejarano, "Female Subject," 135.

16. In fairness I should note that Marga Gomez, an early member of the group, was reunited with Culture Clash for their 1994 production of *Carpa Clash* at the Mark Taper Forum.

She performed material from her immensely successful solo performance *A Line around the Block* and other skits with members of the company.

17. At the biannual Latino Festival Theatre held in the South Bronx in 1990, for example, El Teatro de la Esperanza presented one of the best received plays of the festival, Josefina Lopez's *Real Women Have Curves*. For more information on the festival see Euridice Arratia, "Teatro Festival: The Latino Festival Theatre," *Drama Review* 35 (1991): 176–182. Also in 1990, the University of California at Irvine held "The Representation of Otherness in Chicano and Latin American Theatre and Film" conference where feminist concerns were addressed and debated. See Diana Taylor, review of *The Representation of Otherness in Chicano and Latin American Theatre and Film Conference* at UC-Irvine, 18–20 October 1990, *Theatre Journal* 43 (1991): 377–79. Not all women, of course, are able—or for that matter, willing—to see their work staged in these forums. For all-women performance venues, festivals, and conferences, see Yarbro-Bejarano's essays. For discussions of more recent Latino theatre festivals, see Ed Morales, "Shadowing Valdez," *American Theatre* 9:7 (1992): 14–19; "Welcome to Aztlan," *American Theatre* 10:3 (1993): 38–40; and "Those Who Can, Act: 'Cultural Workers' at Teatro Festival," *Village Voice*, August 3, 1993, 95–6. For an overview of Chicano theatre, see Jorge Huerta, "Professionalizing Teatro: An Overview of Chicano Theatre during the 'Decade of the Hispanic,' " *Theatre Forum* 3 (1993): 54–59.

18. Yarbro-Bejarano, "Female Subject," 145.

19. Ibid.

20. Hector Calderón and José David Saldívar, *Criticism in the Borderlands: Studies in Chicano Literature, Culture, and Ideology* (Durham: Duke UP, 1991), 7.

21. For an insightful critique of *Criticism in the Borderlands* written from the perspective of a Chicana lesbian, see Deena J. Gonzalez, "Masquerades: Viewing the New Chicana Lesbian Anthologies," *Outlook* 15 (1991): 80–83.

22. Miguelina Maldonado, "On the Out Side: Latinos and Clinical Trials," *SIDAhora* 11 (1992): 13.

23. See Alonso and Koreck, "Silences: 'Hispanics,' AIDS, and Sexual Practices."

24. Crimp, *AIDS: Cultural Analysis/Cultural Activism*, 3.

25. See Dante Ramos, "A Second Wave," *New Republic*, June 5, 1995, 29.

26. Alonso and Koreck, "Silences: 'Hispanics,' AIDS, and Sexual Practices," 118.

27. Calderón and Saldívar, *Criticism in the Borderlands*, 7.

28. Ibid.

29. Eve Kosofsky Sedgwick, *Epistemology of the Closet* (Berkeley: U of California P, 1990), 1. Sedgwick is not addressing Latino studies specifically; her quote reads, "[*Epistemology of the Closet*] will argue that an understanding of virtually any aspect of modern Western culture must be, not merely incomplete, but *damaged* in its central substance to the degree that it does not incorporate a critical analysis of modern homo/heterosexual definition . . . " (my emphasis).

30. Otoniel Martinez-Maza, Diana M. Shin, and Helen E. Banks, *Latinos and AIDS: A National Strategy Symposium* (Los Angeles: Center for Interdisciplinary Research in Immunology and Disease, 1989), vii.

31. Alice Villalobos, "AIDS and the Latino/a Community," *ACT UP/Los Angeles Newsletter* 5 (1990): 10.

32. Both Ledesma and Olivias are quoted in Doug Sadownick, "Family among Strangers: Crossing the Borders in Gay L.A.," *LA Weekly*, June 23, 1989, 12–20.

33. Ibid. Highways has since become an important location for Latino queer artists to perform their work. I should add that I joined the Highways Board of Directors in 1995.

34. Chela Sandoval, "U.S. Third World Feminism: The Theory and Method of Oppositional Consciousness in the Postmodern World," *Genders* 10 (1991): 1–24.

35. Sandoval, 16. Yvonne Yarbro-Bejarano has already demonstrated how Sandoval's theory of oppositional consciousness provides fresh insight for critical formations in theories of difference and gay and lesbian studies. See her essay "Expanding the Categories of Race in

Lesbian and Gay Studies," in *Professions of Desire: Lesbian and Gay Studies in Literature,* ed. George E. Haggerty and Bonnie Zimmerman (New York: MLA Publications, 1994).

36. George Lipsitz, *Time Passages: Collective Memory and American Popular Culture* (Minneapolis: U of Minnesota P, 1990), 159.

37. Ibid., 154.

38. For an in-depth discussion of Los Angeles Latinos and poverty, see Mike Davis, *City of Quartz: Excavating the Future in Los Angeles* (London: Verso, 1990). In "The Hammer and the Rock," a chilling chapter on inner-city social conditions, Davis explains how "poverty is increasing faster among Los Angeles Latinos, especially youth, than any other urban group in the United States" (315).

39. All quotes are from the author's unpublished performance text. *Downtown* premiered at Highways Performance Space in Santa Monica, California, November 30 and December 1–2, 7–9, 1990.

40. For an excellent discussion of kinship and conflict as it pertains to lesbians and gay men, see Kath Weston, *Families We Choose: Lesbians, Gays, Kinship* (New York: Columbia UP, 1991).

41. Saldívar is describing specifically Tomas Rivera's foundational Chicano novel, *Y no se lo tragó la tierra/And the Earth Shall Not Devour Him.* See his *Chicano Narrative: The Dialectics of Difference* (Madison: U of Wisconsin P, 1990), 77.

42. On "classic" drag, see chapter 1 of Sue-Ellen Case, *Feminism and Theatre* (New York: Routledge, 1988). But see also Marjorie Garber, *Vested Interests: Cross-dressing and Cultural Anxiety* (New York: Routledge, 1991), for a different reading of cross-dressing and for a more extensive bibliography.

43. In this sense, his work is similar to *Intimacies,* by Michael Kearns (see chapter 4). Both Kearns and Alfaro attempt to perform fictional characters outside of their subject position; by performing characters of other races and genders, each artist hopes to call attention to the related forms of oppression marginalized people may experience. The success of the intended spectatorial identification with either the performer or the character will, of course, be measured differently by individual spectators.

44. Alfaro is participating in the same action which Tim Miller includes in "Civil Disobedience Weekend" in *Sex/Love/Stories.* See my discussion of Miller's performance in chapter 4.

45. Jan Breslauer, "California Performance," *Performing Arts Journal* 41 (1992): 87–96.

46. Alfaro's *Downtown* was performed as *Pico-Union* on a bill with Chloe Webb's *Walkin' the Walls* and Rocco Sisto's rendition of Dario Fo's *The Tale of the Tiger. True Lies* was performed at the Los Angeles Theatre Center from July 25–September 8, 1991.

47. Most of the reviews of *True Lies,* for example, while favorable of *Pico-Union,* describe in detail Alfaro's sexuality and ethnicity—some even to the extent that they talk about his physical appearance—without going into any discussion of either of the two white performers' sexuality or ethnic background, let alone their physical traits.

48. In his collaborations with other gay and lesbian performers, Alfaro continues to articulate a politics of oppositional consciousness. In *Queer Rites,* for example, Alfaro performs with two white lesbian feminists, Robin Podolsky and Sandra Golvin, and with Doug Sadownick, a Jewish gay male performer. Given that it is already understood that the four performers in *Queer Rites* are queer, it is left up to the four of them to establish points of difference and connection. *Queer Rites* celebrates difference while demonstrating the effects of coalition building and dialogue between seemingly disparate people who meet under the political rubric "queer." *Queer Rites* was performed in the summer of 1991, first at Highways and then at Celebration Theatre in West Hollywood. Unfortunately, *Queer Rites* was not reviewed in any great detail. Rachel Kaplan wrote, however, a very descriptive review of the individual performances in *A Queer Exchange* at San Francisco's 1800 Square Feet. These performances developed into the collaborative *Queer Rites.* See Kaplan's review in the *San Francisco Bay Times,* March 1991, 50.

49. See Yvonne Yarbro-Bejarano's contribution to *Entiendes? Queer Readings/Hispanic Writings*, ed. Emilie Bergmann and Paul Julian Smith (Durham: Duke UP, 1995).

50. All quotes are from the authors' unpublished performance script. *Deep in the Crotch of My Latino Psyche* premiered at Highways Performance Space, July 9–11 and 14–16, 1992.

51. Chela Sandoval, 15.

52. Guillermo Reyes, "Radio SIDA" for Teatro VIVA!, unpublished performance skit. My thanks to Monica Palacios and Luis Alfaro for providing me this transcript and also to Guillermo Reyes.

53. AIDS statistics were provided by the staff at the AIDS Information Library in Philadelphia.

7. November 1, 1992

1. Raymond Williams, *Resources of Hope: Culture, Democracy, Socialism* (London: Verso Books, 1989), 322.

2. Tony Kushner, *Angels in America, Part One: Millennium Approaches* (New York: Theatre Communications Group, 1993), 10. All further citations of *Millennium Approaches* are from this edition.

3. Bruce Weber, "Angels' Angels." *New York Times Magazine*, April 25, 1993, 48.

4. The delays were primarily due to last-minute editing of *Perestroika* and fine-tuning certain production elements such as staging.

5. The January 1992 issue of *HIV/AIDS Surveillance*, published through the U.S. Department of Health and Human Services, reported 206,392 cumulative cases of AIDS in the United States through December 1991 (*HIV/AIDS Surveillance*, 8). The number of cases between January 1, 1992, and October 31, 1992, according to the November 6, 1992, issue (vol. 41:44; 840) of the *Morbidity and Mortality Weekly Report* was 39,229; adding these two figures totals 245,621. Although the *Morbidity and Mortality Weekly Report* is published weekly, it does not report AIDS cases on a week-by-week basis; consider, however, that in the month of November 1992, 3,749 cases of AIDS were newly reported (*Morbidity and Mortality Weekly*, December 1, 1993).

6. Michael Taussig, *The Nervous System* (New York: Routledge, 1992), 11.

7. As reported in the year-end edition of *HIV/AIDS Surveillance*, February 1993, 17. The numbers, reflecting deaths through December 1992, are reported as "case fatality rates" and divided into two groups: 169,623 adults and 2,267 children. It's important to remember that these are the numbers of the very administrations that allowed AIDS to spread throughout their twelve years of tenure. There are no numbers available for the countless people whose deaths are unrecorded or who died of "undiagnosed" AIDS.

8. Judith Butler, *Bodies That Matter: On the Discursive Limits of "Sex"* (New York: Routledge, 1993), 14.

9. See for example Robert Rafsky's "An Open Letter to Bill Clinton," published on the eve of the elections, *QW*, November 8, 1992, 21–22. But see also Jeffrey Schmaltz, who writes one year later, "Whatever Happened to AIDS?" *New York Times Magazine*, November 28, 1993, 56–60, 81, 85–86. Both of these writers died of complications due to AIDS. While there is no record of Clinton's response to Rafsky other than his comments to him during a confrontation in New York at the time of the presidential primaries, Clinton centered his December 1, 1993, World AIDS Day address on Schmaltz's essay.

10. Raymond Williams, *Modern Tragedy* (Stanford, Stanford UP, 1966), 60.

11. Ibid.

12. Tony Kushner, *Angels in America, Part Two: Perestroika* (New York: Theatre Communications Group, 1994), 124. All further quotes from *Perestroika* are from this edition.

13. Williams, *Modern Tragedy*, 59.

14. For Williams, a structure of feeling is an affective process which includes a vast array of social and political experience which may fall outside of, or beyond, "recognizable systemic elements." Williams, *Marxism and Literature* (New York: Oxford UP, 1978), 133.

15. Walter Benjamin, "Theses on the Philosophy of History," in *Illuminations*, ed. and trans. Hanna Arendt (New York: Schocken, 1969), 257. All further quotes are from this edition.

16. Consider Benjamin's writing: "But a storm is blowing through Paradise; it has got caught in [the angel's] wings with such violence that the angel can no longer close them. The storm irresistibly propels him into the future to which his back is turned, while the pile of debris before him grows skyward. This storm is what we call progress" (257–58).

17. I am less interested here in offering a definitive reading of Kushner's angel. The multiple and contradictory possibilities of meaning deserve a more thorough examination. Rather, I am interested in situating a type of reading that contextualizes the angel within a discussion of theatre and history.

18. The idea of an "ideology of containment" is set forth by Kushner in interviews. See, for example, Susan Cheever, "An Angel Sat Down at His Table," *New York Times*, September 13, 1992, H7. Kushner explains: "Containment is the idea that there is some sort of viral presence in the body or the body politic that has to be proscribed or isolated or crushed. Containment demonizes the other, whether it's Communism or AIDS or Jews. It's a politics that comes completely out of fear as opposed to out of hope." The idea of "the long revolution" is, of course, from Raymond Williams. See *The Long Revolution*. Williams, it needs to be noted, did not address the lesbian and gay movement, nor did he discuss the AIDS activist movement in his writings. However, since Williams describes continually in his writings the struggles of oppressed groups, his ideas are indispensable for my analysis. The enactment of this ideology of containment is articulated by nearly all of the characters in *Millennium Approaches*, from Louis's concern at his grandmother's grave—"I hope she stays put" (24)—to Sister Ella Chapter's concern for her friend, Hannah Pitt—"Stay put" (83).

19. I address these critics in chapter 2.

20. For the best discussion on this topic, see David Savran, "Ambivalence, Utopia, and a Queer Sort of Materialism: How *Angels in America* Reconstructs the Nation," *Theatre Journal* 47:2 (May 1995): 207–228.

21. See David Savran's interview with Tony Kushner, "Tony Kushner Considers the Longstanding Problems of Virtue and Happiness," *American Theatre*, (October 1994): 100.

22. John Lahr, "Beyond Nelly," *New Yorker*, November 23, 1992, 127.

23. Once again, I want to reference Stephen J. Bottoms's important work on the proliferation of representations of Cohn in contemporary theatre and performance; see "Re-staging Roy: Citizen Cohn and the Search for Xanadu," *Theatre Journal* 48:2 (1996): 157–184.

24. On this idea of heteronormativity see Michael Warner's introduction to *Fear of a Queer Planet: Queer Politics and Social Theory*, ed. Michael Warner (Minneapolis: U of Minnesota P, 1993). Warner's introduction unpacks the violence embedded in heteronormative social arrangements and proceeds to articulate a more efficacious political practice. One point that I find especially useful critiques notions of kinship that rely—if not insist—on biological reproduction as intrinsic: "Het culture thinks of itself as the elemental form of human association, as the very model of intergender relations, as the indivisible basis of all community, and as the means of reproduction without which society wouldn't exist" (xxi). On this idea see also Eve Kosofsky Sedgwick, "How to Bring Your Kids Up Gay," published in the same volume and reprinted in her collection of essays, *Tendencies*.

25. Una Chaudhuri, *Staging Place: The Geography of Modern Drama* (Ann Arbor: U of Michigan P, 1995), 259.

26. Frank Rich, *New York Times*, November 10, 1992, B1.

27. Judith Butler, "Critically Queer," *GLQ: A Journal of Lesbian and Gay Studies* 1:1 (1993): 23

28. For an intelligent and politically inspiring account of kinship and community between and among lesbian and gay people, see Weston, *Families We Choose*.

29. It is significant to note that the black actor who plays Belize also doubles as Mr. Lies. Mr. Lies (Harper's "imaginary friend") functions for her in a way that can be read as analogous to the relationship between Belize and Prior insofar as both black characters are the pri-

mary support—imagined or available—for them. Whether or not these representations are the standard fare of the white imaginary, which continually places blacks and other people of color in subservient roles, should be the topic of wide debate, discussion, and critical analysis. Much more also needs to be said regarding the ubiquity of what Marlon Riggs and other queer African Americans have described as the rage for "negro faggotry" in popular culture, including white gay culture. See his essay "Black Macho Revisited: Reflections of a Snap Queen," in *Brother to Brother: New Writings by Black Gay Men*, ed. Essex Hemphill (Boston: Alyson Publications, 1991). As for my own position, I happen to identify with Belize and his politics, and his overall response to AIDS. For me, this process of identification is a form of valorization. And while the limits of his representation are all too clear, I think it is essential to note Kushner's acknowledgment of the roles queers of color play in mainstream lesbian and gay culture and community. If Kushner errs, he may err on the side of portraying Belize too heroically. This fetishization of lesbian and gay people of color as a type of political catalyst is ubiquitous among the left. I have written elsewhere about this process as it relates to Latino gay men. See "Tropical Fruit," in *Tropicalizations: Transcultural Representations of Latinidad*, ed. Francis R. Aparicio and Susana Chavez-Silverman (Hanover: U of New England P, 1997). The contributions of lesbians and gays of color in the history of the modern lesbian and gay community are extensive. See, for starters and for a bibliography, Martin Duberman, *Stonewall* (New York: Dutton, 1993).

30. But Harper too survives and endures. Her final speech on a plane to San Francisco remains one of the most moving moments in the two plays. Her perestroika includes not only her rejection of Joe, but a thrilling vision of global healing.

31. For an in-depth discussion of this topic, see Cindy Patton, *Inventing AIDS*, especially chapter 1.

32. Douglas Crimp, *AIDS: Cultural Analysis/Cultural Activism*, 6.

33. Allan M. Brandt, *No Magic Bullet: A Social History of Venereal Disease in the United States Since 1880, with a New Chapter on AIDS* (New York: Oxford UP, 1987), 4.

34. Weber, 58.

35. Michael Callen, "A Miracle Cure?" *QW*, November 15, 1992, 35–38.

36. Eric Bentley, "The Theatrical Occasion," in *The Life of the Drama* (New York: Atheneum, 1967), 181.

37. See Jonah Barrish, *The Anti-theatrical Tradition* (Berkeley: U of California P, 1981).

38. These are Bentley's examples; see his essay for their context.

39. Victor Turner, *From Ritual to Theatre: The Human Seriousness of Play* (New York: PAJ Publications, 1982).

40. Richard Schechner, "Toward a Poetics of Performance," in *Performance Theory: Revised and Expanded Edition* (New York: Routledge, 1988), 170.

41. Peggy Phelan, *Unmarked: The Politics of Performance* (New York: Routledge, 1993), 146. But see also her "Reciting the Citations of Others; or, a Second Introduction," in *Acting Out: Feminist Performances*, eds. Lynda Hart and Peggy Phelan (Ann Arbor: U of Michigan P, 1993), 13–31.

42. Consumption may entail the saving of theatre programs or the purchase of merchandise related to the production.

43. For a full discussion of this important topic, see Susan Bennett, *Theatre Audiences* (New York: Routledge, 1990).

44. Avram Finkelstein documents the context for the first political funeral for an AIDS activist—Mark Fisher—on November 2, 1992, in "Furious Burial," *QW*, November 15, 1992, 10.

45. Williams, *Modern Tragedy*, 199.

46. Charles Ludlam, *Camille*, in *The Complete Plays* (New York: Harper and Row, 1989).

47. Michael Kearns writes in a press statement: " 'It changed my life,' I told friends after seeing *Camille* fifteen years ago. And I was serious. Ludlam's gay soulfulness, not to mention his outlandish queerness, forced me to examine my role in the theatre. It was as if Ludlam's

impassioned rendition of Camille—sometimes over-the-top, often subtlely underplayed—stuck a spiritual chord in me which invited me to open myself up to limitless possibilities as an actor. A *gay* actor. When my hero died of AIDS in 1987, it seemed appropriate that I simultaneously mourn the loss and pay homage to him by playing his most famous role. After confirming my own positive HIV-status, I became more determined than ever to bond with Ludlam by playing Camille. HIV didn't exist when Ludlam, as the lovestruck courtesan, was taking her final breath and coughing her final cough. However, even without death at his doorstep, Ludlam knew Camille intimately: the vanity which camouflaged her low self-esteem; the laughter which hid her tears; the brittleness which disguised her fragility. I, too, know Marguerite Gautier; Ludlam, Camille, and I are sisters under the skin. But what will distinguish and ignite the Artists Confronting AIDS production of *Camille* is AIDS consciousness, including my overpowering connection to Ludlam, which will infuse this romantic, tragic love story." Michael Kearns, "Why Camille?" Statement for the 1993 production of *Camille*.

48. See my discussion of Artists Confronting AIDS in chapter 2.

49. Raymond Williams, *Towards 2000* (London: Hogarth P, 1983), 268.

50. Raymond Williams, "The Practice of Possibility," in *Resources of Hope* (London: Verso, 1989), 322.

8. Negative Energies

1. I want to call attention to what is meant by seroconversion throughout this chapter. *Seroconversion* is often used interchangeably with *HIV infection*, but they are not necessarily the same. According to William Johnston, who provides a useful distinction in *HIV Negative: How the Uninfected Are Affected by AIDS*, " 'seroconversion' refers not to HIV infection but to a biological event made evident by two HIV tests: the movement from the absence to the presence of HIV antibodies in the blood stream. In popular usage, 'seroconversion' often refers to the psychological event of learning one is HIV-positive after learning one was HIV-negative" (318).

2. The ELISA test first became available in the spring of 1985. The ELISA and Western blot tests detect the presence of antibodies to HIV, rather than HIV itself. In *Inventing AIDS*, Cindy Patton explains that "the test doesn't actually look for the 'antibody' to HIV but detects—reacts with—certain proteins which, in sero-epidemiological studies of North Americans and Northern Europeans, appear in the blood of people who have mounted an immunologic response to HIV. . . . ELISA and Western blot are not tests in the popular sense of absolute diagnostic value, but rather are chemical reactions that indicate that a particular biochemical process has occurred in the blood of the subject" (33).

3. Initially most AIDS activists were strongly against gay men testing. See Cindy Patton's *Sex and Germs: The Politics of AIDS*, where she writes that "[a]lmost immediately, influential members of the AIDS activist community came out strongly against the test and discouraged gay men from getting it. They argued that the test placed seropositive men in undue mental stress and endangered them should the test results be obtained by an employer or insurance company" (35). Moreover, in 1985, there were no available treatments for people testing positive. Others, however, advised gay men to take the test at anonymous sites, hoping that the test would promote behavior change. The debates over testing are discussed by Patton in *Inventing AIDS* and in *Fatal Advice*.

4. See the personal testimonies of HIV-negative gay men in William Johnston, *HIV-Negative: How the Uninfected Are Affected by AIDS*.

5. Walt Odets, "Why We Stopped Doing Primary Prevention for Gay Men in 1985," *AIDS and Public Policy Journal* 10:1 (1995): 2.

6. David Savran, "Ambivalence, Utopia, and a Queer Sort of Materialism: How *Angels in America* Reconstructs the Nation," *Theatre Journal* 47:2 (1995): 215.

7. Johnston, *HIV-Negative*, 120.

8. Walt Odets, *In the Shadow of the Epidemic: Being Negative in the Age of AIDS*, 146–47.

9. Simon Watney, "Perspectives on Treatment," in *Practices of Freedom: Selected Writings on HIV/AIDS* (Durham: Duke UP, 1994), 194.

10. On early efforts and accounts of discrimination, see Dennis Altman, *AIDS in the Mind of America* (New York: Anchor P, 1986), esp. chapter 4.

11. Walt Odets, "AIDS Education and Harm Reduction for Gay Men: Psychological Approaches for the 21st Century," *AIDS & Public Policy Journal* 9:1 (1994): 4, 11.

12. See his "AIDS Education and Harm Reduction for Gay Men," cited above.

13. Patton, *Inventing AIDS*, 20.

14. The structure of volunteer-based emotional support systems for people with AIDS contributed to this individuation. "Buddies," for example, were paired up with a "client." The nature of these relations was confidential. Buddies and other emotional support volunteers were unable to discuss their volunteer work and the issues around it, except with other "buddies" in confidential, supervised support meetings.

15. See Philip M. Kayal, *Bearing Witness: Gay Men's Health Crisis and the Politics of AIDS*, for a detailed discussion of AIDS volunteerism and activism based on the history of GMHC in New York City.

16. Patton, *Inventing AIDS*, 21.

17. Richard Morrison, "We Are All HIV-Positive: A Conversation with Diamanda Galás, Singer, Composer, Performance Artist, AIDS Activist," *Art and Understanding* (January/February 1993): 29.

18. Gregg Bordowitz, "Boat Trip," *American Imago* 51:1 (1994): 106.

19. On AIDS widows, see Paul Monette's *Borrowed Time: An AIDS Memoir* and *Afterlife*. On "magnetic relations," see Mark Schoofs, "Love in the Age of AIDS," *Village Voice*, August 1994.

20. Johnston, *HIV-Negative*, 97.

21. Odets, *In the Shadow of the Epidemic*, 106.

22. See Odets and Johnston on gay men's desire to test HIV-positive.

23. See Michaelangelo Signorile, "Out in America," *Out*, October 1994, and Michael Warner, "Why Gay Men Are Having Risky Sex," *Village Voice*, January 31, 1995, 33+.

24. This is not to suggest, by any means, that the HIV antibody test resolves this suspense; rather, my point is that before the HIV antibody test introduced the idea of an HIV status, which involves its own specific suspense and "drama," gay men had no way of knowing their relationship to HIV/AIDS. The possibility of succumbing to AIDS-related symptoms and opportunistic infections haunted gay men in a particular way that contributed to this notion of inevitability and arbitrariness. HIV testing involves a similar dynamic; many gay men, for example, have much uncertainty regarding their HIV status before testing. HIV antibody testing detects the presence of HIV antibodies and does not confer an AIDS diagnosis. Testing HIV-positive, in other words, is not a symptom of HIV.

25. Rebecca Ranson, *Warren*. I have discussed many of these early plays in previous sections of the book.

26. These characters are based on real-life friends and family members of Rebecca Ranson and Warren Johnston; Sam Allen, the basis for the character Sam, died of AIDS in 1992.

27. Larry Kramer, *The Normal Heart*, 38. All further citations of the play are from this edition.

28. Williams, *Modern Tragedy*, 16.

29. Take, for example, a recent article in the *Village Voice* on post-AIDS plays. David Finkle speculates on the future of AIDS plays without once suggesting that HIV-negatives and their issues can be the subject of an AIDS play. David Finkle, "Going On: The Post-AIDS-Play Play," *Village Voice*, August 29, 1995, 78–80.

30. Terrence McNally, *The Lisbon Traviata*, in *Three Plays by Terrence McNally*, 69. This short exchange was added to the second version of the play, which opened in New York City at the Promenade Theatre on October 31, 1989. An earlier version of the play, which opened on June

4, 1985, at the Theatre Off Park in New York City, is published in *Out Front: Contemporary Gay and Lesbian Plays*, ed. Don Shewey (New York: Grove P, 1988).

31. Harvey Fierstein, *Safe Sex*, 107–108.

32. It may be useful to turn momentarily to HIV prevention methods to make this point. HIV prevention entails a series of prevention strategies specific to people's relation to HIV. These distinctions, as Walt Odets explains, fall into three categories: primary prevention, secondary prevention, and tertiary prevention:

> In the instance of HIV and the gay communities, traditional use of the terms would define primary prevention as the effort to prevent currently uninfected men from contracting HIV; secondary prevention as the effort to prevent infected with HIV from progressing to clinical disease; and tertiary prevention as the effort to minimize the impact of clinical HIV disease, extending the quality—and perhaps the quantity—of life. . . . The uninfected, the infected but asymptomatic, and the clinically ill have been perceived as having different medical needs, psychosocial issues, and prognoses, and thus as requiring different prevention objectives. ("Why We Stopped," 1)

Furthermore, effective prevention efforts must differentiate between an "outcome" population and a "target" population. In HIV-prevention campaigns, the outcome population should be the uninfected, since the outcome of the prevention plan is to stop the spread of HIV among this group. A target population refers to the population that might be addressed in order to achieve the goals of the primary prevention. In a primary prevention campaign for HIV-negative gay men (the "outcome" population), for example, HIV-positive gay men, who necessarily share in the infection process of uninfected gay men, can be addressed as the target population. Before the HIV antibody test, primary prevention efforts were directed to an outcome population of asymptomatic gay men. Since at the time there was no means to differentiate between the infected and uninfected, primary prevention campaigns were universalized to accommodate as many of the outcome population as possible. With the availability of the HIV antibody test, AIDS service organizations finally had the means to establish specific primary-prevention campaigns for the uninfected, and specific secondary-prevention campaigns for the newly established category of "HIV-positive." Unfortunately, as Odets makes painfully clear, most AIDS service organizations stopped doing primary prevention for gay men in 1985. The HIV antibody test, he argues, "provided the means for distinguishing the outcome populations of distinct primary and secondary prevention efforts that could each address the issues and needs of its outcome population" (2). Rather than developing differentiated prevention campaigns for the uninfected and the infected, AIDS education remained undifferentiated. The only beneficial exploitation of the HIV antibody test was the newly discovered secondary-prevention potential for people testing HIV-positive. Primary prevention, on the other hand, Odets continues, "seemed to remain unrecognized and unacknowledged" (3).

33. Many AIDS plays and performances, however, do differentiate in terms of the spectator's sexual orientation.

34. Paul Rudnick, *Jeffrey* (New York: Plume, 1994), 1. All further citations of *Jeffrey* are from this edition.

35. Frank Rich, "Critic's Notebook," *New York Times*, February 3, 1993, B1+.

36. Michael Feingold, review of *Jeffrey*, *Village Voice*, January 26, 1993, 87.

37. On this issue, see Douglas Crimp, "How to Have Promiscuity in an Epidemic," *AIDS: Cultural Analysis/Cultural Activism*.

38. Johnston writes that "because being HIV-negative is highly valued, and because it is something that can be threatened by sexual intercourse, I liken it to virginity. Testing HIV-negative is a kind of 'revirginization' for many gay men. It seems to offer 'another chance' to those of us who have had sex we fear might have been unsafe" (121). Johnston's concept of "revirginization" is still problematic. Virginity is always a commodity offered to another. It

involves both exchange and loss. For gay men to assume "revirginalization," suggests that this new virginity is to be offered as a thing of value to someone else.

39. José Muñoz, "Dead White: Notes on the Whiteness of the New Queer Cinema," 5. Muñoz analyzes how "whiteness" in the film version of *Jeffrey* is understood as "an image of ideality and normativity that structures gay male desires and communities." Steve and Jeffrey, who are both white gay men, participate in the maintenance of whiteness as an ideality, which comes into crisis with the revelation that Steve is HIV-positive. While Muñoz's essay is specifically concerned with the film version, his ideas are relevant to the New York staging of *Jeffrey* that I am discussing.

40. It's interesting to note that while the play does not differentiate between its audiences around the question of serostatus, the marketing of the play differentiates its audiences along sexual orientation. In ads in publications for gay readers, the *Jeffrey* logo shows Jeffrey in his underwear, the same ad directed at mainstream theatergoers shows Jeffrey fully dressed in a T-shirt and jeans. See Stuart Elliot, "Advertising: When a Play Has a Gay Theme, Campaigns Often Tell It as It Is," *New York Times*, June 25, 1995, D23.

41. It is important to note that Steve, unlike earlier representations of people with HIV, bears no visible trace of HIV; he is, in fact, in all realms, as Muñoz demonstrates, an imprint of the normative ideal—for Jeffrey, for the others in the play, and for his audiences. There is an irony therefore in Steve's disclosure of his HIV status and Jeffrey's silence around his, since Steve is the character who may be more vulnerable to rejection. In other words, since Steve has no visible trace of HIV, Steve has no reason to reveal his HIV status other than his own personal politics on the matter.

42. Richard Corliss, "Profile: Paul Rudnick," *Time*, May 3, 1993, 66.

43. Northrop Frye, *The Anatomy of Criticism* (Princeton: Princeton UP, 1957).

44. In an op-ed piece for the *New York Times*, he writes: "Gay writers, drawing on the repartee that is a form of gay soul, use camp, irony, and epigram to, if not defeat the virus, at least scorn and contain it." Paul Rudnick, "Laughing at AIDS," *New York Times*, January 23, 1993, A15.

45. See Paul Morrison, "End Pleasure," *GLQ: A Journal of Lesbian and Gay Studies* 1:1 (1993): 53–78.

46. This is not to suggest that Jeffrey's issues are not "real" or that he has no "life." The point here is that Rudnick doesn't develop Jeffrey's issues throughout the play.

47. See David Richards, review of *Love! Valour! Compassion! New York Times*, November 2, 1995, C13+; Vincent Canby, "McNally, True, but Vaguely Neo-Chekhovian," *New York Times*, November 6, 1994, H5+; and David Kaufman, review of *Love! Valour! Compassion! The Nation*, December 19, 1994, 774.

48. Terrence McNally, *Love! Valour! Compassion!* (New York: Plume, 1995), 120–21.

49. McNally inserts an interesting commentary on this idea of competition. At one point, Perry spots Buzz and James in the canoe and challenges them to compete for shore: "PERRY to BUZZ and JAMES: You want to race?" (122). Arthur immediately scolds his lover. Buzz, preoccupied with his lover's discomfort and already in a hurry to get back to the shore, mishears Perry: "BUZZ to JAMES: Grace. I thought he said something about grace" (123).

50. Here acknowledgment must also go to Joe Mantello, who directed the production at Manhattan Theatre Club, which was subsequently transferred to Broadway. Mantello highlights the scene so that it stands out as a significant moment in the production; his choices, which include foregrounding the couple at the front of the stage and doing away with props, keeps the audience's focus on the conversation and the mood of the moment, which is enhanced by other production elements such as lighting, costume, and sound. The canoes are represented by boxes of light (the lighting was designed by Brian MacDevitt), and the actors, wearing boating hats, mime paddling to the sound of water breaking. A word also on the actors, who deserve special mention: The Broadway cast included John Hickey as Arthur and Anthony Heald as Perry. Both actors brought nuance and depth to two roles which, on the

surface, seem dull. Their performances were generally overlooked by the media, which praised the work of Nathan Lane (Buzz) and John Glover (John/James Jeckyll), who played the characters with HIV. Heald was, however, nominated for a Tony Award, as was Stephen Bogardus (Gregory), both actors lost to John Glover in the featured actor category. Nathan Lane was not nominated for best actor. (Tony Award nominations are determined by an appointed jury of theatre professionals.) The performances by Hickey and Heald were further eclipsed by the media attention directed to Randy Becker (Ramon), who performs much of the time in the nude. While the production includes various moments of frontal nudity, Becker's good looks and physical attributes were singled out; for an amusing parody of this phenomenon see "Naked Truths," in the "Talk of the Town," *New Yorker*, February 13, 1995, 13.

51. Odets also addresses this in "Why We Stopped Doing Primary Prevention for Gay Men in 1985," when he writes about the comparable ethical responsibilities between HIV-negatives and HIV-positives surrounding the consequences of transmission: "The idea that the uninfected man has a comparable ethical responsibility might be founded in the idea that he has a responsibility to *his community* to remain uninfected—although it would be difficult to equate this 'ethical violation' with the knowing infection of another individual" (12, original emphasis).

52. And its effect on the audience. Bobby and Ramon also circulate as the law of desire in the world of the play and, by extension, in the world of gay culture. Their moments of full frontal nudity are meant to mark their desirability, and the other, older characters respond accordingly. While Bobby and Ramon signal the play's desirable bodies, Buzz's body is read as comically overweight and definitively undesirable. In a telling moment in act 2, Buzz appears "wearing an apron, heels, and little else" (80), only to have Perry snidely demand that he put on his clothes: "Nobody wants to look at that" (81). Nathan Lane's seminude entrance in the scene is played as comic, and although the other characters join in the spirit of Buzz's lightheartedness, Perry's comment lingers. This scene follows a very poignant and theatrical moment between Buzz and James, the two characters with HIV. Buzz asks James to show him his lesion, and when James does so, Buzz kisses it. While the moment is meant to convey, among other things, their nascent romance, the juxtaposition of the two scenes secures the logic of seroconcordance that the play promotes.

53. Odets, "Why We Stopped," 21.

54. Ramon, for example, insists on speaking as a person of color; Bobby too must continually remind the others that he is blind.

55. I thank Eric Severson at the University of Minnesota for first posing the question of the John/James double casting to me.

56. Chay Yew, *A Language of Their Own*, author's script, copyright 1995, page 2. *A Language of Their Own* is scheduled be published along with Yew's earlier play, *Porcelain*, by Grove Press. Thanks to Chay Yew for providing me a copy of this play.

57. Yew, *A Language of Their Own*, 16.

58. Drake's title refers to the night of his twenty-second birthday—June 27, 1985—and his attendance of Kramer's *The Normal Heart* at the Public Theatre in New York. The performance, Drake explains, changed his life. In 1996, he became an editor of *POZ*.

59. David Drake, *The Night Larry Kramer Kissed Me* (New York: Anchor Books, 1994), xiv.

60. Tim Miller, *Naked Breath*, unpublished performance script, p. 32. *Naked Breath* premiered at Highways Performance Space in Santa Monica, California, in February 1994. All quotes are from this performance script.

61. Tim Miller and David Román, "Preaching to the Converted," *Theatre Journal* 47:2 (1995): 181.

62. The possibility of a false-negative or false-positive test result still confirms that a retesting will eventually determine either an HIV-negative or an HIV-positive test result.

63. In part, this cultural phenomenon results from the conflation of *HIV-negative* and *HIV-positive* with two other terms, which set up a related binary: *infected* and *uninfected*. The terms

infected and *uninfected* do not circulate culturally as terms to describe gay men primarily because as descriptives they can enter into official culture only through the mediated power of biomedical science, which translates these terms into *HIV-positive* and *HIV-negative*. *Infected* and *uninfected* are intelligible only if they convey the nature of an infection. Before the discovery of HIV as the agent of infection that leads to what we know as AIDS, *infected* and *uninfected* were the terms gay men used to describe their presumed relation to the unfolding epidemic of disease and death. This presumption was verifiable only through the set of diseases associated with the epidemic. Uninfected gay men, on the other hand, had no way to verify their relationship. It was not until the availability of the HIV antibody test in 1985 that uninfected gay men who were and remained sexually active could verify that they had not been exposed to the alleged virus that can lead to AIDS. With this new means to determine one's relation to HIV, infected and uninfected gay men adopted the language of biomedical science—*HIV-negative* and *HIV-positive*—and began to forge identities around these two terms of medical discourse. Uninfected gay men were finally able to divest from the possibility of their eventual progression to AIDS under the newly established category of HIV-negative. See also Ruth Finkelstein, "Gay Men Have Worked It All Out? Entering the Fray over Safe Sex Practices," *Gay Community News*, Spring 1995, 10–11, 21.

64. I feel compelled to point out that simply replacing *HIV-positive* and *HIV-negative* with *infected* and *uninfected* does not abort the force of the binary and its associated characteristics. *Infected* and *uninfected* are no more "natural" than *HIV-positive* and *HIV-negative*. The point here is that *HIV-negative* is "unnatural" insofar as it emerges from the official practice of biomedical science. One could also argue that *infected* and *uninfected* are the more "natural" terms in that they do not inflect the ideological weight of biomedical science. But this too would be a mistake. *Infected* and *uninfected*, while ostensibly the more "pure" conditions of the body before the intrusion of the practice of HIV-antibody testing, nonetheless are absorbed into the logic of a binary through their oppositional pairing, through the logic of the either/or. As such, *infected* and *uninfected* are thus positioned to be located along the hierarchical power system inherent in all binary structures.

Afterword

1. Quoted in Thomas H. Maugh II, "Studies of Combined HIV Drugs Promising," *Los Angeles Times*, July 12, 1996, A8.

2. Lawrence K. Altman, "India Quickly Leads in HIV Cases, AIDS Meeting Hears," *New York Times*, July 8, 1996, A3.

3. As of the summer of 1996, there are nine drugs sold in the United States; five of these were approved by the Federal Drug Administration (FDA) in 1996. Three of these recently approved drugs are protease inhibitors.

4. *Los Angeles Times*, July 4, 1996.

5. Lawrence K. Altman, "Landmark Studies Change Outlook of AIDS Treatment," *New York Times*, July 14, 1996, A10.

6. The prices of the drugs vary depending upon the pharmaceutical companies that manufacture the drugs and the pharmacies that distribute them. On this topic, see Anne-Christine D'Adesky, "Rich Man's Drug," *Out*, August 1996, 62–65, and John Gallagher, "The Money Pit," *Advocate*, September 3, 1996, 29–30.

7. Reported by Altman, "India Quickly Leads in HIV Cases."

8. David W. Dunlap, "In the AIDS Fight, Bells of Hope from Vancouver," *New York Times*, July 15, 1996, A6.

9. Larry Kramer, "A Good News/Bad News AIDS Joke," *New York Times Magazine* July 14, 1996, 27.

10. Reported by Maugh, "Studies of Combined HIV Drugs Promising."

11. Dunlap, "In the AIDS Fight, Bells of Hope from Vancouver."

12. See David W. Dunlap, "Surviving with AIDS: Now What?" *New York Times*, August 1, 1996, B3.

13. Dunlap, "In the AIDS Fight, Bells of Hope From Vancouver."

14. Gabriel Rotello, "The Risk in a 'Cure' for AIDS," *New York Times*, July 14, 1996, A17.

15. See Thomas H. Maugh II, "High-Risk Sex on Rise, Conference Told," *Los Angeles Times*, July 9, 1996.

16. Michael died in December of 1993, and Jim died in July of 1994.

17. Dunlap, "In the AIDS Fight, Bells of Hope From Vancouver."

18. Stefani Eads, with photography by Carolyn Jones, "*Rent* Collection," *POZ* August/ September 1996, 56.

19. The *POZ* feature points out that William Finn's 1993 musical *Falsettos* had one HIV-positive character and *Angels in America* had two. We could also add *Love! Valour! Compassion!* which also had two, and *As Is*, which had one major character with AIDS.

20. The plot of *Rent* is quite complicated, a situation made all the more difficult due to Larson's death. While *Rent* is not a work-in-progress, the artistic team was still working on the story, as it is entitled to do, during the dress rehearsal run at the New York Theatre Workshop. The three-page plot synopsis distributed with the press kit for the Off-Broadway run differs from the three-page plot synopsis eventually published in the Broadway playbill. I base my comments on the Broadway plot synopsis and on performances I attended at the Nederlander Theatre in June of 1996.

21. Mark and Maureen, for example, are representative of the struggling artists who must continually negotiate a politics around the commodification of their work. Mimi, Roger, and Angel, who can also be defined as struggling artists, face more immediate financial constraints and have fewer opportunities to pursue their creative endeavors within a commodity-driven market. Joanne, on the other hand, is a civil rights lawyer and represents a different class altogether. The point here is that the community of *Rent* is composed of individuals of diverse backgrounds based on class as well as race, ethnicity, sexuality, and sero-status. Consider too that Larson includes secondary characters from the ensemble who perform various roles including "the homeless," one of whom actually points out the economic differences between the *Rent* community and the nameless homeless people who live in the same East Village neighborhood.

22. John Istel, "I Have Something to Say: An Interview with Jonathan Larson," *American Theatre* (July/August 1996): 16.

23 Ibid., 17.

24. The cover image does not identify the actors or the roles, a detail that obscures the difference between Adam Pascal and Daphne Rubin-Vega, and Roger and Mimi, the roles they perform in *Rent*.

25. Jack Kroll, "Love among the Ruins: A Musical for the '90s Jumps a Generation Gap," *Newsweek*, May 13, 1996, 56.

26. Douglas Crimp, "Right On, Girlfriend!" in *Fear of a Queer Planet*, ed. Michael Warner. (Minneapolis: U of Minnesota P, 1993), 304. Crimp is not the only AIDS activist to raise this concern. AIDS activists have been outspoken on this problem since the early 1990s.

27. Jonathan Larson, *Rent: Original Broadway Cast Recording*, SKG Music; unpaginated lyrics. All quotes from *Rent*'s lyrics are from this source.

28. Michael Sommers, review of *Rent*, *Star-Ledger*, February 14, 1996, 49.

29. Bruce Vilanch, "Notes from a Blond Column: Letter from Broadway," *Advocate*, July 23, 1996, 49.

30. Michael Greif, the director of *Rent*, explained to *Out* that he and Larson disagreed on this scene. Greif, who is gay, wanted the scene to convey more anger: "I come from a much more cynical and suspicious place than Jonathan comes from, and when I first encountered the lyric "No day but today," I thought, Wait a minute. But we worked on it, and now a character

gets to express that distrust, but to admit that today *was* a miracle." Tim Allis, "Rent Soars on Broadway," *Out*, May 1996, 122.

31. And here a word must said in tribute to the original New York cast and especially *Rent*'s director, Michael Greif, whose commitment to Larson's vision is evident throughout the production. The *Rent* cast has deservedly been praised for their ensemble performance—they received a 1996 Obie. Their talent, when considered alongside the exceptional circumstances of Larson's death under which they must perform nightly, brings forth performances that are among the most memorable I have experienced in the theatre. Many of the cast members were Larson's friends, and certainly all of them were part of his extended community, which suggests that these moments of memorialization and renewal signify the cast's own efforts to perform these very acts for themselves. While I don't want to overemphasize this point, as if to imply that tragedy brings forth genuine artistry, it would be a mistake not to recognize and call attention to the *Rent* community's own personal investment in these performances. This reality undoubtedly informs my own experience of this particular cast's performance, as I imagine it does for many others lucky enough to have seen them. And while Larson's death was not due to AIDS, it's also worth remembering that so many of the works discussed throughout this book share and enact a similar investment in memorialization.

32. The challenge for artists interested in confronting AIDS through performance, therefore, is not to abandon these conventions of AIDS theatre but rather to animate them with the specific affects of the community to whom they are addressed. I have written on this issue as it relates to lesbian and gay performance in my collaboration with Tim Miller. See our "Preaching to the Converted," *Theatre Journal* 47:2 (1995): 168–188.

33. But even here conflict and contradiction emerge through the collaborative process of creating theatre. Lynn Thomson, *Rent*'s dramaturg, for example, filed a lawsuit against Larson's estate "to assert my right to be compensated and acknowledged" for her various contributions to *Rent*, contributions that Larson himself publicly acknowledged. See Lynn M. Thomson, "The Rewards of Collaboration," *Parabasis* 4:1 (1997): 11–13. Thomson filed her lawsuit in November 1996, some months after I drafted this section. For more information on the lawsuit, see William Grimes, "On Stage and Off," *New York Times*, November 29, 1996, B3. On a related note, Sarah Schulman, the acclaimed lesbian writer and activist, has alleged that *Rent* was based on her 1990 novel, *People in Trouble*. I heard of Schulman's discontent with *Rent* from various sources while I was drafting this afterword in the summer of 1996. At the time, this information was anecdotal and seemed outside of my immediate concern of discussing the relationship between *Rent* and AIDS. However, in her address to the Key West Literary Seminar's conference on "Literature in the Age of AIDS," held in January 1997, Schulman raised issues similar to those I have been addressing here about the role of AIDS in contemporary culture. "Fiction and Action in the Age of AIDS," Schulman's essay based on this talk, was published in *Harvard Gay & Lesbian Review*, Spring 1997, 1.

34. Quoted in Simi Horwitz, "*Rent*: The Musical Theater's New Lease on Life," *Theater Week*, April 29–May 5, 1996, 24.

35. Richard Zoglin, "Lower East Side Story," *Time*, March 4, 1996, 71.

36. Kroll, "A Downtown *La Boheme*," 67.

37. Ibid.

38. Unsigned photo caption for *Rent* review, *New York Times*, February 25, 1996, B1.

39. Margo Jefferson, "*Rent* Is Brilliant and Messy All at Once," *New York Times*, February 25, 1996, B5.

40. *Theater Week*, in its "Broadway Business" column, reports ticket sales for *Rent* at between 99 and 100% since its April opening. These prices reflect box office purchase; phone orders add substantial service charges.

41. There are also twenty-dollar standing-room tickets that are available day-of-sale but are sold at 10:00 AM. Tickets also may become available through cancellations. These tickets

sell at full price as they become available. For *Rent*, the lines form for these tickets early on in the day. *Rent* is not available at the discounted TKTS booth in Times Square.

42. Obviously, if the performance is sold out, access remains a problem regardless of one's economic or class status. The point here is that lower-income theatregoers have less access than those who can afford tickets at full price. For those who can afford tickets, access is either postponed or, for the more impatient and financially able, secured at a higher price through scalper sales.

43. Both the *New York Times* and the *Los Angeles Times* ran features on the July 12 auditions. See Ralph Blumenthal, "Calling All Unsung Superstars: *Rent* Needs Singers," *New York Times,* July 13, 1996, A13, and Patrick Pacheco, "Many Are Called but Few Will Be Chosen for *Rent,"* *Los Angeles Times,* July 18, 1996, F10. *New York Times* quotes an agent who favorably described one actor as "authentic." There is also a peculiar irony here as well: if, in the 1970s, the characters of *A Chorus Line* were meant to represent the marginal and disempowered, that very breed of actor is now less likely to comply with *Rent's* 1990s notions of "authentic" and "marginal."

44. While no people with AIDS spoke during the televised programming during prime time, people with AIDS did address the delegates at other times during the convention. Also I should state that the performance of the *Rent* cast was held on the eve of the issue of the compact disc of the original Broadway cast soundtrack from DreamWorks SKG. Steven Spielberg, Jeffrey Katzenberg, and David Geffen, the cofounders of DreamWorks, are major contributors to the Democratic party, which led some people to suggest that the performance was a political payback. See Francis X. Clines, "Chicago Diary," *New York Times,* August 29, 1996, A13.

45. Frank Rich, "East Village Story," *New York Times,* March 2, 1996, A16.

Works Cited

Abbate, Carolyn. "Opera; or, The Envoicing of Women." In *Musicology and Difference: Gender and Sexuality in Music Scholarship*. Ed. Ruth A. Solie. Berkeley: U of California P, 1993. 225–258.

ACT UP/NY Women & AIDS Book Group. *Women, AIDS, & Activism*. Boston: South End P, 1990.

Adair, Peter, dir. *Absolutely Positive*. 1990.

Alexander, William. "Clearing Space: AIDS Theatre in Atlanta." *Drama Review* 34:3 (1990): 109–128.

Alfaro, Luis. *Downtown*. Performed at Highways Performance Space in Santa Monica, CA. November 30, December 1–2, 7–9, 1990.

Alfaro, Luis, Alberto Araiza, and Monica Palacios. *Deep in the Crotch of My Latino Psyche*. Performed at Highways Performance Space. July 9–11 and 14–16, 1992.

Allis, Tim. "*Rent* Soars on Broadway." *Out*, May 1996, 86+.

Almaguer, Tomás. "Chicano Men: A Cartography of Homosexual Identity and Behavior." *differences* 3:2 (1991): 75–100.

Alonso, Ana Maria, and Maria Teresa Koreck. "Silences: 'Hispanics,' AIDS, and Sexual Practices." *differences* 1:1 (1989): 101–124.

Altman, Dennis. *AIDS in the Mind of America*. New York: Anchor P, 1986.

Altman, Lawrence K. "India Quickly Leads in HIV Cases, AIDS Meeting Hears." *New York Times*, July 8, 1996, A3.

——. "Landmark Studies Change Outlook of AIDS Treatment." *New York Times*, July 14, 1996, A10.

——. "Rare Cancer Seen in 41 Homosexuals." *New York Times*, July 3, 1981, A20.

Anderson, Benedict. *Imagined Communities: Reflections on the Origin and Spread of Nationalism*. Revised edition. London: Verso, 1991.

Anderson, Scott P. "Hollywood Bowl AIDS Benefit—Meager Crowds, Major Problems." *Advocate*, October 13, 1983, 21.

Apple, Jackie. "Notes on Teaching Performance Art." *Performing Arts Journal* 50/51 (1995): 121–125.

——. "Performance Art Is Dead! Long Live Performance Art!" *High Performance* 17:2 (1994): 54–59.

Arratia, Euridice. "Teatro Festival: The Latino Festival Theatre." *Drama Review* 35:2 (1991): 176–182.

Artists Confronting AIDS. *AIDS/US*. Unpublished script, 1986.

——. *AIDS/US II*. Unpublished script, 1990.

——. *AIDS/US/Women*. Unpublished script, 1993.

Artists Involved with Death and Survival. *The A.I.D.S. Show*. In *West Coast Plays 17/18*. Ed. Robert Hurwitt. Los Angeles: California Theatre Council, 1985.

Arvanette, Steven C. "Thousands in Vigil Demand Millions for AIDS." *New York Native,* May 23, 1983, 9–10.

Athey, Ron. "Casebook: *Four Scenes in a Harsh Life.*" *Theatre Forum* 6 (Winter/Spring 1995): 59–68.

Auslander, Philip. "Going with the Flow: Performance Art and Mass Culture." *Drama Review* 33:2 (1989): 119–136.

Barrish, Jonah. *The Anti-theatrical Tradition.* Berkeley: U of California P, 1981.

Beaufort, John. Review of *Six Degrees of Separation. Christian Science Monitor,* June 26, 1990, 22.

Beebe, Barbara. "Pomo Afro Homos: Brian Freeman Talks about *Dark Fruit* and the State of the Black Gay Community." *B&G* 3:3 (1992): 11–14.

Belsey, Catherine. *Critical Practice.* New York: Methuen, 1980.

Benjamin, Walter. *Illuminations.* Trans. Hanna Arendt. New York: Schocken, 1969.

Bennett, Susan. *Theatre Audiences.* New York: Routledge, 1990.

Bentley, Eric. "The Theatrical Occasion." In *The Life of the Drama.* New York: Atheneum, 1967.

Bergman, David, ed. *Camp Grounds: Style and Homosexuality.* Amherst: U of Massachussetts P, 1994.

———. *Gaiety Transfigured: Gay Self-Representation in American Literature.* Madison: U of Wisconsin P, 1991.

Berlandt, Konstantin. "Cowley Services at MCC." *Bay Area Reporter,* December 16, 1982, 10.

———. "Gay Victim Dances over Death." *Bay Area Reporter,* November 11, 1982, 1+.

Bersani, Leo. "Is the Rectum a Grave?" In *AIDS: Cultural Analysis/Cultural Activism.* Ed. Douglas Crimp. Cambridge: MIT Press, 1987. 197–222.

Bérubé, Allan. *Coming Out under Fire: The History of Gay Men and Women in World War Two.* New York: Plume Books, 1990.

Bluestein, Ron. "Images of Survival: The Struggle for New Values and Views." *Advocate,* January 22, 1985, 25–26.

Blumenthal, Ralph. "Calling All Unsung Superstars: *Rent* Needs Singers." *New York Times,* July 13, 1996, A13.

Bommer, Lawrence. Review of *One. Advocate,* December 22, 1983, 52.

Boone, Joseph Allen. *Tradition Counter Tradition: Love and the Form of Fiction.* Chicago: Chicago UP, 1987.

Bordowitz, Gregg. "Boat Trip." *American Imago* 51:1 (1994): 105–125.

Bottoms, Stephen J. "Re-staging Roy: Citizen Cohn and the Search for Xanadu." *Theatre Journal* 48:2 (1996): 157–184.

Brandt, Allan M. *No Magic Bullet: A Social History of Venereal Disease in the United States since 1880, with a New Chapter on AIDS.* New York: Oxford UP, 1987.

Brantley, Ben. "A Little Infamy Goes a Long Way." *New York Times,* October 29, 1994, B13.

Brecht, Bertolt. *Brecht on Theatre.* Trans. John Willett. New York: Hill and Wang, 1964.

Brecht, Stefan. *Queer Theatre.* London: Methuen, 1986.

Breslauer, Jan. "California Performance." *Performing Arts Journal* 41 (1992): 87–96.

Brigham, Roger. "Interview with Magic Johnson." *Advocate,* April 21, 1992, 34–39.

Broder, Michael. "High Risk, Low Priority: Society Turns a Double Blind Eye on AIDS in the Black Community." *BLK* 3:7 (1991): 7–14.

Bronski, Michael. *Culture Clash: The Makings of a Gay Sensibility*. Boston: South End P, 1984.

Burnham, Linda Frye. "Getting on the Highways: Taking Responsibility for the Culture in the '90s." *Journal of Dramatic Theory and Criticism* 5:1(1990): 264–277.

———. "*High Performance*, Performance Art, and Me." *Drama Review* 30:2 (1986): 15–51.

Bush, Larry. "Thousands March Nationwide to Demand Federal Action on AIDS." *Advocate*, June 9, 1983, 8.

Butler, Judith. *Bodies That Matter: On the Discursive Limits of "Sex."* New York: Routledge, 1994.

———. "Critically Queer." *GLQ: A Journal of Lesbian and Gay Studies* 1:1 (1993): 17–32.

———. "The Force of Fantasy: Feminism, Mapplethorpe, and Discursive Excess." *differences* 2:2 (1990): 105–125.

Cady, Joseph. "AIDS on the National Stage." *Medical Humanities Review* 6:1 (1992): 20–26.

Calderón, Héctor, and José David Saldívar. *Criticism in the Borderlands: Studies in Literature, Culture, and Ideology*. Durham: Duke UP, 1991.

Callen, Michael. *Surviving AIDS*. New York: Harper Collins, 1990.

———. "A Miracle Cure?" *QW*, November 15, 1992, 35–38.

Campbell, Bobbi. Letter to the editor. *Christopher Street*, December 1983, 6.

Canby, Vincent. "McNally, True, but Vaguely Neo-Chekhovian." *New York Times*, November 6, 1994, H5+.

Carlson, Marvin. *Performance: A Critical Introduction*. New York: Routledge, 1996.

Carr, C. "Life's Rich Pageant." *LA Weekly*, August 7, 1992, 39.

———. *On Edge: Performance at the End of the Twentieth Century*. Hanover: UP of New England, 1993.

Case, Sue-Ellen. *Feminism and Theatre*. New York: Routledge, 1988.

———. "Performing Lesbian in the Space of Technology: Part I." *Theatre Journal* 47:1 (1995): 1–18.

———. "Toward a Butch-Femme Aesthetic." In *Making a Spectacle: Feminist Essays on Contemporary Women's Theatre*. Ed. Lynda Hart. Ann Arbor: University of Michigan Press, 1989. 282–99.

Cecci, Robert Lee. "Dear Mr. President." *New York Native*, May 23, 1983, 10.

Centers for Disease Control. "Update." *Morbidity and Mortality Weekly Report*, November 6, 1992, 840.

———. "Update." *Morbidity and Mortality Weekly Report*, December 1, 1992, 949.

Chaudhuri, Una. *Staging Place: The Geography of Modern Drama*. Ann Arbor: U of Michigan P, 1995.

Cheever, Susan. "An Angel Sat Down at His Table." *New York Times*, September 13, 1992, H7.

Chesley, Robert. *Night Sweat*. In *Hard Plays/Stiff Parts*. San Francisco: Alamo Square P, 1990.

———. "Profile of Ethyl Eichenberger." *Advocate*, August 8, 1983, 52.

Clement, Catherine. *Opera, or the Undoing of Women*. Trans. Betsy Wing. Minneapolis: U of Minnesota P, 1988.

Clines, Francis X. "Chicago Diary." *New York Times*, August 29, 1996, A13.

Clum, John M. *Acting Gay: Male Homosexuality in Modern Drama*. New York: Columbia UP, 1992.

——, ed. *Staging Gay Lives: An Anthology of Contemporary Gay Theater*. Boulder: Westview P, 1996.

Corbin, Steven. "The Fire Baptism." *Frontiers*, June 19, 1992, 78.

Corliss, Richard. "Profile: Paul Rudnick." *Time*, May 3, 1993, 66.

Crimp, Douglas. "Accommodating Magic." In *Media Spectacles*. Ed. Marjorie Garber, Jann Matlock, and Rebecca Walkowitz. New York: Routledge, 1993. 254–266.

——, ed. *AIDS: Cultural Analysis/Cultural Activism*. Cambridge: MIT Press, 1987.

——. "Mourning and Militancy." *October* 51 (1990): 3–18.

——. "Portraits of People with AIDS." In *Cultural Studies*. Ed. Lawrence Grossberg, Cary Nelson, and Paula Treichler. New York: Routledge, 1992. 117–130.

——. "Right On, Girlfriend!" In *Fear of a Queer Planet*. Ed. Michael Warner. Minneapolis: U of Minnesota P, 1993. 300–320.

——, with Adam Rolston. *AIDS Demographics*. Seattle: Bay Press, 1990.

Dace, Tish. Review of *Night Sweat*. *Advocate*, July 10, 1984, 46.

D'Adesky, Christine-Anne. "Rich Man's Drug." *Out*, August 1996, 62–65.

Davis, Mike. *City of Quartz: Excavating the Future in Los Angeles*. London: Verso, 1990.

Davy, Kate. "Constructing the Spectator: Reception, Context, and Address in Lesbian Performance." *Performing Arts Journal* 29 (1986): 43–52.

——. "Fe/male Impersonation: The Discourse of Camp." In *Critical Theory and Performance*. Ed. Janelle G. Reinelt and Joseph Roach. Ann Arbor: U of Michigan P, 1992. 231–247.

Denneny, Michael. "AIDS Writing and the Creation of a Gay Culture." In *Confronting AIDS through Literature: The Responsiblities of Representation*. Ed. Judith Laurence Pastore. Urbana: U of Illinois P, 1993. 36–54.

Diamond, Elin. "Mimesis, Mimicry, and the 'True Real.' " In *Acting Out: Feminist Performances*. Ed. Lynda Hart and Peggy Phelan. Ann Arbor: U of Michigan P, 1993. 363–382.

Dickman, Ken. "Lypsinka: The Real Voice of a Show Biz Phenomenon." *San Francisco Sentinel*, July 18, 1991, 19.

Dolan, Jill. *The Feminist Spectator as Critic*. Ann Arbor: U of Michigan P, 1988.

——. "Lesbian Subjectivity in Realism: Dragging at the Margins of Structure and Ideology." In *Performing Feminisms: Feminist Critical Theory and Theatre*. Ed. Sue-Ellen Case. Baltimore: Johns Hopkins P, 1990. 40–53.

——. *Presence and Desire: Essays on Gender, Sexuality, Performance*. Ann Arbor: U of Michigan P, 1993.

Drake, David. *The Night Larry Kramer Kissed Me*. New York: Anchor Books, 1994.

Drukman, Steven. "Gay-Gazing at *The Lisbon Traviata*, or: How Are Things in *Tosca, Norma*?" *Theatre Topics* 5:1 (1995): 23–34.

Duberman, Martin. *Stonewall*. New York: Dutton, 1993.

Dunlap, David W. "In the AIDS Fight, Bells of Hope from Vancouver." *New York Times*. July 15, 1996, A6.

——. "Surviving with AIDS: Now What?" *New York Times*, August 1, 1996, B3.

Dyer, Richard. "Coming to Terms." In *Out There: Marginalization and Contemporary Cultures*. Ed. Russell Ferguson, Martha Gever, Trinh T. Minh-ha, and Cornel West. Cambridge: MIT Press, 1990. 289–98.

——. *Heavenly Bodies: Film Stars and Society*. New York: St. Martin's Press, 1986.

Eads, Stefani, with photography by Carolyn James. "*Rent* Collection." *POZ*, August/ September 1996, 56–61.

Elliot, Stuart. "Advertising: When a Play Has a Gay Theme, Campaigns Often Tell It as It Is." *New York Times*, June 25, 1995, D23.

Erickson, Jon. "Appropriation and Transgression in Contemporary American Performance: The Wooster Group, Holly Hughes, and Karen Finley." *Theatre Journal* 42:2 (1990): 225–236.

Feingold, Michael. Review of *Jeffrey*. *Village Voice*, January 26, 1993, 87.

Felshin, Nina, ed. Introduction. *But Is It Art? The Spirit of Art as Activism*. Seattle: Bay P, 1995.

Féral, Josette. "Performance and Theatricality: The Subject Demystified." *Modern Drama* 25 (1982): 170–81.

Fierstein, Harvey. *Safe Sex*. New York: Atheneum, 1987.

Finkelstein, Avram. "Furious Burial." *QW*, November 15, 1992, 10.

Finkelstein, Ruth. "Gay Men Have Worked It All Out? Entering the Fray over Safe Sex Practices." *Gay Community News*, Spring 1995, 10+.

Finkle, David. "Going On: The Post-AIDS-Play Play." *Village Voice*, August 29, 1995, 78–80.

Forte, Jeanie. "Women's Performance Art: Feminism and Post-Modernism." In *Performing Feminisms: Feminist Critical Theory and Theatre*. Ed. Sue-Ellen Case. Baltimore: Johns Hopkins UP, 1990. 251–269.

Foucault, Michel. *The History of Sexuality: Volume I, An Introduction*. Trans. Robert Hurley. New York, Random House, 1978.

Freeman, Brian. "Pomo Afro Homos Presents *Fierce Love*." *Outlook* 14 (1991): 58–62.

Freiberg, Peter. "Thousands March Nationwide to Demand Federal Action on AIDS." *Advocate*, June 9, 1983, 8.

Frye, Northrop. *The Anatomy of Criticism*. Princeton: Princeton UP, 1957.

Gallagher, John. "The Money Pit." *Advocate*, September 3, 1996, 29–30.

Garber, Marjorie. *Vested Interests: Cross-dressing and Cultural Anxiety*. New York: Routledge, 1991.

Gay Men's Health Crisis. "A Letter." *New York Native*, May 23, 1983, 8.

———. "A Letter." *Christopher Street*, July 1982, 17.

———. "Thanks to You, We're a Hit!" *New York Native*, April 26, 1982, back page.

Geer, Richard Owen. "Of the People, by the People, and for the People: The Field of Community Performance." *High Performance* 16:4 (1993): 28–31.

Gevisser, Mark. "Gay Theater Today." *Theatre* 21: 3 (1990): 4–51.

Goldbard, Arlene. "Postcript to the Past: Notes toward a History of Community Arts." *High Performance* 16:4 (1993): 23–27.

Goldberg, Roselee. *Performance Art: From Futurism to Present*. Revised and enlarged edition. New York: Harry N. Abrams, Inc. 1988.

Gomez, Jewelle and Barbara Smith. "Taking the Home out of Homophobia: Black Lesbians Look in Their Own Backyards." *Outlook* 8 (1990): 32–37.

Gómez-Peña, Guillermo. "The Multi-Cultural Paradigm." In *Warrior for Gringostroika*. St. Paul, MN: Graywolf P, 1993.

González, Deena J. "Masquerades: Viewing the New Chicana Lesbian Anthologies." *Outlook* 15 (1991): 80–83.

Gross, Larry. *Contested Closets: The Politics and Ethics of Outing*. Minneapolis: U of Minnesota P, 1993.

Grover, Jan Zita. "AIDS: Keywords." In *AIDS: Cultural Analysis/Cultural Activism*. Ed. Douglas Crimp. Cambridge: MIT Press, 1987. 17–30.

———. "AIDS, Keywords, and Cultural Work." In *Cultural Studies*. Ed. Lawrence Grossberg, Cary Nelson, and Paula Treichler. New York: Routledge, 1992. 227–239.

———. Introduction. *AIDS: The Artists' Response*." Exhibition catalogue. Columbus: Ohio State University, 1989.

———. "Visible Lesions: Images of the PWA in America." In *Fluid Exchanges: Artists and Critics in the AIDS Crisis*. Ed. James Miller. Toronto: U of Toronto P, 1992. 23–52.

Grusen, Lindsey. "Black Politicians Discover AIDS." *New York Times*, March 9, 1992, A7.

Guare, John. *Six Degrees of Separation*. New York: Vintage Books, 1990.

Guarino, George Charles. Letter to the editor. *Washington Blade*, July 1, 1983, 21.

Hachem, Samir. Review of *A.I.D.S. Show*. *Advocate*, July 8, 1986, 36–37.

Hagedorn, Jeff. *One*. Unpublished manuscript, 1983.

Haile, Mark. " 'It Can Happen to Anybody. Even Me, Magic Johnson.' " *BLK* 3:9 (1991): 20–25.

Harding, Rick. "Springfield's Shame." *Advocate*, December 19 1989, 8–9.

Harris, William. "Demonized and Struggling with His Demons." *New York Times*, October 23, 1994, H31.

Hartmann, Paul-Francis. "Stars to Take AIDS Show on the Road." *Bay Area Reporter*, August 25, 1983, 1+.

Hecht, Rob. "An Odd Blessing: An Interview with Michael Kearns." *Spectrum* 34 (1992): 42–58.

Heim, Chris. "Thousands March Nationwide to Demand Federal Action on AIDS." *Advocate*, June 9, 1983, 8.

Helbing, Terry. "A Boom Time for Theater." *Advocate*, January 21, 1982, 43+.

Hilbert, Jeffrey. "The Politics of Drag." *Advocate*, April 23, 1991, 42–47.

Hockenberry, Clint and Carlene Cheatam. "Being 'AIDSed Out': This Is Not the Time." *Washington Blade*, October 7, 1983, 39.

Hoffman, William M. *As Is*. New York: Vintage, 1985.

———, ed. *Gay Plays: The First Collection*. New York: Avon Books, 1979.

Holleran, Andrew. "The Spectacle at the Bottom of the Shaft." *New York Native*, May 23, 1983, 18–19.

Horwitz, Simi. "*Rent*: Musical Theater's New Lease on Life." *Theater Week*, April 29, 1996, 22+.

Huerta, Jorge. "Looking for the Magic: Chicanos in the Mainstream." In *Negotiating Performance: Gender, Sexuality, and Theatricality in Latin/o America*. Ed. Diana Taylor and Juan Villegas. Durham: Duke UP, 1994. 37–48.

———. "Professionalizing Teatro: An Overview of Chicano Theatre During the 'Decade of the Hispanic.' " *Theatre Forum* 3 (1993): 54–59.

Irvine, Janice. "National AIDS Vigil: Coming at a Low Time?" *Gay Community News*, October 7, 1983, 1–2.

Istel, John. "I Have Something to Say: An Interview with Jonathan Larson." *American Theatre*, July/August 1996, 16+.

Jamison, Laura. "Queer Like Me." *Village Voice*, October 8, 1991, 101–102.

Jefferson, Margo. "*Rent* Is Brilliant and Messy All at Once." *New York Times*, February 25, 1996, section 2, page 5.

Johnston, William. *HIV Negative: How the Uninfected Are Affected by AIDS*. New York: Insight Books, 1995.

Jones, James W. "The Sick Homosexual: AIDS and Gays on the American Stage and Screen." In *Confronting AIDS through Literature: The Responsibilities of Representation*. Ed. Judith Laurence Pastore. Urbana: U of Illinois P, 1993. 103–123.

Jones, Therese, ed. *Sharing the Delerium: Second Generation AIDS Plays and Performances*. Portsmouth, NH: Heinemann, 1994.

Jones, Wendell, and David Stanley. *AIDS! The Musical!* Performance run August 1–4 and 8–11, 1991, at Highways Performance Space, Santa Monica, CA.

———. "Authors' Notes." In *Sharing the Delerium: Second Generation AIDS Plays and Performances*. Ed. Therese Jones. Portsmouth, NH: Heinemann, 1994. 208–9.

Joseph, Miranda. "Constructing Gay Identity and Community: The AIDS Plays of Theatre Rhinoceros." *Theatre Insight* 3:1 (1991): 6–11.

Juhasz, Alexandra. *AIDS TV: Identity, Community, and Alternative Video*. Durham: Duke UP, 1995.

Kanellos, Nicolas. *A History of Hispanic Theatre in the United States: Origins to 1940*. Austin: U of Texas P, 1990.

Kaplan, Rachel. Review of *Queer Exchange*. San Francisco Bay Times, March 1991, 50.

KARR. "Porn Corner." *Bay Area Reporter*, September 9, 1982, 32.

Kaufman, David. Review of *Love! Valour! Compassion! Nation*, December 19, 1994, 774.

Kayal, Philip, M. *Bearing Witness: Gay Men's Health Crisis and the Politics of AIDS*. Boulder: Westview P, 1993.

Kearns, Michael. "Gay Dramatists Pen New Works to 'Age of AIDS.'" *Advocate*, January 22, 1985, 24–5.

———. *Intimacies/More Intimacies*. In *Gay and Lesbian Plays Today*. Ed. Terry Helbing. Portsmouth, NH: Heinemann, 1993.

———. *Rock*. Video of May 30, 1992, performance at Sushi's Performance Gallery in San Diego, California.

———. *T-Cells and Sympathy: Monologues in the Age of AIDS*. Portsmouth, NH: Heinemann, 1996.

———. "Why Camille?" Statement for the 1993 production of *Camille* at Highways Performance Space, Santa Monica, CA.

Kirkpatrick, Melanie. Review of *Six Degrees of Separation*. Wall Street Journal, June 25, 1990, 16.

Kleinberg, Seymour. "Dreadful Night." *Christopher Street*, September 1983, 38–46.

Koehler, Robert. Review of *AIDS! The Musical! Los Angeles Times*, August 7, 1991, F9.

Koestenbaum, Wayne. *The Queen's Throat: Opera, Homosexuality, and the Mystery of Desire*. New York: Poseidon P, 1993.

Kondo, Dorinne. "The Narrative Production of 'Home,' Community, and Political Identity in Asian American Theatre." In *About Face: Performing Race in Fashion and Theater*. New York: Routledge, 1997.

Kramer, Larry. "A Good News/Bad News AIDS Joke." *New York Times Magazine*, July 14, 1996, 27+.

———. *Reports from the Holocaust: The Making of an AIDS Activist*. New York: St. Martin's P, 1989.

———. *The Normal Heart*. New York: New American Library, 1985.

Kroll, Jack. "A Downtown La Boheme." *Newsweek*, February 26, 1996, 67.

———. "Love among the Ruins: A Musical for the '90s Jumps a Generation Gap." *Newsweek*, May 13, 1996, 56+.

———. Review of *Six Degrees of Separation*. *Newsweek*, June 25, 1990, 76.

Kuleike, Stephen. "Good Friends Raising Funds for AIDS." *Advocate*, August 18, 1983, 25.

———. "Thousands March Nationwide to Demand Federal Action on AIDS." *Advocate*, June 9, 1983, 8.

Kushner, Tony. *Angels in America, Part One: Millennium Approaches*. New York: Theatre Communications Group, 1993.

———. *Angels in America, Part Two: Perestroika*. New York: Theatre Communications Group, 1994.

Lahr, John. "Beyond Nelly." *New Yorker*, November 23, 1992, 127+.

Larson, Jonathan. *Rent: Original Broadway Cast Recording*. SKG Music, 1996.

Lassell, Michael. Review of *AIDS/US*. *LA Weekly*, April 11, 1986, 42.

Lawson, D. S. "Rage and Rembrance: The AIDS Plays." In *AIDS: The Literary Response*. Ed. Emmanuel S. Nelson. New York: Twayne, 1992. 140–154.

Leverett, Jim. "Ron Vawter." *Village Voice*, May 3, 1994, 96.

Lipsitz, George. *Time Passages: Collective Memory and American Popular Culture*. Minneapolis: U of Minnesota P, 1990.

Lorch, Paul. "KS Diagnosis, Takes Life." *Bay Area Reporter*, December 23, 1982, 1+.

Ludlam, Charles. *Camille*. In *The Complete Plays*. New York: Harper and Row, 1989.

Lypsinka. *I Could Go on Lip-Synching*. Program note, Callboard Theater in Los Angeles, California, Spring 1991.

MacDonald, Eric L. "Theatre Rhinoceros: A Gay Company." *Drama Review* 33:1 (1989): 79–93.

Maldonado, Miguelina. "On the Out Side: Latinos and Clinical Trials." *SIDAhora* 11 (1992): 13.

Marks, Jim. "Brouhaha Erupts over AIDS Office Location." *Washington Blade*, July 22, 1983, 5.

———. "Series of AIDS Fundraisers Planned." *Washington Blade*, April 15, 1983, 17.

Marshall, Stuart. "Picturing Deviancy." In *Ecstatic Antibodies: Resisting the AIDS Mythology*. Ed. Tessa Boffin and Sunil Gupta. London: Rivers Oram P, 1990. 19–36.

Martinez-Maza, Otoniel, Diana M. Shin, and Helen E. Banks. *Latinos and AIDS: A National Strategy Symposium*. Los Angeles: Center for Interdisciplinary Research in Immunology and Disease (CIRID), 1989.

Martz, Steve. " 'I Don't Want to Die of Red Tape.' " *Washington Blade*, August 5, 1983, 1+.

Matson, Jeffrey. Review of *Night Sweat*. *New York Native*, July 2, 1984, 51.

Maugh, Thomas H. "High-Risk Sex on Rise, Conference Told." *Los Angeles Times*, July 9, 1996, A8.

———. "Studies of Combined Drugs Promising." *Los Angeles Times*, July 12, 1996, A8.

McConachie, Bruce A. "Historicizing the Relations of Theatrical Production." In *Critical Theory and Performance*. Ed. Janelle G. Reinelt and Joseph R. Roach. Ann Arbor: U of Michigan P, 1992. 168–178.

——. "Towards a Postpostivist Theatre History." *Theatre Journal* 37:4 (1985): 465–486.

McNally, Terrence. *Love! Valour! Compassion!* New York: Plume, 1994.

——. *The Lisbon Traviata*. In *Three Plays by Terrence McNally*. New York: Plume, 1990.

Mercer, Kobena. "Skin Head Sex Thing: Racial Difference and the Homoerotic Imaginary." In *How Do I Look? Queer Film and Video*. Ed. Bad-Object Choices. Seattle: Bay P, 1991. 169–210.

——. *Welcome to the Jungle: New Positions in Black Cultural Studies*. New York: Routledge, 1994.

Meyer, Richard. "Rock Hudson's Body." In *Inside/Out: Lesbian Theories, Gay Theories*. Ed. Diana Fuss. New York: Routledge, 1991. 258–288.

——. "This Is to Enrage You: Gran Fury and the Graphics of AIDS Activism." In *But Is It Art? The Spirit of Art and Activism*. Ed. Nina Felting. Seattle: Bay P, 1995. 51–83.

Mifflin, Margot. "Performance Art: What Is It and Where Is It Going?" *Art News*, April 1992, 89+.

Miller, Alan. E. "Young, Gifted, and Fierce." *BLK* 3:8 (1991): 9–13.

Miller, Tim. *My Queer Body*. In *Sharing the Delirium: Second Generation AIDS Plays*. Ed. Therese Jones. Portsmouth, NH: Heinemann, 1994.

——. *Naked Breath*. Unpublished performance script, 1994.

Miller, Tim, and David Román. "Preaching to the Converted." *Theatre Journal* 47:2 (1995): 169–188.

Monette, Paul. *Afterlife*. New York: Avon, 1990.

——. *Borrowed Time: An AIDS Memoir*. New York: Harcourt Brace Jovanovich, 1988.

——. "Sleeping under a Tree." In *Last Watch of the Night*. New York: Harcourt Brace, 1994.

Moraga, Chérrie. *Loving in the War Years*. Boston: South End P, 1983.

Morales, Ed. "Shadowing Valdez." *American Theatre*, July 1992, 14–19.

——. "Welcome to Aztlan." *American Theatre*, March 1993, 38–40.

——. "Those Who Can, Act: 'Cultural Workers' at TeatroFestival." *Village Voice*, August 3, 1993, 95–6.

Morris, Charles. Letter. *San Francisco Sentinel*, November 11, 1982, 4.

Morris, Mitchell. "Reading as an Opera Queen." In *Musicology and Difference: Gender and Sexuality in Music Scholarship*. Ed. Ruth A. Solie. Berkeley: U of California P, 1993: 184–200.

Morrison, Paul. "End Pleasure." *GLQ: A Journal of Lesbian and Gay Studies* 1:1 (1993): 53–78.

Morrison, Richard. "We Are All HIV-Positive: A Conversation with Diamanda Galás, Singer, Composer, Performance Artist, AIDS Activist." *Art and Understanding*, January/February 1993, 27–29.

Muñoz, José. "Dead White: Notes on the Whiteness of the New Queer Cinema." *GLQ: A Journal of Lesbian and Gay Studies*. Forthcoming.

Newman, Karen. "Directing Traffic: Subjects, Objects, and the Politics of Exchange." *differences* 2:2 (1990): 41–54.

Newton, Esther. *Mother Camp: Female Impersonators in America*. Chicago: U of Chicago P, 1979.

Odets, Walt. "AIDS Education and Harm Reduction for Gay Men: Psychological Approaches for the 21st Century." *AIDS & Public Policy Journal* 9:1 (1994): 1–16.

——. *In the Shadow of the Epidemic: Being HIV Negative in the Age of AIDS*. Durham: Duke UP, 1995.

——. "Why We Stopped Doing Primary Prevention for Gay Men in 1985." *AIDS & Public Policy Journal* 10:1 (1995): 1–31.

O'Loughlin, Ray. "Gay Culture." *Advocate*, December 11, 1984, 80–82.

Pacheco, Patrick. "Many Are Called but Few Will Be Chosen for *Rent*." *Los Angeles Times*, July 18, 1996, F10.

——. "Self-Hate Crimes." *Los Angeles Times*, August 2, 1992, 72.

Padgen, Phillip. "*Warren*: A Moving Tribute to a Friend." *Advocate*, January 7, 1986, 72.

Page, Clarence. "Deathly Silence: Black Leaders and AIDS." *New Republic*, December 2, 1991, 15–18.

Pally, Marcia. Review of *As Is*. *Advocate*, April 16, 1985, 33–34.

——. Review of *The Normal Heart*. *Advocate*, May 28, 1985, 40–2.

Palmer, Vernon W. "The Life You Save Could Be Your Own." *Washington Blade*, October 7, 1983, 17.

Patrick, Robert. *Pouf Positive*. In *Untold Decades: Seven Comedies of Gay Romance*. New York: St. Martin's P, 1988.

Patton, Cindy. *Fatal Advice: How Safe-Sex Education Went Wrong*. Durham: Duke UP, 1996.

——. *Inventing AIDS*. New York: Routledge, 1990.

——. *Last Served? Gendering the HIV Pandemic*. London: Taylor and Francis, 1994.

——. "Safe Sex and the Pornographic Vernacular." In *How Do I Look? Queer Film and Video*. Ed. Bad-Object Choices, Seattle: Bay P, 1991. 31–50.

——. *Sex and Germs: The Politics of AIDS*. Boston: South End P, 1985.

Perry, David. "Black, Fierce, and Funny: New Performance Group Crafts Stories of Black Gay Life." *Advocate*, July 2, 1991, 86–87.

Phelan, Peggy. "Money Talks." *Drama Review* 34:1 (1990): 4–15.

——. "Money Talks, Again." *Drama Review* 35: 3 (1991): 131–42.

——. "Reciting the Citations of Others; or, a Second Introduction." In *Acting Out: Feminist Performances*. Ed. Lynda Hart and Peggy Phelan. Ann Arbor: U of Michigan P, 1993. 13–31.

——. *Unmarked: The Politics of Performance*. New York: Routledge, 1994.

Pomo Afro Homos. *Dark Fruit*. In *Staging Gay Lives: An Anthology of Contemporary Gay Theatre*. Ed. John Clum. Boulder: Westview P, 1996.

——. *Fierce Love: Stories from Black Gay Life*. In *Colored Contradictions: An Anthology of Contemporary African-American Plays*. Ed. Harry J. Elam, Jr. and Robert Alexander. New York: Plume, 1996.

Popham, Paul. "April 8, 1982, Speech." *New York Native*, April 26, 1982, 13.

Postlewait, Thomas. "Historiography and the Theatrical Event: A Primer with Twelve Cruxes." *Theatre Journal* 43:2 (1991): 157–78.

——. "Towards a Postpositivist Theatre History." *Theatre Journal* 37:4 (1985): 465–486.

Rafsky, Robert. "An Open Letter to Bill Clinton." *QW*, November 8, 1992, 21–22.

Ramos, Dante. "A Second Wave." *New Republic,* June 5, 1995, 29.

Ranson, Rebecca. *Warren.* Unpublished manuscript, 1984.

Reinelt, Janelle G. "Feminism(s): Introduction." In *Critical Theory and Performance.* Ed. Janelle G. Reinelt and Joseph Roach. Ann Arbor: U of Michigan P, 1992. 223-25.

———. "Feminist Theory and the Problems of Performance." *Modern Drama* 32 (1989): 48-57.

Reyes, Guillermo. "Radio SIDA." Unpublished performance script, 1993.

Rich, Frank. "A Guidebook to the Soul of a City in Confusion." *New York Times,* July 1, 1990, C1+.

———. "Critic's Notebook." *New York Times,* February 3, 1993, B1.

———. Review of *Angels in America, Part One. New York Times,* November 10, 1992, B1.

———. Review of *Six Degrees of Separation. New York Times,* June 15, 1990, C1.

———. "East Village Story." *New York Times,* March 2, 1996, A16.

Richards, David. Review of *Love! Valour! Compassion! New York Times,* November 2, 1995, C13+.

———. Review of *Six Degrees of Separation. Washington Post,* July 12, 1990, 13.

Riggs, Marlon. "Black Macho Revisted: Reflections of a Snap Queen." In *Brother to Brother: New Writings by Black Gay Men.* Ed. Essex Hemphill. Boston: Alyson Publications, 1991.

———. "Meet the New Willie Horton." *New York Times,* March 6, 1992, A19.

———, dir. *Tongues Untied.* Frameline, 1989.

Robertson, Chris. "Thousands March Nationwide to Demand Federal Action on AIDS." *Advocate,* June 9, 1983, 8.

Robinson, Amy. Review of Pomo Afro Homos' *Fierce Love. Theatre Journal* 44:2 (1992): 225-227.

Rofes, Eric. "A Healing Performance: *Immunity Mandala*—a Community Ritual." *Gay Community News,* October 29, 1983, 14-15.

Román, David. "Performing All Our Lives: AIDS, Performance, Community." In *Critical Theory and Performance.* Ed. Janelle Reinelt and Joseph Roach. Ann Arbor: U of Michigan P, 1992. 208-221.

———, with Tim Miller. "Preaching to the Converted." *Theatre Journal* 47:2 (1995): 169-188.

———, with Alberto Sandoval. "Caught in the Web: Latinidad, AIDS, and Allegory in *Kiss of the Spider Woman, the Musical." American Literature* 67:3 (1995): 553-585.

Ross, Andrew. *No Respect: Intellectuals & Popular Culture.* New York: Routledge, 1989.

Rottelo, Gabriel. "The Risk in a 'Cure' for AIDS." *New York Times,* July 14, 1996, A17.

Rubin, Gayle. "The Traffic in Women: Notes on the 'Political Economy of Sex.' " In *Toward an Anthropology of Women.* Ed. Rayna Reiter. New York: Monthly Review, 1975. 157-210.

Rudnick, Paul. *Jeffrey.* New York: Plume Books, 1994.

———. "Laughing at AIDS." *New York Times,* January 23, 1993, A15.

Saalfield, Catherine. "On the Make: Activist Video Collectives." In *Queer Looks: Perspectives on Lesbian and Gay Film and Video.* Ed. Martha Gever, John Greyson, Pratibha Parmar. New York: Routledge, 1993. 21-37.

———, with Ray Navarro. "Shocking the Pink: Race and Gender on the ACT UP Frontlines." In *Inside/Out: Lesbian Theories/Gay Theories.* Ed. Diana Fuss. New York: Routledge, 1991. 341-372.

Sadownick, Doug. "ACT UP Makes a Spectacle of AIDS." *High Performance* 13 (1990): 26–31.

——. "Family among Strangers: Crossing the Borders in Gay L.A." *LA Weekly,* June 23, 1989, 12–20.

Saldívar, Ramon. *Chicano Narrative: The Dialectics of Difference.* Madison: U of Wisconsin P, 1990.

Sandoval, Alberto. "So Far from National Stages, So Close to Home: An Inventory of Latino Theater on AIDS." *Ollantay* 3:2 (1994): 54–72.

——. "Staging AIDS: What's Latinos Got to Do with It?" In *Negotiating Performance: Gender, Sexuality, and Theatricality in Latin/o America.* Ed. Diana Taylor and Juan Villegas. Durham: Duke UP, 1994. 49–66.

Sandoval, Chela. "U.S. Third World Feminism: The Theory and Method of Oppositional Consciousness in the Postmodern World." *Genders* 10 (1991): 1–24.

Saslow, James M. "AIDS Awareness and Action Nationwide." *Advocate,* June 23, 1983, 14–15.

Savran, David. "Ambivalence, Utopia, and a Queer Sort of Materialism: How *Angels in America* Reconstructs the Nation." *Theatre Journal* 47:2 (1995): 207–228.

——. *Communists, Cowboys, and Queers: The Politics of Masculinity in the Work of Arthur Miller and Tennessee Williams.* Minneapolis: U of Minnesota P, 1992.

——. "Tony Kushner Considers the Longstanding Problems of Virtue and Happiness: Interview with Tony Kushner." *American Theater,* October 1994, 100+.

Schechner, Richard. *Performance Theory: Revised and Expanded Edition.* New York: Routledge, 1988.

——. "Ron Vawter—For the Record: An Interview with Richard Schechner." *Drama Review* 37: 3 (1993): 17–41.

Schmaltz, Jeffrey. "Whatever Happened to AIDS?" *New York Times Magazine,* November 28, 1993, 56+.

Schoofs, Mark. "Love in the Age of AIDS." *Village Voice,* August 16, 1994, 21+.

Schweikhart, Gary. "Thousands March Nationwide to Demand Federal Action on AIDS." *Advocate,* June 9, 1983, 8.

Sedgwick, Eve Kosofsky. *Between Men: English Literature and Male Homosocial Desire.* New York: Columbia University P, 1985.

——. *Epistemology of the Closet.* Berkeley: U of California P, 1990.

——. *Tendencies.* Durham: Duke UP, 1993.

Seligmann, Jean, with Michael Reese. "A Family Gives Refuge to a Son Who Has AIDS." *Newsweek,* August 12, 1985, 24.

Shatzky, Joel. "AIDS Enters the American Theatre: *As Is* and *The Normal Heart.*" In *AIDS: The Literary Response.* Ed. Emmanuel S. Nelson. New York: Twayne, 1992. 131–139.

Shepherd, Michael. "Review of 'AIDS Benefit' at Don't Tell Mama." *New York Native,* May 23, 1983, 53.

Shewey, Don. "Introduction." In *Out Front: Contemporary Gay and Lesbian Plays.* Ed. Don Shewey. New York: Grove P, 1988.

Shilts, Randy. *And the Band Played On: Politics, People, and the AIDS Epidemic.* New York: St. Martin, 1987.

Shirley, Don. Review of *AIDS/US. Los Angeles Times,* May 31, 1986, C11.

Signorile, Michaelangelo. "Unsafe Like Me." *Out*, October 1994, 22+.

Simmons, Ron. "Some Thoughts on the Challenges Facing Black Intellectuals." In *Brother to Brother: New Writings by Black Gay Men*. Ed. Essex Hemphill. Boston: Alyson Publications, 1991.

Solomon, Alisa. "AIDS Crusaders ACT UP a Storm." *American Theatre*, October 1989, 39+.

——. "Art Attack: What Do Plato and Pat Buchanan Have in Common?" *American Theatre*, September 1992, 19–24.

Sommers, Michael. "Beyond Off-Broadway: Just What Is the State of Gay Theatre?" *Genre Magazine*, Summer 1991, 31.

——. Review of *Rent*. *Star-Ledger*, February 14, 1996, 49.

Spurier, Jeff. "Blood of a Poet." *Details*, February 1995, 106+.

States, Bert. "Performance and Metaphor." *Theatre Journal* 48:1 (1996): 1–26.

Sterns, David Patrick. Review of *Six Degrees of Separation*. *USA Today*, June 19, 1990, C3.

Stewart, Charles. "Double Jeopardy: Black, Gay, (and Invisible)." *New Republic*, December 2, 1991, 13–15.

Stewart, Karl. "My Knights in Leather." *Bay Area Reporter*, November 18, 1982, 28.

——. "My Knights in Leather." *Bay Area Reporter*, December 23, 1982, 26.

Taussig, Michael. *The Nervous System*. New York and London: Routledge, 1992.

Taylor, Diana. Review of *The Representation of Otherness in Chicano and Latin American Theatre and Film* Conference at UC–Irvine, 18–20 October 1990. *Theatre Journal* 43:3 (1991): 377–79.

Thompson, Mark. "Children of Paradise: A Brief History of Queens." In *Gay Spirit: Myth and Meaning*. Ed. Mark Thompson. New York: St. Martin's P, 1987. 49–68.

Timmons, Stuart. "Playwright Stephen Holt: Haunted by Life's Ironies, Fever of Unknown Origin." *Advocate*, December 9, 1986, 53–54.

Trebay, Guy. "Ron Athey's Slice of Life." *Village Voice*, November 1, 1994, 38.

Treichler, Paula A. "AIDS, Homophobia, and Biomedical Discourse: An Epidemic of Signification." In *AIDS: Cultural Analysis/Cultural Activism*. Ed. Douglas Crimp. Cambridge: MIT P, 1987. 31–70.

Turner, Dan. "The Ultimate Disconnection." *Bay Area Reporter*, December 15, 1983, 26.

Turner, Victor. *From Ritual to Theatre: The Human Seriousness of Play*. New York: PAJ Publications, 1982.

United States Department of Health and Human Services. "Case Fatality Rates." *HIV/AIDS Surveillance*, January 1992, 8.

——. "Case Fatality Rates." *HIV/AIDS Surveillance*, February 1993, 17.

Vilanch, Bruce. "Notes from a Blond Column: Letter from Broadway." *Advocate*, July 23, 1996, 49.

Villalobos, Alice. "AIDS and the Latino/a Community." *ACT UP/Los Angeles Newsletter* 5 (1990): 10.

Vittoriano, Larry. "*Warren*: A Moving Look at Tragedy of AIDS." *Au Courant*, June 10, 1985, 10+.

Walder, Joyce. "David Hampton." *People*, March 18, 1991, 99–100.

Wallace, John. "Something to Do on a Saturday Night." *New York Native*, September 12, 1983, 11.

Walter, Dave. "AIDS Vigil Brings High Emotion, but Low Turnout." *Washington Blade*,
    October 14, 1983, 1+.
———. "AIDS Vigil, Black Conference This Weekend." *Washington Blade*, October 7,
    1983, 1+.
Warner, Michael. Introduction. *Fear of a Queer Planet*. Ed. Michael Warner. U of Min-
    nesota P, 1993.
———. "Why Gay Men Are Having Risky Sex." *Village Voice*. January 31, 1995, 33+.
Watney, Simon. "Missionary Positions: AIDS, 'Africa,' and Race." *differences* 1:1
    (1989): 83–100.
———. *Policing Desire: Pornography, AIDS, and the Media*. 2d ed. Minneapolis: U of
    Minnesota P, 1989.
———. *Practices of Freedom: Selected Writings on HIV/AIDS*. Durham: Duke UP, 1994.
Weber, Bruce. "Angels' Angels." *New York Times Magazine*, April 25, 1993, 48.
West, Cornel. "The New Cultural Politics of Difference." In *Out There: Marginaliza-
    tion and Contemporary Cultures*. Ed. Russell Ferguson, Martha Gever, Trinh T.
    Minh-ha, and Cornel West. Cambridge, MA: MIT P, 1990. 19–36.
———. *Race Matters*. New York: Vintage, 1993.
Weston, Kath. *Families We Choose: Lesbians, Gays, Kinship*. New York: Columbia UP,
    1991.
White, Allen. "A Celebration of Life: Choreographer's Dance with Death." *Voice*, No-
    vember 19, 1982, 6.
———. "CMC Carnival." *Voice*, November 19, 1982, 11.
———. "Cover Story: Leo Ford." *Voice*, October 22, 1982, 39.
———. "Cowley Memorial." *Voice*, December 3, 1982, 18.
———. "Hollywood AIDS Show Flops." *Bay Area Reporter*, September 1, 1983, 1+.
———. "Hollywood Stars Still Avoid Gay-Colored Charities." *Bay Area Reporter*, Sep-
    tember 8, 1983, 1+.
———. "KS Foundation Needs More Support." *Bay Area Reporter*, July 22, 1982, 11.
———. "Megatron Man Dies." *Voice*, November 19, 1983, 4.
Williams, Albert. " 'Cornucopia' Raises $11,000." *Gay Life*, November 25, 1982, 1+.
———. " 'Cornucopia' Shows Set for Nov. 20." *Gay Life*, November 18, 1982, 18.
———. "Human Element Explored in *One*." *Gay Life*, August 11, 1983, 1+.
Williams, Raymond. *Marxism and Literature*. New York: Oxford UP, 1978.
———. *Modern Tragedy*. Stanford: Stanford UP, 1966.
———. *Resources of Hope: Culture, Democracy, Socialism*. London: Verso Books, 1989.
———. *Towards 2000*. London: Hogarth P, 1983.
Witchel, Alex. "Impersonator Wants to Portray Still Others, This Time, Onstage."
    New York Times, July 31, 1990, C1.
———. "The Life of Fakery and Delusion in John Guare's *Six Degrees*." *New York
    Times*, June 21, 1990, C17.
Yarbro-Bejarano, Yvonne. "The Female Subject in Chicano Theatre." In *Performing
    Feminisms: Feminist Critical Theory and Theatre*. Ed. Sue-Ellen Case. Baltimore:
    Johns Hopkins UP, 1990. 131–149.
———. "Expanding the Categories of Race in Lesbian and Gay Studies." In *Profes-
    sions of Desire: Lesbian and Gay Studies in Literature*. Ed. George E. Haggerty &
    Bonnie Zimmerman. New York: MLA Publications, 1994. 124–135.

Yew, Chay. *A Language of Their Own*. New York: Grove P, 1997.

Yingling, Thomas. "AIDS in America: Postmodern Governance, Identity, and Experience." In *Inside/Out: Lesbian Theories, Gay Theories*. Ed. Diana Fuss, New York: Routledge, 1991. 291–310.

Zoglin, Richard. "Lower East Side Story." *Time*, March 4, 1996, 71.

Zweig, Ellen. "The Best Kept Secret." *American Book Review*, August-September 1994, 14.

Index

David Román is an assistant professor of English at the University of Southern California.